£50.00 OA

ALBANIA AND THE ALBANIANS

Pinter Reference
a division of **Pinter Publishers Ltd.**
25 Floral Street, London WC2E 9DS, United Kingdom

First published in 1994

Distributed exclusively in the USA and Canada by St. Martin's Press, Inc., Room 400, 175 Fifth Avenue, New York, NY 10010, USA

British Library Cataloguing in Publication Data
A CIP catalogue record for this book is available from the British Library

ISBN 1 85567 010 0

Library of Congress Cataloging-in-Publication Data
Hall, Derek, R.
    Albania and the Albanians / Derek Hall.
      p.   cm.
    Includes bibliographical references and index.
    ISBN 1–85567–010–0
    1. Albania.   I. Title.
DR910.H35   1994
949.65–dc20   94–2633
                                 CIP

Typeset by Mayhew Typesetting, Rhayader, Powys
Printed and bound in Great Britain by SRP Ltd, Exeter

To Alan Burnett, who bears the responsibility for awakening the author's interest in Albania a quarter of a century ago.

Contents

List of figures

List of plates

All photographs are by the author.

List of tables

List of boxes

Preface

Albania has been unfortunate in that the romance of her story has appealed to many, and the propaganda in her history has been peculiarly partisan. (Winnifrith, 1992b, p. 11)

This brief volume has been written during a time of enormous and unprecedented change for Albania and her neighbours. Within a context of instability and upheaval throughout the Balkans, it aims to provide the reader with a background understanding of the evolution of Albania and the Albanian nation, with a view to better appreciating the likely role of Albania and the Albanians in the common European home of the twenty-first century.

Albania has held both a strategic and peripheral position (Figure 0.1). The country has sat astride strategic trade routes, and has acted as a meeting ground of races and religions since Roman times. But foreign interests have often been able to control the country's major routeways and strategic ports by playing off one Albanian group against another. The country has been located on the edge of two worlds since the separation of the Roman Empire. This division was intensified when the Turks took over the Byzantine Empire, and Albania was anchored to the western edge of the Muslim world. The Strait of Otranto between Albania and Italy became a virtually unbridgeable cultural, political and technological divide from 1500 to 1913 (Ackerman, 1938), and again from 1944 as Albania became the south-western outpost of communist Europe.

Albania is certainly different, as this book will attempt to reveal. On paper, a twentieth-century creation, the country claims direct descendance from classical and pre-classical times. Albania feels hard-done-by because the major powers left as many Albanians outside of the country's borders as within them when the great and good, armed with poor maps and thick pencils, drew lines over the Balkans in the wake of Turkey's disintegration. For a country which has taken itself very seriously, and whose schoolchildren can quote more Byron — who extolled the land and its people — than many British counterparts ever could, Albania's size, language and location have condemned it to a peripheral and superficial consideration by many in the West. Mention of King Zog, Gegs and Tosks is still sufficient to invite jocularity in some; allusions to Lilliputia and Ruritania litter the literature, and pejorative references to an Albanian this or that in joke form are still commonplace. I make no apologies to my Albanian friends for mentioning these apparent insults to Albanian honour, but simply point out that, in a vacuum of ignorance, the need to overcome such perceptions will not be insignificant in Albania's attempts to join mainstream Europe.

An alternative western perception has been through old Cold War lenses: with Albania viewed as the least known element of a monolithic communist Eastern Europe. Yet the country's individuality emphasised both its own distinctiveness and the diversity of those other far from homogeneous lands east of the Elbe. Because of successive ruptures in relations with its political patrons and economic supporters — Yugoslavia in 1948, the Soviet Union in 1961, and China in 1978 — the country's 'communist' post-war development path was punctured by a series of economic and political

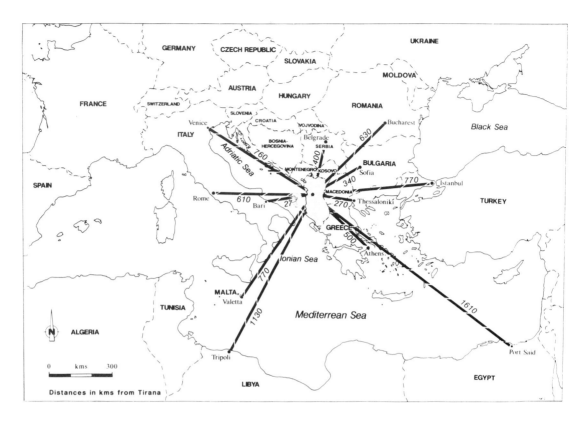

Source: after Mason *et al.*, 1945, p. 2.

Figure 0.1 *Albania's strategic location*

crises. Its smallness, sense of nationhood and historic vulnerability to predators, which had bequeathed many Albanians an Islamic religion yet distinctly Albanian culture, nurtured a 'communist' political leadership which used the fear of external aggression as a force for internal unity. In the vacuum of increasing isolation, this climate spawned one of the most enduring Stalinist personality cults together with an economic and technological inertia which were to set Europe's least developed country into a spiral of social and financial impoverishment.

I here place the term 'communist' in inverted commas, since, even more so than in the rest of Central and Eastern Europe, the post-war political ideology of Albania was essentially a nationalism infused with regionalism and the strong self-interest of a small ruling group, employing Marxist ideology and invoking Stalinist methods (some would say more so than in Stalin's USSR) as a buttress to power and a justificatory veneer.

The accession of this ruling group and its subsequent 'politics' are reasonably well documented elsewhere (Amery, 1948b; Skendi, 1948, 1956a; Gunther, 1949, pp. 127-8; Ingber, 1949; V.R., 1950; Dedijer, 1951; Seton-Watson, 1956; Wolff, 1956; Burks, 1961; Logoreci, 1967, 1977; Pano, 1968, 1970, 1977a, 1977b, 1982, 1984; Lendvai, 1969; Birch, 1971; Peters, 1971; Prifti, 1972a, 1978, 1979; Marmullaku, 1975) and are addressed in this volume only where they illumine the evolution of development policies for Albania.

In its post-communist transitional path, Albania's distinctiveness has been maintained, again not necessarily with positive consequences:

Table 0.1 *Changing foreign perceptions of Albania*

As beautiful as fairyland . . . as unknown as the heart of Africa	Scriven, 1919, p. 75.
An extraordinary country	Lyall, 1930, p. 167.
A living museum of everything medieval	Ackerman, 1938, p. 262.
China's beach-head in Europe	Hamm, 1963.
The deep-red land of Marxist mystery	Gardiner, 1976, p. 9.
Defiant	Myrdal and Kessle, 1978.
Stern and wild	Newby, 1985, p. 108.
Like coming home	Dewar, 1990.
A collage of fantasies	Glenny, 1990, p. 143.
Europe's Bangladesh	Milivojevic, 1992, p. 15.
The sort of place that makes surrealists weep for joy	Barber, 1993.

political reform in Albania started later than in the rest of Eastern Europe, and economic reform initially proceeded at a very slow rate, with limited privatisation, a hesitant liberalisation of prices, incomplete legal frameworks, industrial paralysis due to raw material and energy shortages, food shortages requiring a dependency on aid shipments, and, for the 1991–92 period, a rapid turnover of governments. Since spring 1992 and the electoral victory of the Democrat-led grouping, the pace of economic reform has hastened. Albania remained highly centralised long after other Central and Eastern European states had begun to liberalise their economies, and for most purposes a private sector had been eliminated. Albanian enterprises have been subjected to a low level of efficiency, even by East European standards. The country has experienced by far the highest sustained rate of natural growth of population of any European country, and has maintained by far the highest proportion of rural dwellers, which, even by the 1990s, made up almost two-thirds of the total population. Emphasising the country's economic vulnerability, in the early 1990s post-communist transition, Albania experienced hyperinflation, unemployment and soaring currency exchange rates at a far higher level than most other Central and Eastern European societies. Through all of this Albania has maintained the lowest level of economic development in Europe (Minxhozi, 1992).

Until the post-communist fragmentations of Yugoslavia and the Soviet Union, Albania was Eastern Europe's smallest country. The potential for a small country to adapt relatively quickly, supported by a substantial resource wealth, provides the basis for optimistic longer-term forecasts for the country's future role.

Because, or perhaps in spite of, the country's peripheral yet buffer status, isolation yet international role, smallness yet strength of character, a number of commentators on matters Albanian appear to have had some difficulty in reaching a consensus on even the most basic matters. This has been partly attributable to ideological sympathies and partly to nationalist leanings, but often it has been due to an appalling ignorance, as alluded to earlier. On the one hand, perceptions of Albania have had to adapt to very dramatic changes in the country's circumstances over the past eighty-odd years (Table 0.1). On the other hand, the general lack of readily available knowledge of the country meant that transmitted images and information were vulnerable to bias of presentation and interpretation, witting or otherwise, on a scale greater than for most other European societies. First-hand reports of brief and manipulated visits (e.g. Harrington, 1967; Abulafia, 1976; Hall and Howlett, 1976; Jenkins, 1976; Meynell, 1985), while usually worthy in themselves, were a poor and often misleading substitute for measured analysis based on intimate knowledge. Further, many Westerners preferred to bask in the 'romantic' images portrayed by such earlier visitors as Edward Gibbon, Lord Byron, Edward Lear and Edith Durham.

Another set of obfuscations arises from the

use in Albanian of definite and indefinite cases as well as several other noun complications in the portrayal of proper- and place-names. To maintain some degree of consistency for non-Albanian speaking readers, indefinite forms ('Shkodër' rather than 'Shkodra') are used in the text and on the maps. An exception to this rule is the use of the 'Westernised' (and definite form) 'Tirana' for the capital (rather than 'Tiranë'). Further confusion can result from the variations in place-name use arising from the partisan employment of competing Balkan languages. What is 'Kosova'/'Kosovë' to Albanians is 'Kosovo' to Serbs and probably most Westerners. While mindful of sensitivities and the emotive nature of this topic, the more familiar forms (to Western readers) of region- and place-names located outside of the Albanian state are normally employed in this volume. Alternative names are presented in Appendix I.

This volume is concerned with discussing the context and future for a 'sustainable' development path for Albania. Key elements of any future social and economic development would appear to be: (a) the development and growth of agriculture and food industries within an essentially private farming sector; (b) enhanced energy development and mineral exploitation, employing environmentally friendly high-quality technology ascertained through inward investment; (c) the development of 'appropriate' tourism, taking cognisance of the country's fragile cultural and physical environment; and (d) trade and light manufacturing, particularly based upon indigenous skills and crafts, which should be developed in at least a supporting role.

All the above require a sufficient medium-term injection of aid and investment to permit the country's infrastructure, not least its transport and communications systems, to be able to support a sustainable development strategy which emphasises both harmonious economic growth and an equitable distribution of the fruits of that growth. These are issues which are addressed in subsequent chapters, following a discussion of 'Albanian-ness' and an assessment of the inheritance of almost half a century of Balkan Stalinism.

The first chapter of this book aims to set the

contemporary context for Albania's development path. It briefly examines the fragility of the Balkans as a setting within which to place the overall evolution of the Albanian state and its natural resource base.

Chapter 2 explores the components of Albanian national identity: ethnicity; language and oral tradition; national symbols; religion; and the diaspora. Within an historical perspective, these key elements in any understanding of 'Albanian-ness' are discussed and set against the context of current events.

The third chapter evaluates the major socio-economic dilemmas now confronting the country that have resulted directly or indirectly from policies pursued during the communist years. While a high population growth rate was encouraged, the immediate impact on women's role in society, as well as other negative consequences such as housing, health and education problems, were submerged in propaganda and the fog of inadequate information. Underlying all such considerations was the question of human rights.

Chapter 4 attempts to clarify the economic development path of Albania as the basis for a background understanding of the country's condition in its post-communist transition. It illumines in particular the country's low level of development prior to the Second World War, and patterns of development under the communists.

The following chapter, Chapter 5, complements the previous two by assessing the critical problem of the environmental legacy of almost half a century of neo-Stalinist policies of industrialisation and economic exploitation. It evaluates the requirements for avoiding environmental disaster under the country's new developmental circumstances.

Chapter 6 examines the far from stable and auspicious domestic and international circumstances within which Albania's post-communist pathway has been set. The country's tortuous political re-emergence entailed some dynamic final months of communist rule, followed by a year of upheaval, before 1992 heralded a totally non-communist central government and a freeing of economic and diplomatic shackles.

Next, the Balkan dilemma, and Albania's

position within it, is discussed in Chapter 7. Albania's independence and recognition just prior to the First World War, brought the drawing of new international boundaries which excluded half of the Albanian nation. Rather than being encompassed within the new Albanian state, most of these people found themselves in what became Yugoslavia, an essentially Slav state dominated by not necessarily sympathetic Serbs. Now, with rapid political and economic change taking place in Albania, violent disintegration in Yugoslavia, and all-round Balkan instability, this discrepancy is crucial to an understanding of, and is a contributory factor to, Albania's delicate relationship with its Balkan neighbours. It is, of course, not the only factor.

Chapter 8 examines both the domestic and external environments for Albanian economic restructuring and the attraction of inward investment, noting in particular the constraints and the potential of the country's infrastructure.

The following chapter, Chapter 9, looks at the three major areas of development which appear vital for Albania's future well-being: food and agriculture; minerals and energy; and tourism. Balance between these three elements, their roles and methods of development, needs to take place within a strategy seeking to establish a sustainable development path for the country.

The final chapter, Chapter 10, argues in conclusion that for Albanian development to be sustainable into the next century, policies must take full regard of the need to constrain the degradation of Albania's important ecosystems and to enhance the social, cultural and economic well-being of the host population. In so doing, they should not disregard the lessons of the country's immediate past.

As a citizen of a country with whom Albania had no diplomatic relations due to outstanding mutual disputes, the author first managed to visit the country in 1974. Although I made repeated visits to Albania subsequently, in later years acting as a holiday tour guide, the circumstances of these visits were inevitably constrained until the 1990s. The simple fact of wanting to return was sufficient to inhibit action and enquiry, often to an excruciatingly frustrat-

ing degree, not only out of self-interest but also so as not to compromise the guides, drivers and other Albanians with whom officially sanctioned contact was made, not to mention those whom one was supposed not to befriend.

In those strained circumstances, which noticeably eased through the 1980s, I did, however, come to make a number of friends, although they knew that I knew that they were not necessarily being their true selves, and nor necessarily was I. Despite the unavoidable anathema of being herded around in a group, controlled and self-censored, travelling in this relatively pristine country, both as a tourist and as a tour guide, was not without its lighter side. There was the very English willowy retired civil servant, for example, pointing out to an Albanian guide in the 1970s, that, contrary to the leader's wishes, a personality cult appeared to have grown up around Enver Hoxha, and perhaps he should be told.

Then there was Spresa, who, on an 'un-Christmas' December tour in the mid-1970s declared that she would never take a husband as she was forever wedded to the Party and to comrade Enver. She would spend many a long hour at the front of the tour bus together with the driver bellowing hearty patriotic songs at the shrinking tourist group behind, many of whom would be gripping their seats with white knuckles as the apparently time-expired vehicle bounced into and out of pot-holes and negotiated blind hairpin bends on unmetalled mountain roads, all the while the driver having at most one hand on the wheel while energetically gesticulating the actions of the song or manipulating the inevitable cigarette (or both) with the other. When Spresa castigated the inhibited British for their lack of pride, a feeble single verse of 'Onward Christian Soldiers' was proffered, and that response more out of ironic bravado from the wits on the back seat than out of any sense of commitment. Spresa is now happily married with a family.

Despite its recent media exposure in the West, Albania remains an unknown country. Even the most recent studies to hand on politics (Schöpflin, 1993) and gender (Funk and Mueller, 1993) in Eastern Europe largely ignore Albania. Yet with more informed Western texts on the country (e.g. Winnifrith, 1992b; Grothusen, 1993) and the greater ability both of outsiders to research and explore Albania (e.g. Jones, 1993) and of Albanians to express themselves and reveal their country to the outside world (e.g. Neza and Hanka, 1993), our knowledge of matters Albanian will gradually improve. To be able to *understand* Albania and the Albanians, however, requires a great deal more: at the very least it requires open minds and hearts.

Grateful thanks are due to Neil Purvis for the cartography, and to WWF UK for financial support for a visit made to Albania in December 1993. I am pleased to be indebted to a wide range of friends for their support, advice and inspiration during an obsessional journey through the Albanian maze over the past quarter-century. Particularly warm regards are extended to those who have remained on the Illyrian shores to help build a new Albania. Many thanks to my parents, and to the indulgent production team at Pinter: Nicola Viinikka, Jane Evans and Patrick Armstrong and the meticulous anonymous copy editor.

Glossary of abbreviations and acronyms

AAIB	Arab Albanian Islamic Bank
AIB	Arab Islamic Bank
ASA	Azienda Strada Albania
asl	above sea level
ATA	Albanian Telegraphic Agency
BIS	Bank for International Settlement
BBC	British Broadcasting Corporation
BK	*Balli Kombëtar* political party
BSZEC	Black Sea Zone of Economic Co-operation
CEPP	Committee for Environmental Preservation and Protection
CMEA (COMECON)	Council for Mutual Economic Assistance
CSCE	Conference on Security and Co-operation in Europe
DAPA	Democratic Alliance Party of Albania
DP	Democratic Party
EBRD	European Bank for Reconstruction and Development
EC	European Community/Commission
EKHF	Environment Know-How Fund
EU	European Union
FAO	Food and Agriculture Organisation
FYP	Five-year plan
FYR	Former Yugoslav Republic
G-24	Group of 24 'Western' (including Japan) most industrialised nations
GCC	Gulf Co-operation Council
GEF	(World Bank) Global Environment Facility
GWh	gigawatt hours
ha	hectare
HSH	Hekurudhë Shqiperisë (Albanian Railways)
HTC	higher-type agricultural co-operative
IBRD	International Bank for Reconstruction and Development
ICO	Islamic Conference Organisation
IDA	International Development Association
IDB	Islamic Development Bank
ILO	International Labour Organisation
IMF	International Monetary Fund
IUCN	World Conservation Union (the International Union for the Conservation of Nature)
JV	joint venture
K	thousand
kg	kilograms
km	kilometres

kph	kilometres per hour
kV	kilovolts
m	metres
MAP	Mediterranean Action Plan
METAP	Mediterranean Technical Assistance Plan
MFN	Most Favoured Nation
mn	million
MTS	machine and tractor station
MWh	megawatt hours
NATO	North Atlantic Treaty Organisation
nd	not dated or no data
NEM	New Economic Mechanism
np	not paginated
PLA	Party of Labour of Albania
PPNEA	Association for the Protection and Preservation of the Natural Environment
PSRA	People's Socialist Republic of Albania
RA	Republic of Albania
RAPA	Republic of Albania People's Assembly
RFE/RL	Radio Free Europe/Radio Liberty
RP	Republican Party
SDP	Social Democratic Party
SHAPE	Supreme Headquarters Allied Powers Europe (of NATO)
SIMSA	Società Italiana delle Miniere di Selenizza-Albania
SPA	Socialist Party of Albania (the former communist Party of Labour of Albania)
t	tonnes
TEMPUS	(EC) Trans-European Mobility Programme for University Studies
UAE	United Arab Emirates
UHR	Union for Human Rights (representing the Greek ethnic minority following the banning of OMONIA as an ethnic-based political party)
UN(O)	United Nations (Organisation)
UNDP	United Nations Development Programme
UNEP	United Nations Environment Programme
UNHCR	United Nations High Commission for Refugees
UNRRA	United Nations Relief and Reconstruction Agency
WB	World Bank
WHO	World Health Organisation
WTO	World Tourism Organisation
WWF	Worldwide Fund for Nature
ZiP	*Zëri i Popullit*

PART I

Albania and the Albanians

1

Albania for beginners

1.1 Territory and state

1.1.1 Albanian origins

As a group from which present-day Albanians claim direct and uninterrupted descent, the Illyrians inhabited territory over much of what is now the western Balkans. They were an Indo-European people who settled here around 1000 BC. Classical writers – the likes of Herodotus, Livy, Pliny and Strabo – spoke of them as being tall and well-built, good fighters and fond of drinking (Marmullaku, 1975, p. 5). Albanians argue that their sense of territoriality is based upon this Illyrian presence which long predated Slav migrations to the area, that theirs has been a history of territorial compaction rather than of expansionism, and that southern Illyria, roughly coinciding with present-day Albanian-inhabited lands (Figure 1.1), was characterised by a high level of economic, social and cultural development before Roman occupation (Buda, 1980). Even so, Illyrians were disunited and failed to live harmoniously with their neighbours. Alongside agriculture and hunting, sea piracy was a major occupation. Under that infamous tactician Pyrrhus, they invaded southern Italy in the third century BC and inflicted serious defeats upon the Roman armies. Unification of the more advanced Illyrian tribes and

territories took place over several centuries. This paved the way for a convergence process which continued after Roman occupation alongside a territorial 'involution' which took place as succeeding foreign invasions impacted upon the region.

The Arbër culture of the early Middle Ages (Table 1.1) is seen by Albanians as a continuation and further development of Romanised Illyrian elements, extending over a territory which included Montenegro, Macedonia, Epirus and Corfu (Anamali, 1969, 1972). Despite conquests by Bulgarians and Serbs in the ninth and tenth centuries, the term *Albans*, which emerged in the eleventh century, was no longer just the name of a society in direct line of descent from the ancient tribe mentioned by Ptolemy and subsequently fused with other Illyrian groups: it had assumed a territorial character.

According to Buda (1980) and other Albanian commentators, divergences in language and other cultural characteristics became more pronounced *after* the Ottoman occupation of the fifteenth century brought an interruption to the natural evolution of the Albanian people and a separation in terms of administration and identity.

Following the collapse of Stefan Dušan's Serbian state at the hands of the Turks at Kosovo Polje in 1389, Albanians penetrated

3

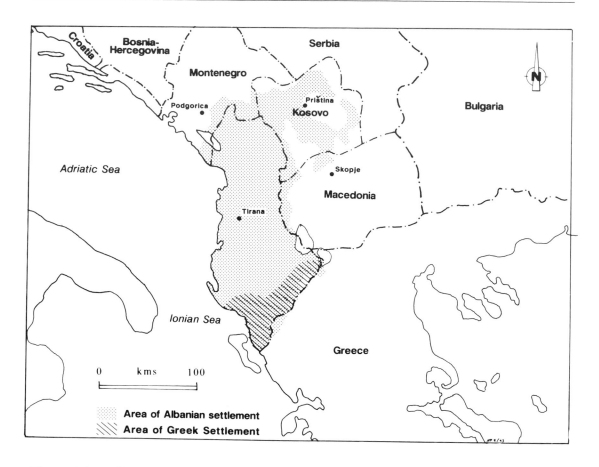

Figure 1.1 *Albanian-inhabited lands*

into western and northern Macedonia and to Dubrovnik on the southern Dalmatian coast. Although significant numbers of Albanians had remained in these territories in the intervening years (no small point of contention with Serb historians), from 1690 they also re-colonised in large numbers such areas as Kosovo, Novi Pazar, Niš, Ipek (Peć), Djakovë and Gusinj, which had been inhabited by Illyrians before Slav expansion had taken place.

The Ottomans found it convenient to entrust the administration of Albanian territories to native pashas or beys (*begs*) but no single ruler held sway over all Albanian lands: one would be played off against another, as were highland chieftains. Partly to prevent a union of beys and pashas, Constantinople indulged the growing strength of two local dynasts – the Bushatlis in the north, based in

Shkodër, and that of Ali Pasha Tepelena in the south, with its court in Janina – such that both established virtually independent hereditary principalities (Skendi, 1967, p. 21). Ali Pasha, a Bektashi renowned for both diplomatic skills and ruthlessness, maintained contacts with all the major European powers, not least Napoleon Bonaparte, Lord Nelson and the Russian Tsar, and his court was visited by many eminent Europeans. One such visitor was Lord Byron in 1809, who was inspired to devote a canto of *Childe Harold* to Albania and the Albanians.

During the 1820s, however, the Sultan concluded that the power of these two groups had to be curtailed, permitting a re-emergence of the old beys who, none the less, soon found themselves in opposition to Turkey's increasingly centralist policy.

Table 1.1 *Key dates in Albanian history*

BC	
*c.*5000	Pelasgians migrate to the Balkans at the beginning of the Bronze Age.
*c.*1000	Illyrians travel from Central Europe to settle in the western Balkans.
7th–5th centuries	Greeks from Corfu and Corinth colonise the Albanian coast: founding of Epidamnos and Apollonia.
5th–3rd centuries	The flowering of the state of Illyria.
435	Conflict between the independent city-state of Epidamnos and the island of Corfu.
250	The Illyrian state extends from the River Krka in Slovenia to present-day Albania.
229–168	Roman invasion of the Illyrian coast, after Illyrian piracy threatens Adriatic trade. The Illyrian kingdom is reduced to a narrow strip between Dubrovnik and Lezhë. Building of the Via Egnatia from Dyrrachium (Epidamnos) on to Constantinople; centres of high culture are established in Dyrrachium and Apollonia.
167	The Illyrian kingdom is brought under Roman rule.
AD	
6–9	Illyrian tribes are overwhelmingly crushed, and begin to be gradually Romanised, some Illyrians entering the Roman army and administrative bodies as civil servants.
2nd century	Illyrians become known as Arbërs; Christianity spreads.
160–927	Slavonic tribes occupy the mountain districts of Albania.
395	Division of the Roman Empire. Arbëria becomes part of the Eastern, Byzantine Empire.
5th century	Invasion by Goths, Avars and Celts; they ravage the Balkan provinces, stay a short time and move on. Huns invade Kosovo.
529–640	Invasion of Albanian lands from Central Europe by Slavic tribes, ending Byzantine authority. The Romanised Illyrian population withdraws into the coastal towns and the mountains of the interior of northern Albania.
851	Invasion of the area by Bulgars, who stay until *c.*1010.
1054	Schism in the Christian Church between Orthodox (Eastern) and Roman Catholic (Western) branches, affects Albanian Christianity.
1081	Normans enter Albania from Italy, and govern until 1100.
1096	Armies of the First Crusade march through Albanian lands.
1180	Serbs conquer the provinces of Shkodër and Prizren.
1190	Proclamation of the feudal state of Arbëria in northern Albania, with Krujë as its capital.
1204	Crusaders conquer Constantinople, thereby hastening the decline of the Byzantine Empire. Michael Comnenus, a member of the Byzantium Imperial family, founds the Despotate of Epirus, incorporating southern Albania and depriving Byzantium of the Albanian coastal region.
1272	Charles I of Anjou, King of Naples, enters Albania from northern Italy, establishes the Kingdom of the Arbërie, and proclaims himself 'King of Albania'. The interior of Albania continues to be ruled by Byzantine and Serbian princes until 1356. Roman Catholicism spreads.
1344	Albania is incorporated into the Kingdom of Serbia under Stefan Dušan (1331–58), together with Macedonia, Thessaly and Epirus. After his death, Albania falls to native chieftains, and the Norman knight Balsha establishes a dynasty at Shkodër until 1421, fending off Serbs and Bulgarians. Large numbers of Albanians move south, capturing Janina and Arta.
14th–15th century	Rise of an independent Albanian principality governed by three families: Dukagjin (north), Kastriot (centre), and Arianit (south). At the close of the 14th century the Venetians establish themselves at Durrës, Shkodër and Bar.
1352	The Ottoman conquest of Europe begins.
1389	Defeat of the Serbian state by the Turks at Kosovo Polje (on the 'Field of Blackbirds').

1431	The Turks capture Janina, take a large part of Albania under their control and establish two sandjaks: Albania and Dibrës.
1433	Mass uprising against the Turks between Shkodër and Vlorë, led by Arijanit Shpata.
1442	Gjergj Kastrioti (Skanderbeg) (1405–68) resigns from the Turkish army, enters Krujë with 300 Albanians, proclaims independence of the principality of Kastrioti, and raises his red family flag with its black double-headed eagle.
1444	Covenant of Lezhë: Albanian League of Princes convened by Skanderbeg to resist the Turks.
1448	Skanderbeg concludes a peace treaty with Venice in order to have a free hand in fighting the Turks.
1450	Five-month siege of Krujë by Sultan Murad broken by Skanderbeg with assistance from King Alfonso I of Naples.
1457	With a 60,000-strong army the Turks take most of lowland Albania but are repulsed at Krujë.
1466	Sultan Mohammed II conquers Albania but fails to occupy Krujë.
1468	Death of Skanderbeg, at Lezhë. He is succeeded as C-in-C of the Albanian army by Lekë Dukagjini, after whom the 'Canon of Lekë' is named. This sets out the norms and rules governing life and behaviour of individuals and tribal organisation in northern Albania under Turkish domination.
1478	Critically, Krujë falls to the Turks under Mohammed II who also retrieves Lezhë from the Venetians, but Shkodër holds out.
1479	Peace between the Turks and Venice sees the latter giving up Shkodër, but keeping Durrës, Ulcinj and Bar. An annual tribute is thenceforth paid to the Turks for trading rights on the Black Sea coast.
1501	Ottoman control of Albanian lands is complete: Durrës is taken from the Venetians.
1555	First book in the Albanian language published – a liturgical book of prayers.
16th century	Almost every part of Albania is Christian: Orthodoxy is dominant in the south and Roman Catholicism in the north.
16th–17th centuries	Tens of thousands of Albanians are forced to emigrate due to hunger and oppression, mainly to southern Italy. Others become assimilated Muslims, turn to brigandage, or join the Turkish army. Yet others travel all over the Ottoman Empire as traders, artisans and manual workers.
1635	First Latin–Albanian dictionary and grammar published.
1749–1796	Karamahmut Pasha Bushatli rules northern Albania from Shkodër.
1785–1822	Ali Pasha Tepelena rules southern Albania and Epirus from Janina. Visited by Byron in 1809.
1821	Greek wars of independence.
1829	The Albanian Literary Society is founded in Constantinople. In 1885 it transfers to Bucharest.
1830	400 Albanian chieftains are massacred by the Turks at Monastir.
1878	The Albanian Question is discussed at the Congress of Berlin.
1878	The League for the Defence of the Albanian Nation is founded in Prizren, 10 June. The first Albanian newspaper, *Drita*, is published.
1881	The Turks ban the League of Prizren.
1887–1902	First authorised Albanian school, Korçë.
1908	The Albanian National Congress, at Monastir, chooses the Latin alphabet for written Albanian, 21 November.
1909	First Albanian teachers' training school, Elbasan.
1910–1913	Balkan Wars.
1912	Proclamation of Albanian independence, at Vlorë, 28 November.
1913	Conference of Ambassadors, London, recognises Albanian independence.
1920	Congress of Lushnjë demands withdrawal of foreign troops from Albanian soil.
1924	June 'Bourgeois-democratic' revolution led by Bishop Fan Noli. December: Ahmet Zogu with foreign support overthrows Fan Noli.

1928	Ahmet Zogu crowns himself King Zog I.
1939	Italian invasion and occupation, 7 April.
1941	Italian establishment of a 'Greater Albania' incorporating Kosovo.
1943	Germans replace Italians as occupying power, September.
1944	Partisans seize control under the leadership of Enver Hoxha, 29 November.
1946	Corfu Straits incident: two British destroyers are mined off the Albanian coast, 22 October. Albania is condemned by the United Nations; the International Court of Justice awards £840,000 damages to Great Britain, but Albania disclaims responsibility (it is generally assumed that Yugoslavia, on Albania's behalf, placed the mines), and refuses to recognise the ruling. In response, Britain refuses to return Albanian gold looted by the Nazis and subsequently held for safe keeping in the Bank of England. Diplomatic relations are not restored until 1991.
1948	Cominform break with Yugoslavia: Albania is saved from being absorbed by its Slav neighbour.
1953	Death of Stalin.
1956	Khrushchev's 'secret speech' denounces much of what Stalin had done.
1961	Sino-Soviet rift sees Albania leaving the Soviet bloc.
1967	Albanian 'cultural revolution', including the banning of religion.
1968	Albania formally withdraws from the CMEA and the Warsaw Pact following the latter's military intervention in Czechoslovakia.
1976	New constitution. The state now officially known as the People's Socialist Republic of Albania. Article 28 proscribes loans and credit from external sources.
1978	Climax of the rift with China as that country's last technicians and advisors are withdrawn from Albania.
1980	May: Josip Broz Tito dies, to be succeeded in Yugoslavia by a rotating presidency.
1982	Hoxha virtually retires. Ramiz Alia appears to take control of the day-to-day running of the country.
1985	Enver Hoxha dies, 13 April, and is formally succeeded by Alia. The country immediately begins to take a more active role in international affairs.
1987	First economic agreements with West Germany following the re-establishment of diplomatic relations.
1989	Anti-communist revolutions in Eastern Europe: the rapid despatching of the Ceauşescus in Romania in December exerts a significant impact on the Albanian leadership.
1990	Opposition political parties are legalised; the ban on religion is lifted; the 1976 constitution is virtually abolished; preparation for the next five-year economic plan period 1991–95 appears to be abandoned.
1991	First post-war multi-party general elections see a rural-urban split between the communists (Party of Labour of Albania – PLA) and the recently established Albanian Democratic Party (ADP). Ramiz Alia loses his parliamentary seat and becomes a non-party political president. The year sees four different governments: communist monopoly (Alia) to March; communist majority (Fatos Nano) from May to early June; coalition (Ylli Bufi) from July to December; and interim salvation (Vilson Ahmeti) from December to March 1992. Economy in dire straits.
1992	Second multi-party general elections in March/April: communists (now officially renamed socialists (SPA)) finally lose their post-war majority hold on national political power. ADP lead non-communist coalition, although a split appears in their own leadership. In July local elections the SPA makes a comeback. Economic restructuring gets under way. Economy still largely dependent upon aid.
1993	Albanian economy shows signs of the beginnings of a recovery. Alia, Nano and Ahmeti are arrested on corruption charges.

Sources: Davis, 1992, pp. 5–6, 1993b, pp. 25–6; and various.

In response to the Greek Revolution, to strong opposition in northern Albania, and to the massacre of 500 southern beys at Monastir in 1836, new territorial arrangements dividing Albanian-inhabited lands were established to remove any possible basis for Albanian unification. The north now found itself within the Roumelian *eyalet* (province), whose centre was at Monastir. The south was now part of the Janina *eyalet*. (Neither centre was to later fall within a unified sovereign Albanian state.)

When nationalistic sentiment began to emerge, in the middle of the nineteenth century, Albanian lands were divided between the administrative centres of Shkodër, Prizren and Ipek, each designated as *liva* (districts) with a governor, under the auspices of a regular army general. Further complicating the administration of Albanian lands was the fact that while the towns of Prishtinë (Priština), Üsküb (Skopje) and Tetovë (Tetovo) were still governed by native pashas, their higher administration vacillated between Monastir and Sofia. In the highlands of the Shkodër district – Mirditë – a further modification, in cognisance of the special conditions pertaining there, saw the intercession of a 'super chieftain' (*Kapedan*) as vassal to the Sultan through the Shkodër governor.

While Ottoman administrative-territorial organisation largely acted to ease tax collection and related bureaucratic duties in the Albanian lands, its imposition clearly held an intrinsic political character, aimed at pre-empting any attempts at Albanian unification. This was reinforced when a further territorial reorganisation in 1865 separated Albanians into three *vilayets* ('local governments') based upon Shkodër, Janina and Monastir, each in turn sub-divided into a number of districts. Prior to the 1878 Berlin Congress, a Kosovo *vilayet* was added to the mosaic, incorporating Novi Pazar and predominantly Slav-inhabited areas such as Niš, to counterbalance and outweigh Albanian strength and influence:

Obviously the Ottoman government did not want to create homogeneous Albanian *vilayets*, still less give a definite demarcation to the vague geographic expression 'Albania'. (Skendi, 1967, p. 27)

1.1.2 National awakening

Ottoman administrative structure had a profound impact on the type of nationalism that emerged in its former territories. The Turks virtually eliminated the local nobility as they conquered the Balkans, preferring to control their subjects indirectly through religious leaders. Since religious leaders were the most conscious segment of Balkan society, nationalism in the Balkans was strongly influenced by religious identification. Albanians are the exception. (King, 1973, p. 8)

By the 1870s, Albanian patriots of three religious persuasions – Islam, Orthodoxy and Roman Catholicism – had begun expressing their aspirations in terms of a nationalism over and above religious loyalties. Their immediate objective was to prevent Montenegro, Serbia and Bulgaria annexing parts of Albania from a dismembered Ottoman Empire. Such fears were borne out in the Treaty of San Stefano in 1878, which, following a Turkish defeat at the hands of Russia, largely over Bulgaria, provided for substantial tracts of Albanian lands to be transferred to newly independent Slav nations (Sumner, 1937; Stojanović, 1939; Skendi, 1953a). In particular, Russia wished to create a greater Bulgaria, as well as a larger Montenegro and Serbia, thereby satisfying fellow Slavs, while gaining dominance of the region at the expense of both Turks and Habsburgs. Significantly for Albanian aspirations, Austria-Hungary and Britain refused to accept such a situation and the Congress of Berlin was called to consider a revision of the Treaty:

When the San Stefano Treaty was published, the articles concerning Albania caused deep anxiety amongst her people. The movements of the Albanians, which until then had been primarily against the taxes, the draft, and the centralistic policy in general that the Turkish government was attempting to impose, took another turn – they began to be nationalistic. (Skendi, 1967, pp. 33–4)

1.1.3 The role of Kosovo

The significance of the Kosovo lands for Albanian cultural and political aspirations was emphasised with the hosting of the first meeting aimed at securing 'national' rights in Prizren in June 1878. Held prior to the Berlin Congress, the gathering gave birth to the 'Albanian League for the Defence of the Rights of the Albanian Nation'. By referring to themselves as the Prizren 'League', the Albanian patriots used the Turkish term *millet* ('nation') to place themselves within the imperial structure. Little voice was given at this time to full-blown independence.

The strong counter-claims to the Kosovo lands held by both Albanians and Serbs were now to enter the world stage, reinforced by ethnic, linguistic and religious differences. Yet Kosovo is small and has little geopolitical value; it has limited mineral wealth and some good agricultural land, but with chronic over-population it is one of the poorest areas of the Balkans. The question of Kosovo has become particularly intractable because both the Albanians, on the one hand, and the Serbs and, to a lesser extent Montenegrins on the other, are strongly attached to the area and refuse to acknowledge the other's claims.

The Serb view of Kosovo is that it represents the heartland of the original Serbian nation and state: here was where Serbian settlement from the seventh century was focused and where the Medieval Serbian kings were crowned. Stefan Dušan (1331–55), the great Serbian leader, established the seat of his empire here, in Prizren. At Kosovo Polje (on 'The Field of Blackbirds') in 1389 came the fateful defeat of the Serbs at Ottoman hands, a source of such Serbian romantic literature and legend that it has been transformed over the centuries into a moral victory. The area is also closely associated with the Serbian Orthodox Church, an institution synonymous with the history and destiny of the Serbian nation. In 1346, when Dušan was crowned emperor of the Serbs, Greeks, Bulgarians *and Albanians*, the Serbian bishopric of Peć (in Kosovo) was proclaimed a patriarchate, thereby rendering the Serbian church independent of the patriarch of Constantinople.

For reasons of both church and state, therefore, Kosovo is regarded as 'sacred ground' by Serbs. Churches and monasteries dot the landscape as a living testimony to their medieval Slav state. For Serbs to renounce Kosovo would be tantamount to renouncing their national heritage. Albanians, by contrast, are viewed as latecomers and as agents of the Turks in driving Serbs from the area: most notably in causing the flight to Hungary in 1690 of the Serbian patriarch and 30,000 Serbian families, along with retreating Habsburg armies. The cause of several subsequent out-migrations, particularly in the 1737–9 period, are again laid at the door of the Albanians. Certainly, 1690 appears to have been something of a watershed in the demographic history of Kosovo (Jelavich, 1983a, p. 92). The migratory process again was accelerated at the end of both world wars when Serbs and Montenegrins left for the Vojvodina and its rich farmlands, which had previously belonged to Hungarians or Germans. Serbian and Montenegrin sources claim that Albanians have continued to drive Slavs out of Kosovo through economic and psychological pressure (Moore, 1992a, 1992b).

The Albanian view is that theirs is the stronger historical claim to Kosovo. The area had been inhabited by Illyrians, the Albanians' claimed ancestors, at least three centuries before Slavs began appearing in the area to displace them. The major point of contention is the extent of the Illyrian/Albanian presence throughout the period of Serb domination – the Albanian ethnogenesis. Albanians claim a strong continuity.

Either way, by the later decades of the nineteenth century, Kosovo emerged as the cradle of an Albanian rebirth – the land that sparked the drive for freedom and national independence, after nearly five centuries of Turkish domination (Prifti, 1978, pp. 223–5). In that re-awakening, however, the Albanians could call upon no single centre from which national leadership could emerge. Ironically, nationalist sentiment was strongest in towns closest to the Albanian frontiers – Shkodër, Prizren, Dibër and Janina – with Prizren the most active.

Out of the 1878 Berlin Congress (Sumner, 1937; Stojanović, 1939; Skendi, 1953a), parts of northern Albania, including Kosovo, were to be ceded to Montenegro, from whom the

Albanians attempted to prevent possession, pointing out that Montenegrin control of Ulcinj would provide an advance seaport for Russian aspirations, stimulating further annexations. It needed a joint Adriatic naval demonstration and mobilisation of the Turkish army to persuade the Albanians otherwise. Repelling Montenegrins in the north, Greeks in the south and Bulgars to the south-east, as well as taking Turkish controlled towns as their own (Prizren, Prishtinë, Üsküb and Dibër), Albanians called for the establishment of one Albanian *vilayet* (suggested by Britain). They were answered by a Turkish re-occupation, and destruction of the Albanian League. Its leaders were exiled, and Islamicised Albanians remained 'Turkish' soldiers and administrators until 1912.

The failure of the Albanian League emphasised the internal contradictions of Albanian national identity. The people of southern Albanian lands, physically more open to ease of administrative control, opposed less energetically the centralising tendencies of the Porte. Conversely, upland northern groups were largely preoccupied with localised disputes and specific points of contention such as taxation and conscription, and were largely unable to conceive of autonomy in a broader, national sense (Skendi, 1953a, p. 231). Nevertheless, despite its destruction, the League's spirit continued, particularly through nationalistic support and developments in the Albanian diaspora (see section 2.5).

1.1.4 Territoriality

The concept of territoriality – the attachment to and protection of a given area by a self-ascribed group – had two key elements for Albanian national identity. The first element, the need for an administratively unified Albanian-inhabited area, was desired by the Albanians to unite them in such areas as law and practices. With Turkish refusal of the right to Albanian administrative unity, the establishment of such a unified territory acted as a rallying point for Albanian nationalists as an expression of national geographical identity.

The second role of territoriality, that of

protection and defence of a prescribed area against the encroachments and irredentism of neighbours, met with some support from the Turks in their efforts to allay the territorial collapse of their own empire in Europe. Certainly external threats to Albanian land from Greeks, Serbs, Montenegrins, Macedonians and Bulgars, in the face of a weakening Turkey, stirred Albanian nationalists into demanding, and executing, counter-measures to protect their homeland. The various plans put forward by the major powers for Albanian partition merely helped to reinforce such national-territorial emotions.

In 1910, with the empire rapidly falling apart, Albanians in full revolt marched on Üsküb and managed to extract a wide range of concessions from the Turks:

... which seemed to indicate a future policy of decentralisation. The settlement virtually established autonomy for the Albanian *vilayets* of Scutari, Kosovo, Janina and Monastir and was generally accepted among the Albanian tribes. (Helmreich, 1938, p. 98)

But all this came too late. Albanian nationalism was now a pawn in big power diplomacy; Albania, still without recognised boundaries (aside from the Adriatic and Ionian coastline), and with a minimum of infrastructural development was easy prey to small-power imperialism. Turkey's role in determining the area's fate was diminishing fast.

During the First Balkan War, out of which Albania's very existence as a recognisable territory was threatened, Albanian representatives from nearby and overseas met at the southern Albanian city of Vlorë in November 1912. Under the leadership of Ismail Kemal Bey Vlora they proclaimed Albanian independence and set up a mixed Christian–Muslim government. By its very declaration the goal of independence helped to promote the development of an Albanian national identity (Skendi, 1967, p. 472).

1.1.5 International boundaries

Shortly afterwards, the London Conference of Ambassadors 1912–13 formally acknowledged the claims of the Albanians to be regarded as a distinct people, with national traditions and ideals peculiar to themselves and deserving of recognition (Barnes, 1918). None the less, the Conference ceded Kosovo to the Slavs.

Thus, for Albanians at least, a far from complete Albanian state came into existence on 29 July 1913. They felt slighted, particularly since the recent armed struggle against the Turks, from 1909 to 1912, had been spearheaded by Kosovar Albanians whose aspirations subsequently had not been recognised by the great powers. The new country's boundaries were the result of a compromise between the claims put forward by Greece and Serbia, and those urged on behalf of Albania by Austria and Italy (Figure 1.2). Needless to say, none of these interests was altruistically motivated:

Except for the southern boundary between Albania and Greece determined by the International Commission . . . no serious attempt at all was made to draw boundaries in accordance with either ethnical or economic principles . . . . The official statistics put forward by the variously interested Governments and Societies are quite worthless in that they utterly contradict each other. (Barnes, 1918, pp. 14, 15)

Such was the difficult nature of Albanian terrain, inclement weather and international uncertainty that the powers failed to physically demarcate Albania's boundaries before the events of Sarajevo overtook the world. Further, the ruler imposed by the powers on the new state, Prince Wilhelm of Wied, was driven out of the country within seven months of his arrival in March 1914 (Skendi, 1956a; Marmullaku, 1975).

During the First World War, the country was overrun by seven different armies, and barely escaped partition (RIIA, 1939). In accordance with the 1915 'Secret Treaty' of London (whereby Britain, France and Russia had 'bribed' Italy to enter the war on their side (Logoreci, 1977, p. 51)), Italy demanded a mandate over the port of Vlorë and central Albania. This was rejected at the Peace Conference. But only after fierce fighting between Albanians and Italians, and violent demonstra-

tions in a number of Italian cities against the despatch of reinforcements to Albania, were Italy's 20,000 troops eventually withdrawn. France also withdrew from Shkodër and Korçë after Woodrow Wilson's insistence on the principle of self-determination and a disavowal of secret treaties which had rendered peoples and territories little more than objects of barter between larger powers. Wilson's position gave the Albanians reason to look upon the United States as a distant protector: a role which was somewhat difficult to maintain in subsequent years.

Still without fully demarcated and accepted international boundaries, the Albanians held a national congress in January 1920 at Lushnjë and subsequently elected a parliament and government, joining the League of Nations later in the year. The country's borders were finally confirmed in November 1921, with certain minor concessions in Yugoslavia's favour, after counter-claims between Italy and Yugoslavia and a long drawn-out dispute with Greece had prolonged the process. The latter country had sought to bring under its jurisdiction all those parts of the Balkans inhabited by Orthodox Christians. This expansionist doctrine, known as the 'Great Idea', was dealt an apparent final blow in 1922 when Greece was defeated by the Turks in the war in Asia Minor. But during the course of the Second World War, Greeks were to establish a temporary administration over the southern half of Albania in the wake of an Italian retreat from the area.

As for Britain's role,

. . . the offer made to Greece in November 1914 of the whole of Southern Albania up to the Viose, with the exception of Vlore, as an inducement for her to enter the war on our side, sounds peculiarly cynical in that we were proclaiming in the very same breath our allegiance to the cause of small nationalities. (Barnes, 1918, p. 24)

1.1.6 False dawns

Relations with Albania's neighbours during the inter-war period reflected both Albanian

Sources: Helmreich, 1938, p. 256; Lendvai, 1969, p. 174.

Figure 1.2 *Albania: alternative boundaries*

internal politics and rival international territorial aspirations.

The country's first national assembly was convened in March 1920. Elections were held in 1921 and recognisable political parties emerged – the Democratic Party, the Popular Party, the Progressives (who largely comprised feudal landowners), and independents. Ahmet Zogu, a member of one of the leading families of central Albania, initially a member of the Democratic Party, became minister of internal affairs and the gendarmerie in the first government, a coalition, which was formed at the Congress of Lushnjë in 1920. Ingratiating himself with the landowners and the Progressive Party, Zogu gained sufficient support to enable him to become prime minister in 1922. With much power and patronage vested in the hands of the large landowners, the major domestic issue, agrarian reform, began to polarise society.

The Democratic Party, whose platform was based on social reform, left the coalition to form the nucleus of an opposition grouping. But in the elections of December 1923, the opposition, led by Fan Noli, won only 35 out of 95 seats, in the face of considerable intimidation and corruption. However, popular dissatisfaction, coupled with a crop failure which threatened famine, brought about an armed uprising and toppled the new government.

This 'bourgeois democratic' revolution of 10 June 1924 unseated the landowning aristocracy from their positions of power, and Zogu fled to Yugoslavia. A democratic government under Fan Noli announced a number of ambitious social reforms – not least that of agrarian reform – and established diplomatic relations with the Soviet Union. But Noli's government failed to gain sufficient support within the country, while much suspicion and intrigue was cast from without. Before the end of the year, direct intervention from Yugoslavia had overthrown the government and returned Zogu to power. This marked the end of parliamentary government and the restoration of the power of the landowners. Political parties were now banned. A republic was established in January 1925 with Zogu as president. In 1928, having consolidated his

power, he proclaimed Albania a 'parliamentary and hereditary monarchy' with himself as Zog I 'King of the Albanians'.

But Zogu soon turned away from Belgrade to be courted by Italy. Through a series of treaties, an open-door policy and tariff preferences for Italian goods, he undermined efforts to stimulate domestic industry (see section 4.1 below), and managed to isolate the country. Loans and other financial transactions, concessions to Italian firms for exploitation of mineral and other natural resources (section 1.2.5 below), and the employment of Italian experts in key administrative posts imposed upon Albania a semi-dependent role. The Italian-Albanian pact of 27 November 1926, signed in Tirana, placed Albania in complete subserviance to Italy. When, in 1939, Zogu refused to renew the pact, Italians occupied the country. But by then Albania's fate had already been set.

Following the German-Austrian *Anschluss*, to counter possible German penetration into the Adriatic, Count Ciano, the Italian foreign minister, advised Mussolini as early as May 1938 to prepare to annex Albania. Ten days after Germany's occupation of Czechoslovakia on 15 March 1939, Zogu was handed an Italian proposal for an 'agreement' under which Albania would voluntarily become an Italian protectorate. Invasion followed a lapsed ultimatum. Zogu, 'Queen' Geraldine and three-day old Leka took flight, this time to Greece.

1.2 Natural environment and resources

1.2.1 Albania in outline

Now with a population of 3.3 million and an area approximately the size of Wales or the state of Maryland – 28,748 sq km – the Republic of Albania is by far the smallest state of Eastern Europe, or at least it was before Yugoslavia and the Soviet Union disintegrated into smaller fragments (Table 1.2). Now Estonia, Georgia, Latvia, Macedonia and Slovenia are smaller by population, and the

Table 1.2   *Albania: basic data comparisons with Central and Eastern Europe*

Country	Area ('000 sq km)	Population		$ per cap. GNP (1988)
		In millions (1990)	Density per sq km	
Albania	27	3.3	114	930*
Slovenia	20	1.9	95	
Macedonia	26	1.9	73	
Armenia	30	3.3	111	
Moldova	34	4.4	129	
Estonia	45	1.6	36	
Bosnia-Hercegovina	51	4.1[†]	80	
Croatia	57	4.8	84	
Latvia	65	2.7	42	
Lithuania	65	3.8	58	
Georgia	70	5.4	77	
Hungary	93	10.4	112	6,491
(Ex-) GDR	108	16.6[‡]	154	9,361
Bulgaria	111	9.0	81	5,633
(Ex-) Czechoslovakia	128	15.7	123	7,603
Yugoslavia (Serbia and Montenegro)	135	12.0[+]	89	
Belarus	208	10.2	49	
Romania	238	23.3	98	4,117
Poland	313	37.9	121	5,453
Ukraine	506	51.5	102	
Russia	10,500	148.0	14	
Former Yugoslavia				4,898
Former Soviet Union				5,552

Notes:
* 1986 estimate
† estimate
‡ 1988 figures

Sources: *Business Europa*, 1993, 2(1): p. 60; *Europa World Yearbook*, 1992, p. 306; Hall, 1993e, p. 9; author's additional calculations.

last two also by area. Albania extends some 340 km north–south and just 150 km east–west at its widest point. Fundamental to the country's cultural, economic and political evolution is the fact that Albania is largely mountainous and access is difficult, lying as it does between the Dinaric Alps to the north and the Pindus range to the south, and between the Macedonian highland to the east and the Adriatic and Ionian seas to the west. The country does, however, possess the only green, low-lying coastal plain on the whole of the eastern Adriatic shore. Until relatively recently, however, the potential of this area remained largely unrealised, as it remained an undrained malarial swamp.

Of the country's 932 km of land border, most of which is over difficult terrain, 476 km is shared with Montenegro, Kosovo and Macedonia and 256 km with Greece. The coastline, at its nearest points only 65 km from Italy and five kilometres from Corfu, constitutes a further 472 km of state borders.

Albania can be topographically divided into: a sub-alpine and alpine zone, situated north of the River Drin with peaks attaining heights of

Table 1.3 *Albanian land use*

	1976		1985		1987		1989	
	a	b	a	b	a	b	a	b
Agricultural land	1,084	39.6	1,113	40.6	1,111	40.5	1,110	40.5
arable	*666*	*24.3*	*713*	*26.0*	*714*	*26.0*	*707*	*25.8*
permanent pasture	*418*	*15.3*	*400*	*14.6*	*397*	*14.5*	*403*	*14.7*
Forest and woodland	1,080	39.4	1,048	38.2	1,047	38.2	1,046	38.2
Irrigated area	330	12.0	399	14.5	409	14.9	423	15.4
Other land	246	9.0	180	6.6	173	6.3	161	5.9
Land area	2,740	100.0	2,740	100.0	2,740	100.0	2,740	100.0
Total area	2,875		2,875		2,875		2,875	

Notes:

a thousand hectares

b percentage of land area

Sources: DeS, 1991, pp. 178–9, 238, 243; EIU, 1992a, p. 42; FAO *Production Yearbooks*; author's additional calculations.

over 2000 metres; a mountainous zone of alternating deciduous forests of beech and cultivated basins, between the Drin and Osum valleys; a broad Mediterranean and transitional deciduous forest zone with scattered patches of Mediterranean pine south of the Osum valley featuring limestone mountains and valleys; and a coastal plain of phrygana, maquis and cultivation, dissected by numerous rivers (Grimmett and Jones, 1989). Two-thirds of the country contains sedimentary deposits and one-third igneous rock. The coastal zone consists mainly of alluvial material: of 250,000 ha, 220,000 ha have been reclaimed, mostly from mosquito-infested marshland. Of the remainder, 18,000 ha were to have been developed for agriculture and intensive fisheries, and 12,000 ha set aside as nature reserves (Kusse and Winkels, 1990).

Of exploitable land, over a third is covered by forest and bush, 14 per cent to 15 per cent by natural pasture, 40 per cent by cultivation and a further 15 per cent by irrigated land (Table 1.3). The country contains some 3,500 species of flora, with several hundred endemic and sub-endemic species. These are well documented (e.g. Demiri, 1983), and even before political change they were attracting increasing attention in the West (North, 1990; Almond, 1988a, 1988b; Polunin, 1980; also Turrill, 1929). Some 865 specimens are claimed to have curative properties, and Albania has been Europe's leading exporter of medicinal herbs, supplying around 20,000 tonnes worth $20 million.

The country is particularly rich in water resources: average annual precipitation in the upland areas is the highest in Europe at around 1,500 mm, and the average annual water flow is 42,000 million cubic metres (Frashëri, 1988). The sources of Albanian rivers are invariably above 1,000 metres. Rivers flow fast over relatively short courses to the sea and provide substantial hydro-electric potential. Conversely, until large storage lakes were developed in conjunction with major HEP schemes (Koman, Fierzë), navigation of most Albanian waterways was virtually impossible.

1.2.2 Physical divisions

While the country consists essentially of a highland interior and a lowland coast, the distinct northern, central and southern components of both can be further sub-divided (Figure 1.3). About 70 per cent of the country's territory

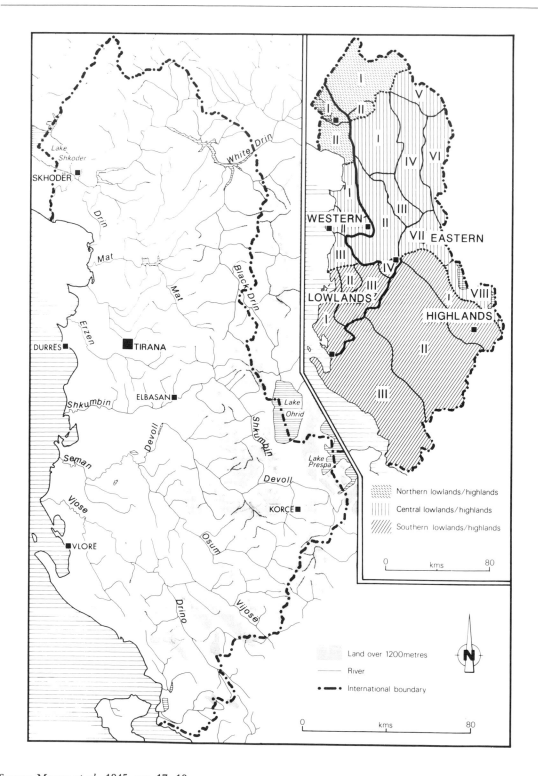

Sources: Mason *et al.*, 1945, pp. 17, 18.

Figure 1.3   *Albania: topographic divisions and drainage*

Key to Figure 1.3: topographic divisions (Mason *et al.*, 1945, pp. 19–56)

I *Western (lowland) Albania*
A. Northern Lowlands
   1. Plain of Shkodër
   2. Plain of Zadrimë
B. Central Lowlands
   1. Plain of Tirana
   2. Plain of Shijak
   3. Plain of Kavajë
C. Southern Lowlands
   1. Myzeqe Plain
   2. Basins east of the Gur i Gomarës coastal hills
   3. Belsh Plateau
   4. Elbasan Plain

II *Eastern (highland) Albania*
A. Northern Highlands
   1. Limestone plateaux
   2. Cukali
B. Central highlands
   1. Mirditë
   2. Western border ranges
   3. Mat Basin
   4. Central ranges between the Drin and Fan-Mat drainage
   5. Frontier range north of the White Drin
   6. Drin Trough and eastern frontier ranges beyond
   7. Çermenikë
   8. Lake region
C. Southern Highlands
   1. Upper Shkumbin Valley and the Plain of Korçë
   2. South-eastern Highlands between the Devoll and Vjosë rivers
   3. Coastal ranges and lowlands

lies above 300 metres and 30 per cent is above 1,000 metres. Albania's mountains are the southern continuation of the Dinaric Alpine range: young folded uplands aligned south-east to north-west and dissected by anticlinal domes and tectonic basins.

Western lowland Albania is characterised by sands, clays and marls broken up into fertile soils. Development of the wide lowland fore-shore, until twentieth century drainage and irrigation, was inhibited by waterlogging and endemic malaria, as the many streams from the highland gorges slow down and deposit considerable quantities of silt and gravel, forming marshes and lagoons. This prograding coast is estimated to have advanced in some places by up to five kilometres since classical times (Pounds, 1969, p. 827). Small, relatively isolated fertile basins – Tirana, Durrës and Vlorë – have dominated the country's economic and political life. Ridges of harder sand-stones and limestones divide the lowland into several distinct coastal plains, and trending south-east to north-west, they form hilly pro-montories on reaching the coast.

The northern lowlands comprise a wide but shallow trough, partly filled by Lake Shkodër. To the south is a level area of alluvium, clay and sand which has been drained for arable cultivation and is dominated by the city of Shkodër, whose hill-top Turkish fortress – Rozafat – presents a commanding view.

In the central lowlands the coastal plain gra-dually widens southwards to Tirana, although also obliquely bisected by low ridges of sands and clays to produce the three plains of Tirana, Shijak and Kavajë, through which major lines of communication pass.

The southern lowlands are composed of another, much larger triangular plain, with its hypotenuse running north-east to south-west from the industrial town of Elbasan, in the centre of the country, to the naval port of Vlorë. The drained lagoons and marsh here present some of the country's most fertile land, with high maize yields and the cultiva-tion of such cash crops as cotton.

In eastern, highland Albania the northern highlands ('North Albanian Alps') consist of a vast limestone upland, continuous with the Montenegrin plateau but more deeply dissected by river gorges and rising to watershed ridges of around 2,500 metres. Quaternary glaciation carved this area into alpine forms, and even in the southerly Shllak region, where the great limestones have been removed to expose older shales, cherts and contorted limestones, gorges as deep as 1,000 metres reveal U-shaped heads.

The central highlands are geologically more complicated, with great limestones denuded to expose sedimentary, metamorphic and volcanic rocks of varied composition and mineral content. To the south, the western border

Plate 1.1   *The Ionian coast at Borsh*

ranges present an upland terrace which is actually an eroded coastline. The strategic significance of this region is legendary within the country – it was the fortress home of the national hero Skanderbeg during his fight against the invading Turks. To the south of Tirana and projecting westwards to the north of the Shkumbin river to separate coastal plains, are the flysch-covered Krrabë 'badlands': dissected and heavily eroded ridges (Papa, 1987). Further east are ranges of serpentine, with remnants of a Cretaceous limestone plateau which thickens northwards (up to 1,200 metres). Transverse gaps and streams break this central highland into often inaccessible masses. Southwards towards Lake Ohrid, mineralised rocks provide the country's major sources of haematite, now linked by rail through the Shkumbin valley to the metallurgical plant at Elbasan. Much of the lowland of the area is under cereals, vegetables, tobacco and orchards, and reed beds around the lakes have been reclaimed for arable cultivation.

The southern highlands represent extensions of the massive limestone anticlines with an overload of flysch eroded into troughs between them, trending north-west to south-east from Greek Epirus to the transverse dislocation between Vlorë and Elbasan. Physical and cultural characteristics reveal continuities with those south of the border – a maquis vegetation giving way to oakwoods on the flysch and to karst moorland interspersed with substantial areas of alpine pasture, and a Greek culture in an area where traditional Albanian tribalism lost its potency far earlier than elsewhere. The wide upland basin of Korçë – with the reclaimed Lake Maliq now a centre of sugar-beet cultivation – represents a prolongation of Lake Ohrid's subsided trough. Cereals, tobacco, vineyards and market gardening have traditionally been associated with this fertile area.

The south-eastern highlands present closely folded limestones, from which the flysch has sometimes been removed. Fertile valley floors are well cultivated and often villages are located up valley sides on the spring line between limestone above and flysch below. This inversion, and the steepness of the lime-

stone escarpment, is the result of overthrust, which becomes more marked closer to the coast. This movement is still in progress, and accounts for the earthquakes experienced in and around the coastal range, such as that of Tepelenë in 1920, and the more recent episodes of April 1969, December 1975 and April 1979. Terracing of hill slopes with olive groves and orchards, particularly along the Ionian coast, has significantly added to the abundance of the area. Within the Dropull valley, high spurs to the south of Tepelenë – a very well fortified position – have traditionally inhibited interaction between the Gjirokastër basin and Albania further north, while the basin is physically open to Greek Epirus and Ioannina to the south. Ironically, it was in Gjirokastër that Albania's Stalinist leader Enver Hoxha was born.

1.2.3 Climate and vegetation

Albania lies on the margin between two major atmospheric regions and between two distinct systems of atmospheric circulation. In winter, caught between the Azores high, extending over southern Europe and into central Asia, and low pressure over the Mediterranean and north Africa, cold, dry northerly winds are brought southwards over Albania. In summer, the Mediterranean low pressure extends northwards, bringing very warm air.

At all seasons, Atlantic and Mediterranean cyclonic depressions provide the major source of rainfall, although they are most extensive and violent in winter. In particular, the deep, virtually land-locked Adriatic trough, overlooked by the Dinaric mountain chains, possesses a low-pressure area of its own, with frequent cyclonic depressions which, once established, bring south-westerly and westerly winds onto the Albanian coast. Moving inland, these are soon forced to rise against the high land, resulting in copious precipitation. They also accelerate the general circulation of Mediterranean sea currents, bringing warmer surface water through the Ionian Sea and into the Adriatic, mitigating the winter cold for coastal regions, while increasing

Plate 1.2   *The southern highlands on the Greek border near Ersëkë*

summer humidity. At all seasons, the local up-draught of warm air brings dramatic thunderstorms, particularly in the mountain valleys.

The Albanian climate is therefore characterised by winter cold and heavy rainfall – annual precipitation in the mountains rises to over 2000 mm with snow cover from early winter to late spring - by wide seasonal and geographical variations in temperature, sometimes violent winds, summer drought and high lowland temperatures. Generally, the interior massifs act to modify climatic effects: the south is sheltered from the intense cold of the winter *bora* wind, while warming influences from the sea are unable to penetrate very far inland, causing the warm, moist and hazy *scirocco* to blow from the south and south-east when depressions approach from Italy. Indeed, mist and haze are not uncommon over the lowlands, as well as the highlands, and the palaeotechnic emissions from relatively recent industrial plants have exacerbated poor visibility with substantial atmospheric pollution over such sheltered urban areas as Tirana, Korçë and Elbasan.

In a country so mountainous, local climates vary considerably according to altitude and aspect. Coupled with such other complications as the periodic flooding of certain low-lying districts, this results in marked local vegetational and botanic variation. However, certain generalisations can be made concerning the country's vegetation, employing the regional divisions found in Figure 1.3.

Coastal Albania is dominated by Mediterranean flora and evergreen hard-leaved vegetation. The coastal lowlands extending southwards to Vlorë encompass a significant portion of the country's arable land. Oakwoods in the north give way to marsh woodlands, maquis and intensive cultivation.

The south has a much rockier and steeper coast, salt marsh and sand stretches being severely restricted. The country's best beaches are, however, to be found here, in small, secluded bays along what has become known as the Albanian riviera (*bregdeti*). Maquis, with the prickly, shrubby kermes oak is abundant, with Greek fir, pines and some beech on the mountains. Hill terracing was notable from the

1960s, with olive and citrus groves particularly ubiquitous in the region.

Both altitude and distance from the coast produce a more continental regime, although towards the south and on seaward facing slopes, Mediterranean influences are exerted. Within highland Albania two vegetational regions can be discerned. The highest points of the North Albanian Alps and central highlands show the most extensively developed forests of white-barked pine and beech – which particularly flourish on the limestone – below which are oak forests. The southern highlands experience conditions less favourable to the beech, but black pine and Greek fir predominate, with dry oakwoods and, in southern low-lying river valleys, maquis scrub.

1.2.4 Water resources

The country is latticed by rivers, often with complex drainage patterns, although the dominant flow is westwards from the mountainous core over a relatively short distance to the sea. As a consequence of this, HEP potential, estimated at 2500 MW, is second only to Norway within Europe. Rates of flow decelerate substantially on reaching the coastal plains, with a consequent silting and the former prevalence of malarial marshes. Despite the length of the major rivers (Drin 281 km, Seman 252 km, Shkumbin 146 km), only the short Bunë, with its source in Lake Shkodër, is navigable. But the commercial value of this has been virtually nil, since for much of its course the river acts as the border with Montenegro.

With a low level of economic development and poor relations with immediate neighbours precluding possible export, Albania's water resource only began to be developed with Italian aid late in the inter-war period. Ironically, the one plant in question, located near Tirana and begun by a fascist dictatorship, was finally completed in 1952 as the 'Lenin' scheme. Subsequently, the northern rivers have been harnessed to an increasing extent, with hydro-power providing some 82 per cent of the country's electricity needs; the River Drin provides 50 per cent of the total. By 1990 the

Drin was said to be generating an annual average 4.5 million MWh. With the planned construction of two further HEP stations, the total was planned to rise to 6.5 million MWh.

Albania's internal waters encompass an area of 64,000 hectares, the major features of which can be found in Figure 1.3. Despite extensive marshland drainage, the country possesses over 150 lakes. These are of four types: (i) tectonic, such as Shkodër (370 sq km within Albanian territory), Ohrid (often referred to in Albania as Lake Pogradec; 367 sq km), and Prespa (285 sq km). These happen to be the country's largest, the first being shared with Montenegro and the other two with Macedonia, with the last also shared with Greece. As such, any fishing potential has tended to be constrained by security considerations; (ii) clastic, such as those of Belsh, in the eastern margin of the Kavajë plain; (iii) glacial, such as those of Lurë and Allaman in the north of the country; and (iv) artificial, usually resulting from HEP projects, such as at Vau i Dëjës and Fierzë on the River Drin.

1.2.5 Mineral resources

Despite its small size, Albania is relatively well endowed with mineral resources: some 30 types are known. The potential for the country is high, but production of most resources has been in decline in recent years, largely due to undercapitalisation, poor management and hopelessly dated technology, as well as domestic instability. Generally, the south-west of the country is rich in hydrocarbons and fuels, particularly petroleum and bitumen, whilst the north-east is rich in metallic deposits, notably chromite, copper and ferrous nickel (Table 1.4, Figure 4.1).

Until 1939, only petroleum and bitumen had any national significance, occurring in Tertiary deposits along the inner edge of the coastal plain between Elbasan and Vlorë. Seepages of burning natural gas ('everlasting fires') had been known in classical times, as attested in the writings of Strabo and Dioscorides, but it was not until the First World War that Italian marine officers reported a seepage of heavy oil

east of Vlorë. Although some borings were made in 1918, further development awaited a more stable political situation. In 1925 concessions were granted firstly to the Anglo-Persian oil company and then to Italian interests. The former were allowed to lapse, while the latter were consolidated into a subsidiary company of the state-controlled railways, Azienda Italiana de Petroli Albania (AIPA), for exploration and development purposes. By 1937 over a hundred wells had been sunk into the tertiary deposits along the inner edge of the coastal plain particularly in the then malarial and swampy Plain of Myzeqe and in the Seman and Vjosë valleys. Relatively difficult and costly to refine, with a high sulphur and asphaltic base, the low level of crude production which resulted was transported by 74-km of Italian-built pipeline from the Kuçovë field to Vlorë for export, primarily to refineries at Bari and Livorno. Thus Albania failed to derive any advantage that well-head refining might have brought it. By 1940 annual production had reached 1.6 million barrels. From a 1960 figure of 60,000 barrels per day, production had declined to 18,000 by 1991, and to half that in the following year (Mining Journal, 1992).

Like the country's copper deposits, Albanian asphalt bitumen has been known for its high quality and has been exported since classical times. Ironically, in a country whose poor infrastructure – particularly its meagre hard surface roads – had inhibited other mineral exploitation, asphalt bitumen was one of the most important exports in the earlier part of the twentieth century. The mine at Selenicë was worked by a French syndicate and initially the raw material was carried across the hills to the exporting port of Vlorë by pack animals. Later, a narrow gauge railway was constructed, which was, in fact the only railway in existence in Albania at the end of the war. By 1938 annual exports had reached 12,000 tonnes.

Chromite ore (48 per cent C_2O_3) occurs widely in upland Albania, although limited in workable form, being associated with intrusive masses of serpentine and other basic igneous rocks. The most extensive and accessible

Table 1.4 *Albania: major mineral deposits*

Mineral		Location	Comments
Chromite:	48% Cr_2O_3 9% silica.	Widely distributed in association with the intrusive masses of serpentine and other basic igneous rocks, although concentrated in workable form in the Kukës, Bulqizë and Pogradec regions.	The country has been the world's third largest producer but output has declined since 1985. Reserves estimated to be fourth largest after South Africa, Russia and Zimbabwe.
Copper:	Low grade sulphides.	Found in iron pyrites mostly between the Drin and Mat valleys in the north of the country.	Worked since ancient times. First copper smelter built by the Italians before the war. Supports the production and export of wire and cables. Total annual refined copper output is estimated at 12,000 tonnes. Copper ore production peaked in 1985.
Iron-nickel:	43% Fe, 1% Ni, 8% SO_2, 4% Cr_2O_3. Of the Lymonithic lateritic type.	West of Lake Ohrid, mined at Guri i Kuq, Pishkash, Prrenjas and Librazhd, and to the north-east of Korçë at Bitincha.	Processed at the Elbasan metallurgical complex via a rail connection.
Lignite:	Seams of between 0.4 and 1.7m thick of varying calorific value.	At the same stratigraphical level as oil sands, in the Krrabë highlands east and south of Tirana, around Memaliaj-Tepelenë, east of Korçë, and near Pogradec. 20 mines in operation, but major technical and geological problems.	Long used for brick-making and lime-burning. Albania lacks hard coal reserves. 2.1 million tonnes produced in 1990, but only 1.1 million in 1991.

Sources: *Albanian Foreign Trade* (various); Mason *et al.*, 1945; Mining Journal, 1992.

deposits lie in the middle Drin valley, near Kukës, in the Mirditë serpentine massif south of the Drin, and in the mountains of both the extreme north-east, and to the south-west of Lake Ohrid (Figure 4.1). In 1940 workable reserves were estimated at half a million tonnes. In that year the first shipment of ore was made to Italy, from a concession at Mëmbisht, near Pogradec. But as was so often the case, crude ore was exported without the possible benefits of any processing and enhancement accruing to Albanian coffers. Output reached a peak in 1942 (36,000 tonnes) and then declined with Italy's fortunes and the progress of the war.

Although worked from ancient times, the country's low-grade sulphide copper reserves only began to be exploited to any extent after 1939, when 6,000 tonnes annual production was being projected (Mason *et al.*, 1945, p. 251). Italian concessions in the Mirditë region, held since 1926, had previously yielded very little ore. Iron ore is relatively ubiquitous within the country, but usually in minor ore bodies. The country's haematite (ferrous nickel) deposits, were thought in the late 1930s to represent about 20 million tonnes, largely found to the west of Lake Ohrid and in the Drin valley. Already of low-grade quality however, pre-war problems of poor access and transport facilities further raised the relative costs of the ore's exploitation and mining was discontinued during the war.

Albania's coal resources are largely comprised of lignite. Estimated at up to 20 million tonnes, the reserves of this fuel are of upper Tertiary age, worked in the hills to the east, and on the Krrabë plateau to the south of Tirana, in the Korçë Basin and at Mamaliaj in the Vjosë valley (Figure 4.1). By 1939, annual production stood at just 7,000 tonnes, representing relatively small-scale working for domestic fuel, brick-making, lime-burning and other local industries (Mason *et al.*, 1945, p. 250). In the post-war period lignite has been burnt by domestic consumers, in a number of industrial processes and in the country's thermal power stations in Tirana and at Korçë, with deleterious atmospheric and health consequences (see section 5.2.1). Consideration of longer-term energy provision has stimulated studies into the potential for low-cost solar, wave, wind, geothermal and photosynthetic means of energy generation (Karadimov, 1989).

In addition to the mineral resources noted in Table 1.4, extracted metals include manganese, chrome, bauxite, copper and nickel; and non-metallic resources extracted include phosphate, calcium, barytes, kaolin, clay, gypsum, salt, dolomite, magnesite, olivinite, marble, sand and quartz. In the late-1980s, annual output amounted to just over two million tonnes of coal and just over one million tonnes each of chromite, ferrous-nickel ore and copper ore (Bërxholi, 1990b).

Additionally, springs of mineralised water are found in many parts of the country. Cold sulphurous springs are the most common, although waters with temperatures of up to 50 degrees centigrade exist near Elbasan and Peshkopi, the former marking the site of a Roman bathing station.

2

Dimensions of Albanian national identity

2.1 Ethnicity

2.1.1 Ethnic self-identity

No Balkan society is immune from the observation that a nation is a group of people united by a common error about their ancestry and a common dislike of their neighbours (Deutsch, 1969, p. 3; King, 1973, p. 5). Although language, literature, religion, customs and historical antagonisms assist the definition of ethnic groups' national ideals, territorial exclusiveness and integrity is vital to assert a separate identity. In the Balkans, however, the complicated patterns of historical migrations meant that over a long period groups became intermixed geographically, rendering territorial exclusiveness here more elusive than elsewhere in Europe, as testified in the horrific nature of Yugoslavia's disintegration.

One of the determining characteristics of Albania has been its ethnic homogeneity. As an ethnic group, the Albanians have avoided assimilation by their Slav, Greek and Italian neighbours – despite centuries of incursion and exploitation by outsiders – such that today's Republic of Albania stands close to being a 'true' nation state. Although more Albanians live outside the country than within it, and in recent years the diaspora has played

an important role in opening up and supporting the country, the increasing ethnic homogeneity of the state may be seen as both a strength and also a source of potential racial intolerance.

According to the most recent, April 1989 census (*Zëri i Popullit*, 9 July 1989; DeS, 1991, pp. 361, 370), 98 per cent of the country's 3,182,417 population were ethnic Albanian. The remaining 2 per cent (64,816) were made up of 58,758 ethnic Greeks and 4,697 Macedonians, 100 Montenegrins and Serbs, and 1,261 others, largely Vlachs (Winnifrith, 1987), living in the south-west of the country, and itinerant Gypsies, who are most noticeable in central Albania, especially around Rrogozhinë. The Greeks were concentrated in the Ionian district of Sarandë, and from Gjirokastër southwards to the Greek border. Many of these left for Greece in the early 1990s. The country's small and poorly documented Jewish community was airlifted to Israel during 1991. Reflecting the high ethnic Albanian growth rate (aside from any official falsification of the statistics), minority groups have proportionately decreased in the past half-century: they made up 5 per cent of the total population in the 1961 census, while in 1939 the figure was estimated at 8 per cent, of whom 50,000 were recorded as Greek-speaking in 1930. Such figures have always been contested, with

Greek sources in particular having claimed in the past that 400,000 Orthodox Christians within the country represented the Greek community.

As a nation, most Albanians actually living in Albania and those 2½–3 million in the former Yugoslavia hold a strong sense of national identity. The Albanian diaspora additionally extends across Europe to North Africa, the Middle East and North America (section 2.5 below).

Present-day Albanians recognise themselves to be direct descendants of the pre-Hellenic, Hallstatt culture Illyrians. Certainly, the Illyrian tribes are regarded as having inhabited the western Balkan peninsula since at least the second millenium BC; and by the end of the third century BC they had consolidated a state centred on the present-day Shkodër. The term 'Albania' is believed to be derived from the name of one particular Illyrian tribe which inhabited what is today north-central Albania. These people were known as the Albanoi, and were mentioned in the second century AD writings of Ptolemy. The term subsequently spread slowly to encompass other Illyrian tribes. 'Albania' as such, appears to have been employed first in thirteenth-century Latin dictionaries. Certainly during the Middle Ages the area was known as 'Arbër' and its people referred to themselves as 'Arbëri' in the north and 'Arbëresh' in the south (as Albanians in Italy and Greece often still do).

Indigenous Albanians today, however, refer to themselves as Shqiptarë and to their country as Shqipëri. These terms appear to have come into use after Albania's occupation by the Turks in the fifteenth century, although the precise source is debated. Some have supposed that these terms are derived from the Albanian word for eagle, *shqiponjë*, and as a consequence the country has often been referred to as the 'land of the eagles'. More likely, however, is the connection of the root *shqip* to the word *shqiptoj* ('pronounce'), from which come *flas Shqip* ('I speak Albanian') and *them Shqip* ('I say in Albanian'):

It seems more reasonable for a medieval Albanian to identify himself not with an eagle, but with those who conversed in his own language compared to the many alien conquerors of his people who did not. (Davis, 1993a, p. 24)

Fuel for the 'eagle school', however, is provided by the fact that the central motif of the country's medieval hero Skanderbeg (section 2.3.2 below) was a double-headed eagle, later adopted for the Albanian national flag itself. That such a motif or similar was also among the emblems adopted by major Central European powers further complicates the picture. Finally, the name of the country's post-independence interior minister, prime minister, president and finally king, Zogu (section 1.1.6 above), means 'bird' in Albanian. 'King Bird of the Land of Eagles' has been too compelling an image for some commentators to ignore.

2.1.2 Gegs and Tosks

Albania's physical geography has contributed significantly, at least until very recently, to the cultural separation of Albanians into two distinct sub-groups. To the north of the Shkumbin river and most characteristically in the remote north-east highlands, Gegs (Ghegs) have predominated. Characterised by Coon (1939, p. 601) as 'Dinaric' in physical type, 'tall, convex-nosed, long-faced', they are anthropologically grouped with other mountain peoples who extend as far north and west as Switzerland. Living in small, dispersed settlements, social organisation amongst Gegs has been based upon traditional clan loyalty.

A council of elders maintained a semi-autonomous rule within *bajraks* (Turkish word for banner) which were territorial-political organisations including one or more clans. The councils of elders were comprised of family headmen who regulated customary law, pasture, forest and water rights, and in particular, the 'Law of Lek'. Derived from a local fifteenth century feudal lord – Lckë III Dukagjini – the canon demanded honour (*besa*), hospitality and pursuit of retribution through the 'blood feud': *koka për kokë* – 'a head for a head' (Durham, 1905, 1909; Mason *et al.*, 1945; Hasluck, 1954; Marmullaku, 1975, pp. 86–9; Lopasic, 1992). This tradition was particularly characteristic of the north-eastern mountain areas of Mbishkodër and Dukagjin (Mirditë).

Although vendettas have long existed in the Balkan peninsula, the blood feud came to be reinvigorated following Turkish conquests of the region. Inefficient Turkish administration was unable to provide adequate protection for its subjects against major crimes, and the blood feud emerged as a common law institution of social control by which clan members had both the right and the duty to avenge a murder by killing the murderer or another member of his family or clan. Rules were strictly observed. A victim could not be a woman, a male child nor a priest. Nor could a murder be committed in a place of worship, nor in the presence of a stranger or a woman:

It appeared that George II had a blood feud with a family of the next valley. As he did not wish to be shot, he issued a periodic warning as he approached, since by the Law of Lek no one could kill him in the presence of a stranger. 'But how will you get back?' I asked him, anxiously . . . 'Oh that's all right' he assured me. 'I shall get a woman to walk back with me'. (Newman, 1936, p. 151)

Fear of revenge was the best guarentee of law and order and was a warning to all those who would transgress tribal law. The council of elders had the power to decree that one clan 'owed blood' to another. The latter then had every right either to kill a member of the first clan, to give a pardon, or even to postpone execution of the sentence for several generations, thus keeping the first clan in a state of servitude through fear.

The social, cultural and economic consequences of the blood feud and of hostilities between various families and clans have been considerable as the following points demonstrate:

(a) To provide refuge, families have lived in fortified houses (*kulla*) built of hard materials. These can be seen in north-east Albania and Kosovo, particularly on the plain of Dukagjin.

(b) Families raised their children to be particularly careful and circumspect in what they said for fear of uttering words which would insult the honour of others. This element of fear and circumspection was easily adapted to the needs of the communist period.

(c) Members of small communities or of the same village have tended not to intermarry, for fear of interference in each others' affairs. This attitude has been seen replicated in the pattern of Albania's foreign relations under the communists (Marmullaku, 1975, p. 88).

(d) Many lives, usually of families' main breadwinners, have been lost. In the 1920s up to 20 per cent of male deaths in parts of the north-east were the result of blood feuds (Lendvai, 1969, p. 180). Visiting the Mat valley in the mid-1930s, Newman (1936, p. 146) reported that with Zogu's attempts to eradicate the blood feud, vendetta murders there had decreased in frequency from one per week to one every six weeks. In Kosovo, such murders were said to be increasing in the 1960s: three communes alone recorded 15 murders and about 30 attempted murders between 1968 and 1970 which were largely attributable to blood feuds (*Politika*, 3 March 1973), although in recent times, attempts by voluntary organisations to end vendettas by extracting pardons from feuding groups appeared to be making some headway.

(e) The impacts on closed families, those which owed blood and lived largely under self-imposed house arrest, were profound. Not least were the economic consequences of untilled fields and the cultural and social implications of restricted movement resulting from suspicion and fear of neighbours. As land was a major source of vendetta disputes, development of the agrarian economy was impeded further than might otherwise have been the case. Certainly the communists' aim to totally collectivise land in Albania and thereby remove individualism and the disputes it provoked, was in part generated by the desire to consign the blood feud to history.

(f) With valley bottoms acting as the boundaries between clan lands, and thus dividing potentially mortal adversaries, communications in this part of the country have long been constrained as a result of such strong forces of tradition.

Although the communists claimed to have eradicated the blood feud within the country itself, it certainly persisted amongst Albanians living in Kosovo, Macedonia and Montenegro, and in Albania's immediate post-communist transition period, the settling of old scores, whether justified in traditional terms or otherwise, re-appeared with some ferocity.

Inhabiting villages in the plains and mountain basins to the south of the Shkumbin river, Tosks have been consistently more susceptible to foreign, especially Greek and Italian, influences. Traditionally they have worn 'petticoats', which, akin to the kilt, were the source of the more effeminate Greek *fustanella*. Most Albanian emigrants, particularly to Italy and the United States, have been of Tosk origin. Environmental and cultural differences evolved a contrasting society to that of the north, yet one based upon variations insufficient to eclipse an Albanian national identity. While tribal organisation had largely been eliminated in the south, up to the eighteenth century certain villages were composed of what could be referred to as small clans – *fare* (literally 'seeds') – headed by elected chieftains (Remérand, 1928).

Under the Turks, Christians were precluded from governmental positions such that the Orthodox members of the south who were not converted pursued craft activities (organised into guilds), business and liberal professions, thus reflecting an altogether more settled, economically oriented and outward-going society than in the north. A complementarity developed in the rural sector under the Turkish *çiflik* (estate) system, whereby Islamicised (or Turkish) landowners provided housing, implements and other farming necessities for the (usually) Christian Orthodox peasant labourers, who in turn delivered up a large proportion of the produce cultivated. Initially the landowners were likely to be *sipatis* – cavalrymen who held military fiefs, but with the empire's military contraction, especially from the eighteenth century, the role of land-owning beys (feudal lords) grew in the southern lowlands, coastal plains and interior basins. Christians in small-scale businesses and the liberal professions could buy small pieces of land (such as around Korçë and Gjirokastër), but the growth of a wealthy land-owning class often left large tracts of land wastefully neglected as some beys became too affluent to bother with cultivation (Durham, 1909).

In the late nineteenth and early twentieth centuries, the children of well placed Tosk families were sent to Western and Central European intellectual centres for their education. Not surprisingly, 'when foreign ideas entered Albania at all, they usually penetrated via the south' (Wolff, 1956, p. 31).

Ironically, it was a Geg, the Muslim Ahmet Zogu, who was to dominate Albanian political life in the inter-war period, once the country had gained its political independence and had achieved some measure of stability. However, at the end of the Second World War the emergent communist leadership was of predominantly southern origin, often having been educated abroad. Enver Hoxha, the party secretary and commander-in-chief of the armed forces, was born in Gjirokastër, and although educated in recently opened Albanian schools, studied in Montpellier and Paris. His father was a labour migrant to the United States (Dede *et al.*, 1985).

2.1.3 Imposed one-ness?

As part of the post-war regime's policy of moulding a unitary Albanian nation, the generic terms 'Geg' and 'Tosk' were not officially recognised – Albanians were simply 'northerners' or 'southerners'. Explicit policies aimed at encouraging intermarriage and intermigration between different regional groups were pursued, in order to overcome long-held local and regional loyalties, and to eradicate traditional distinctions, despite very limited individual mobility.

One of the most notable of these policies was the use of directed labour on major construction projects, such as railway building, and the very explicit intermixing of groups — particularly young people of marriageable age — from different regions of the country on such projects. These youthful workers were also meant to pursue the role of 'revolutionising' the citizens of the areas through which the railway lines were being built. Gatherings with local inhabitants were held to convey socialist ideals and to break down traditional social barriers and aid the intermixing of Albanians from different regional backgrounds (Lani, 1984).

None the less, the traditionally Catholic north and its hostility to the southern communists (particularly those, like Hoxha, with a bourgeois background), wrought what many Albanians and outside observers saw as a communist long-term hidden agenda of exploiting and underdeveloping the north of the country. In addition to the electricity generated by the cascade of hydro-electric power stations developed on the Drin river in the 1970s and 1980s, the region's copper and chrome mines and smelters produced a large proportion of the country's export earnings, yet the employees of these sectors often worked and lived in appalling environmental circumstances. Shkodër, the northern regional capital, and the country's largest centre by population in 1938, had been overtaken by Tirana, Durrës and Elbasan by 1990, with Vlorë catching up fast (see Table 3.13 below).

Ramiz Alia, Hoxha's successor in 1985, was, however, from Shkodër, and did appear to take measures to help redress the previous apparent regional bias. The country's first post-communist president, Sali Berisha, was also a northerner. From the district of Tropojë, adjacent to Kosovo, his background was Muslim, and although some criticism was aimed at him both for establishing close economic ties with the Muslim world and for allegedly showing favour to his own clan in political appointments, given Albania's parlous economic condition, any regional bias in eco-

nomic development was not discernible in the early years of the 1990s.

2.2 Language and oral tradition

2.2.1 The role of language

Language has often been one of the most contentious aspects of national identity: while it divides humans into distinct groups, it is not an adequate criterion of nationality alone. Linguistic characteristics are not fixed or static, they change over time and are shaped by politics as much as politics are shaped by language. In many parts of the world linguistic communities are not of a suitable size to act as the basis of a modern nation state. Yet in the flowering of European nationalism, language was the most frequently invoked attribute in support of national ideals and identity. Nationality and religion did not coincide for the Albanians as they did for their Balkan neighbours, such that the role of language was central to the evolution of Albanian national identity in the nineteenth century, acting both as a common element and as a distinctive cultural and national trait separating Albanians from Turks, Greeks and Slavs.

Within the Indo-European family of languages, Albanian comprises its own sub-group (as do, for example, Iranian and Armenian), although infusions from Greek, Latin, Turkish, Slav and Italian have been inevitably absorbed over the centuries. Ironically, because of the ruggedness, isolation, and relatively poor communications of the area, linguistic influences from adjacent cultures have encouraged significant dialect differences across Albanian-speaking lands. In the post-war period efforts have been made to simplify this complexity through the adoption of a 'standard' Albanian language. In 1952, a 'scientific session' in Tirana, first attempted to clarify and elucidate the problems of evolving a unified language. Twenty years later, the Congress of Orthography adopted uniform phonetic rules of spelling and declared that the Albanian people now possessed a unified literary language, incorporating the basic common elements of the two major dialects, Geg and Tosk (EBNA, 1984, p. 74).

For nineteenth-century nationalist ideals, the role of Abdyl Frashëri, a Bektashi, was emblematic in the Albanian pursuit of overcoming religious differences, whereby for the first time in Balkan history, language, not religion, became the vehicle of national aspirations. This was given especial pertinence because of the Turks' refusal to accept Albanian as a medium of literature and teaching: all nationalities within the empire except the Albanians had their own schools. In Albanian lands, helping to mask the true nature and delineation of an Albanian nation, education was undertaken in Greek for Orthodox Christians and in Turkish or Arabic for Muslims. Three related elements were particularly important in elevating the role of the Albanian language as the prime vehicle for national aspirations: language structure and purity, the evolution of an accepted alphabet, and the role of literature.

2.2.2   Language structure and purity

By the second half of the nineteenth century, a number of scholarly European works had emphasised the ancient antecedence of the Albanian tongue, its cultural associations and structural importance (Skendi, 1967, pp. 113–14). While Greek propagandists attempted to assert that Albanian had Hellenic origins, suggesting for example, that it developed out of Thracian, many others, notably Bopp (1854), pointed to Albanian as holding an independent place within the Indo-European family, thereby emphasising the concomitant ancient independence and separateness of the Albanian people. This relationship has been crucial in the buttressing of Albanian national identity, particularly in relation to the Kosovo question (ASPSRA 1984a, 1985) (see sections 1.1.3 above and 7.1 below).

2.2.3   The evolution of an accepted alphabet

The role of alphabet was in many ways more emotive. By virtue of the Turkish proscrip-

tions on the Albanian language and teaching, any written Albanian became a symbol of nationalist sentiment. Expressed in an alphabet which was again different from that used by the Turks, the Albanian language was thus doubly symbolic. In 1844, Naum Vegilharxhit published a primer employing a new Albanian alphabet of his own making. Believing that Greek, Latin and Arabic alphabets were neither universally acceptable to all Albanians nor able to fully represent Albanian phonetics, he also stimulated nationalist ideals in attempting to preclude foreign political influences transmitted through alien scripts. Various combinational alphabets were employed and experimented with, and the Albanian Society in Constantinople used a basically Latin script devised by Sami Frashëri. At the turn of the century two competing alphabets developed in Shkodër – the *Bashkimi* (Union), using digraphs for sounds not represented by one letter, and the *Agimi* (Dawn) employing diacritics. Whatever the competitive conflicts, the significant factor to emerge was that the Latin script had now gained recognition by Albanians themselves as the medium for their language. Both *Bashkimi* and *Agimi* were totally based upon it, with the consequence that Albanian teaching, clandestine or otherwise, was given a boost and an extra nationalistic dimension.

Adoption of the Latin (rather than Arabic) alphabet for the language's written form at the 1908 Albanian Congress at Monastir (Bitolj) forcefully symbolised an Albanian national and cultural renewal (the British and Foreign Bible Society, with offices in Monastir, had been printing a Latin-alphabet bible in Albanian, with the first dictionary in such a script, since the 1860s (Wolff, 1956, p. 91)). In the same year, the Young Turks gave constitutional guarantees whereby Albanian schools, societies and clubs were opened, newspapers and periodicals were published and distributed. But the nationalistic, implicitly anti-Turkish symbolism of the use of the Latin script soon provoked the Young Turks into suppressing such developments with the result that the Albanian response of revolt against the crumbling empire became even more nationalistic.

2.2.4 The role of literature and oral tradition

A fusion of linguistic purity and patriotic content in Albanian literature was considered the forte of Naim Frashëri (1846–1900), one of the three gifted brothers who embodied Albanian national sentiment in the second half of the nineteenth century. Outside of Albania, the literary activities of expatriate Albanians and their descendants kept alive Albanian writing despite the Ottoman proscriptions. Within the country, with Frashëri as the standard bearer, an 'underground' Albanian literature, full of nationalist content flourished. Indeed, an epic poem depicting the struggles of northern Albanians against the Slavs ran to more than 13,000 verses (Skendi, 1956a, p. 124).

Although the oldest known written document in Albanian only dates back to 1462 (Skendi, 1956a, p. 300), historical evidence from travellers of the time records the existence of written Albanian in the early fourteenth century and possibly earlier. However, with both later Turkish Ottoman and Greek Orthodox proscriptions on written Albanian, the role of oral literature and traditions, myths and stories took on an even greater role, with vernacular folklore and tradition, songs, legends and epics passing orally from one generation to the next, sustaining a national identity and helping to maintain the survival of the native language (Marmullaku 1975, p. 17):

Whatever they could not put down in writing they expressed in their songs, verses, tales, and wise sayings, which going from mouth to mouth, became the patrimony of the whole people. (Xholi, 1985, pp. 26–7)

Alongside songs of romance and marriage, the bulk of Albanian oral poetry has been composed of heroic songs, mostly from the north of the country. They tell of critical events, particularly concerning the vendetta, and the underlying motif is inevitably that of honour (Skendi, 1956a, p. 302). The Albanian diaspora has been important not only in maintaining a written language when it was proscribed within Albania itself, but also in sustaining historic oral traditions. In particular, the songs of Italo-Albanians have remained reflections of the time, following the defeat of Skanderbeg (section 2.3.2 below), when migration from Albania took place. Song cycles tell of wars against the Turks and of the heroism of Skanderbeg.

2.3 National symbols

2.3.1 Material culture

Albanian material culture — military and domestic architecture, costume and textiles, wood, silver and iron-working, pottery, stone and visual art — has long played an important role in contributing to the collective self-image of Albanian-ness, rising above regional, tribal and religious divisions.

Settlement in Albania can been traced back to at least the late Neolithic period, and a number of Bronze age tumuli remain. From the fifth century BC Illyrian castles and towns began to be established, usually on strategic hilltops. Fusing with Greek influences, by the second century BC substantial Illyrian urban centres had been established on protected sites adjacent to the coastal plain. Roman occupation brought road, bridge and aqueduct construction, while from the fifth century both new defensive works and religious buildings were developed. Feudal relations in the Middle Ages saw the rise of centres of artisan production, while, from the fifteenth century, under the Turks, mosques, public baths, and clock towers added new architectural elements. In the countryside, bridges and aqueducts were further developed. By the eighteenth century, the distinctive housing styles of individual urban settlements, such as those of Gjirokastër — fortified two-storey dwellings with large bay balconies — were being forged. Table 2.1 summarises some the major elements of Albanian material culture which have both complemented and moulded Albanian national identity.

2.3.2 Skanderbeg

That 'Shqipëri' is often believed to mean 'land of the eagles' (section 2.1.1. above) may not

Table 2.1   *Summary and exemplification of Albanian material culture*

1. Major archaeological/architectural elements

Illyrian:

Remnant walls and city gates of Lissus (Lezhë) and Rozafat (Shkodër).

Classical:

City ports of Epidamnos/Dyrrachium (Durrës), Apollonia and Butrint, with their urban assemblages, including amphitheatres, hypercausts and mosaics.

Byzantine:

Ecclesiastical architecture and artefacts, such as the tenth century chapel with mosaic within the Roman amphitheatre at Durrës, and the fourteenth century church at Mborjë near Korçë.

Medieval:

Defensive works, such as the XI–XVI century castle at Lezhë, XI–XV century fortifications at Rozafat, XII–XIII century castle at Gjirokastër, remnants of the XII–XV century castle at Krujë made famous by Skanderbeg; Berat's XIII century castle.

Ottoman period:

(a)   Defensive works of local rulers, such as the nineteenth century works of Ali Pasha Tepelena, including the castle at the town of his name (his birth-place);

(b)   preserved mosques in Tirana, Vlorë, Berat (Plate 2.1), and Gjirokastër;

(c)   clock towers in Tirana and Elbasan;

(d)   'Turkish' hump-backed bridges at Mes (near Shkodër) and Mirakë (near Librazhd);

(e)   aqueducts, such as that remaining at Bënça, near Tepelenë;

(f)   public baths, as at Elbasan;

(g)   cobbled streets, as in Gjirokastër, Berat and Krujë, with their often steep gradients;

(h)   wooden 'bazaars', as that partially restored in Krujë; and

(i)   domestic architecture, as in the cores of the 'museum cities' of Berat and Gjirokastër.

2. Ethnographic elements

Textile products:

Linen, wool, silk and cotton use all have an ancient tradition, which reached its climax in the eighteenth and nineteenth centuries. Silk weaving was particularly notable, and the production of women's shawls in the Zadrimë area (south of Shkodër) was outstanding. Aprons, vests, waistcoats, belts, shirt blouses and short jackets were notable from many districts. In addition to clothing, blankets, mattresses, pillows and cradle covers, cushions, hand and saddle bags, tufted bedcovers and floor rugs all had particular regional distinctiveness.

Wood-carving:

A shepherd tradition: water kegs, cradles, distaffs, spoons all gained regional characteristics in relation to the type of wood and nature of carving and chiseling employed. Notable were the water kegs of Kukës, Përmet and Ersekë, the spoons of Mirditë and Gjirokastër, the shepherds' crooks of Gramsh and the distaffs of Shkodër, Gjirokastër and Vlorë. During the Ottoman period, craftsmen of the Albanian school of decorative woodwork, notable for their domestic interior decoration, particularly ornamental ceilings, rosettes, furniture, screens, doors and windows, were employed across the Balkans and Asia Minor.

Silver-working:

The peak of this craft's development took place at the end of the eighteenth century, when dozens of silversmiths' shops flourished in Berat, Elbasan, Shkodër, Tirana and Voskopojë. In the centres of Elbasan and Shkodër more than a hundred families were engaged in the craft. Earrings were particularly notable, including filigree work. Later, decorated small arms became well known.

Iron-working:

Illyrian iron axes, bronze and iron sickles. (Fine examples of vessels, graves, implements and ornaments found in Slovenia.)

Wrought ironwork for domestic decorations, including lamps, later became popular. Exterior elaboration is particularly characteristic of Korçë.

Working of simple materials:

The working of such materials as osier, broom, rushes, straw, reeds and bone horn have often revealed substantial artistry.

Pottery:
This was produced in many locations up to the inter-war period. Notable products were cooking pots, eating bowls and plates, vessels for water, dairy products, oil, chimney pipes, children's toys, tobacco pipes, and religious objects.

Stone-working:
This is known from Illyrian times. Later, notable motif decoration for buildings included suns, flowers and eagles, while fireplaces were produced with geometrical and motif designs. Public amenities such as heads of wells, water fountains, village springs, were often given motifs. Millstones and mortars were ubiquitous.

Icons:
The work of sixteenth-century Onufri is outstanding, as is that of his son Nikolla, and that of the eighteenth-century master David Selenica. Museums have been established at Berat and Korçë.

Sources: Marmullaku, 1975, p. 7; Gjergji, 1978; Senja and Xhafa, nd; Shkurti, 1978, pp. 57–113; Meksi and Thomo, 1981, pp. 99–114; Senja and Kekezi, 1982; Zarshati, 1982; Onuzi, 1987; Dhamo, 1989, pp. 229–40; Karaiskaj, 1989, pp. 49–63; Nallbani, 1989.

be unconnected with the fact that the family emblem of the country's medieval national hero, Gjeorgj Kastrioti (Skanderbeg), was a double-headed eagle, a motif which was adopted for the Albanian national flag.

'Between the fall of the Roman Empire in AD 476 and the fall of the Byzantine Empire in 1453, Albania gained recognition for the first time in her history as a distinct political entity under her own name' (Prifti, 1978, p. 5), when Charles I of Anjou, King of Naples, took Dyrrachium (Durrës) in 1272 and declared a kingdom of Albania (Regnum Albaniae) of which he was to be king (Rex Albaniae). This was not achieved, however, without establishing treaty relations with the Albanian chieftains, who organised their lands from fortified bases such as Krujë. Indeed, a brief independent principality of Albanian chiefs had been set up in 1190.

In 1385, the Albanians' inability to resolve their own internal disputes saw the Ottoman Turks willingly taking up an invitation to intercede. The outcome, repeated so many times in history, entailed a Turkish military victory, extending further than the original dispute warranted, so that by the end of the fourteenth century, Albanian feudal lords were recognising the sovereignty of the Ottoman Sultan over their lands (Skendi, 1967).

As part of their westward and northward expansion, which was to see them taking Otranto and twice threatening the gates of Vienna, the Ottoman Turks, under Sultan Murad II, invaded Albania in 1423, quickly pushing to the Adriatic coast, then largely under Venetian control. While meeting strong resistance, the Turks pursued a largely conciliatory policy, whereby most indigenous landowners maintained their positions in return for three 'forfeits': the payment of tribute, the provision of auxiliary troops when needed, and the compulsory despatching of the feudal lords' sons to the Sultan's court in Constantinople as hostages. It was hoped by the Turks that such a policy would preclude the recurrence of rebellion from Albanian lands.

The son of the feudal lord of Krujë, Skanderbeg was one of the most renowned soldiers in the Turkish army of the early 1440s. Like other well positioned Albanians' sons, he had spent time in the Sultan's court, became Islamicised, and fought fiercely in battle for the Ottoman cause. That half a millenium later Skanderbeg should have been elevated by the communist regime as *the* Albanian national hero, freedom fighter and lauded patriot, is a matter of some historical transformation and no little irony.

Defeated at Niš in 1443 alongside his fellow Muslims at the hands of Christians led by János Hunyadi of Hungary, Skanderbeg abandoned the Turks, and returned to Krujë to denounce Islam and embark upon a holy war against the Ottomans (Skendi, 1980). It has been argued (Wolff, 1956) that Skanderbeg alone helped mould a league of Albanian chieftains into an effective military and

33

Plate 2.1   *The 1827 Bachelors' Mosque situated at the foot of Berat fortress. After 1967 this building became the Museum of Material Culture.*

Plate 2.2 *The National History Museum, situated on the north side of Skanderbeg Square in the centre of Tirana, was completed in 1981. The largest mosaic in the country depicts the communist regime's perception of Albanian-ness. As a somewhat bizarre counterpoint, the Mercedes bus passing in the foreground, easing its way through nonchalant pedestrians and cyclists, was a late-1980s second-hand purchase from Western Europe and still carried the garish colouring, if not the wording, of an all-over advertisement livery.*

political force against the Turks (at the 1444 Congress of Lezhë), and that he was in sole possession of a wider awareness of political strategy. As a symbol of Albanian national unity, therefore, Skanderbeg's future role was secured.

Leading his countrymen for almost 25 years without defeat, one of the major ironies of Skanderbeg's later recognition as a national hero by the world's first self-declared atheist state, was that he received aid from the 'entire Catholic world whose cause he championed' (Noli, 1947, p. 2). Not without reason did successive popes, Alphonse V King of Naples, the Venetian Republic and the City of Ragusa (Dubrovnik) support Skanderbeg's efforts, such that Pope Calistus (1455–8) could declare that 'he stopped the fury of the Turkish tide and prevented it from overruning Christian Europe' (Noli, 1947, p. 74). Indeed, following Skanderbeg's death in 1468 and the inevitable Ottoman victory ten years later, some 10,000 Turks set sail from Vlorë for the Italian mainland, where they captured and held Otranto in the Kingdom of Naples, until 1481.

The subsequent Islamic conversion of many Albanians saw the memory of the national hero fade, particularly in the south, and the songs that once celebrated him and his compatriots became confined to the northern uplands. Having fled from the Turks, Italo-Albanians, free from Islamic dominance, played an important role in perpetuating Skanderbeg's memory. Indeed, he became a nationalist inspiration in the struggle for the liberation of Italy as well as for the freedom of fellow Albanians across the Adriatic, thereby serving 'as an essential link between the two shores' (Skendi, 1968, p. 84).

The elevation of Skanderbeg to the rank of national hero in Albania was largely the work of the writers of the period of national revival (Skendi, 1968). In the nineteenth century, Skanderbeg became the one major symbol of Albanian independence, uniting religious groups in a national ideal. Muslims conveniently forgot that he regained his Christianity to fight a holy war for nearly 25 years against the Turks, just as the later communist leadership did not care to remember his religious

and 'class' affiliations. As an Albanian patriot, Skanderbeg's inspiration was again enrolled to stimulate generations of stories, myths and legends woven around a nationalist theme: one of the most notable poems in the Albanian language is Naim Frashëri's *Skanderbeg* (1899), a lengthy work describing heroic deeds against the Turks. Among the numerous ironies surrounding the projection of Skanderbeg is the fact that the name he is remembered by is a corruption of the Turkish, and implicitly Islamic, Iskander Bey (Prince Alexander, after Alexander the Great of Macedonia), rather than being recalled by his, literally, Christian name Gjergj Kastrioti, which tended not to be emphasised in a later predominantly Islamic nationalist Albania.

Thus, Skanderbeg's example played a crucial role in inspiring later acts of resistance against foreign domination, and provided the necessary self-confidence and will for the ultimate achievement of national independence:

His extraordinary career became in time both the living symbol and the fountainhead of Albanian nationalism (Logoreci, 1977, p. 31).

The post-war communists found it in their interests to harness nationalist symbols: indeed, in its later years Hoxhaism might well be thought of as extreme Albanian nationalism masquerading as socialism. The Day of the Flag was restored as a national day, and emphasising the continuity of Albanian national identity, Skanderbeg's presence was interwoven into the country's post-war development path, as expressed in a number of key localities around the country. Examples of this are described below.

(a) The main square of the capital became Skanderbeg Square, received an equestrian statue of the man, and was considerably enlarged and lined with modern buildings. By contrast, symbolising the superior role of nationalism over communism, the statues of Lenin and Stalin (the latter once located in the square) were less prominantly displayed some distance away to the south (until their removal in 1990/1).

(b) In the northern plain town of Lezhë –

site of the Illyrian and classical Lissus, where Skanderbeg convened the Albanian League in 1444, and later died in 1468 – to mark the quincentenary of his death, the ruined Franciscan church of Shën Koll (St Nicholas), which had been converted into a mosque during the Ottoman period, was declared a national monument, and promoted as Skanderbeg's burial place. No evidence can be found of the burial today: the Turks were said to have desecrated the site and removed his remains.

(c) In the 1960s Krujë was declared a 'hero city' (although it is in practice a rather sparse hillside town of 12,000 people at an elevation of 600 metres). An equestrian statue of Skanderbeg gazes down on what passes to be the town's main square. On the outcrop upon which the medieval fortress once stood, a Skanderbeg museum, one of the better post-war architectural works (designed by Hoxha's daughter Pranvera), was constructed in the early 1980s in the form of a medieval castle. With its still unweathered limestone dominating the skyline, this contemporary representation of Skanderbeg ably articulated the significance of such symbols for the moulding of an Albanian national identity.

2.3.3 The Hoxha cult

The post-war leadership's rhetoric of such heritage and lineage incorporated the Hoxha personality cult. This programmed mass sycophancy was required as a vehicle for galvanising a sense of internal unity and cohesion. Inevitably, it grew as the country became more isolated and its leadership more paranoid about external (and internal) threats. Senility also played its part. Indeed, whenever Hoxha could not or would not appear in public, a closely guarded double, who had been subjected to plastic surgery is claimed to have taken his place (Jones, 1993).

Not content with almost 50 volumes of his *Works* and an all-pervading presence in Albanians' hearts and minds, two days after his

death a special Plenum of the Central Committee, held on 13 April 1985, 'took several decisions to immortalize the work and name of Enver Hoxha' (Alia, 1988, p. 469). It approved unanimously proposals to apply his name to the University of Tirana, to the country's Pioneers' Organisation, to Durrës seaport and to the agricultural co-operative of Plasa in Korçë district. Monuments to the dead leader would be erected in Tirana, Gjirokastër and Korçë, and enormous piles were subsequently erected in the capital's Skanderbeg Square and in a dominant position on the hillside of his birthplace. Already the restored main street of artisans' dwellings in Shkodër had been named after him, and, in 1988, the eightieth anniversary year of his birth, a 'space-age' Enver Hoxha Museum was opened in Tirana ('the pyramid'), housing displays of a wide range of costly, imported, high-technology hardware. The same year saw Hoxha's successor, Ramiz Alia, publish the laudatory volume *Our Enver* (Alia, 1988), his only 'major' work.

Completed in July 1988 this volume personified the continuity which appeared necessary to maintain Party unity and national cohesion. As Hoxha's successor, Ramiz Alia, later to be seen by some as a pragmatic reformer, perpetuated the Stalinist stance in his sycophancy of Hoxha in a book written in almost biblical terms, interweaving the Skanderbeg symbolism with a deification of the communist leader:

For 500 years on end our people have kept alive the legendary figure of Skanderbeg and have been kept alive by it. Just as the battles and deeds of Skanderbeg inspired the Albanians' patriotism and spirit of the resistance even in the most dramatic moments of the life of the nation, so the name and work of Enver Hoxha will remain through the centuries a banner of the struggles of our people for socialism and the prosperity of the Homeland.

With his majestic work Enver Hoxha will always inspire the communists and the people of great deeds, to ceaseless progress. He will always be present in the joys and worries of our society. The present and future generations will be guided by his teachings. Facing any major problem, facing any difficulty or obstacle, they will seek the advice of Enver.

Plate 2.3   Enver Hoxha, in his characteristic baggy trousers, being venerated in marble by heroic workers, peasants and servicemen, at Himarë, on the Ionian coast.

And Enver will help them. He will give them the answers through his work. (Alia, 1988, pp. 481–2)

Just two years later, in September 1990, Alia, now presenting himself as a reforming pragmatist, addressed the United Nations on its 45th anniversary. Emphasising his country's centuries-old role in European affairs and its desire to become an active participant in contemporary events in the continent, Alia's speech broke new ground by avoiding any mention of Hoxha. He did, however, highlight the historic position of Skanderbeg.

At the June 1991 tenth and final congress of the (communist) Party of Labour of Albania (PLA), a keynote opening speech pointed to the many 'illusions and mistakes' of the Hoxha era, and implicitly criticised Alia for showing 'sentimental attitudes' to friends and collaborators. The congress went on to re-evaluate the past, changed the party's name, replaced most of the old guard with a new technocratic leadership, and set the scene for the discrediting of Hoxha. Thus, having risen to heights of deification after his death, Hoxha's personality cult, as a central element of Albanian national identity, came to an abrupt halt. This took place despite a strong rearguard defence by loyal supporters focused around his widow Nexhmije, who maintained a strong political presence as chairman of the Party-affiliated National Democratic Front until arrested in 1992 and sentenced to seven years imprisonment in the following year. Yet the path away from 'Hoxhaism' was dogged by continuous internal divisions at the highest levels until the communists were finally swept from political power in April 1992.

2.3.4 Symbolism and rhetoric of 'self-reliance'

Successively colonised by Greeks, Romans, Huns and Visigoths, by succumbing to Turkish domination in the fifteenth century, Albania was effectively removed from 'Europe' for almost half a millenium. Just as independence was gained from the waning Ottoman Empire prior to the First World War, the country was to be overrun by several armies and become a pawn in major power diplomacy. During the inter-war period, Albanian interests were increasingly subordinated to Italian economic aspirations, which culminated in military occupation on Good Friday 1939. Following Italian capitulation, Axis occupation continued under the Germans. Therefore, by the time of the country's liberation by Yugoslav-backed communist partisans in 1944, Albanian national pride was in sore need of restoration.

Under the communists, following the establishment of a socialist republic in 1946 ideological purity, and economic and cultural independence were to become obsessive. Not requiring the intervention of the Soviet Red Army in ridding the country of its occupiers, the close Albanian–Yugoslav relationship almost saw the smaller of the two neighbours being absorbed by the larger, until, in 1948, Tito's Yugoslavia was expelled from the Soviet bloc (Cominform) for standing up to Stalin on the question of Soviet economic exploitation. This allowed Hoxha to purge all opposition to his then far from secure leadership position as pro-Yugoslav traitors. Albania thus found herself to be the Soviet Union's only direct outlet to the Mediterranean, a strategic significance acknowledged by the development of a Soviet naval base and submarine facility off Vlorë. The Soviets and Czechs also wished to exploit Albania's resources for tourism purposes, although the Albanians had other ideas (see section 4.4).

Following the Sino-Soviet rift of 1961, the Albanians found themselves fulfilling an ideological role as China's mouthpiece in Europe (Hamm, 1963; Prifti, 1968). While representing a significant international relationship, Albania later made it clear that the link with China never matched — economically or ideologically — the strength of that which had existed with the Soviet bloc. In the period of deteriorating relations which was to culminate in the withdrawal of all Chinese personnel in 1978, a new Albanian constitution was published in 1976. Article 28 of this constitution forbade the undertaking of loans, credits or joint ventures with any capitalist, imperialist or revisionist government or institution:

> The granting of concessions to, and the creation of, foreign economic and financial companies and other institutions or ones formed jointly with bourgeois and revisionist capitalist monopolies and states, as well as obtaining credits from them, are prohibited. (PSR of Albania, 1977, p. 17)

Implicitly, this still permitted such activity with 'true socialist' and developing countries, although this was often (conveniently) overlooked by commentators (Sandstrom and Sjöberg, 1991, p. 944). The cynical might argue that Article 28 was concocted to formally undermine any subsequent Chinese claims for the repayment of loans and grants provided to Albania over the previous decade and a half (or indeed Soviet claims for the period before that). None the less, the new constitution institutionalised 'self-reliance' where autarky had been the previous goal. Although the Albanian leadership was not to elevate this to the 'scientific' and conceptual pretensions of the North Korean 'juche principle' (Foster-Carter, 1986; Hall, 1986b), Article 28 encapsulated the way in which the country's leadership, looking to an history of foreign domination, argued the need to call upon what it saw as Albanian deep-rooted pride (Gurashi and Ziri, 1982).

While this constitutional position projected a face of ideological steadfastness, it represented a considerable constraint on foreign economic relations and a major stumbling block to economic development and 'modernisation'. Such an approach also expressed itself in the promotion of Albanian culture and its distinctiveness. In this way, the outgoing and innovative nature of a small nation which had historically impressed itself on a wider world stage (section 2.5), was now circumscribed by the dogmatic belief that 'self-reliance' was the very epitome of the Albanian character. This was grafted on to the self-perceived role of Albania as lone practitioner of true Marxism-Leninism, in the face of Soviet post-Stalin and Chinese post-Mao revisionism.

Apart from United Nations membership, Hoxha refused to permit Albania to take part in any international forum which was seen to be being undermined by the two superpowers. Thus Balkan gatherings were not graced with an Albanian presence, since Tirana argued that Bulgaria and Romania, as Warsaw Pact members, were merely surrogates of Soviet imperialism, while Greece and Turkey, as part of NATO, represented American imperialism. Albania was also the only European country not to be a signatory to the Helsinki accords on human rights (see section 3.1 below).

Ideological self-isolation brought an ever-closer intertwining of communist ideology – as interpreted by the Albanian leadership – and national culture, in an effort to justify an increasingly anachronistic international stance:

> The Party of Labor of Albania preserved, developed and enriched this progressive centuries-old national culture of the Albanian people, gave it a new, socialist content and placed it in the service of the socialist construction of the country . . . by preserving and developing all the healthy and progressive elements of the national culture of the past and of the popular tradition, the artists and writers . . . assist the Party in the communist education of the masses, in preparing them to cope with the imperialist-revisionist ideological aggression. . . . Let them call us savages, because the drum and the bagpipe are played on our stage, or because we have given pride of place to dances of men in wide breeches and woollen caps. For us the important thing is to defend the Homeland, to defend the people, Marxism-Leninism and socialism. And these we defend when we defend everything which is national in form and socialist in content. (Xholi, 1985, pp. 20, 29, 31–2)

The stance of relative self-reliance restricted the country's access to modern technology and thus its capacity to more effectively exploit and process its natural riches. In particular, the oil, chrome and copper industries were faced with increasing productivity problems. A weakening world chromium price in the late 1980s did not improve matters. The consequences of poor quality, deriving from low technology together with poorly trained and motivated mass mobilisation, simply fed back into the system.

As in a number of other developing-state socialist societies, mass mobilisation was favoured by the Albanian authorities to remove, or at least ameliorate, bottlenecks in supply and certain infrastructural development areas. While articulating 'self-reliance' at a group level and thereby reinforcing ideological beliefs, the use of mass 'voluntary' labour reflected a number of other facets of Albanian international isolation and domestic order: the lack of modern technology, and in some cases any technology at all, the lack of funds, and the availability of substantial surplus labour which might have been otherwise misappropriating its time.

The definition of 'voluntary' donation of labour and services appeared to be a rather loose one in the Albanian context, and owed its pedigree both to the pre-war corvée system, a form of tax whereby every adult male was bound by law to give ten days' free labour to the state (or pay someone else to do it for them), and to Stalinist methods of mass mobilisation, whereby both 'volunteers' and other groups (including convict labour) were employed on major construction works. This was seen in its most extreme form in response to earthquake damage (for example in 1967, 1969, 1975, 1979, 1983 and 1988) (Smith, 1979; Popović and Milić, 1981; Qerimi, 1981; Dede, 1983; Neza and Hanka, 1993, p. 40).

Disrupting production, aggravating the housing problem and causing no small measure of human grief, a succession of devastating Balkan earthquakes have had their epicentres actually within or close to the borders of Albania. In November 1975 150 houses were destroyed and 810 damaged in the Sarandë district in the south. As in 1967 and 1969, all outside aid was refused. In April 1979, an earthquake of 7¼ degrees magnitude on the Richter scale, with its epicentre close to the Albanian-inhabited town of Ulcinj in Montenegro, caused great damage in northern Albania. Five hundred villages were severely damaged, 17,000 houses were demolished, 35 people were killed, 350 were injured and 100,000 were rendered temporarily homeless. The village of Dajçi, south of Shkodër, was completely destroyed, killing 15 of its inhabitants. The towns of Shkodër, Lezhë, Peshkopi and Kukës were all affected. For such a small

country, the burden of repair and reconstruction was substantial, yet all international aid was again refused. Instead, 'voluntary' workers drafted in from all over the country helped in the rapid reconstruction efforts, aiming in six months to eliminate the physical consequences of the earthquake. This was financed by the equally 'voluntary' offering of a working-day's pay from every worker in the country, thereby emphasising the dogma that such work was undertaken relying solely on Albania's 'own efforts'.

The collective construction of housing through mass mobilisation emerged in 1968 when a pioneer programme was launched in Tirana during the country's 'cultural revolution'. The general principle involved in voluntary construction efforts was similar to the Soviet Gorkii method (Stretton, 1978), and the later (from 1971) more successful Cuban micro-brigade system (Hall, 1981b, 1989), but did differ in some significant respects. Groups of volunteers were organised within the framework of their residential area or place of employment. Unlike the Cuban system, in which voluntary workers undertake such construction during their normal working time whilst their colleagues back at the workplace attempt to compensate for their absence, the Albanian voluntary principle depended upon construction being undertaken by comrades *in addition* to their normal work patterns – that is entirely in their 'free' time. Otherwise, the principle was similar: the state, through the executive committee of the local people's district council, provided building materials, and technical assistance was made available by state building organisations (Pajcini, 1983).

Final allocation of such housing was supposed to be a matter of full meetings of all persons at the workplace, given that co-operation based upon the place of employment was the usual basis for activity. However, it was the trade union's role, perhaps in conjunction with the enterprise director, to designate final dwelling allocation, according to 'the existing living conditions of each worker and his contribution to the construction of these buildings' (Anon, 1983, p. 8). As other socialist societies found, while mass mobilisation may have been ideologically important and sustaining, resultant poor work quality and low productivity tended to see such methods phased out (with the exception of a revival of the Cuban micro-brigade system in the later 1980s (Hall, 1989)). For example, voluntary housing construction undertaken on behalf of the Korçë Knitted Goods Combine over the two decades up to 1990, had managed to provide just two blocks, housing some 30 families, for a total workforce of some 4,000. On the other hand, in Durrës in the early 1980s the number of homes built with voluntary labour was said to equal that of those built by state building enterprises (Anon, 1983).

The country's railway system was expanded partly through the mobilising of large numbers of young people required to undertake manual work for at least one month every year. Organised into brigades of some 30 strong, they helped lay track-bed and aid the construction of ancillary works such as walls and embankments. For example, 17,000 such young 'volunteers' were involved in the building of the 22 km Laç–Lezhë section of the Durrës–Shkodër railway line, 7,000 were mobilised for the Lezhë–Shkodër section, and 31,000 were required for the inauguration of the 80 km branch line into the northern hills from Milot to Rreshen and Klos (Çoçoli, 1989). A similar mobilisation of youth was employed for the terracing and tree-planting efforts undertaken in upland areas from the 1960s to the 1980s, most notably along the Ionian coast (Anagnosti, 1985). In this way, young women and men from different parts of Albania were drawn together and inter-regional marriages amongst them were encouraged.

By the late 1980s, such 'volunteer' youth labour represented the only remaining example of 'mass mobilisation' in Europe (apart, perhaps, from the deployment of volunteer Romanian coal-miners in urban 'peace-keeping' activities). While mass mobilisation as self-reliance precluded the need for technology – indeed, it was one consequence of its absence – it also required substantial internal social control mechanisms. Once those mechanisms were relaxed, as they were in the early 1990s,

'voluntary' mass mobilisation was just one of a range of dogmas which quickly evaporated.

2.4 Religion

2.4.1 Not a unifying factor

Albanian national identity has tended to coincide with race and language, rather than with religion. Geographically midway between Rome and Constantinople, Christian Albanian lands had been divided between a Roman Catholic north and an Orthodox south ever since the religious schism of 1054. Religious differences, though marked, proved of little lasting importance in constraining Albanian national unity. Although the Roman Catholic north and Orthodox Christian south were Islamicised following the Turkish conquests in the fifteenth century, the process was often slow and uneven (Hasluck, 1929; Skendi, 1956b). Only in the south did religion take on a socio-economic significance wherein a small group of landowning Muslim beys held sway over a largely Christian Orthodox peasantry. The mountainous nature of the north-east and the predominance there of clan-organised pastoralism precluded such relationships.

Reflecting the relatively pragmatic approach taken by the Turks to local affairs within their empire, a large proportion of northern Albanians remained Roman Catholic long after Ottoman conquest. The first 35 years of Ottoman rule saw less than 3 per cent of the population becoming Muslim. By 1610, there were still ten Roman Catholics for every Muslim in Geg lands (Skendi, 1967, p. 8). Indeed, even with conversions among the menfolk, Geg women often maintained their Catholic Christianity. During the seventeenth century, however, the advantages of conversion to Islam became increasingly apparent. Avoidance of taxes and wider administrative employment opportunities within the empire were available to converts. A diminishing number of Catholic clergy was further depleted following the Catholics' support of their north-Italian co-religionists in the 1645 Turko-Venetian War. Further, the Pasha of

Ipek (Peć) deported large numbers of mostly Catholic north-Albanians to the plain of Serbia. Following the Albanian revolt of 1689 and the retreat of supporting Austrian armies from the area, forced conversions to Islam began to be undertaken.

By the second half of the seventeenth century, Elbasan, the most central town in the country, was also the most oriental. Berat too was now predominantly Muslim: by 1670 19 of the city's 30 sections were of such a persuasion (Skendi, 1956b).

Christian Orthodoxy in the south of the country was accorded a very different role to that of Catholicism in the north. Since the Ottoman capture and transformation of the Byzantine capital in 1453, the Patriarchate of Constantinople had been favoured with protection of the Sultan. In this way Mehmet II hoped to gain the allegiance of Orthodox Christians in the Balkans, and granted old rights and privileges to the Ecumenical Patriarch. Thus, for three centuries Islam remained a relatively elitist faith in the south. In 1515, for example, in Gjirokastër district there lived 12,257 Christian families compared to just 53 Muslim households, while in the district of Vlorë, the 1,206 Islamic families there were vastly outnumbered by 14,304 Christian households (Skendi, 1967, p. 10). Greek schools were established in and around the southern Albanian lands at St Nahum (Sveti Naum, sixteenth century), Korçë and Vlorë (eighteenth century). In particular, Voskopojë grew as the first important centre of Greek culture in Albanian lands, exerting great influence over Orthodox Albanians. By the eighteenth century it had attained a population of 40,000, predominantly Vlachs and Albanians. Most significant in this development was the Ottoman refusal to recognise or allow the use of the Albanian language: the Greek Orthodox church more than willingly complied.

During the eighteenth century Voskopojë gave way in importance to Janina; by this time Islamic pressure was being exerted upon Albanian Orthodox Christians. In particular, following the 1768 Russo-Turkish war, reprisals were taken against those whom the Turks considered allies of the Orthodox Russians,

and forced conversions were undertaken. From now on, with increasing Islamic predominance, foreign, and particularly Western perceptions of the Albanians, would closely associate them with their Ottoman co-religionists. This would further emphasise the apparently negative role of religion in the nationalist cause.

Of greatest positive significance in the relationship between religion and national identity, however, was the development of an Islamic sect, often connected to the whirling dervishes, known as Bektashism. Its leading personalities tended to be strong Albanian nationalists with a sense of literary tradition and, not least, Bektashi groups were often instrumental in smuggling into Albania works of literature printed in Albanian outside of the country. This faith was embraced by perhaps a third of all Albanian Muslims. Believed to have originated in the thirteenth century, in the Anatolian frontier regions of Islam, Christianity and pantheism, Bektashism was thought to have been introduced into Albania in the fifteenth century by the Janissaries. Its significance rested in an ability to present both a more tolerant form of Islam compared to the rigid religious prescriptions of the Turks, and a competing faith in its Shia sympathies (as opposed to the Ottoman Sunni faith).

Bektashi leaders played an important part in the Albanian national movement, mediating between other religious groups and providing a more outward-looking cultural receptacle for external influences (Hasluck, 1925; Birge, 1937; Jacques, 1938). Naim Frashëri who, towards the end of the nineteenth century, strove to establish a unified written language and glorify the Albanian past in a literature of its own, was a leading Bektashi.

Orthodox Albanians of Albania did not join forces with the Greeks in their war of independence against the Turks (1821–9). The Orthodox Albanians who did participate lived in Greece, particularly those of the Peloponnesus, descendants of the Albanians who emigrated there during the fourteenth century. Apart from being surrounded by Muslims such that any revolt would be fruitless, the Orthodox Albanians in Albania possessed an Orthodox Christian consciousness rather than any Greek national one. On the other hand, Muslim Albanians who sided with the Turks were not necessarily motivated by religious reasons but had been promised rewards by the Turkish high command for their military service. Any struggle between Orthodox and Muslim Albanians during the Greek Revolution was therefore not looked upon as motivated principally by religion (Skendi, 1956b).

The establishment of the first Albanian Orthodox Church, in the United States in 1908, was rather belated, but at least in its symbolic discarding of the Greek shackles it acted as a rallying point for Albanian nationalists of all religions (see section 2.5.2 below).

In an inter-war period dominated by the Muslim Zog, the Bektashi Order, expelled from Turkey, became an important national influence (Birge, 1937; Irwin, 1984). However, the localised strength of Roman Catholicism in the north and Orthodoxy in the south, their 'external' inspiration and potential divisiveness (Kennedy, 1939), meant that religion was a relatively easy target for the post-war communist government, seeking to establish its own national unifying emblems.

2.4.2   Atheism imposed

As part of the country's (debatably Chinese-inspired) 'cultural revolution' (Pano, 1974), Hoxha announced in February 1967 the beginning of campaigns against bourgeois attitudes, the unequal status of women, a pervading spirit of individualism, and religious practices. The latter, whose inauguration was subsequently attributed to a spontaneous movement by Durrës students, culminated in the closure of all the country's 2,169 places of worship and the imprisonment of many clergy. Albania declared itself, in September of that year, to be the first state-sponsored atheist country. Religion, it was argued, was a divisive force and a source of external subversion, representing the interests of Albania's predatory neighbours: Italy (Roman Catholicism), Serbia and Greece (Orthodoxy), and Turkey (Islam).

The attempted elimination of religion actually passed through several phases in the post-

war period (Skendi, 1956a, pp. 293–9; Logoreci, 1977): the 1967 proscription was merely the ultimate action of a long process of attrition. Initially, when still relatively insecure, the regime pursued a somewhat moderate policy but from the late 1940s attitudes hardened. The land reform law of August 1945 deprived religious organisations of almost all of their property, and a law of November 1949 required all religious communities to develop among their members a sense of loyalty towards 'people's power' and the (then) People's Republic.

Islam was first to be subjected to state interference and control, probably because it was less well organised than the Christian churches. By excluding Bektashis from formal recognition as part of the Muslim community, the state accentuated Sunni-Bektashi differences. Within the faith, two leading Bektashi communist-sympathisers were murdered as traitors near Tirana in 1947 by dervishes of their own order. Discouragement of, then restriction on, mosque attendance and Islamic teaching was followed by the gradual closure of mosques. In the Orthodox Church, bishops loyal to the regime and willing to establish close relations with the Russian Orthodox Church in Moscow were installed: others were imprisoned or executed.

As the Roman Catholic church had played an important role in keeping alive the Albanian language and cultural traditions during the period of Ottoman occupation, the communist regime appeared to have decided to obliterate from popular memory all traces of its historic contribution (Logoreci, 1977, p. 154). For example, it had been Roman Catholics, alongside the country's Bektashi intellectuals, who had supported adoption of the Latin alphabet in 1908; the Orthodox had wanted a Greek alphabet and many Muslims preferred Arabic. Indirectly, without the Roman Catholic presence in northern Albania, Austria-Hungary and Italy would have been bereft of a reason to stop the partition of Albania between Orthodox neighbours which had been threatened since the 1878 Treaty of San Stefano (Peyfuss, 1992, pp. 131, 132).

Despite this, the Vatican was seen as an

alien institution hostile to communist rule, and certainly some of the most vehement opposition to that rule from within Albania came from Catholic sources. Most of the post-war communist leadership hailed from the south of the country; Roman Catholicism had been rooted in the north, with the archbishopric located at Shkodër.

As early as 1945 the Church was attacked as an instrument of the Vatican, and the Apostolic Nuncio to Albania was arrested and expelled after being denounced as a foreign agent. In the following year several prominent Albanian Catholic clergymen were tried for subversion, imprisoned or executed. Such crude acts against the faith and its adherents were followed in 1951 by a government decree nullifying the independence of the Roman Catholic Church. This severed all links with Rome and established a 'national' church subservient to the state.

Persecution and suppression continued until, in 1967, teams of young 'revolutionaries' similar to Mao's 'red guards' in China, were sent on a national crusade to persuade the population to remove religion from their lives. The country's 1946 constitution, not replaced until 1976, did, none the less, guarantee all citizens the freedom of conscience and of faith.

In the early 1970s, an anti-religious museum was established adjacent to Shkodër's erstwhile Roman Catholic cathedral. Nationally, parents were discouraged from giving their children names which held any religious connotation; and official lists of Illyrian and other appropriate names were published. By 1976 such lists had become prescriptive. Article 37 of the country's constitution published in that year declared that:

. . . the state recognises no religion whatsoever and supports atheistic propaganda for the purpose of inculcating a scientific, materialistic world outlook in people (PSR of Albania, 1977, p. 20),

and the 1977 penal code held severe provisions for 'religious propaganda'.

Four factors were important, these were that:

(a) religion was seen by the post-war regime as a divisive rather than unifying force for Albanian national identity (despite, or perhaps because of, the fact that Albanians of different faiths had come together in the national reawakening in the second half of the nineteenth century);

(b) religion was viewed as acting as a trojan horse for alien influences and potentially hostile foreign powers;

(c) both the above perceptions were particularly motivated by the mutual hostility of religion and communist ideology; and

(d) being divided between three competing faiths, institutionalised religion was unable to withstand the onslaughts of the Hoxha regime.

At the individual level, religious faith could not be so easily eradicated: 'crypto-atheism', whereby Albanians outwardly went along with the regime, but secretly continued their religion at home, appears to have been widespread, despite the wide net of *Sigurimi* informers.

Soon after Hoxha's death, the anti-religious museum in Shkodër was closed, being declared no longer appropriate. Although in the mid-1970s one or two multi-coloured booklets in French translation had been published concerning icons and religious murals (Anamali and Adhami, 1974; Dhamo, 1974; Popa, 1974), it was not until after the closing of the atheist museum that postcards depicting religious objects appeared, and new museums and old churches containing substantial religious artefacts were opened to both domestic and foreign visitors. Most notable were the Museum of Medieval Art at Korçë and the Onufri Museum, a former Orthodox cathedral, in Berat.

2.4.3 Religious freedoms

By mid-1990 the communists were declaring that the crime of disseminating religious propaganda was to be removed from the statute book, and religious belief would be a matter for individual conscience. This was indeed a

45

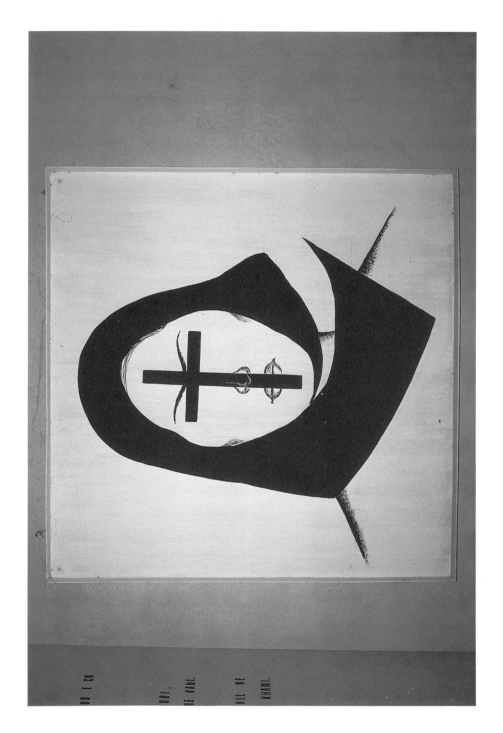

Plate 2.4 *One of the several striking exhibits in Shkodër's long-closed atheist museum.*

major step away from the Hoxha line; but no religious institutions were to be reopened nor clerical posts to be permitted, a position which was to change dramatically by the end of the year.

The Second Balkan Foreign Ministers' Conference, held in Tirana in October 1990, saw Albania become a signatory to a declaration on human rights including freedom of religion. It also witnessed an attack from Greece on Albania's position on that very subject. Encouraged by these developments, mid-November saw 5,000 Albanian Catholics breaking the 23-year-old state ban on religion by holding and attending a public mass in Shkodër. This met no hindrance from the state authorities. Led by Father Simon Jubani, who had been released only the previous year from an incarceration begun in 1967, this was the first religious service to be held since the 'cultural revolution'. The ball had begun to roll. Unable to keep up with events, in the same week Alia confirmed that the constitution should be reformed to permit formal religious activities. But his response to the rapid re-emergence of public religion symbolised a loss of control over national events and the retro-active nature of the communists' waning months of administrative power.

The order of Mother Theresa had become active in Albania during 1990, following a visit in August 1989 from the ethnic Albanian, Skopje-born Gonxhe Bojaxhiu herself. In the past, some criticism of Mother Theresa had been voiced concerning her silence over the fate of Catholics in Albania, but her claimed position had been that she was an unofficial ambassador of the Albanian people when she met religious and civic leaders around the world, and always avoided getting involved in public controversy with Tirana (Zanga, 1989b).

The Vatican later reported (*Osservatore Romano*, 18 October 1991) that only 39 elderly Roman Catholic priests had survived communist rule in Albania, each having spent an average of ten years in prison. The Italian Bishops' Conference donated $50,000 for a new seminary in Shkodër, but foreign priests would be required until an adequate training programme for Albanian lay-workers could fill the vacuum left by a generation devoid of formal religious knowledge and practical experience. Church spokesmen argued that there had developed a strong interest in religion amongst young people, who predominated at the re-introduced masses. Post-communist religion certainly became fashionable. But the wearing of crucifixes came to be as much a symbol of anti-communism and 'freedom' as of any deeply-held Christian beliefs. Indeed, many young crucifix-wearers professed no religion at all or declared themselves to be Muslim, in both circumstances regarding their appendage as a fashionable item of clothing and symbol of newly won self-expression.

Islam was a couple of months behind the Roman Catholic church in inaugurating public services in Albania. Nevertheless, several hundred worshippers gathered in the central Tirana Ethem Bey mosque on 18 January 1991 for the first legal Islamic observance for 23 years. Acting Chief Mufti Ibrahim Bala, in his seventies, led the faithful in prayer, while some 15,000 onlookers gathered in Skanderbeg Square outside. The Mufti had been forced to take a job as a teacher during the ban on religion, but now the training of both clerics and religious educators was underway. The Bektashi Order, with its World Council of Elders based in Tirana, was also reconstituted.

Easter 1991 saw the autocephalous Albanian Orthodox Church re-establishing itself with celebrations in Tirana. However, following the installation of Sali Berisha as the country's president in April 1992, a row ensued over his compliance with a decision taken in Istanbul during the communist period to appoint a Greek archbishop.

In April 1993 John Paul II paid the first ever papal visit to Albania. In Shkodër he ordained two archbishops (for Shkodër and Durrës) and two bishops. By now there were some 65 Roman Catholic priests and nearly 200 monks and nuns within the country. The Pope took the opportunity of his visit to praise religious tolerance within Albania, and President Berisha used the pontiff's comments to rebut suggestions that the country was

Plate 2.5   *An Islamic noticeboard – in Albanian and Arabic – publicises the 1993 Ramadan for those passing Tirana's now battered ex-Palace of Culture.*

moving too close to the Islamic world (EIU, 1993c, p. 43), with Saudi and Kuwaiti finance helping to construct a number of new mosques.

By this time, several religious groups were jostling in the free market atmosphere to compete in making converts of the 'godless' Albanians (Hajrizi, 1993). Baptists, Jehovah's Witnesses, Seventh Day Adventists, Baha'is, Mormons and mainstream Evangelists were so vigorously attempting to fill the perceived spiritual void that proposals were being put forward in parliament to outlaw any missionary activity not connected to Albania's four established faiths. However, President Berisha was said to be ready to veto any such proposals which prevented freedom of religion. Significantly, no political party has a specific religious affiliation.

2.5 The diaspora

2.5.1 *Supranational enterprise*

A distinguishing feature of Albanian national character has been its ability to adopt, adapt, and even capitalise upon the requirements of conquering imperial powers, even when proclaiming fierce self-determination. Overcoming physical and cultural isolation and smallness of numbers, this response to culture contact has seen Albanians rise to positions of extreme influence over territory far greater than a self-contained, independent Albania would have otherwise permitted. The tragedy of much of the country's post-war history has been that by imposing relative self-isolation on the country and its people, Hoxha and his clique prevented this natural innovative and expansive characteristic. As a consequence, the country's role on the world stage in recent decades has become renowned largely for its negative qualities.

The Illyrians, eventually conquered by the Romans in 167 BC (although the Dalmatians, an Illyrian tribe to the north of present day Albania, held out against Rome until 46 BC), made their presence strongly felt within that Empire. Their prowess in conflict brought them renown as some of the best soldiers under Rome's control, which, from 247 AD, was exerted by emperors themselves of Illyrian origin. Claudius II, Aurelian and Probus were notable in this respect, while Diocletian (emperor 284–305) managed to preserve the Empire by transforming a number of its institutions, and Constantine (324–337), a fellow Illyrian, was instrumental in transferring the Empire's capital to Byzantium and proclaiming Christianity as the official religion.

Just as the Illyrians, who were unable to maintain a unified state of their own, served and ruled Rome and Byzantium, so the Albanians . . . served and ruled the Ottoman Empire (Wolff, 1956, p. 26).

After Turkish conquest, the embrace of Islam enabled large numbers of Albanians to acquire property and to have the opportunity of rising within Ottoman political and administrative ranks. The term Crypto-Christianity has been employed (Wolff, 1956) to refer to those who professed Islam for reasons of personal or family advantage, but who in private practised Christianity. These were particularly numerous in Ipek (Peć), the Kosovo plain and between Elbasan and Berat.

Echoing Illyrian successes within the Roman Empire, Albanian administrators and politicians attained the highest positions open to them within Ottoman lands. Some 27 grand viziers were said to have come from Albanian backgrounds. Mehemet Ali, an Albanian tobacconist, rose through the ranks of the Turkish army to attain governorship in 1805, and subsequently independent rule, of Egypt. In 1801 he had co-operated with the British to drive Napoleon and his French army out of Egypt. Ali's dynasty was to last until the abdication of Farouk in 1952.

2.5.2 *The role of emigration and emigrés*

The mobility patterns of northern and southern Albanian groups have revealed marked variations over time. These differences were significant in the process of awakening and sustaining an Albanian national ideal. While northern groups experienced migratory expansion and contraction, being subject to the pressures of Slav and later Turkish constraint, southern Albanians have contributed to the development of a wide diaspora.

In the south, large-scale Albanian emigration, especially to southern Italy and Sicily, took place after Turkish conquest and continued until 1744. By 1886 there were recorded 181,738 Italo-Albanians, while the Italian census of 1907 revealed that numbers had increased to 208,410. At this time a further 60,000 expatriate Albanians and their descendants could be found in the United States, notably around Boston and New York. Significant Albanian colonies had also established themselves in Romania, Bulgaria, Egypt and Turkey proper, with Albanian societies later appearing as far apart as Buenos Aires and Odessa. Some of these were to render far greater assistance to the Albanian national cause than others, reflecting the internal contradictions of Albanian national identity in lacking the cohesion which religious uniformity could bring to other nationalist groups. Yet the continued Ottoman proscription on Albanian teaching and literature provided a focus for such groups: perpetuating, enhancing and giving national identity to the Albanian mother tongue.

By virtue of sheer numbers and physical proximity, the Italo-Albanians have been seen as the most significant overseas group in stimulating Albanian national identity. Referring to themselves as Arbëresh, the majority of Italo-Albanians adhere to the Uniate Church, with its cathedral, the church of the Martorana, in Palermo. This body preserved the Orthodox liturgy while recognising the Pope, thus offending neither Catholic nor Orthodox Albanians. A nationalist literature began to emerge among this group during the middle of the nineteenth century. This movement was spurred on by Italy's wish to further its influence in the Mediterranean, and by the fact that in the 1870s the country's premier, Francesco Crispi, was himself an Italo-Albanian from Sicily. But even prior to higher political considerations, in the 1860s a group of Italo-Albanians had established contact with Albanian patriots in Albania proper (particularly in Shkodër), Egypt and elsewhere, to encourage Albanian literary activity.

It was not until the later 1890s, however, that collective action within Italo-Albanian circles began to crystallise. Two nominally cultural congresses were held in 1895 and 1897 in Calabria. They took on an implicit political dimension, supporting the loosely constituted Società Nazionale Albanese. From these meetings, a four-point programme emerged, calling for a unified Albanian alphabet, the compilation of an Albanian dictionary, the foundation of an Albanian national society, and the establishment of wide-ranging relations with Albania itself. An Albanian language newspaper was subsequently launched, appeals for unity were made to indigenous Albanians, and memoranda were sent to the Sultan requesting freedom for the Albanian language and teaching within Ottoman lands. Not all of the Italo-Albanian proposals necessarily made sense, especially when they involved Italo-Albanian 'union'. Many indigenous Albanians were suspicious of political arguments which carried the support (if only implicit) of the Italian government. In Italy, there were those who saw nothing short of armed revolution and insurgence as the way towards Albanian freedom. Other Italo-Albanians favoured a more moderate course, advocating reform and autonomy for the homeland, rather than revolution and independence.

While the activity of the Italo-Albanians certainly provided a strong impetus to the Albanian national movement and gave the Albanian problem greater prominence in West European thinking, differing perceptions of aims and methods, suspicion of hidden political agendas, and divisions of cultural background limited the value of the movement.

Elsewhere, the most important nationalist impetus came from the Albanian colony in the United States. Dominated by migrants from the Korçë region, this group benefited from a freedom of action not attained elsewhere in the diaspora. In 1905, an Albanian society was established in Buffalo, New York State, and in the following year a weekly publication in Albanian appeared in Boston. Both argued for

BOX 2.1   *Diaspora case study: Albanians in Australia*

In 1921 there were only some ten Albanians in Australia. By 1947 their numbers had risen to 1,400; in the census of 1976 1,492 stated their place of birth as Albania. During the financial year 1979/80, 22 persons arrived in Australia from the country (DEYA, 1983). The great increase in Albanian migration to Australia occurred during the period 1925–8 (Price, 1963). This arose partly from the migration in 1925–6 of Albanians who had returned to their country from the United States, but who then could not return to the US because of that country's quota laws of 1922–4. By 1940 over 120 villages and towns of south-east Albania were represented in Australia, although fewer than one-third of these had representatives in Australia before 1924 (Price, 1963, p. 96).

In the late 1920s and 1930s, Albanian migrants nominated their friends and relatives. There was a large disproportion between the number of men and women as most early Albanian migrants were males. This was largely due to the fact that many migrants had no intention of leaving Europe on a permanent basis, but came to Australia for short-term reasons. Some left their country to avoid persecution or danger; others came to earn money with which they could return home to improve their family properties. In the early stages of migration many came from the same village and community. On arrival, they tended to settle in areas already inhabited by Albanians from their region. This can be seen in the early concentrations of Albanian settlers in Shepperton, Victoria and Moora in Western Australia. Many Albanians who arrived before 1940 established themselves in horticulture, market gardening, sugar-cane growing and tobacco farming. Some also settled in the dairy or mixed-dairying regions of Victoria in the 1930s (Price, 1963, pp. 110–11, 150–51).

Within the chain migration processes of southern Europeans in Australia, there were certain patterns of work activity that a particular group undertook. For example, migrants from the Korçë area tended to concentrate in agriculture and unskilled labouring in Western Australia, Victoria and Queensland, whereas the majority of those from Gjirokastër started small catering businesses in Perth, Melbourne and Sydney. These migrants did not stay in one place, but moved frequently during the first period of settlement. An examination of the patterns of migrants from the village of Rakvicke, near Korçë, found that during the early years of high mobility two-thirds of the male migrants concerned were single, a quarter were married but had left their wives in Albania, and the remainder had either married in Australia or had brought their wives out from Albania to join them (Price, 1963, pp. 175–6).

Gradually, such men gathered their families around them, either by bringing out their families from Europe or by marrying British Australian women or those from their own ethnic background, and setting up home in Australia. A reduced level of movement followed, tending towards more congenial surroundings in more profitable areas or nearer to friends and compatriots. For example, Albanians, along with Bulgarians and Dalmatians who had become well established at Broken Hill, left there in the late 1920s and 1930s for the market gardening and poultry farming areas of outer Sydney (Price, 1963, pp. 180–82).

Although during the depression years of 1929–33 the chain migration of some European groups practically ceased, the sponsoring of womenfolk and friends in other groups continued. The chains from the Korçë district, however, were rather different. They did not start active life until 1927–8, and were thus just beginning their first stage when the depression took hold. But the global economic situation did not have such a severe impact on the immigration of new settler chains, and the sponsorship of male compatriots from the district during the later 1930s was much stronger than for most other immigrant groups. This reflected the continuing desire for the first generation of immigrants to be joined by their male friends and relatives. Indeed, many Korçë settlers had not reached the point of bringing out their womenfolk when World War II interceded, preventing them from doing so. At the end of the war, the new political circumstances in Albania made it equally difficult to emigrate, such that, with migrants from the Korçë district making up the bulk of Albanian settlers in Australia, the proportion of Albanian women in the antipodes has been lower than that of any other southern European migrant group (Price, 1963, pp. 189–90).

During the late 1920s and 1930s, about one-third of Albanians arriving were married, and of these, two-thirds still had their wives in Albania when they were naturalised about ten years later. Of those arriving single, less than 10 per cent had married when naturalised,

BOX 2.1   *Continued*

again on average ten years later. By 1947 the sex ratio of Albanians in Australia was a mere 9.8 females per 1,000 males, a figure which had only risen to 16.0 by 1954 (Price, 1963, p. 96). By the time of the 1976 census, however, the balance had improved with, of 1,492 recorded Albanian migrants, 417 females and 1,075 males, a ratio of 388 per thousand (DEYA, 1983, p. 11).

One of the more notorious links between Albanians and Australia in recent years was the marriage in 1976 of the Albanian pretender Leka, son of Zogu, to the Australian beauty queen Susan Cullen Ward of New South Wales (Eisenhuth, 1977; Ashton, 1979). As the self-styled King Leka and Queen Suzani the couple have made private visits to Australia meeting members of the Albanian community.

the use of the Albanian language and the opening of Albanian schools in the homeland and supported the major cultural demands of the Albanian national leaders.

As noted earlier (section 2.4), it was in the United States that the very first Albanian Orthodox Church was founded. Since 1880, the establishment of such an autocephalous church had been a principal aim of Albanian nationalists in order to rid themselves of Greek, Bulgarian and Serbian chauvinism under the guise of matters Orthodox. It was considered by many to be second only in importance to establishing the recognition of the Albanian language. As neither the establishment of an Albanian church, nor even the use of Albanian in other church services was possible in Albania itself, developments elsewhere in the Albanian world were therefore crucial. The colony in Bucharest failed in its attempts in this direction, and it was left to the intransigence of a Greek priest in Boston – who refused to officiate over the funeral of an Albanian nationalist – to stimulate sufficient nationalist reaction for the founding of the first Albanian Orthodox Church (St George's). In March 1908, with American-educated Fan Noli ordained as priest (by the Russian archbishop of New York), the first litany in Albanian was celebrated. But of course, its role was not simply religious, as that would only appeal to Orthodox Albanians:

. . . as an institution established in order to detach them from the Patriarch of Constantinople, whose policy was to hellenize them and unite them with Greece, it acquired a broader and national significance. (Skendi, 1967, p. 163)

Of the other overseas groups, that in Bulgaria was perhaps the most influential. Published in Sofia, the fortnightly *Drita* ('the light'), had popular appeal, particularly in Albania south of Tirana and Durrës. In 1879, the Society for the Printing of Albanian Writings was established by expatriates in Constantinople, who employed a mixed, mostly Latin alphabet for periodicals and inspirational pamphlets. Following Turkish suppression of the Prizren League, however, the Society was forced to move to Bucharest in 1884 to continue its nationalist propaganda activities and link up with other groups there. In Brussels, an Albanian newspaper began to be published at the turn of the century. Anti-Turkish in content, it was edited by Ismail Kemal Bey Vlora (who later led the first Albanian parliament). Financed from Austria (Helmreich, 1938), the paper was later printed in London.

Throughout the communist period a number of expatriate groups met regularly and promoted material of both an informative and polemical nature. Perhaps the most vociferous was the National Democratic Committee for a Free Albania, based in Paris, which through its news-sheet, *The Albanian Resistance*, attacked the plight of Albanians both in their nation state and in 'enslaved Kossovo'. In the United States, the New York based 'Free Albania' National Committee regularly published *Shqipëria*. In the post-communist period, the newspaper *Illyria* has been gaining in stature there.

With 'self-reliance' an increasingly hollow dogma, the communist leadership in its waning months began turning to the Albanian diaspora for little short of economic salvation. It was, after all, preferable to be bailed out by fellow ethnic Albanians, however deep and long they had been anti-communist, rather than go cap-in-hand to other nationalities. Here could now be seen in the cold blue light of a new dawn the supremacy of nationality over ideology. Thus a crucial feature of Alia's trip to the US in September 1990 to take part in the United Nations' 45th anniversary celebrations was his stopover in Boston, the social and cultural centre for Albanian Americans. Alia visited the important shrine of St George's Albanian Orthodox Church, and at a dinner in Boston attended by some 600 largely well heeled Albanian Americans, he paid tribute to the United States, which, he said, had sheltered Albanians from Kosovo, Macedonia and Montenegro, and had afforded them the opportunity to progress (Zanga, 1990d). This was indeed a different voice to that which, only months before, had condemned US superpower imperialism and had continued to prevent Americans from entering Albania.

Although Boston has been an important focus for the Albanian-American community, New York, and particularly the Bronx, where Albanians own a third of all privately held property, including 35 per cent of the district's pizzerias, now has the largest US Shqiptar community, with a population of an estimated 150,000. A third of this group are from Kosovo, 15,000 having fled from there since 1981 (Greenberg, 1992).

Since 1990, the role of the diaspora has been somewhat mixed. Albanian Americans have moved into publishing, catering and the taxi business in Albania, with some degree of success. On a grander investment level, Iliria Holdings, registered in Switzerland but fronted by Kosovars, signed some of the first contracts for funding inward investment in tourism, property and economic development following Tirana's change of direction. With the coming to power of the Democratic Party, however, those contracts were cancelled and the circumstances of Iliria Holdings were put under investigation.

The overall role of the diaspora in attaining Albanian independence and maintaining a healthy debate on the nature of Albanian national identity has been significant. Certainly

PART II

The legacy of Stalinism

3

The social inheritance

3.1 Human rights

3.1.1 The Mediterranean gulag

In moulding the country's population to fit the Hoxha model of Albanianism, the Party and state went to extreme lengths to exclude foreign interference and to eradicate long-held religious differences and tribal rivalries within the country. Through its self-imposed isolation, the state was able to evade much international scrutiny of its human rights practices. By virtue of its membership of the United Nations in 1955, however, Albania was bound by the UN Charter to uphold human rights, a commitment which it flagrantly ignored. Between 1945 and 1956 an estimated 80,000 political arrests were made (out of a population then less than two million), of whom 16,000 died in prison. In 1961 there existed some 14 camps for political prisoners (Hamm, 1963, p. 53), and by the mid-1970s the number was estimated at 18, situated near mines, industrial centres, construction sites, large irrigation and agricultural reclamation schemes (Logoreci, 1977, pp. 197–8).

Particularly pernicious was the systematic deprivation of contact with the outside world. This assisted the regime's claim that Albania was close to paradise on earth, simply because it prevented Albanians from gaining any other experience with which to compare their own

circumstances, apart from the bad old days of pre-communist Albania, whose official history was suitably re-written. Such deprivation had the long-term effect of stultifying thinking, expression, knowledge, imagination and achievement at individual, group and national levels. (Although that is not to underestimate the ingenuity and innovation which was required to sustain an adequate living within an economy of shortage).

Not only were there draconian bureaucratic, social and border controls which made it virtually impossible for Albanians to leave their own country or, indeed, their own region, but few foreigners were permitted entry, and those who were extended the privilege of being Albania's guests were closely accompanied. In the unlikely event of non-official Albanians finding themselves in conversation with a foreigner, they were obliged to immediately report this to the police. Complications would no doubt arise in such circumstances, but even more trouble was likely if such an event occurred without it being self-reported: sufficient numbers of *Sigurimi* ensured that knowledge of such a conversation would be recorded.

At this time mail was routinely censored, telephone calls were monitored and, until Hoxha's death in 1985, Albanians were forbidden from watching foreign television

57

broadcasts. No foreign literature was available, apart from classic works prescribed for educational purposes, and the monopoly press was state run, albeit with specific journals and newspapers for such groups as the youth and trades unions. Incoming foreigners were searched for literature, particularly for that of a political, religious or titillating nature (see Box 2), and overseas visitors in their turn were not permitted to obtain (although they were rarely aware of it) such newspapers as the party daily *Zëri i Popullit*. Harsh treatment awaited anyone foolish enough to actually attempt to enter the country 'unconventionally' (e.g. see Balyrakis, 1974).

In summary, the major human rights abuses under communism (Frey *et al.*, 1990, pp. iii–vi) entailed methods intended to maintain subservience to the big lie – that Albania was paradise on earth. These included the following.

(a) Restrictions on freedom of expression: journalism, media, art and writing were exclusively state-sponsored. Individuals working in these fields were trained in state-controlled institutions and were dependent upon government commissions. Albanian citizens' rights of free expression and association were greatly diminished through fear of informants and of long, harsh prison terms.

(b) The abolition of religion: as the world's first self-proclaimed atheist state (section 2.4), Albania was unique in constitutionally forbidding all aspects of religion. The 1967 prohibition was the 'logical' conclusion to a largely uncoordinated programme of coercion, intimidation, and violence aimed at clergy and their congregations. An extensive security network enforced the anti-religion decrees.

(c) Intrusion into family life: privacy and protection of the family were abused particularly in the regime's paranoid search for signs of religious activity. Child and adult informants, and the interception of mail were the most common methods employed. The Albanian constitution did not prevent such practices.

(d) Torture and detention: an extensive system of prisons and labour camps held individuals in unspeakable conditions because of their political or religious beliefs. Physical and psychological torture was carried out by local police, prison guards and the *Sigurimi*. The state exploited detainees as a slave labour force in the often dangerous working environments of the country's mining and construction industries.

(e) Restrictions on personal movement: travel outside the local area or residential relocation within the country required prior written authorisation. Attempted escape from the country was considered to be treason, punishable by at least ten years imprisonment and possibly by the death sentence. Relatives of those who attempted an escape were persecuted, denied access to employment and education opportunities, and were liable to suffer internal exile and detention (e.g. see Modiano, 1984). Movement within the country was closely monitored, and individuals who were travelling or relocating even with official permission were liable to harassment.

Internment settlements were dotted around the country. One such was Savra, on the outskirts of Lushnjë, some 64 km south of Tirana. The village consisted of two nucleations, with ordinary villagers and internees separated. Those exiled to Savra, usually the entire families of political prisoners or of those who had escaped abroad, could be confined there without the need for any outward signs of an internment camp. Roll-calls took place three times a day. Detainees, whose identity cards were confiscated, were allowed to move around only in the immediate vicinity of Lushnjë (Partos, 1992).

(f) Economic and social rights: while some gains in the field of economic and social rights were made, particularly in access to education and health care, this was counterweighed by food shortages and extensive rationing, low salaries and a scarcity of consumer goods.

(g) Discrimination against minorities: the abolition of religion particularly disrupted the life of the Greek community, whose identity was based upon common religious, as well as ethnic, bonds. The state attempted to remove the use of many Greek personal and place-names. Internal exile and other dispersal mechanisms were used to dilute the strength and to reduce the size of areas designated as Greek, thereby causing them to lose their minority status, including the right to Greek language schooling. Greek could not be spoken in most public institutions and ethnic Greeks were afraid to speak their own tongue outside of the home. Attempts to create a uniform Albanian nation through the suppression of cultural identity clearly violated ethnic minority rights. The official, truthful, if cynical, argument was that minorities enjoyed the same rights as other Albanian citizens.

3.1.2 Re-establishing the rule of law

Reflecting change in Eastern Europe, domestic unrest and human rights pressure from abroad (Amnesty International, 1984; Frey *et al.*, 1990), in 1990 Albania began to acknowledge the need to cultivate its image, and made it known that it no longer wished to be excluded from the CSCE process. In a blatant and often crude attempt to ease a path towards admission to CSCE, early in 1990 the Albanian government announced it would embark on the long haul of bringing the country's procedures and practices into line with much of the rest of Europe. An early sign was the country's Internal Affairs Ministry's publication of statistics on political prisoners (*Zëri i Popullit*, 21 February 1990). But although the United Nations sessions on human rights in Geneva had examined the Albanian case for seven successive years, Tirana's first reaction to charges levelled against the country was to refuse to discuss them.

In May 1990 the People's Assembly approved a number of changes relating to the judicial system, virtually on the eve of the first ever visit to Albania by a UN Secretary General. Pérez de Cuéllar was arriving specifically to examine the country's human rights situation.

Under the 1976 constitution defence lawyers had been banned and there was no right of appeal. It was easy to offend. Draconian penal codes of 1977 and 1980 had provided for minimum punishments of ten years' imprisonment with hard labour for 'anti-socialist propaganda', and the death sentence was available for 34 offences, including illegal cross-border escape. Border guards were still shooting would-be escapees in 1991 (Amnesty International, 1989; Traynor, 1991). In 1990, a justice ministry and a legal profession, both banned in 1967, were to be re-established, and the authority to try penal offences was removed from village, ward and town courts.

Additionally, a number of hasty pronouncements were made on the lifting of restrictions on personal movement.

(a) All Albanian citizens would be eligible for a passport. For foreign travel they would either need to apply through the official travel agency, or prove that friends or relatives abroad would pay all their costs. In practical terms this new 'freedom' appeared largely academic for most Albanians, although experts and students would now be sent abroad for further education and technical specialisation.

(b) The offences of leaving the country without official permission, of creating foreign or joint companies, and of receiving credits from abroad, would no longer be regarded as treasonable, capital offences: the crime of attempting to flee the country was downgraded to 'illegal border trespassing'.

(c) The administrative restriction of residential rights would be abolished: such restrictions in future would only be applied to persons convicted of a penal offence.

Such declarations substantially raised public expectations, but a continuing political power struggle within the PLA stifled them. When it became painfully apparent that some of the declared measures were not to be carried out after all – notably the question of access to passports – the storming of foreign embassies in Tirana by large numbers of would-be emigrants followed. Eventually the Albanian authorities temporarily relented to permit the exodus of several thousand Albanians from the embassies and out of the country.

It was painfully apparent from the notably bad press that the Albanian government received around the world as a consequence of these events, that official manoeuvring had been counter-productive. As a result, the May 1990 application to join the CSCE met with the granting of mere observer status; full membership was finally bestowed only in June 1991. The Council of Europe was prepared to give Albania no more than observer status, a response which appeared vindicated in February 1992 when the ethnic Greek minority party Omonia was banned, and anti-Greek violence broke out in Sarandë.

However, the internal security police, *Sigurimi*, was disbanded in July 1991 and replaced by a new National Information Service, the function of which remained both obscure and ambiguous.

In an interview with the Internal Affairs Minister Simon Stefani in 1990, *Zëri i Popullit* reported that although various foreign sources had estimated the number of political prisoners in Albania to be between 20,000 and 40,000, there were in fact only 3,850 people in 'penal settlements and re-education stations'. Stefani argued that no person was sentenced for religious activity, and that four death penalties for political crimes had been passed during the 1980s, with three or four persons a year under sentence of death for ordinary crimes. In response to foreign reports claiming large numbers of Greek minority prisoners, Stefani argued that these numbered just 35, and that none had been sentenced for grave political crimes. However, in the last days of 1990 and first few weeks of 1991, more than 11,000 Albanians, many ethnic Greeks, braved snow and freezing conditions to flee across the border to Greece. Constantine Mitsotakis, the Greek prime minister, visited Albania in an effort to stem the flow and promised that Greece would help Europe's last communist state as it moved towards reform. Albania assured Greece that refugees could return 'without consequences', but turned down a request to grant amnesty to those who fled illegally.

The release of all political prisoners was one of the main demands of the country's new opposition parties, following their legalisation in December 1990. In the same month Arben Puto, who had previously co-authored one of the communists' key re-interpretations of Albanian history (Pollo and Puto, 1981; also Puto, 1981), now found himself chairman of the newly formed Forum for the Defence of Human Rights and Fundamental Freedoms. As the country's first independent human rights group, this became the official local monitoring group of the Helsinki Federation for Human Rights in the following year. The Forum sponsored the establishment of the Association of Former Political Prisoners and Victims of Persecution.

By the spring 1991 elections, 563 people had been released since mid-1990, a number several times higher than the previously admitted official figure of 85 political prisoners. This left just 120 people languishing in prison for political offences, with an additional 150 arrested during the violent demonstrations of December 1990. In March the government announced that although it had recently released all political prisoners, 64 people were still being held on such charges as sabotage, hijacking, terrorism, and espionage. Puto claimed in May 1991 that over a hundred political prisoners were still being held (Crawshaw, 1991).

On 30 September 1991 the People's Assembly passed a law declaring all former political prisoners to be innocent except those who had committed acts of terrorism resulting in death or other serious consequences. In the following month Albania acceded to the International Covenants on Civil and Political Rights and on Economic, Social and Cultural Rights (Amnesty International, 1992, p. 53).

Following the Democratic Party's victory in the spring 1992 elections, all remaining political prisoners were released. The Association of Former Political Prisoners and Victims of Persecution subsequently claimed to represent the interests of some 700,000 people — approaching a quarter of the total population. Its aim was to press the authorities into providing them with compensation as well as homes, jobs and education. Those of pensionable age received 600 leks a month (then about $5), roughly half of the average monthly pay.

Many former victims wanted the prisons, labour camps and internment settlements preserved as museums, and this was to be the likely fate of Burrel prison. By contrast, former communists wanted them converted into grain storage depots. Other former internees argued that the Enver Hoxha museum, a posthumous hi-tech shrine to the leader's personality cult, should be converted into a museum dedicated to the victims of his regime (Crawshaw, 1991).

After their release, many former internees were housed temporarily in holiday accommodation on the Adriatic coast in and around the Durrës Beach area. Means for their integration into post-communist society have included the opening up of three-month study courses on the new legal and civic circumstances of the country, in the hope that they could be trained to take up administrative or similar forms of employment. For the 1991–92 and 1992–93 academic years, those former political prisoners who wished to enter higher education were exempted from all admission requirements (Koenig, 1993, p. 23). The children of rehabilitated internees swelled the ranks of those Albanians, stimulating the growth of correspondence courses (Lamani, 1993).

3.2 The demographic legacy

3.2.1 Context

Albania's communist rulers had aimed to have a population of four million by the twenty-first century by maintaining birth rates and lowering infant mortality: recent mass emigration and changing attitudes to birth control suggest 3.5 million to be a more likely figure (Figure 3.1). Between 1982 and the end of the century the rural population was to have increased by 42 per cent, and the urban population by 44 per cent, although the annual absolute increase in the rural population had remained considerably higher than the urban (Skenderi and Vejsiu, 1984, pp. 33–5). By the early 1980s, Albania's average annual population increase was running

at 2.2 per cent (Fincancioglu and Dinshaw, 1982), Europe's highest national figure, but below that for Albanians within Kosovo, where the rate was about 2.6 per cent. Indeed, by the middle of the next century, based on differential rates of natural increase alone, there would be more Albanians outside of the country than within it.

Until recently, little attention had been paid to the country within major demographic appraisals of Eastern Europe by 'Western' authors (Besemeres, 1980; Kosinski, 1977; Kostanick, 1977; McIntyre, 1975). This has, in part, reflected the unique and distinctive position of Albanian demographic patterns and various data problems, although several studies have been undertaken in Albania by Vejsiu and associates (Vejsiu, 1981, 1982a, 1982b, 1987, 1989, 1990; Vejsiu and Bërxholi, 1987; Bërxholi, 1985a, 1988; Bollano, 1988, 1991).

3.2.2 Pre-war conditions

High birth and death rates – the latter reflecting the significant effect of infant mortality and blood feuds – characterised pre-war Albania's demographic structure and early position within the 'demographic cycle'. The estimated population in 1938 was just over a million, an increase of 40,000 on the 1930 census figure for the country (Table 3.1). The country's natural increase for the 1930–38 period was just 5.06 per cent; this was significantly lower, because of high death rates, than that for Bulgaria (13.8 per cent) and Romania (14.0 per cent) (Mason *et al.*, 1945, p. 129). According to League of Nations (1941) figures, general birth rates for 1938 and 1939 were respectively 34.4 and 27.9 per thousand, higher than any other European country and approximately twice the rate for England and Wales at the time. Yet even these figures are considered to be underestimated, since birth registration in Albania was incomplete, especially in the north of the country. The birth tax of half a gold franc acted as an effective deterrent to registration. General death rates for the two years were recorded as 17.6 and 15.1 per thousand, again among the highest in Europe. Although registration of deaths was

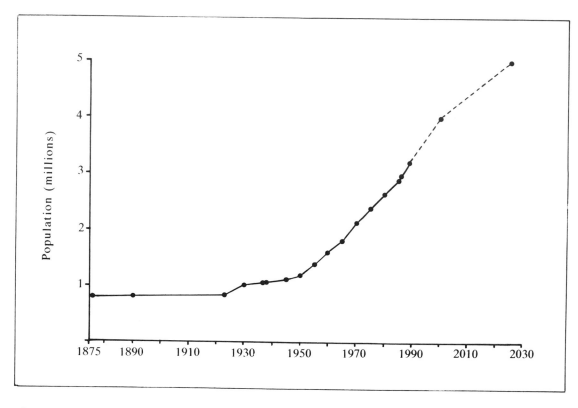

Sources: Mason *et al.*, 1945, p. 129; Bërxholi and Qiriazi, 1986, p. 56; DeS, 1991, p. 35.

Figure 3.1   *Albanian population growth, 1876–2025*

Table 3.1   *Albania: population and religious affiliation by prefecture, 1938*

Prefecture	Area (sq.km)	Population nos	density (p.p.sq.km)	Muslim	Orth.[†]	RC[‡]
				Religion* %		
Berat	3,932	160,497	40.8	73	27	0
Durrës	1,596	83,727	52.5	85	8	7
Elbasan	2,955	105,145	35.6	92	8	0
Kosovo	2,135	48,541	22.7	81	0	19
Korçë	3,312	160,256	48.4	60	40	0
Gjirokastër	4,142	154,157	37.2	51	49	0
Tirana	850	53,084	62.7	96	4	0.3
Vlorë	1,360	54,369	40.0	66	34	0.04
Shkodër	4,870	137,748	28.3	38	1	61
Dibër	2,386	88,159	36.9	80	2	18
Totals	27,538	1,045,683	38.0	69.3	20.4	10.2

Notes:
* Excluding 0.1% Protestants and Jews. The percentages are based upon an estimate of 1927.
† Christian Orthodox
‡ Roman Catholic

Source: Mason *et al.*, 1945, p. 129.

certainly more complete than that of births, there was no standard death certificate form, the posting of registers was always in arrears, and very little information on cause of death was recorded. The majority of villagers died without seeking a doctor: by the mid-1920s over half of the country's 2,540 villages had never been visited by one (Haigh, 1925).

With an average 1938 population density of 38 persons per square kilometre (p.p.sq.km) (compared to 55 for Greece and 60 for Yugoslavia), lowest densities were to be found in the northern highlands, with an average of 14 p.p.sq.km (Figure 3.2, Table 3.1). The highest densities were around the northern city of Shkodër (then the second largest settlement after Tirana), in the fertile Korçë basin, and on the cultivated margins of the coastal plain, with over 80 p.p.sq.km. By contrast, adjacent unreclaimed, malarial districts of the coastal lowlands revealed low densities of 20 or fewer persons per square kilometre. Endemic in all areas below 1,200 metres, malaria was at this time hyper-endemic in parts of the coastal plains and river valleys (Hackett, 1944). The country's bad reputation had been established during the First World War when the disease debilitated Austrian soldiers and Italian marines. It also killed three-quarters of the Romanian prisoners of war interned in Albania, and on repatriation of the remainder new strains of parasite were introduced into Romania on a sufficient scale to significantly modify that country's epidemiology. Malariologists of the Rockefeller Foundation helped establish an Institute of Hygiene in Tirana in 1938, together with a series of malaria stations in the principal towns.

Under subsequent Italian guidance, useful anti-malarial works were undertaken. One of the more notable was at Durrës, where, adjacent to the port, a 15 square kilometre marsh was cleared of mosquitos within two years by reversing the action of an automatic tide gate to admit, rather than exclude sea water at high tide, thereby creating a saline lagoon. The cost of the scheme was more than covered by profits from a fishing concession. More comprehensive Italian plans for malaria eradication and land reclamation – 200,000 hectares at a cost of 1,200 million lire (Prampolini, 1941; von Luckwald,

1942) – were never realised, and much that had been achieved was destroyed in the war.

3.2.3 Population growth and structure

3.2.3.1 Pro-natalism. Although the country's post-war birth rate had declined under the communists from 43.3 per thousand in 1960 to 32.5 in 1970, 26.5 per thousand in 1980 (Anon, 1984) and 25.2 in 1990 (Table 3.2, Figure 3.1), there remained a very explicit pro-natalist policy and access to contraceptive methods was exceptional. This in part reflected the population's Islamic and Roman Catholic backgrounds, but also indicated the atheist state's desire to maintain high manpower levels for the country's future military and economic strength, and for youthful revolutionary fervour to submerge old beliefs. As a result of a halving of the death rate since the 1950s (and a notable improvement in infant mortality rates (Sjöberg, 1990a)), the country's natural increase of 2 per cent per annum – about five times the European average – placed severe pressures on the country's ability to feed itself by the end of the 1980s.

A continued demographic growth rate of 2.2 per cent per annum was to achieve a population of four million by the end of the century: between 1982 and 2000 the rural population was to increase by 830,000 and the urban population by more than 380,000 (Skenderi and Vejsiu, 1983, p. 161). This period would see an increase of about 65 per cent of the population of pensionable age – an issue of no little concern to the authorities.

Certainly, while the population of Albania is young, particularly in the cities, an increase in numbers of citizens of pensionable age had been taking place at a higher rate than for population growth as a whole. In the last decade of communist rule, measures were still being undertaken to stimulate birth rates in the face of a gradual long-term decline. In 1981 the period of paid pregnancy leave from the workplace was extended from one-and-a-half to six months, and it was noticeable that 22,000 more births were recorded for the four-year period after this measure than for the four years

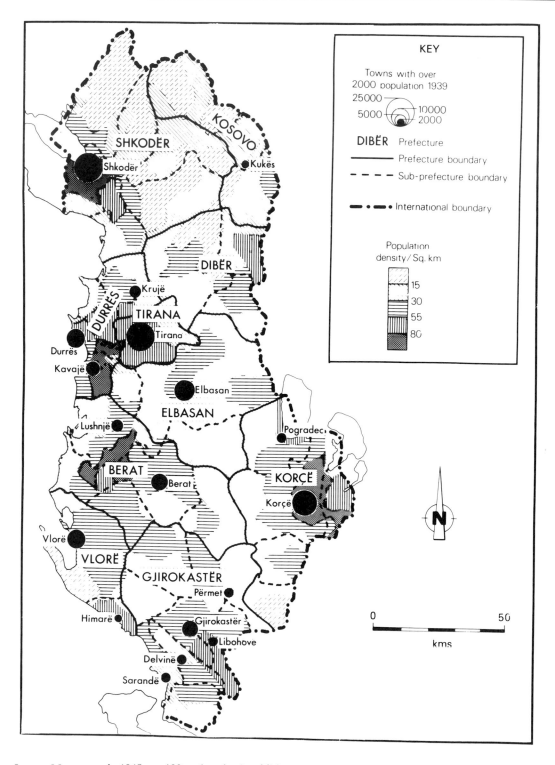

Sources: Mason *et al.*, 1945, p. 130 and author's additions.

Figure 3.2   *Albania: administrative areas, population density and towns of over 2,000 population, 1939*

Table 3.2 *Albania: demographic indicators, 1950–90*

| | | Per thousand inhabitants | | | |
Year	Birth rate	Death rate	Natural increase	Marriages	Divorces
1950	38.5	14.0	24.5	10.1	0.8
1960	43.3	10.4	32.9	7.8	0.5
1970	32.5	9.2	23.3	6.8	0.7
1980	26.5	6.4	20.1	8.1	0.7
1985	26.2	5.8	20.4	8.5	0.8
1989	24.7	5.7	19.0	8.6	0.8
1990	25.2	5.6	19.6	8.9	0.8

Source: DeS, 1991, p. 41.

preceding it. As a corollary, infant mortality was said to have been halved between 1979 and 1985 as improved health and welfare facilities were developed, particularly in the countryside. Shop prices of children's articles were deliberately lowered and the need to emphasise pre-school education was acknowledged, particularly for a previously unrecognised category – 'low income families' (Vejsiu, 1987, p. 32). Emphasis was also given to the 'protection and strengthening of the health of women' and of their domestic facilities, although little subsequent evidence of this was observable.

Birth and death rates took on a greater demographic significance under the communists given that international migratory movement was virtually nil. After an initial post-war burst of rural to urban migration, internal mobility was almost wholly sponsored by the state, particularly in relation to labour requirements for major construction projects.

3.2.3.2 Regional variations. None the less, regional variations in demographic growth reflected a picture of diversity which, for such a small and supposedly egalitarian country, was notable (Hall, 1986a, 1987a). For the period 1960–73 for example, there were significant differences in the population growth rates between the northern and southern upland areas. High birth rates in the northern alps compared to the relatively low rates of the southern uplands have been partly accounted for by religious differences, with the north traditionally strongly Roman Catholic as opposed to the Orthodoxy of the extreme south (Borchert, 1975, p. 179). This factor is at best questionable. Although the official abolition of all religion in 1967 had little effect on relative birth rates in the short term, despite incomplete data, for 1960–73 the two northern districts with by far highest growth rates in the country – Mirditë and Krujë – were also the only two to contain three major new towns each, the construction and subsequent development of which would have significantly contributed to population growth, initially through in-migration and later by natural increase. In the southern districts by contrast, only one or two major new towns were established before the mid-1970s (Hall, 1986a).

By the mid-1980s local variations in birth and death rates were still significant (Table 3.3). By 1990, claimed expectation of life at birth had risen to an average of 72.2 years (from 38.3 in 1938 and 53.5 in 1951), with the rate for women being 75.4 and for men 69.3 years (DeS, 1991, p. 36). At 113.3 inhabitants per square kilometre in 1990 (compared to just 28 in 1923), Albania had the highest population density in the Balkans (Vejsiu, 1990; DeS, 1991; Schmidt-Neke and Sjöberg, 1993).

3.2.3.3 Unshackled youth. By 1985 37 per cent of the population were under 15 years of age, and almost 75 per cent were under 40 (Begeja, 1984, p. 36). By this time, three-quarters of all Albanian citizens had been born into and educated within the framework of Albanian socialism: the average age of the population was

65

Table 3.3 *Albania: regional demographic patterns, 1990*

District*	Total Population ('000s)	% urban	Pop. Density per sq.km	Rates per thousand, 1985 Births	Deaths	Natural increase
Berat	180.5	39.1	175.7	24.8	4.9	19.9
Dibër	153.8	13.2	98.1	32.7	6.6	26.2
Durrës	251.0	49.8	296.0	24.1	6.0	18.1
Elbasan	248.7	40.6	167.9	26.5	5.2	21.2
Fier	251.1	29.4	213.7	25.1	4.8	20.3
Gramsh	44.8	18.2	64.4	24.7	4.9	19.8
Gjirokastër	67.4	40.7	59.3	23.2	6.7	16.5
Kolonjë	25.3	29.6	31.4	22.9	5.0	17.8
Korçë	218.2	34.4	100.1	24.1	6.2	14.9
Krujë	109.9	38.6	181.0	26.2	5.2	21.0
Kukës	104.7	16.6	78.7	35.1	6.1	29.9
Lezhë	63.5	20.1	132.6	24.9	4.7	20.2
Librazhd	73.9	12.0	72.9	28.9	6.1	22.8
Lushnjë	137.8	22.9	193.6	25.6	4.7	20.9
Mat	78.8	19.8	76.6	29.2	5.7	23.5
Mirditë	51.7	15.4	59.6	26.9	5.2	21.7
Përmet	40.4	24.0	43.5	22.8	5.4	17.4
Pogradec	73.3	27.4	101.1	25.9	6.1	19.8
Pukë	50.3	12.1	48.6	30.6	6.2	24.5
Sarandë	89.5	30.3	81.5	22.1	5.1	17.0
Skrapar	47.6	36.3	61.4	25.2	4.4	20.8
Shkodër	241.5	34.9	95.5	24.6	6.0	18.6
Tepelenë	51.0	28.2	62.5	25.9	5.0	20.8
Tirana	374.5	67.6	302.5	21.1	5.7	15.3
Tropojë	46.0	21.9	44.1	28.0	5.9	22.1
Vlorë	180.7	49.0	112.3	24.1	5.7	18.4
Albania	3,255.9	36.1	113.3	25.2	5.6	19.6

* *Note*: normally the names of districts would be rendered in Albanian in the indefinite form. In this volume they are rendered in the definite form, the same as for specific place-names.

Sources: DeS, 1991, pp. 37, 49, 51, 63.

just 26 years (Skenderi and Vejsiu, 1983, p. 156; Sjöberg, 1989a, p. 97).

During the 1980s the number of secondary school pupils increased by about 15 per cent, and higher school students by 65 per cent. By the mid-1980s this generation no longer shared, nor saw the contemporary relevance of, the aspirations of fiercely defended independence and national individuality held by their parents' and grandparents' generations, and which, to a large extent, had sustained but also severely constrained post-war Albania. The post-Hoxha abolition of the ban on watching foreign television broadcasts helped to promote the familiarity of neighbouring societies' lifestyles and thereby to accelerate the pace of growing discontent with life in the People's Socialist Republic of Albania.

By the late 1980s, although the country's leaders continued to denounce Soviet *perestroika*, adjustments to remove 'outmoded' mechanisms and ways of thinking had seen public debate criticising conservative attitudes towards young people. This was a debate which had been rumbling since at least 1984 when the party theoretical paper *Rruga e Partisë* and the daily *Zëri i Popullit* highlighted slackening discipline among the country's youth (Biberaj, 1985, p. 38).

The ability to tune into foreign and particularly Italian television broadcasts from 1985 was crucial in forming young people's attitudes and aspirations. That university students were in the vanguard of demands for change at the end of 1990 was significant. The Albanian youth had developed a collective outlook which did not conform or coincide with the older generations' ways of acting or thinking. This is still apparent today. The fact that most young people are still forced by economic circumstances to live with their parents, often even after marriage, is building up pressures which may yet express themselves forcefully: the generations have moved apart yet still have to share the same roof.

3.2.3.4 A growing working-age population. Representing 58 per cent of the total population, the number of Albanians of working age would increase more rapidly than the total population towards the end of the century, a position regarded as desirable by the communist authorities in order to provide a sufficient labour force for future tasks (Vejsiu, 1989). This attitude, held even into 1990, suggested a maintainance of the 'self-reliance' stance and indicated a lack of faith in any technological modernisation taking place in the near future. Those of working age as a proportion of the total population increased from 55 per cent in 1980 to 57.8 per cent in 1990 (DeS, 1991, p. 36). This meant that annually new jobs needed to be found for 70,000 new recruits to the labour market (Brogan, 1990, p. 183). Total employment officially increased from 1.122 million to 1.433 million over the same decennial period, a growth of 27.7 per cent (DeS, 1991, p. 54).

A growing working population together with policies encouraging large families required the provision of appropriate pre-school care and education for children whose parents were not able to be with them during the working day. Although not compulsory, pre-school education has been an important component of the country's economic and social structure, not least because under the communists it exposed children to 'socialist education' at an early age. Infants and children under the age of three could be placed in day care or overnight accommodation for fees payable by parents and their employers. For children aged three to six years, state-funded kindergarten, administered from the Ministry of Education, had a centrally prescribed curriculum which included language development, physical education and basic natural science, arithmetic, art and music. In 1991 the Ministry aimed to enrol 85 per cent of all five-year-olds into kindergarten by 1995 (Koenig, 1993, p. 8).

3.2.4 Urbanisation, rural development and migration

Albania has maintained the lowest level of urbanisation in Europe – just 35.5 per cent of the population were recorded as living in towns in the 1989 census; an increase of 2 per cent over 1979 (DeS, 1991, p. 361). Three factors accounted for this low figure: first, an explicit rural-led development programme which, despite industrialisation, has seen agriculture and agro-industry as being of prime economic importance to the country's development; second, the maintenance of a higher natural increase of the rural population; and lastly, constraints on rural to urban migration, such that the officially quoted figure for this movement in the later 1980s was just 0.4 per cent of the rural population per annum (Hall, 1987a; Sjöberg, 1989a). Between 1950 and 1986 the amount of arable land in the country had been doubled, through terracing, irrigation, drainage and desalination schemes, much of this in difficult upland areas. These were just the districts first abandoned, with social unrest and economic chaos, in the early 1990s. A 250 per cent increase in population over the 1950–86 period saw the amount of arable land per person actually decrease by 10 per cent. This process accelerated during the 1980s.

As a consequence, and with post-war policies emphasising rural development, Albania has been distinctive in having a rural population which has been increasing in absolute if not in relative terms (32,000 per year). Unlike some

Eastern and many Western European countries, such rural increases have not been statistical quirks resulting from suburbanisation or the growth of dormitory commuter settlements.

During the 1951–5 period of early industrialisation, the country's urban population increased by 52 per cent, about 80 per cent of which was attributable to in-migration (Geco, 1970). High rural emigration rates in those early post-war days began to create serious knock-on effects for rural development, such that, for example, the increase in agricultural output for 1956–60 was only 5 per cent instead of a planned target of 79 per cent (Borchert, 1975). Between 1950 and 1960 rural-to-urban migrants numbered about 130,000, representing 40 per cent of rural areas' natural increase during that period (Vejsiu, 1987, p. 36), or an overall annual national migration rate of ten per thousand. By the end of the 1950s, however, rural-to-urban migration had been sufficiently contained to be of secondary importance to natural increase in contributing to urban growth (Geco, 1973). Average annual rural-to-urban migration rates of 3.5 per thousand total population were reported for the 1960s and 2.7 per thousand for the 1970s (Misja and Vejsiu, 1982, p. 13). From the mid-1970s rural-to-urban migration slowed down substantially to a level of six to seven thousand persons per year by the mid-1980s (a migratory rate of about two per thousand population, although sources failed to indicate levels of urban-to-rural migration) (Skenderi and Vejsiu, 1983, p. 161; 1984, p. 34).

Policies discriminating positively in favour of rural development, and particularly of upland areas, encouraged high rural population growth rates: between 1970 and 1978 it represented 72 per cent of the national increase (Hall, 1987a). However, some Albanian authors argued that there continued to be an over-concentration of activity in the Durrës-Tirana-Elbasan 'core area'. Here, 26 per cent of the country's urban population, over 38 per cent of total industrial output, more than 50 per cent of national light industrial production and over 58 per cent of the country's engineering could be found (Qemo and Luci, 1983, p. 238). It was argued that migration to these areas should be further restricted.

Although at a much lower level than in the rest of Eastern Europe, some rural-to-urban commuting took place. Towards the end of the communist period about 120,000 people (6.3 per cent of the rural population) were said to be working in industry and other urban employment sectors but living in rural homes (Skenderi and Vejsiu, 1983, p. 162). However, with at that time no private ownership of cars and a somewhat rudimentary national public transport system, the physical nature of such commuting was somewhat less sophisticated than elsewhere.

In the upheaval of the early 1990s, rural poverty and the demise of bureaucratic constraints on internal mobility saw large numbers of people migrating to urban areas. In the year between the spring 1991 and 1992 general elections, Tirana's population was increased by 30,000 in-migrants, equivalent to 10 per cent of the capital's population (EIU, 1992c, p. 44). Spontaneous settlements developed on the periphery of the city and on open spaces such as the botanical gardens (see Chapter 5).

3.3   Welfare provision

3.3.1   Incomes

Up to the early 1960s, Albanian pay scales were similar to those in the rest of socialist Eastern Europe. After the break with the Soviet bloc in 1961, a shortage of suitably qualified experts saw the emergence of income differentials between and within sectors as a result of the need to encourage the acquisition of better qualifications. Physically difficult jobs also offered higher remuneration. Consequently, by the mid-1960s, workers in the highest paid sector, transport (Table 3.4), received an average income of 71 per cent more than those in food, the lowest paid sector (Lika, 1964). Income differentials of up to 4:1 within individual employment sectors were also thought to have occurred (Schnytzer, 1982, p. 113). In response to this, attempts began in 1967 at equalisation, by reducing the highest salaries. All incomes above 1,200 leks per month were cut (the minimum salary would

Table 3.4 *Albania: distribution of the working population by economic sector, 1960–90*

	1960	1970	1980	1985	1988	1990
	Year: percentage of total					
Industry	15.1	19.2	21.8	22.3	22.9	23.6
Construction	11.4	9.1	9.1	8.0	7.0	6.8
Agriculture	55.6	52.2	51.4	51.3	51.7	47.0
Transport and communications	2.0	2.3	2.5	2.9	2.9	2.0
Trade*	5.9	5.9	4.8	4.8	4.8	1.8
Education and welfare	3.4	4.7	4.6	4.5	4.5	4.5
Health	2.7	2.6	3.0	2.8	2.9	2.9
Public service	–	–	–	–		5.0
Others	3.9	3.2	2.8	3.4	3.3	6.4
Total	100.0	100.0	100.0	100.0	100.0	100.0

Note: * for 1990 designated as 'Trade-catering'.

Source: KPS, 1989, p. 59; DeS, 1991, p. 77; author's additional calculations.

have been about 500 at this time), although this was to some extent compensated for by the abolition of all forms of income tax. However, 'supplementary' payments were still significant in making up wage packets, and official claims that the ratio between highest and lowest pay ranged from 1:2.5 to 1:3 appeared a little unreal.

In April 1976 income equalisation was taken further, particularly in regard to urban-rural and upland-lowland differences. This entailed measures to reduce: (a) all salaries above 900 leks by between 4 per cent and 25 per cent; (b) incomes of teachers and scientists by 14 per cent to 22 per cent; and (c) bonuses for scientific titles, degrees and publications by up to 50 per cent, together with the abolition of other bonuses and payments. On the other hand, wages of state farm workers were raised, albeit linked to plan fulfilment. All specialists were to be paid according to their field of specialisation and not in relation to the district or institution in which they worked. Finally, certain unspecified 'disproportions' observed in the wages of workers in the fishing and maritime transport sectors were to be adjusted.

The reported consequences of these measures were to see the ratio between the average pay of workers (that is, urban and state-farm employees) and the salary of a ministry director,

brought down from 1:2.5 to 1:2. This ratio was often wrongly quoted subsequently as representing the whole range of Albanian incomes (Bollano, 1984). It was only a comparison of sector averages, and excluded the co-operativist peasantry. Other income ratios officially quoted included that between workers and the director of the same enterprise at 1:1.7, and the lowest and highest rates of workers within the same branch, at 1:1.65 (EBNA, 1984, pp. 171–2).

The 1976 pronouncement on the need to reduce rural–urban differentials was not new. Indeed, between 1971 and 1975, while national average per capita real income increased by 14.5 per cent, that for rural workers increased by 20.5 per cent compared to only 8.7 per cent for urban workers. (Also, in 1972 the co-operativist peasantry were provided with state pensions for the first time.) In addition, neither was attention to improving upland areas new: the major slogan for the 1966–70 plan period – 'let us take to the hills and mountains and make them as fertile and as beautiful as the plains' – had symbolised that. But by explicitly referring to the need for priority to be given to the improvement of living standards in rural and upland areas, the 1976 signals were suggesting that all was not as well as it should have been.

Table 3.5 *Albania: spatially expressed equalisation policies*

'Pro-rural'	'Pro-upland'
1. 'Socialising' household work to ease the burden of women and to raise living standards: establishment and extension of bakeries, creches, kindergarten, dining halls, public baths, launderies, clinics, maternity homes.	1. Each co-operative was allotted blocks of orchards, olive groves or vineyards with 50% state coverage of development costs.
2. Compulsory eight-year school system.	2. Encouragement of auxiliary activities – production of building materials, food processing, handicrafts.
3. Extension of part-time education course.	3. Rustication of urban workers and youths.
4. Electrification, enabling increased mechanisation of farm work and higher productivity.	4. Mutual help between upland and lowland co-operatives.
5. Rustication of urban workers and youth in mass campaigns for harvesting and construction projects.	5. State support for irrigation projects.
6. Raising co-operativists' pensions.	6. Reduction of 9%–15% in the price of nitrogenous fertilisers.
7. Improved housing – more than half of the peasantry live in dwellings built since the start of collectivisation.	7. Defraying of storage and transport costs by MTSs for co-operatives.
8. Co-operativists' voluntary contribution to construction and securing of local materials.	8. Exemption from paying interest on state loans.

Source: Hall, 1987a, p. 55.

Various subsequent rural development policies aimed at positive discrimination in favour of rural rather than urban areas and of uplands rather than lowlands (Table 3.5). However, as Sjöberg (1989b, 1991a, 1991b) and others have emphasised, there were additional dimensions to rural retention policies, most notably administrative restrictions on the movement of rural dwellers. Further, introduction of higher-type agricultural co-operatives (section 4.2) and the rural intensification programme of the 1980s militated against regional economic equalisation.

One consequence of this policy was a faster rise in rural incomes than urban: while for 1960–70 the rate was 140 per cent greater, for 1971–80 it was up to three times greater. From 1980 to 1982 per capita income in the countryside rose by 28 per cent compared to 4.1 per cent for the population as a whole. The 1980 rural population, at 1.75 million, was greater than the country's total population in 1960 (1.61 million), and was viewed by the communists as reflecting the success of a policy which attempted to prevent unplanned rural-to-urban migration and to ensure the country's upland areas were not depopulated (Papajorgji, 1982). Even so, Skenderi and Vejsiu (1983, p. 161) talked about the demographic imbalance in some of the country's north-eastern uplands resulting from out-migration of young females. Self-criticism began to appear:

. . . in some instances the physical movements of the population are expressions of lack of proper co-ordination in the plan of territorial distribution between the material elements of productive forces and the sources of labour (Qemo and Luci, 1983, p. 236).

It was not until the turn of the decade, however, that the facade began to be rent asunder. With the collapse of raw material and energy supply, and the introduction of an 80 per cent guaranteed payment for those laid off as a consequence, it was announced in September 1990 that the minumum wage would be raised from 350 to 450 leks per month, with differential increases above 450. This would result in the average wage rising from 523 to 570 leks per month. The move was likely to have an inflationary effect at a time when consumer goods were already in short supply (EIU, 1990e, p. 42).

Four months later the communist authorities announced a series of concessions to striking coal-miners in an effort to stop labour unrest spreading. A special session of the council of ministers decided that all miners would receive a 30 per cent–50 per cent pay increase, depending upon their length of service. Basic pay was 1,000 leks a month. The council ruled that the concessions would apply to all Albania's 30,000 miners, not just to those who had been striking at the 3,000 strong Valias pit for a 200 per cent increase. By this time, however, inflation was beginning to bite.

3.3.2 Medical provision

It is in the areas of health and education that past claims and reality appear to have most noticeably diverged (compare Anon, 1973a, with Hamilton and Solanki, 1992). Before the war there were some eight state hospitals within the country, and an institute of hygiene was founded in Tirana in 1938 with the co-operation of the Rockefeller trustees (Mason *et al.*, 1945, p. 224). Ambulance stations and medical officers were provided in all municipalities, while travelling medical officers, introduced in 1932, visited villages, examining schoolchildren and dispensaries. Founded in 1922, the Albanian Red Cross maintained a number of services, largely in the capital.

The communists introduced a wide-ranging insurance scheme in 1947, and most medical treatment, although not medicaments, was provided free. Comprehensive improvements to the health service introduced in the 1950s saw a substantial building and training programme throughout the 1960s and 1970s, albeit disrupted, as other areas of development, by the political break with the Soviet Union. By 1980, for example, according to official statistics there were 70 hospital beds per thousand population compared with ten in 1938, while the proportion of physicians and dentists had risen to one for every 597 persons from 1: 8,527 in 1938 (Table 3.6). Direction of medical personnel to the country's more remote areas, however, only

gained momentum during the 'cultural revolution' of the mid-1960s, by which time, following the loss of Soviet assistance, most medics were receiving their training solely within Albania. In rural areas in 1962 there was only one doctor for every 24,717 persons, a discrepancy significantly reduced (in official statistics at least) to 1:5,800 by 1969. By 1971 every village was said to have its own medical centre. These steps were vital with a population still two-thirds rural and often extremely isolated.

As noted earlier (section 3.2.3), mortality rates, including infant mortality, were greatly reduced during the communist period. A number of endemic diseases were brought under control, including malaria, tuberculosis and syphilis. By the early 1980s there were some 800 medical institutions distributed across the country, with most major urban centres having more than one hospital catering for in-patients. Rural health centres and mobile teams were said to cover all inhabited settlements: more than 80 per cent of health and medical institutions were located in the countryside (Miho, 1977, p. 62; Preza and Bekteshi, 1978, pp. 7–8; Kallfa, 1984, p. 162; Sjöberg, 1991a, pp. 152–3). By 1990, there was an average of four hospital beds per thousand population (Table 3.6), although the figure varied between districts from eight in Tirana to two in the mostly lowland districts of Fier, Krujë and Lushnjë, and the remoter inland district of Librazhd (DeS, 1991, p. 123).

While little statistical evidence of quality was ever revealed, limited empirical observation provided a mixed picture of apparently reasonable primary care systems but with shortages of most basic technical requirements. Internal debate also focused on shortcomings in medical research (Logoreci, 1977, p. 185). However, informed analysts such as Sjöberg (1991a, p. 154) could argue from the fragmented evidence that with health centres and other stationary medical services largely found in locations commensurate with settlement rank size, there appeared to be a reasonably equitable geographical distribution of health resources during the 1970s and 1980s. The role of mobile teams was, however, questionable in emergencies where substantial shortcomings in

Table 3.6 *Albania: extent and general distribution of health and education facilities, 1938–90*

	1938		1969/70		1978/9	1988		1990
	a	*b*	*a*	*b*	*a*	*a*	*b*	*a*
All medical institutions	10	0	238	54.6	882[†]	894[‡]	53.8[≠]	884
Medical beds	820	0	13,750	9.2	16,414[†]	18,800		19,000
Beds per 1000 population	1.0	0	7.1		6.6	5.1		4
Population per doctor[+]	8,527		1,181	c	583	572		585
Kindergarten	23*	0	1,423	73.4	2,667[†]	3,251	76.4	3,926
Primary schools	643	82.3	1,374	86.4	1,539	1,691	86.5	1,726
Secondary/ technical schools	11	0	115	7.0	265	485		513

Notes:

a   number
b   % rural
*   none existed in 1938, these data are for 1950
†   data for 1980
‡   comprising: 730 maternity homes, 158 hospitals and 6 spas
≠   refers to hospitals only
c   in rural areas in 1962 there was only one doctor for every 24,717 persons, a discrepancy reduced to 1: 5,800 by 1969.
+   includes dentists

As ever, the data need to be treated with some caution: while the above come from original or translated Albanian sources, significant discrepancies appeared during their compilation for this table.

Sources: Klosi, 1969, 53–5; DPS, 1974, pp. 205, 223; Anon, 1979, 23–4; Selala, 1982, p. 24; BBC SWB EE/ W1315 A/6 22 November 1984; Hall, 1987a, p. 56; KPS, 1989, pp. 4, 130–1, 159–161; DeS, 1991, pp. 90–3, 121–3; author's additional calculations.

the physical infrastructure, particularly during severe winter conditions, rendered swift and effective mobility difficult. Mountain villages were particularly vulnerable in this respect.

Following the collapse of Albanian support systems, Western media attention (e.g. Hamilton and Solanki, 1992) focused on major shortcomings in the country's health-care system. Many rural hospitals lacked basic diagnostic facilities, while much of the equipment in urban hospitals was obsolete and patient conditions were poor. In Shkodër, for example:

Patients have to arrive early at the . . . . polyclinic in order to see a specialist, as there is no appointments system. The decrepit building with its peeling paint lacks glass in many of the windows.

Patients bring their bicycles into the clinic to avoid having them stolen, and stand about smoking as they wait for hours in the corridor. Blood stained phlegm stains stairs and landings. (*Medical Monitor*, 1991, p. 5)

While medical staff training was of a relatively high standard, the limited pharmaceuticals industry and lack of hard currency to import drugs and equipment meant that health workers had no choice but to prescribe inappropriate or time-expired medicaments. The dogma of self-reliance had exacerbated this problem, and only the small political élite had been able to leave the country in order to gain access to better medical treatment.

Ironically, since the country's borders have been prised open, large numbers of young professionals have left Albania to further debilitate the country's services. In 1991 alone some 200 doctors were reported to have gone to France. In that year the World Health Organisation (WHO) reported on the urgent need to keep district and central health care facilities functioning: maternal and infant mortality levels were a particular cause for concern. The WHO emphasised the need for a hygiene programme, one of the targets of which would need to be a reduction of roundworm infestation. The parasite was widespread: 40 per cent of urban and up to 80 per cent of rural children were found to be affected. With faeces used to fertilise the soil, ascaris eggs were being ingested by children and babies taken into the fields by their working mothers and eating the soil containing eggs. Improving methods of excreta disposal was therefore a key objective.

Pneumonia and diarrhoea were the major causes of infant mortality, while the incidence of viral hepatitis was increasing. Respiratory diseases accounted for around 40 per cent of all infant deaths, and a quarter of hospital admissions of young children were thought to be linked to malnutrition. Premature births were associated with a quarter of all infant mortality, and 12 per cent of births weighed less than 2.5 kilograms (*Medical Monitor*, 1991). By mid-1993, however, it was being claimed that deaths in childbirth had halved since 1990, reflecting the legalisation of abortion and a ban on allowing pregnant women to continue to work in heavy manual jobs such as mining and construction.

Following World Bank prompting, the Ministry of Health conducted a survey of the location and use of the country's 16,000 hospital beds. As a consequence, 65 small hospitals were to be transformed into health centres with day beds, and overall bed provision was to be reduced by 3,000 (*ATA*, 18 February 1993). Means of transforming the rest of the country's medical provision would follow.

3.3.3 Education

3.3.3.1 Pre-Communist education. Under the Ottomans, writing and printing in the Albanian language were forbidden, although from 1891 Korçë's Kyrias Institute for girls held surreptitious classes in the language and for a short time the Normal School at Elbasan was given some latitude. With nominal independence, the provisional government of Ismail Kemal Vlora promoted education in the south of the country, while between 1915 and 1920 the various foreign armies of occupation opened schools in the areas under their control.

In 1920, a ministry of public instruction was created, set with the task of trying to establish a national school system in a newly emergent country whose people were 80 per cent illiterate. An education law was passed in 1921 and 452 schools were established, employing 647 teachers. The Normal School at Elbasan and the French Lycée at Korçë became secondary schools. The American Junior Red Cross opened a technical school in Tirana, using English as the medium of instruction. By 1922 seven boarding schools with 450 pupils had been developed for children in sparsely populated regions. Italian professional schools were founded during 1927–8, and two years later the American Near East Foundation opened an agricultural school for boys and a domestic economy school and teachers' course for girls.

Under the monarchy, most schools were nationalised in 1933, and in the following year education became compulsory but free for children between seven and 13 years old. Italian schools were taken over on the grounds that they were becoming training grounds for fascism. In 1934, however, the attempt to close Greek schools was condemned by the Hague Tribunal, and the whole question of Greek schools in Albania, and Albanian schools in Greece, was examined by the League of Nations Council, which insisted that the communal Greek schools in the south of the country should be reopened, albeit as state schools. Secondary schools were reorganised in 1938.

Generally, the Albanian state-school system was poorly supported. Without a university, higher education overseas – particularly in France and Italy – was necessary. In 1938, 16 state scholars were studying abroad, while a further 429 were overseas at private expense.

One particularly interesting development of the Zogu era was the founding of the 'National Education' (*Eni Kombëtar Gjlmenie Shqiptare*) organisation, which was intended to oversee the physical, moral and civil education of Albanian youth. This included developing comradeship between boys and girls as a corrective to the traditional low status given to women in society. While formally resembling both Hitler Youth and communist Young Pioneer movements, the organisation was not overseen by any one political party. Its headquarters was located within the Ministry of Education until February 1939 when it was transferred to a new Ministry of Popular Culture, and the organisation executed its mission through recognised sporting and artistic associations (Mason *et al.*, 1945, pp. 220–3).

3.3.3.2 Changing educational influences under communism. Education was axiomatic to the communists' post-war development programme, and was pursued with characteristic vigour (Table 3.6). In 1944 an Office of Education was established to oversee a reorganisation of education based on Marxist-Leninist precepts. Reforms of 1946 saw the introduction of pre-school education, and schools were established in hitherto unprovided regions of the country. Compulsory education was now extended to children between seven and 14 years. The trade unions, youth movements and women's organisations were all mobilised, so that by 1955 illiteracy was said to have been eliminated for every Albanian under 40 years of age.

General Soviet-style principles were established and the opening of vocational and technical secondary schools was a reflection of this. Albanian students and scholars now visited the USSR, while Soviet textbooks, teaching materials and instructors flowed in the opposite direction. Russian became the compulsory foreign language in schools and tertiary institutions. In 1956 Soviet-inspired polytechnic education was introduced, whereby work-oriented schooling led on to specialised and narrowly focused training for industry. Technology, agriculture and manual skills were emphasised in the classroom, while outside productive work acted to relate academic learning and everyday life. Schoolchildren were required to work on local gardening projects or in agricultural co-operatives; older students went into co-operatives or factories. In 1957, the State University of Tirana was formed from a number of existing higher education institutes.

By the end of the decade, however, the Sino-Soviet rift was reaching a climax which would see Albania supporting the Chinese position. The 1960s were therefore characterised by policies aimed at reducing or eliminating Soviet influence, not least in education. Ironically more emphasis needed to be given to Soviet-style polytechnic education in order to train Albanians taking over work previously undertaken by Soviet advisors. In 1961, when relations were finally broken off, Albanian students and scholars in the USSR, and Soviet citizens in Albania returned home. Russian language classes were no longer compulsory. An eight-year elementary and four-year secondary school education structure was instituted and schools for training skilled workers were established. Much needed part-time evening, correspondence and seasonal programmes for working adults were also introduced.

The period of Chinese influence saw educational and cultural exchanges taking place with the world's most populous state, and English became the most widely studied foreign language, often using Chinese learning materials. The level of productive work demanded of students was virtually doubled. Military training and physical education were made compulsory following Albania's formal withdrawal from the Warsaw Pact in 1968 (in response to the invasion of Czechoslovakia, although the country had effectively left the organisation after the Sino-Soviet split).

Education reforms in 1970 aimed at consolidating post-Soviet trends, the underlying dogma being to combine learning, productive work, physical education and military training in order to produce the elusive 'new (Albanian) socialist man'. Compulsory education was extended to eight years, with the school starting age now reduced to six. A uniform system of separate elementary and secondary school programmes was introduced, and all secondary school curricula were standardised, to comprise 55 per cent academic work, 27 per cent production and 18 per cent military training and physical education. Students wishing to enter higher education were first required to work in productive labour for a year, and on completion of higher education, there was a further requirement of nine months productive work and three months military training. Part-time programmes for working adults now paralleled full-time programmes. Centres for higher education were extended to new locations, and in 1971 the Academy of Sciences, with constituent research institutes, was established.

The isolation which followed China's withdrawal of support was accompanied by a notable slowing of technological development with increasing material obsolescence and intellectual bankruptcy. Extensive censorship, restrictions on personal freedom and inflexible state control only exacerbated the situation.

3.3.3.3 Education and political change. Following changes elsewhere in Central and Eastern Europe, students were in the forefront of demands for social and political change (see Chapter 6). Tirana students took to the streets in December 1990 and pushed the communists into legalising opposition political parties. After the communist victory in the spring 1991 general elections, students continued to push for reform through hunger strikes and the symbolically momentous toppling of Hoxha's statue in the centre of Tirana. Across the country, students demanded improvements in their living and working conditions. In response, the government closed all higher education institutions apart from Tirana's faculty of medicine. Students completed courses through correspondence and were allowed to return to take their final examinations.

During the summer of 1991 some reforms were introduced. New legislation was passed formally removing politics and ideology from education instruction; production practice and military training requirements were also removed.

3.3.3.4 Higher education and research. Successive waves of emigration during the early 1990s saw many thousands of educated people leave the country in search of better economic opportunities. Many of the country's teachers and university staff have left: an estimated 2,000 had departed by the end of 1991. Students have also emigrated. The concurrent attempts to overhaul and restructure the administrative organisation of higher education, to replace the ideologically dominated curriculum base, and to overcome the morale-sapping domestic economic and social position, are hardly aided by depleted staff resources, especially as a notable proportion of those who have left are of the younger, more dynamic elements of the academic community. The former political affiliations of those remaining also creates internal tensions.

For its post-communist aid and guidance in educational reform, Albania has turned chiefly to the European Community and the United States. Some educational institutions, business programmes and social organisations established academic exchange programmes and assistance projects, and late in 1991 Albania was included in the EC TEMPUS higher education training assistance programme. Mobility of Albanian students and scholars was beginning to increase, although hampered by visa regulations in receiving countries and restricted access to a passport in Albania itself, a situation which was to be ameliorated with 1993 regulations governing the overseas passage of Albanian businessmen and scholars.

In Albania's search for an appropriate post-communist development path a strong education and research capability is essential. Academically, Albanian higher education suffered from outdated teaching methods, lack of contact or familiarity with external developments, both empirical and conceptual, severely limited equipment and materials, poor teaching environments, and a lack of motivation or incentive to innovate.

Under the communists, the Albanian Academy of Sciences undertook research – largely in support of the country's economic development and cultural self-image – and

Table 3.7 *Albania: institutions of higher education*

Name (pre-1991 name in parentheses)	Year founded	No. of students (1991)
1. Academy of Arts (Higher Institute of Arts)	1966 (merger of 3 institutions)	700
2. Agricultural University (Higher Agricultural Institute) Branches in Durrës, Lushnjë and Vlorë	1951	4,076
3. Aleksander Xhuvani University of Elbasan (Aleksander Xhuvani Higher Pedagogical Institute of Elbasan (originally the Normal School)	1909	1,305
4. Eqrem Çabej University of Gjirokastër (Eqrem Çabej Higher Pedological Institute of Gjirokastër)	1971	812
5. Higher Institute of Physical Culture (Vojo Kushi Institute of Physical Culture)	1958	328
6. Higher Military Academy	nd	nd
7. Higher Military School in Vlorë	nd	nd
8. Higher Unified Military School	nd	nd
9. Luigj Gurakuqi University of Shkodër (Higher Pedagogical Institute in Shkodër)	1957	1,682
10. Polytechnic University of Korçë (Higher Agricultural Institute of Korçë until 1992)	1971	c1,000
11. Polytechnic University of Tirana (engineering faculties of the University of Tirana)	July 1991	4,435
12. University of Tirana (State University of Tirana, 1957–85; Enver Hoxha University of Tirana, 1985–February 1991)	1957	8,812
13. V.I. Lenin Higher Party School	Closed 1991 as the higher education institution of the Party of Labour	

Note: all located in Tirana unless otherwise indicated.

Source: Koenig, 1993, pp. 38–42.

convened seminars and meetings. The country's sole university, established in 1957, pursued an essentially pedagogic role. A number of teacher training and agricultural colleges are scattered around the country. The latter, such as that at Kamëz to the north of Tirana were closely linked to state farms.

Including the military academies, there are 12 higher education institutions (Table 3.7): since 1991 a number of former colleges have become universities. Also, Tirana University was divested of its engineering faculty, which became a separate Polytechnic University (Narayan, 1991).

Subsequent discussion centred around the need for a post-university institute that could offer structured higher degree programmes and the elimination of the Soviet-style system of Candidate of Sciences and Doctor of Sciences awards in favour of degree structures congruent with those more familiar in Western Europe and North America (Koenig, 1993).

Documentary and technical resources have been severely limited. For half a century ideological diktats permitted only a narrow field of literature to be available: that which was ideologically safe in not deviating from the Albanian interpretation of Marxist dialectical analysis, reinforcing the cosy view that Albania was pursuing the only logical path of development.

University libraries lack security, and individual departments are now developing their own resource centres. It is apparent, however, that in some cases at least, Western gifts of desperately required books are either disappearing from secured rooms or being salted away in eminent men's bookcases to be employed for prestige rather than for urgent educational purposes. Referring students to library resources for independent study was not a notable pursuit in Albanian higher education. 'Dictation' in both senses of the word was the norm. Too independent thought and inquiry was not encouraged; the stultifying effect of such intellectual straight-jacketing may take a generation to shake off.

Nevertheless, with Albania's inclusion in the EC TEMPUS programme, whereby higher education institutions from at least two EC member countries provide assistance in restructuring higher education in at least one Eastern Europe society, the staff of the country's universities now have better opportunities to upgrade teaching methods and to embrace new areas of disciplinary development. One of the TEMPUS priority areas is environmental management (Chapter 5), recognising Albania's vulnerability during the period of transition and beyond, particularly in relation to its relatively fragile physical and cultural environments. Institutional and course flexibility is now required to meet rapidly changing national and international skills demands. Societies such as Albania need to be able to benefit from the global diffusion of information and innovation, for which a substantial transfer of skills and technology is required. But this must be appropriate to meet the needs of sustainable development paths (Hall, 1992d).

3.3.4 Domestic recreation

Albanians have long flocked to the coast in summer, the range of coastal resorts used for domestic tourism being far wider than that previously made available to foreigners (see Figure 3.3), not least because of infrastructural constraints.

The greatest concentration of both international and domestic tourism accommodation and activities is focused in and around Durrës Beach. This is the country's most extensive beach and a wide range of accommodation is situated closeby, including hotels, villas and apartment blocks, as well as stable-like terraced huts both on and off the beach. Shops, kiosks, a post office, cinema, circus site and other facilities are ranged along the main road which backs onto the beach area. During 1991 and 1992, when conditions were hardly conducive to tourism, some of the holiday apartments were used to house former political prisoners as a short-term measure during their period of rehabilitation. To the south of the international hotel complex are villas and gardens, also adjacent to the beach, high walled and guarded, formerly the preserve of the communist *nomenklatura*. South beyond these are further public beaches, such as Golem, a holiday centre for the young pioneers organisation. No longer politically affiliated, the pioneers have continued in the post-communist era, providing organised activities and recreation for Albanian youth. It remains to be seen how far such organisations will be supplanted eventually by the resurgence of scouting and guiding, as in other parts of post-communist Europe (Sizeland and Hall, 1992).

Second in importance is Vlorë, where Adriatic and Ionian seas meet. With several sandy bays – notably at Dhërmi, Himarë and Borsh – the coast extends south to Sarandë, where the tourist hotel used by foreign tour groups has been a favourite for Albanian honeymooners. Facing the island of Corfu and enjoying spectacular sunsets, the town is claimed to receive a daily average of eight hours sunshine.

As Gardiner (1976, p. 57) observed:

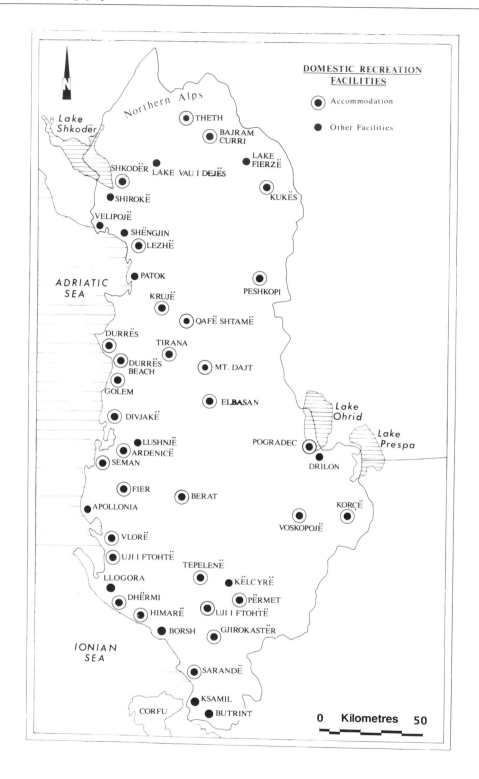

Figure 3.3 *Albania: major domestic recreation centres*

Sarandë marks the southern limit of Bregdeti 'the coast', the red riviera . . . I would nominate it for the title of the most beautiful sixty miles of Mediterranean shore. That it is also the least developed goes without saying. Cruise passengers in the Adriatic see this shoreline through binoculars, but they don't see the half of it – not the frying-pan-shaped inlets, the lake-isles of Porto Palermo, the turquoise gulfs near Dhërmi and Borsh, the rivers of olives and avalanches of orange and mandarin bushes which flow down from the heights of Llogora . . . a littoral made for tourism, a littoral where hardly a tourist has ventured if you except the young Albanians who caper in the sea in the vicinity of a State holiday home.

The northern part of the Adriatic coast was selectively developed for domestic recreation in the late 1970s and early 1980s. Shëngjin is noted for its fine sand, although marine pollution resulting from industrial effluent disposal has posed problems. Patok has been developed close to the industrial new town of Laç (EBNA, 1984, pp. 218–19).

Inland, the country's lakes and mountains have been exploited almost exclusively for domestic use. Albania shares three major lakes with its neighbours, and of these Shkodër and Ohrid are by far the most significant. One of the first young pioneers' holiday homes was established on Shkodër lakeside, while Pogradec on the western shore of Ohrid is the country's most important lakeside resort, with beach and other recreational facilities. Here, as elsewhere, water sports, particularly those employing motorised craft, tended to be restricted, both by economic circumstances, and by the tight control on population movement in border areas.

In the alpine north-east mountains some winter-sports development has taken place, but foreign tourists were usually limited to stop-overs in the towns of Kukës and Peshkopi. Still relatively inaccessible to large vehicles, the health resort and walking centre of Theth is possibly the best known focus for domestic recreation in the region. From here, peaks of up to 2,600 metres are accessible as are lake resorts in the heart of the Albanian Alps. Domestic facilities also exist in mountain resorts located close to the capital, particularly on Dajt, where

there is a pioneers' summer camp and winter skiing facilities; at Qafë Shtamë with its bungalow accommodation set among towering pines, in the centre of the country; and in the south-east at Korçë and Voskopojë, the latter also being a popular centre for children and winter sports.

Provision of heavily subsidised holiday centres for workers and children had been made by trade unions and enterprises in a number of locations since the early socialist period. The last large trade union hotel developments included that on the hillside overlooking Korçë, and the complex on the water's edge just south of Sarandë. In 1990 some 60,000 workers and children spent their summer vacations in the network of holiday homes (DeS, 1991, p. 128; see also Table 3.8). While on their annual paid holiday, workers and their families paid a third of the real cost of their stay in such accommodation (EBNA, 1984, p. 220). Normally, however, because of limited availability, trade union-sponsored holiday accommodation was not available to the same family for two consecutive years.

By 1993, although trades unions and enterprises still owned holiday accommodation, most subsidies had been removed such that with inflation the cost of this type of holiday had increased dramatically and was out of the reach of most Albanians.

Three alternative means of gaining access to holiday accommodation have existed. At the top end of the range, significant numbers of Albanians spent their holidays in Albturist-operated hotels. The cost of such accommodation would be extremely high by Albanian standards, and personal connections were no doubt useful in securing a booking.

Secondly, local authority facilities, including beach huts, have been available for renting, but could usually be booked only via an office in the holiday location, and not from one's home area. Such facilities could be used by individuals as well as being block-booked by trade unions to accommodate workers from other parts of the country.

Finally, the mode which appeared to be increasingly important during the 1980s, as domestic recreation increased, as formal

Plate 3.1 *Holiday home with its own 'magic mushroom' on Dajt mountain. Clearly some Albanians have been just a little more equal than others*

Table 3.8 *Albania: holiday homes for workers and young pioneers, 1950–90*

	1950	1960	1970	1980	1990
Holiday home places					
For workers	583	2,365	2,140	2,960	3,206
For pioneers	1,450	3,860	4,650	5,000	4,350
Numbers using accommodation					
workers	3,682	14,250	14,181	24,235	40,500
pioneers	4,283	12,965	13,571	15,765	19,500

Source: DeS, 1991, p. 128.

accommodation failed to meet demand, and as economic regulations became looser, was the private renting out of accommodation. This practice became common in such holiday centres as Durrës, Sarandë and Pogradec, where local residents sub-let rooms in their state flats to vacationing families usually on a two-week basis. Such transactions were not undertaken through formal advertisement, but by word of mouth. In Pogradec, for example, it was estimated that in summer approaching 80 per cent of the town's households hired out rooms, with the result that during the season Pogradec's population doubled from 30,000 to 60,000. The usual rate charged was said to be 200 Leks (a 1990 figure: then about ten days' average income) for one room for a family of four for two weeks. This represented a useful source of income for appropriately located households, although given the relatively small size of Albanian apartments, it would also exert substantial pressures of space. The privatisation of state flats has increased this practice considerably (section 3.5.7. below).

Non-residential excursions and day trips have been an important mode of recreation. Both on an individual and a collective basis, such activities had to rely on public transport. This entailed individual trippers taking overcrowded trains, such as for the hour's journey from Tirana to Durrës, perhaps supplemented by further road travel, as from Vlorë or Ballsh in order to reach the southern resort of Sarandë. Collective groups on the other hand – co-operative, enterprise, state farm or school

outings – usually had their own transport, albeit an unreliable time-expired Skoda bus.

More passive forms of recreation have followed patterns similar to those of the West, if only in delayed form. Between 1960 and 1990, during which period television was inaugurated within the country, attendances at cinemas were reduced by 79 per cent, even though numbers of cinemas increased from 72 to 108. Between 1980 and 1990 attendances at 'artistic performances' declined by 22 per cent (DeS, 1991, pp. 109, 112–13).

In the post-communist era, several trends quickly developed to radically modify domestic recreational patterns and processes:

(a) the 1991 legalisation of private motor vehicle ownership saw a rapid influx of second-hand vehicles and their use for recreational journeys. This in its turn opened up access to a far wider range of localities than was available previously. By so doing, however, such a development also exposed and put additional pressures on an inadequate road infrastructure. It also increased environmental pressures both on the recreational areas themselves and on roadside locations chosen to dump quickly expired vehicles in a country with limited experience of the driving or maintenance of sophisticated Western motor vehicles;

(b) the removal of former constraints on domestic population movement permitted Albanians to move freely about their own country should they now wish to do so;

81

(c) economic collapse brought substantial unemployment and the irony that although large numbers of people now had more time on their hands to indulge in recreational activities, they largely lacked the financial means to do it. The simultaneous growth of private cafe-bars did, however, provide one relatively inexpensive means of spending recreational time. For most young people, forced by economic circumstance to live with their parents, this offered a welcome safety valve against inter-generational conflict;

(d) for those able to afford it, television could now play a much larger role in Albanian daily life. Satellite broadcasts (dish and decoding facilities) became available for the cost of about $120 (4–6 months average salary). By the end of 1993, the pervasive presence of satellite dishes in both rural and urban residential areas was perhaps one of the more surprising landscape features to symbolise the new Albania;

(e) in mid-1993 the concept of the recreational weekend finally arrived in Albania. In July of that year a five-day 40-hour working week officially replaced the previous 48-hour six-day requirement. 'Albanians celebrated with hundreds of cars heading out of cities to favoured tourist spots on the morning of Saturday, July 3'. (EIU, 1993e, p. 44)

3.4   The position of women

Viewed historically, the qualities for which Albanian women are most often admired are those of a martial type: heroism in battle, the spirit of self-sacrifice, loyalty to menfolk fighting for freedom, and devotion to country. (Prifti, 1975c, p. 111)

Maybe. Certainly, the communist regime extolled a whole range of historic figures as role models: Teuta, queen of the Illyrians, who defied the might of the Roman Empire in the third century BC; Illyrian women who hurled themselves from towers rather than fall into the hands of the enemy (a practice later to be

undertaken by northern Greek women in defiance of Ali Pasha Tepelena); Skanderbeg's mother, Voisava a 'long-suffering but unbowed woman' (Prifti, 1975c, p. 111), and his sister Mamica, who was said to have surpassed many male chieftains in battle. Less pugilistic 'patriotic virtues' were also claimed:

. . . it was mainly the womenfolk who persevered and carried on the cultural traditions, the language, and the customs . . . (Buda, 1961, pp. 10–11)

of the country through the period of Ottoman domination.

3.4.1   Trapped by Balkan traditions

For most women traditional Albanian life was characterised not only by poverty and immobility, but by discrimination and inequality with men, reinforced by a wide range of cultural norms. According to the Canon of Lek Dukagjini, formulated in the Middle Ages (section 2.1.2 above):

'. . . the husband is entitled to beat his wife and to tie her up in chains when she defies his word and orders . . . The father is entitled to beat, tie in chains, imprison or kill his son or daughter . . . The wife is obliged to kneel in obeisance to her husband'. (quoted in Ash, 1974, p. 233)

A woman's purpose in life was to bear children and work in the house, and although women were usually far too insignificant to be directly involved in a blood feud, according to:

. . . the Law of Lek, if all the men of a family are killed in a vendetta, then the eldest unmarried girl must become the man of the house. This had been the fate of my guide; her brother had been shot only a few weeks before the date of her wedding, so she had promptly renounced marriage for ever, donned trousers, and picked up the gun. For the rest of her life she would live as a man. (Newman, 1936, p. 151)

While the Canon subjugated women particularly in the northern uplands, religion abetted their oppression in the rest of the country. In some Muslim areas polygamy was the norm and arranged marriages were widespread. By Islamic law a man was permitted four wives and could divorce any of them by a simple unilateral declaration. The birth of a girl was considered a misfortune and a burden on the family. A boy was 'the pillar of the house', while a girl was merely thought of as 'destined for another home', and an old Albanian saying reinforced this notion: 'even the beams of the house shed tears when a girl is born' (Prifti, 1975c, p. 112). Marrying off a daughter could be an intolerable financial burden for the parents, perhaps requiring them to work for years simply to pay off the debts incurred. Female infanticide was not unknown. The patrilineal nature of highland life in particular meant that the names and exploits of ancestors in the male line would be known for up to perhaps 20 generations back, while those in the female line would tend to be forgotten after two or three generations (Hasluck, 1954, p. 25).

Two Korçë sisters played a prominent role in the nationalistic projection of Albanian women during the waning decades of the Turkish occupation. In 1891 Sevasti and Parashqevi Qiriazi opened the first Albanian school for women, and in 1909 the latter helped to establish the first society of Albanian women, known as 'The Morning Star', the chief aim of which was to educate women. Both activities were based in Korçë and helped to elevate that town as one of the most progressive in the country.

In the immediate pre-war period there were just 21 female teachers in the country, a couple of women doctors and no female engineers, agronomists or chemists. In 1938 the country could boast an official total of 668 'working women' (Ash, 1974, p. 235). Only 2.4 per cent of secondary school students were girls (EBNA, 1984, p. 212).

3.4.2 Women and the family

Despite a post-war constitution guaranteeing women equal rights with men and banning the wearing of the veil, many of the old social practices were not eradicated but were simply adjusted to meet new requirements. The patriarchal system survived as a way of life in the countryside, especially in the highlands, although the authority of the master of the family was considerably reduced. Marriage and divorce were regulated by the 1946 constitution. The law on marriage required the nuptial contract to be entered into before an official of the local people's council, and strong penalties were prescribed for any clergyman performing a religious ceremony before its civil equivalent had taken place.

An interesting early example of Albanian sociological research entailed 54 married couples living in the northern town of Rrëshen being surveyed on the arrangement of their marriage (Uçi, 1969). In this essentially rural upland region pre-war marriages were invariably arranged by the parents. In the 1960s survey, 26 (48 per cent) of the couples had chosen their own partners, 15 (28 per cent) had married on the initiative of their parents, but with their own consent, and 13 (24 per cent) had been married by arrangement between their parents without their consent. As part of the 'cultural revolution', during the 1966 campaign to transform social relations in rural areas, it was claimed that 3,718 engagements undertaken according to the old customs were broken off.

The legal age for contracting marriage was set at 18 for both sexes, but persons as young as 16 years of age could marry with the permission of the People's Court. In such cases, the minors did not require parental consent, and the law considered them 'emancipated' (DEYA, 1983, p. 9). Marriage was theoretically based on the full equal rights of both spouses, who, theoretically, had the right to choose their own occupation, profession and residence. Thus the concept of the head of the family, recognised by pre-communist civil law and so important for Albanian family life, was substantially undermined (Keefe *et al.*, 1971, pp. 74–9). Marriage rates increased from 5.8 per thousand in 1938 to 8.5 by 1985, one of the highest levels in Europe.

The Family Code of 1965 established equality of access to divorce for either spouse. Although a rising trend (from 850 in 1960 to 2,024 in 1980 and to 2,675 in 1990 (KPS, 1989, p. 57; DeS, 1991, p. 72)), in practice, the person suing for divorce had to present her or his case to a

Table 3.9 *Albania: proportion of women in the work-force, 1960–90*

	1960	1970	1980	1985	1988	1990
Industry	27.8	44.2	43.6	44.0	44.3	44.5
Construction	5.7	9.4	9.0	8.5	8.5	9.5
Agriculture	43.8	52.8	52.2	52.5	52.3	52.2
Transport and communications	6.7	14.9	15.8	15.4	17.2	15.9
Trade	39.6	39.6	53.3	54.1	53.1	54.5
Education and culture	41.4	48.7	50.5	52.8	53.0	53.0
Health	72.3	77.5	78.7	79.7	79.4	80.5
Others	19.6	37.9	38.3	41.7	39.5	21.3
Total	35.9	45.3	45.9	46.6	46.8	45.1

Source: KPS, 1989, p. 60; DeS, 1991, pp. 78–9; author's additional calculations.

council of the People's Court and answer in public any questions put to them, thereby reflecting a lack of domestic privacy and embodying the 'snooping' nature of the state.

Equal rights included, of course, the equal right and virtual requirement to have a job. This was commonplace in Eastern Europe as of course it was in much of post-war Western Europe (Corrin, 1992). Many women had to work outside the home to supplement the generally low wages of their husbands. Subsidised day-care nurseries were set up to make it easier for mothers to work, but also to give the regime an early opportunity to indoctrinate the children. In 1981 the period of paid maternity leave was extended to six months, with the woman's right to return to her job protected by law (Bërxholi and Qiriazi, 1986, p. 61). By that time, women made up 46 per cent of the economically active population: proportions in the light and food industries, education and health ranged from 58 per cent to 80 per cent, and 52 per cent of workers in agriculture were women (Table 3.9).

In addition to being expected to work, under communism Albanian women were given little choice but to procreate: there was virtually no birth control availability nor public discussion of it. The Stalinist practice of presenting medals and awards to successfully fecund women persisted into the 1980s: on the first birthday of the eighth surviving offspring, the accolade

of 'Heroic Mother' was bestowed, while third, second and first class awards of 'Mother's glory' were made to women with between four and seven children. In 1978 there were 13,000 mothers with more than seven children (Begeja, 1984, p. 37). The year 1988 saw 2,899 live births – 3.6 per cent of the total – of a seventh child or above (compared to figures of 7,010 and 10 per cent in 1960) (KPS, 1989, pp. 45, 67; DeS, 1991, p. 53). As a consequence of this, 96 women became 'Heroic Mothers' within the year, bringing the country's total to 1,194. By 1990, when such accolades were no longer used, there were 2,473 live births of a seventh child or above, representing 3 per cent of total live births. Of those women giving birth to a seventh child or above in 1990, 102 were under 30 years of age, and, incredibly, four were younger than twenty (Table 3.10).

By the mid-1980s all urban births and 98 per cent of rural deliveries were said to take place in medical institutions (hospitals or maternity homes): it was claimed that each village had a doctor, midwife, nurses and a medical establishment (Begeja, 1984). However, with lowering reproduction rates, in 1981 the party leadership had declared that the country's birth rate should always remain higher than that of the 1980 level, and an improvement in maternity provision soon began to show results (section 3.2.3). Whereas the average number of births for the 1978–81 period had been 71,400, for 1982 the

Plate 3.2 *Women breaking arable land with basic implements, near Pogradec, April 1991*

Table 3.10 *Albania: live births by age of mother and birth order, 1990*

Age group of mother	Birth order								
	1st	2nd	3rd	4th	5th	6th	7th and above	Unknown	Total
Below 20	2,109	223	18	3	0	0	4	16	2,373
20–24	16,205	6,831	1,340	197	38	12	22	128	24,773
25–29	8,741	12,279	6,230	2,292	729	181	76	130	30,658
30–34	1,830	4,247	4,679	2,966	1,712	1,011	594	77	17,116
35–39	377	619	991	857	732	809	1,039	24	5,448
40–44	66	55	107	113	137	199	641	9	1,327
45–49	6	7	5	13	12	17	78	3	141
Above 50	8	3	4	6	4	3	17	0	45
Unknown	79	45	28	8	11	5	2	66	244
Totals	29,421	24,309	13,402	6,455	3,375	2,237	2,473	453	82,125

Source: DeS, 1991, p. 53; author's own additional calculations.

figure was 77,300 (Skenderi and Vejsiu, 1983), representing a rate of 27.7 per thousand (Anon, 1984a).

The year 1982 saw an 18 per cent decrease in infant mortality rates, particularly marked in the two to five-month age group, corresponding to the very period of extended maternity leave granted in 1981 (Skenderi and Vejsiu, 1983, pp. 158–9). As a consequence, the death rate continued to decline: from 10.4 per thousand in 1960 to a 1986 figure of 5.7 per thousand. However, by 1986 the birth rate had also fallen further to 25.3 (and was down to 25.2 per thousand by 1990 (DeS, 1991, p. 51)). Significantly, the tenth Congress of the Women's Union of Albania, held in June 1988, failed, for the first time in the Congress's history, to make an appeal for large families, and unusually, spent little time discussing demographic policy. Rather than attempting to return to previously high levels of natural increase, the Albanian authorities appeared to have taken a more pragmatic approach and turned their attention to preventing further decline to levels comparable with other parts of Europe. Increasingly uncertain food supplies, poor housing and lack of consumer goods, not least for children, were all clear deterrents against large families.

Indeed, average family sizes had diminished substantially, most noticeably in the towns and cities. Urban families with more than ten members represented only 0.8 per cent of the total in 1980, compared to 2.2 per cent in 1960. In rural areas, however, the respective figures were 6.3 and 9.1 per cent. By the end of communist rule the average family size was less than five. Most flats appeared to be built to meet the needs of families of this size, although by 1989 the average urban family size was just 3.9 people (DeS, 1991, p. 364). Single person households had been reduced to 3.3 per cent of all households by 1979 (compared to a 1930 figure of 9.2 per cent, and a UK figure of over 50 per cent), representing just 0.6 per cent of the total population (Begeja, 1984, pp. 22–3).

As in other state socialist societies, canteens at both workplace and local residential area were provided to lighten the woman's load, as were launderettes and labour-saving devices to assist women to combine their roles of workers and mothers, for them to 'be delivered from the drudgery of household chores' (Ash, 1974, p. 236). All of this presupposed that such chores were the woman's responsibility (e.g. see Nickel, 1989). Even by the mid-1970s, a text sympathetic to the regime could argue that while men were learning to take their full share of domestic responsibilities, they had not taken readily to such changes (Ash, 1974, pp. 236–7). Indeed, when a social survey of a cross-section of 450 Tirana residents was undertaken by Tirana University in 1986 (Tarifa and Barjaba, 1986, 1990), it was concluded that:

The overburdening of women with housework and child care reduces the time they have available for cultural activity and for raising their cultural and professional level (Tarifa and Barjaba, 1990, p. 13).

Although the survey showed that 62 per cent of Tirana families had a washing-machine and 53 per cent had a refrigerator – figures by far the highest in the country – 80 per cent of female workers spent more than two hours a day on housework compared to only 20 per cent of male workers. This difference was even more pronounced on non-working days when 63 per cent of female workers spent more than three hours on housework (with 30 per cent spending more than five hours), compared to only 14 per cent of male workers. A similar picture was presented when looking at the division of responsibilities for the care of children Whereas 47 per cent of women in the sample spent between 1.5 and three hours a day looking after children, only 15 per cent of men devoted this amount of time to child care, a figure which ranged from 12 per cent for manual workers to 19 per cent for intellectuals.

Such figures hide the hardship of having to queue for bread at 4.30 am before starting an eight hour shift at 6 am, and of having to make small amounts of groceries last and please all of the family:

In Albania the monthly ration for a whole family is two pounds of meat, two pounds of cheese, ten pounds of flour, less than half a pound each of coffee and butter. Everywhere, the bottom line is bread .... Every mother ... can point to where communism failed, from the failures of the planned economy (and the consequent lack of food, milk), to the lack of apartments, child-care facilities, clothes, disposable diapers, or toilet paper. The banality of everyday life is where it has really failed, rather than on the level of ideology. (Drakulić, 1992, p.18)

Jeta Kapllani stumbled out of bed at three o'clock yesterday morning, staggered half asleep from her fourth floor flat down the stairs to the ground floor carting pots, pans and buckets. She was fetching the day's water supply for her family of four, a chore that takes her 90 minutes before dawn every day. Power cuts and water shortages are endemic in Tirana .... The water – cold only – comes on every morning between three and five .... The Albanian male's aversion to water-fetching is replicated across the entire spectrum of everyday manual tasks .... No self-respecting male would be seen dead doing 'woman's work' for fear of being the laughing stock of his mates. (Traynor, 1993b)

3.4.3 Female access to education and employment

In 1967, when declaring the state atheist, the regime made much of the argument that organised religion had been one of the major sources of female oppression, and that the young women of Albania had a right to throw off the shackles which had bound their mothers and grandmothers to the home and which had denied a vocational education for women Unquestionably, female educational opportunities improved considerably during the period of state socialism (Table 3.11), which is not to say that it might not have improved further under alternative conditions: female education lagged behind that for males until the 1970s. In the first half of that decade a campaign was being waged for more training facilities: 37 per cent of all technicians were women, but the proportion of females receiving specialist training and being engaged in higher education was considered unsatisfactory. Certainly the proportions of female students in part-time education and women teachers above primary level revealed in Table 3.11 are low, although in education as a whole, female employment has been relatively high (Table 3.9).

In 1967 for example, Alia pointed out to a Central Committee plenum on women that the great majority of women in production were engaged in simple, unskilled labour; by 1973 they only accounted for 5.6 per cent of directors of industrial enterprises and only 3 per cent of agricultural co-operative heads (Prifti, 1975c, pp. 112, 125).

Table 3.11 *Albania: proportion of females in education, 1970–90*

	1970	1980	1985	1988	1990
8-year schools					
Total students	46.9	47.2	47.5	47.8	47.9
full-time students	47.4	47.9	48.0	48.1	nd
part-time students	42.9	23.7	22.4	22.5	nd
total teachers	48.0	50.3	51.8	53.6	nd
Secondary schools					
total students	40.9	44.7	45.1	44.9	44.8
full-time students	45.2	52.1	51.8	51.6	nd
part-time students	36.5	39.1	33.9	30.8	nd
total teachers	28.2	35.3	38.2	39.9	nd
Further and higher education					
total students	32.5	49.6	45.4	50.3	nd
full-time students	29.7	47.8	46.6	50.8	nd
part-time students	34.5	52.3	41.6	48.1	nd
total teachers	14.6	20.1	23.6	26.0	nd

Note: nd: no data.

Source: KPS, 1989, pp. 132–5; DeS, 1991, p. 95; author's additional calculations.

With political change came a re-evaluation of the question, posed across the erstwhile state socialist world, as to whether a woman's right to work, as guaranteed under communist law and ideology, was indeed a form of emancipation or simply one more aspect of state exploitation. Women often felt forced to work outside of the home (in addition to the inevitable domestic chores), and were likely to be treated at the workplace within the confines of sexual stereotypes (Bren, 1992). Across Eastern Europe any development of women's roles took place within a vacuum, by dint of communist party diktat and largely without any commensurate comprehensive change in social attitudes. As a consequence, such communist impositions have not proved themselves sufficiently well rooted to prosper through recent changes. Reports by the United Nations Commission on the Status of Women and the Committee on the Elimination of Discrimination Against Women have confirmed that the reform process across the region has been eroding such advantages that women gained under the communists while further damaging their current status (Einhorn, 1991).

In particular, women have been unable to take advantage as readily as men of new economic opportunities. Exhausted by the double burden of work inside and outside the home, women are reluctant to take on jobs with private firms that demand even more working hours and do not guarantee maternity leave or child-care benefits: the mechanics of the market economy do not value domestic work or child care. The result is that women have the same double burden as before, but this is now augmented by new economic difficulties. As unemployment has risen, women have been expected to be the first to be displaced (Rosenberg, 1991; Szalai, 1991; Bren, 1992; Williamson, 1992) and discrimination is often overt in, for example, newspaper job advertisements for foreign joint ventures (Fong and Paul, 1992).

3.4.4 Women in political and social organisations

The Union of Albanian Women was established in 1943 as the Union of Anti-Fascist Women of

Table 3.12 *Albania: proportion of female deputies in the People's Assembly, 1945–87*

Date of elections	Total	Deputies No. of women	Female % of total
2.12. 1945	82	6	7.3
28.5. 1950	121	17	14.0
30.5. 1954	134	15	11.2
1.6. 1958	188	17	9.0
3.6. 1962	214	25	11.7
10.6. 1966	240	39	16.3
20.9. 1970	264	72	27.3
6.10. 1974	250	83	33.6
12.11.1978	250	81	32.6
14.11.1982	250	76	30.4
1.2. 1987	250	73	29.2

Source: KPS, 1989, p. 29.

Albania. The name change came about at its second congress, held in 1946, when Nexhmije Hoxha was elected its president. Indeed, the organisation was little more than a party vehicle for manipulating Albanian women, with its leading figures being for many years the wives of party and state leaders. It was:

... a single, well organized, and centrally directed effort with clearly defined goals ... and ... like other mass organizations in Albania, was conceived and created by the Albanian Party of Labor in order to carry out more effectively its program (Prifti, 1975c, p. 128).

By carrying out its high mission as a revolutionary organization of the masses of women, under the leadership of the Party ... in a lofty revolutionary spirit, it is gathering around itself and training in its bosom thousands of worker, co-operativist and intellectual women who have hurled themselves enthusiastically into the great battle for the complete construction of socialist society in Albania (Anon, 1978, pp. 39–40).

Compared to India, Sri Lanka, Israel, the Philippines, Britain and Norway, in no East European socialist state did a woman manage to achieve the highest political office (Childs, 1988), and despite pretensions to equality in these societies few women appeared to be able to attain significant positions in their own right.

As noted above, wives of leaders often took key positions, and Nexhmije Hoxha continued as Chairman of Albania's Democratic Front organisation after her husband's death, acting as a rallying point for embittered reaction to subsequent 'revisionist' government, until her arrest and imprisonment.

Although thousands of girls were drawn into organised sports activities and the young pioneers movement, and in the 1960s and 1970s there were 300,000 members of the Women's Union (Ash, 1974, p. 235; Prifti, 1975c, p. 121), women played a less active public role than the communists claimed to be their wish. In 1967 women made up only 12.4 per cent of Party membership, and although by 1973 this figure had risen to 24 per cent, women were seen as being weakly represented at the higher levels of the Party hierarchy. Employing a quota system rather than recognising merit, the proportion of female deputies of the People's Assembly approached one-third of the total (Table 3.12), comparable to other Central and East European societies of the time (Childs, 1988, p. 251). A similar proportion was also quoted for female members of the supreme court (EBNA, 1984, p. 214). Being guaranteed a certain number of political posts, such women are now regarded in retrospect as little more than 'ornaments', and the role of women in post-communist Albanian political life has sub-stantially diminished (Weyr, 1992; see also Drakulić, 1990).

3.4.5   Equality with democracy?

Just before the spring 1992 general elections which brought the Democratic Party to full government, Albania held its first beauty contest. What is one person's expression of freedom is another's symbol of exploitation; and so it was that 25 women aged between 15 and 23 competed to be Miss Albania for a 3,000 lek prize and the promise of overseas travel, the latter providing a greater attraction than the former. The female choreographer of the show argued that the event was to prove, if nothing else, that Albanians were 'capable of living a normal modern life' (McDowall, 1992). Such a spectacle was far from representing normality, however. Participants complained of having to be 'feminine' and 'attractive' on the catwalk, only to return to homes where basic necessities were minimal and where water and electricity were scarce and erratic.

A new government office for women and a Forum for Albanian Women have now been established; but as in other parts of 'liberated' Eastern Europe, 'freedom' is bringing rising levels of crime against the person – not least rape – as well as the more obvious crimes against property (e.g. McDowall, 1991a). Pornography is also now being sold on the streets of Tirana for the first time in the country's history, through the medium of four different magazines. At the time of writing, no Albanian women's group appeared to have arisen to challenge such developments as had occurred in other post-communist societies (e.g. Bren, 1992), and neither had there emerged any lesbian or gay and lesbian organisation (see also Rieder, 1991).

While longer-term freedoms of contraception, mobility and employment and the inevitable onslaught of Western modernity on traditional values, may assist an improvement in the posi-tion of Albanian women, there are clearly other factors which may yet diminish it (Buckley, 1992; Corrin, 1992; Edmundson, 1992).

3.5   Housing and planning

3.5.1   Settlement development

Albania's internal administrative system had always been at best tenuous. Under Zogu, a prefectoral system with several levels of authority operated in subordination to the Ministry of the Interior, but was responsible to the king for political control and for the supervision of foreigners and their affairs. In 1942 the Axis powers added annexed territories to the ten provincial prefectures.

Public works and basic infrastructure were minimal. In urban areas streets were usually irregular and narrow, ill-paved and poorly lit: Italian electric light companies served just a handful of settlements by the end of the 1930s. With the exception of Korçë, served by a 250kW HEP station, most urban and industrial power supplies were derived from internal combustion diesel engine plants. Drainage systems were exceptional and water supply was limited to private wells and cisterns with a few public fountains. Most towns suffered water shortages during the long dry summer, and later Italian plans for aqueduct projects in Durrës, Tirana, Berat, Gjirokastër and Vlorë were overtaken by the war. Sarandë was notable for having piped water fed from a reservoir above the town, filled by pumping from wells.

The settlement system was generally char-acterised by poor construction methods, inade-quate sanitation and hygiene, and little urban development. Two inter-war decades of inde-pendence briefly witnessed some suburban development in Tirana (founded in 1614 but only decreed the country's capital in 1920), Durrës, Shkodër, Korçë and Vlorë along 'European' lines to serve a small administrative and middle-class elite, with central Tirana laid out along Italian architectural lines as a modern capital (Plate 3.3). Villa development at recrea-tional spots such as Himarë on the Ionian Coast, and on Lake Ohrid near Pogradec, remained relatively isolated oases of bourgeois decadence for the very few. Wartime devasta-tion and impoverishment curtailed further developments along these lines.

Post-war town and country planning policies

Plate 3.3 *Skanderbeg Square looking south to the main university building, from the Hotel Tirana. Government ministry buildings, built in the 1930s, dominate the middle distance. Taken before the ban on private motor transport was lifted, the photograph brings out the dark staining made by the regular patterns of bus movements. Traffic is no longer allowed to cross the Square between the fountains and Skanderbeg's statue, as the articulated bus is doing in this 1989 view*

Table 3.13   *Albania: urban population growth, 1938–90*

	Urban population ('000s)						% urban population growth		
	1938	1945	1960	1970	1979	1990	1938–60	1960–79	1970–90
Tirana	25.1	59.9	136.3	171.3	190.2	243.0	443.0	39.5	41.9
Durrës	10.5	14.2	39.9	53.8	65.9	85.4	281.0	65.2	58.7
Elbasan	12.7	34.3‡	29.8	41.7	61.1	83.3	134.6	105.0	99.8
Shkodër	25.3	14.7‡	43.3	55.3	64.7	81.8	71.1	49.4	47.9
Vlorë	9.9	12.7	41.4	50.0	56.4	73.8	418.2	36.2	47.6
Korçë	21.2	24.6	39.4	47.3	52.6	65.3	85.8	33.5	38.0
Fier	1.4	7.3	14.4	23.0	32.4	45.2	928.6	125.0	96.5
Berat	9.6	11.9	18.7	25.7	33.3	43.8	94.8	78.1	70.4
Lushnjë	4.0	5.5	12.5	18.9	22.0	31.5	212.5	76.0	66.7
Kavajë	7.3	9.7	14.2	18.7	20.9	25.6	94.5	47.2	36.9
Gjirokastër	8.8	9.4	14.1	17.1	19.4	24.9	60.2	33.3	45.6
Kuçovë†	–	–	10.3	14.0	17.2	22.3	–	67.0	59.3
Pogradec	2.5	4.9	7.8	10.1	13.1	20.1	212.0	67.9	99.0
Patos	–	–	–	8.9	12.0	16.7	–	–	87.6
Sarandë	3.0	1.5	6.0	8.7	10.8	16.4	100.0	80.0	88.5
Kukës*	2.0	1.1	–	6.1	9.5	14.3	–	–	134.4
Laç	–	–	–	6.1	9.5	13.6	–	–	123.0
Krujë	4.5	5.9	6.3	7.9	9.6	13.6	40.0	52.4	72.2
Peshkopi	–	2.0	nd	nd	nd	13.3	–	–	–
Burrel	–	–	–	–	–	11.2	–	–	–
Total urban	160.0		502.5	719.0	881.8°	1176.0	214.1	75.5	63.6
Total rural	880.4		1123.9	1416.6	1681.6°	2079.9	27.7	49.6	46.8
Total popn.	1040.4		1626.3	2135.6	2563.4°	3255.9	56.3	57.6	52.5

Notes:

† Known during the communist period as Qytet Stalin (Stalin City)

* Old Kukës was drowned by the lake below Fierzë HEP dam: the inhabitants were moved to a new town with the same name.

‡ An apparent inconsistency in the data. The 1945 figures for Shkodër and Elbasan appear to have been transposed in the original source and the false figures perpetuated in subsequent Albanian calculations (e.g. Bërxholi and Qiriazi, 1986, p. 66)

◇ 1978 figure.

Sources: Mason *et al.*, 1945, pp. 265–303; DPS, 1974, pp. 22, 30; Bërxholi and Qiriazi, 1986, p. 66; Hall, 1987a, p. 48; DeS, 1991, pp. 35, 38–9; author's additional calculations.

appeared to seek four not necessarily compatible goals: (a) reduction of socio-economic differentials within society; (b) provision of guaranteed living standards and facilities; (c) preservation and enhancement of agricultural land; and (d) promotion of monuments to past glories, in architecture, archaeology, customs and motifs.

By the 1990s some two-thirds of the country's population still lived in rural areas,

and while, at 35.5 per cent, Albania's proportion of urban population was the smallest in Europe, it was more than double the 1938 share of 15.4 per cent. Of the country's 3,454 recognised settlements, 67 were regarded as towns or cities. Of the total urban population in 1990, 80 per cent was found in the 20 largest settlements with populations of more than 10,000 (DeS, 1991, pp. 35, 38–9) (Table 3.13).

3.5.2 New towns

As in other state socialist societies, the establishment of post-war new towns was one of the more explicit dimensions of state-directed spatial development, although Albanian policies were never quite as draconian as Ceauşescu's attempted 'systematisation' of Romanian rural settlement (Turnock, 1986, 1991a, 1991b). In Albania 'new towns' usually accompanied the opening up of new economic areas, both for industrial and agricultural development. Official sources varied as to the number of such new settlements (Anon, 1982b, p. 497, quoted the total as 32; Vejsiu, 1982b, p. 20, suggested 'about 40'; Bërxholi and Qiriazi, 1986, p. 65, were certain it was 42), though it was clearly fewer than 50. Residential areas were invariably made up of apartment blocks incorporating service facilities for the workers and their families employed in several categories of economic activity:

(a) mineral extraction centres, often located in remote areas, such as Bulqizë (chromite extraction), Prrenjas (iron-nickel), Memaliaj and Valias (lignite);

(b) mineral processing centres, such as Kurbnesh, Kukës and Rubik (copper), Ballsh, Patos and Cërrik (petroleum);

(c) new heavy manufacturing plants in locations previously sparsely populated, such as Fushë-Krujë (cement), and Laç (chemical fertilisers);

(d) new centres of food processing, such as Maliq (sugar beet), and Çorovodë (food and drink);

(e) 'pioneer' state farms, carved from virgin land, such as Lukovë and Ksamil (both characterised by terraced citrus groves);

(f) relocated centres adjacent to areas drowned by the lakes of HEP schemes, such as Kukës and Bajram Curri;

(g) administrative centres for the remote districts, such as Burrel, Ersekë, Rreshen and Pukë; and

(h) an agricultural college and centre of wheat production – Kamzë.

Outline growth figures for the largest new towns (Kucovë, Patos, Cërrik) were noted in Table 3.13. Figures for the smaller centres have been less accessible, but, for example, Ballsh was planned for a tenfold increase in its population between 1970 and 1985 (which stood at 5,700 by 1989), commensurate with the construction and operation of the country's most advanced oil refinery there. Over the same period Bajram Curri trebled its population from 2,800 to 7,400 (Anon, 1972a; DeS, 1991, p. 38).

New town development added an impetus to the growth of the country's urban population and assisted its wider regional distribution (Hall, 1986a). Overall, however, the actual proportion of the country's total population living within urban areas rose slowly, even though in absolute terms it was significant (Table 3.13). Additionally, the largest urban settlements – those which most benefited from the rapid, if brief, early post-war rural-to-urban migratory flows – continued to retain their pre-eminence within Albania's settlement system. But, with increasing population pressure and very little remaining reclaimable agricultural land, a pressing need was for the establishment of more dynamic rural growth centres and better communications with the more remote regions of the country (Hall, 1987a). After the loss of Chinese assistance in the mid- to late-1970s, however, a lack of industrial expansion and innovation and the significant absence of 'new' technologies from Chinese sources saw retrenchment and consolidation of both economic and settlement development policies.

3.5.3 Housing and spatial planning administration

Under the communists, elected people's councils carried out administrative responsibilities at village, city and district levels. They were charged with economic and cultural matters and directed affairs of the various bodies under their aegis, while being responsible to the higher organs of state power. They met just twice a year, between which time their work was undertaken by executive committees elected from their membership. These supervised and administered a number of permanent

93

Table 3.14   *Albania: pre-1992 administrative units and divisions*

Rrethi	Area (sq km)	Cities	City quarters	Regrouped or 'unified' villages	Villages
Berat	1,027	3	23	29	133
Dibër	1,568	2	8	34	200
Durrës	848	4	29	20	123
Elbasan	1,481	3	27	28	217
Fier	1,175	4	22	25	151
Gramsh	695	1	4	15	91
Gjirokastër	1,137	2	7	15	91
Kolonjë	805	2	0	14	74
Korçë	2,181	3	18	37	194
Krujë	607	5	10	13	63
Kukës	1,330	2	8	27	113
Lezhë	479	2	3	12	59
Librazhd	1,013	2	2	17	64
Lushnjë	712	1	8	22	114
Mat	1,028	4	3	18	78
Mirditë	867	3	0	16	70
Përmet	929	2	4	19	94
Pogradec	725	1	5	16	68
Pukë	1,034	2	0	20	74
Sarandë	1,097	3	9	17	99
Skrapar	775	2	5	18	99
Shkodër	2,528	2	20	29	190
Tepelenë	817	2	6	18	76
Tirana	1,238	4	62	23	151
Tropojë	1,043	2	0	12	64
Vlorë	1,609	4	23	25	98
Total	28,748	67	306	539	2,848

Source: DeS, 1991, p. 12.

departments. Twenty-six districts (*rrethi*) acted as the largest internal administrative units and these were sub-divided into localities, made up of a number of villages constituting a territorial unit. At the same level, the 'regrouped' or 'unified village', comprised several villages forming a distinct territorial and economic unit, on the basis of which regrouped co-operatives were set up. They numbered 539 by 1990 (an increase of 95 over 1985). In the countryside the 2,848 villages acted as the basic unit of administrative division, while 67 cities and major inhabited centres shared equal urban functions. Larger cities were administratively divided into quarters or precincts, of which there were 306 by 1990 (an increase of 99 over

1985). Table 3.14 indicates the distribution of these units.

The executive committees of the district people's councils (and of the people's councils of city quarters in the larger urban centres) guided the planning and construction of new dwellings and determined the allocation of those built by state building enterprises. Each town had its own structure plan, which was supposed to be continuously updated through consultations between the *rrethi* administrations, branch offices of the Institute of Town Planning and Architecture, and central ministries. For example, the plan for Vlorë city, published in 1972, covered a period of up to 25 years and envisaged a more than doubling of the city's population to 120,000 by the end of the century. Both a major expansion of the urban area and a comprehensive redevelopment of the city centre were planned, the latter encompassing a new city hall, palace of culture, theatre, tourist hotel and market-place, interspersed with pools, fountains and greenery. New residential districts would incorporate public gardens, schools, kindergartens and creches, shops and playgrounds (Anon, 1972a).

3.5.4 Housing trends

By the end of World War Two, over 62,000 houses – possibly a quarter of the total stock – had been damaged or destroyed, and with generations of neglect, the Albanians' post-war housing task was arguably the most formidable in Europe in relative terms. Early efforts to improve housing conditions and keep pace with population growth, saw 185,000 new flats and houses built between 1945 and 1970. At an average of 7,400 dwellings per year, however, this effort fell short of the country's requirements by a substantial amount at a time when the annual population increase was between 40,000 and 50,000 (Table 3.15). Further aggravated by the ravages of earthquakes, the housing question was subject to rare public debate in 1967, when Hoxha spoke of a national housing crisis which was particularly critical in urban areas. While citing rapid industrialisation and a high birth rate as contributory factors, the party secretary appeared unable to offer a solution to the problem. In 1971 the matter was again raised by a leading party official who argued that if such social problems as housing were not frankly discussed in public, forcefully expressed social discontent could result (Logoreci, 1977, p. 147). One approach of particular significance in the 1970s, was to further emphasise rural development to the extent of rusticating urban youths and cadres – on a basis not dissimilar to Chinese practice. The aim was to ease the pressure on urban areas and enhance food production; but these policies in their turn required an extension of rural house-building programmes to meet the

needs of these urban-to-rural migrants (Shehu, 1976, p. 71; Hoxha, 1977a, p. 61).

By the 1980s it was being claimed that over 80 per cent of the total population lived in accommodation built since 1944 (Alia, 1986, p. 5). Since at least the mid-1970s, this had meant the almost continuous erection of blocks of apartments in urban areas, while in the country-side dwellings normally comprised one- or two-storey family houses for the co-operative peasantry, with a greater likelihood of small blocks of flats for state-farm workers.

A number of general trends in dwelling completion and state investment in housing by five-year periods (Table 3.15) were evident:

(a) a continued increase in the number of dwellings constructed up to the 1966–70 period, and then a falling off, to some extent relating to the relative decline of the country's birth rate; despite an apparent resurgence in the 1980s, plan targets continued not to be realised;

(b) with declining population growth rates and increasing numbers of new dwellings constructed, the country appeared to be beginning to catch up with its quantitative housing problem. However, the 'housing quotient' ignores the additional need for new housing to replace existing stock. Given that 20 per cent of existing dwellings were built before the war, and that much could still be considered to be inadequate, there remained a substantial task of replacement by the end of the 1980s. This effort became constrained by the physical limits placed upon the expansion of built-up areas in order to conserve valuable agricultural land. Belatedly, the abandoned 1986–2005 20-year development plan for Tirana pointed to the need to pay special attention to building quality (Sulko, 1988);

(c) with the state enrolling an urban voluntary construction programme to boost its own urban efforts from the late 1960s, urban self-build housing was squeezed, both through shortages in individual time for such construction and in the availability of building materials. By contrast, self-build

Plate 3.4   *The port city of Vlorë, 1990: preserved mosque, 1970s apartments, bicycles and articulated buses, but then still carless streets*

Table 3.15 *Albania: dwelling completions and state-housing investment by five-year periods, 1945-90*

FYP Period	Dwellings built	State No.	State %	Self-build Urban	Self-build Rural	State sector investment mn leks[†]	%[‡]	Housing quotient[æ]
1945–50	12,114	1,114	9.2	–	11,000	[six years]		8.0
1951–55	26,110	7,596	29.1	1,619	16,895	165	6.7	6.6
1956–60	47,413	11,734	24.7	3,514	32,165	292	6.2	5.0
1961–65	44,693	15,808	35.4	2,091	26,794	429	6.6	5.3
1966–70	73,213	29,045	39.7	2,382	41,786	579	5.7	3.7
1971–75	61,908*	32,038[∓]	51.8	1,476	28,394	862	5.6	4.8
1976–80	56,390[+]	26,326	46.7	1,240	28,824	790	4.3	4.3
1981–85	75,362	41,187	54.7	1,388	32,787	1045	5.9	3.1
1986–90	75,522[◇]	37,799	52.1	1,082	32,641	1166	6.0	3.3

Notes:

† Million leks at 1981 prices.

‡ Percentage of total state investment for five-year period.

æ Annual increase in population per new dwelling.

* 80,000 new dwellings had been the plan target.

∓ State flats now include those constructed by voluntary labour.

+ 65,000 new dwellings – 42,000 rural, 23,000 urban – had been planned for this period, the significant shortfalls suggest disruptions in the wake of the break with China.

◇ The projected plan figure had been 85,000.

Sources: DeS, 1962, p. 53, 1968, p. 27, 1991, pp. 255, 260; Shehu, 1971, pp. 36, 101, 1976, p. 30; DPS, 1974, p. 21; Anon, 1977, p. 41, 1984a, pp. 29, 106, 114, 1985a; Hoxha, 1977a, p. 61; Misja and Vejsiu, 1982, p. 4; BBC, 1983, SWB EE/W1265/A/9 1 Dec, 1988a, SWB EE/0039 C1-4 4 Jan, 1988b, SWB EE/0043 C1-11 8 Jan, 1990, SWB EE/W0113 A/5 1 Feb; Mihali, 1984; Alia, 1986, p. 60; Çarçani, 1986, pp. 15, 57, 58; author's additional calculations.

rural housing maintained its pre-eminent role in the countryside, even though numbers declined after a 1966–70 peak;

(d) a relatively steady, if declining proportion of state investment appeared to have picked up in the 1980s with greater all-round state spending;

(e) the state's share of new housing, compared with other Central and East European societies, tended to increase, attaining a level of just over half of all new dwellings by the late 1980s, the majority of which were urban; and

(f) average annual new dwelling completions fluctuated, although in the post-war period there was an overall upward trend.

Urban apartments were constructed with between one and three rooms in addition to a kitchen and a bathroom with piped water (Kuke, 1983, p 14). No lifts were provided, even for blocks of up to six storeys, as imported technology would have been required. Given Albanian hardiness, this omission was perhaps less of a problem than in more pampered societies.

For the heating of dwellings, solid fuel appears to have been dominant. It usually comprises either poor quality lignite, the burning of which has exacerbated atmospheric pollution, or firewood, which is collected widely. The extent of domestic solid-fuel burning is reflected in the fact that appropriately equipped cooking ovens manufactured in Tirana would be prominently exhibited in the 'white goods' section of the capital's economic achievements exhibition (Gurashi and Ziri, 1982). Outward signs of their use are the stacks of firewood often to be seen on apartment balconies, even in mid-summer, and the flue pipes emerging from the roofs and occasionally sides, of apartment blocks. Natural gas has been employed for heating in areas adjacent to the country's oilfields, and oil-fired central heating systems have been provided in later developments in upland areas.

3.5.5   Communal infrastructure

By the mid-1980s, just over half of the country's then 2,703 villages had adequate access to a water supply (Shkodra and Ganiu, 1984, p. 36; Meksi, 1987, p. 13). Of the remainder, 1,100 villages were considered 'without water' because of their distance from the nearest springs, or because water supplies were seasonal. The aborted 1986–90 plan had intended to bring drinking water to all remaining villages and inhabited centres. Parts of the systems in Tirana, Durrës and Vlorë were also to be upgraded. Under the plan, each village would have a tap for every 60 to 70 residents, or group of ten to 12 dwellings – the equivalent of 60 litres of water per day per inhabitant (Meksi, 1987).

Great publicity was given to the fact that every village in the country was in receipt of electricity by October 1970. The subsequent 1971–75 plan period saw the completion of telephone links to all villages, and a striving (not then completed) to make all villages accessible for motor transport through an extension of the rural road network.

The proportion of floorspace devoted to such functions as retailing facilities varied considerably: central place accessibility played an important role. For example, in the centrally located blocks of the upland new towns of Burrel and Bajram Curri, ground floor shops characterised most of the five-storey square blocks constructed in the 1970s and 1980s. At the other end of the country on the 'pioneer' state farm of Ksamil – close to the country's south-western border – of the settlement's 15 four-storey blocks, only one had shops on its ground floor in the late 1980s, and another a communal buffet. Separate, single-storey buildings provided a communal laundry, buffet and food shop. In the mid-1970s the country's 3,750 rural shops (Skarço, 1984, pp. 3–4), represented

one retail outlet for more than 400 rural dwellers.

More traditional rural settlements had some degree of central place patterning grafted onto them, with certain villages being singled out for the location of a post office and telephone, polyclinic, school, creche, kindergarten, library and house of culture, public baths, public service office, *MA-PO* (People's Store) 'supermarket', other shops and at least one buffet, this list appearing to comprise the top end of the rural service provision hierarchy (Basha, 1986, p. 30).

Other communal facilities included underground defensive shelters, the entrance to which would be found in courtyards or open space between apartment blocks.

3.5.6   Housing tenure

Under the communists, there existed two basic housing sectors: (a) state, involving rented accommodation; and (b) private, representing the most important element of 'personal property' ownership available to Albanian citizens.

The state sector dominated the urban housing market for much of the post-war period, but made an impression in rural areas only in the 1970s and 1980s (Table 3.15 above). By building apartment blocks in the countryside, particularly at state-farm centres, differentials between town and country, both tangibly and symbolically, were seen to be reduced. By the time new post-communist policies were introduced in the early 1990s, about 60 per cent of the total population lived in flats, most of which fell into the state sector, whether urban or rural. Over 80 per cent of Tirana's population were living in state-built apartments (Lleshi, 1977; Basha, 1986, p. 16; Carter, 1986). Sixty per cent of rural dwellers lived in state-owned dwellings, many of which were not apartments.

In the 1980s, typical rent levels for urban apartments were about 3.5 per cent, 5.5 per cent and 7 per cent of average incomes for one-, two- or three-room dwellings respectively, each with kitchen and bathroom (Anon, 1985b, p. 22). However, given that most households would comprise at least two wage-earners, as the right to work was forcefully pursued, the proportion of family income spent on rent was effectively a half of these figures. While official sources claimed to have abolished income tax, payments for such services as water and electricity were additional to housing costs.

The private owner-occupied sector fell into two distinct groups. Pre-socialist housing, firstly, comprised those dwellings which survived threats of compulsory purchase and demolition for reconstruction. In urban areas in particular, they usually did so on the grounds of their architectural or historic merit. Areas of traditional housing in a number of towns, notably Berat and Gjirokastër, were put under state protection, but not ownership, for this purpose (Riza, 1971, 1975, 1978, 1981a, 1981b; Anon, 1973a; Suli, 1982; Muka, 1985; Strazimiri, 1987). In most cases, the dwellings in these areas were either family houses of one or two storeys, or larger buildings perhaps divided between two or three families. Owner-occupation appears to have been the predominant form of tenure.

Self-built dwellings, the second owner-occupied group, were largely developed in rural areas. Although private self-building could take place in both urban and rural areas under the communists, the primacy of state-sector activities and planning regulations presented major obstacles to the urban private self-build sector. The state theoretically provided credits for the construction of such dwellings, to take place within a plot of up to 300 square metres, but made a point of denying such funds for the purpose of outright purchase of existing houses. Such a plot usually included provision for a personal garden.

In the majority of agricultural co-operatives, most dwellings were single-family, privately owned houses built with family funds. Each co-operative had its own physical development plan which contained a 'yellow line' to indicate the limit of expansion for the built-up area. Each co-operative family requiring a new dwelling received a plot of about 500 square metres within this designated area.

Every family also had its personal garden, usually adjacent to its home and typically devoted to grapes, apples, potatoes and tomatoes. Co-operative members were allowed to keep chickens, rabbits, bees and limited numbers of other livestock, and anything was permitted to be grown in the plot for family consumption or to be sold either to the co-operative or in the nearest town. Personal physical access to the latter may have been difficult, and most households appeared to sell straight to the co-operative, despite the lower prices usually received. The average size of garden was around 1,000 sq. m. per family, although between the mid-1960s and mid-1970s co-operativists' plots were reduced in size by between a half and two-thirds, and their livestock was cut by half (Skarço, 1984, p. 58). Subsequent events overtook the ultra-Stalinist aspiration to phase out the gardens completely within ten years.

Dwellers in private owner-occupied housing retained rights of inheritance, at least for their offspring. Private houses could be sold but not for speculation. They could also be rented if, for legitimate reasons, the owner or his family did not live in part or all of the dwelling. The rent could not exceed that paid for state-owned properties, and no more than one dwelling could be owned. A private rented sector of sorts therefore existed under Albanian communism.

3.5.7 Restructuring and privatisation

A continuing major problem has been a shortage of housing stock. With continued high birth and marriage rates, housing supply, with annual construction rates in the 1980s of at most 6,000 rural and 9,000 urban dwellings, was not able to keep pace with demand, despite the infusion of mass mobilisation concepts into housing construction. A shortage of flats, particularly for newly married couples, had long been a cause for concern (Biber, 1980, p. 551). New urban apartments were inhabited before services and outer facades were completed, and problems of quality control were abundant.

Following Hoxha's death, rather as in China after Mao, such 'revolutionary' policies as youth rustication were gradually, and quietly, scaled down, and came to an abrupt halt in 1991. With economic restructuring during 1991–92, there was an immediate increase in the prices of building materials and consequently of housing, the cost of which rose tenfold; the state's investment in this field was curtailed and 13,000 homes were left unfinished. However, during the period of 'national stability' and provisional governments from June 1991 to March 1992, when much social, economic and administrative upheaval took place, it was alleged (*Rilindja Demokratike*, 4 May 1993) that some 2,000 illegal construction licences were issued in Tirana by functionaries who involved themselves in lucrative property activities. It was claimed that not only did town-planning staff fail to control and prevent illegal development, but were themselves, together with their families, deeply involved in corrupt activity.

From November 1992 300 million leks was made available for housing completion. A national housing construction enterprise was established to distribute the credit and to raise further funding by creating new sources of investment. One longer-term consequence of taking on foreign technology for building construction was likely to see consequent higher elevations for apartment blocks, with the greater use of pre-fabrication, installation of lifts and improved service provision.

The privatisation of state housing was a high priority. Undertaken by the communist authorities in most other East European societies long before the events of 1989 (Sillince, 1990; Hegedüs *et al.*, 1992), selling state housing to its sitting tenants theoretically had the double advantage to the national exchequer of shifting the burden of upkeep from the public to the private sector, and of soaking up people's savings, thereby both making available more funds for central government use and hopefully checking inflationary pressures and demand for imported consumer goods. However, as recent high levels of inflation had acted as a strong disincentive to savings, it was unlikely that a significant proportion of the population would have adequate funds to be able to invest in housing. The exceptions would include urban dwellers working the black market and those with relatives and friends abroad sending back hard currency remittances.

As a consequence, in January 1993 a new housing privatisation law was announced which dispensed with earlier plans to make most families, except those of political prisoners, pay something towards the purchase of their homes. Under the revised scheme, homes with one room built before 1970 and pre-1965 structures with two rooms could be taken over by their tenants free of charge. For other dwellings, a sliding scale of up to 40,000 leks was to be levied as the purchase cost. All households acquiring their home were to receive a one-off payment of 2,600 leks to aid repair and maintenance, an admission of the poor quality of many state-owned properties. Some 200,000 state properties were available for acquisition, 80,000 of those being located in the capital where a special commission was set up to speed up the privatisation process. Within a short time, therefore, it had become apparent that:

Tirana residents are eager to rent out their dingy two- or three-room flats, just bought from the state for about $200, to the incoming foreigner for several hundred dollars a month. That's what you get in the West, they argue. That's the market economy. The flat comes replete with power cuts, cold water two hours a day, no hot water, quaintly pre-modern sanitation and kitchen facilities (Traynor, 1993a).

A new land law had been passed in July 1992 which, theoretically at least, permitted a domestic private property market to be developed. Outright purchase would not be permissible for foreigners. The new law based the price levels for land to be leased or sold upon the interaction of four weighted factors: (a) land productivity, divided into five categories; (b) location, again divided into five classes, including one for tourist areas, which rendered a factor of at least three times the next highest value category; (c) purpose of activity, divided into six categories, with tourism again having the highest price weighting; and (d) length of lease, with five time periods. Rent levels of land leased to foreigners would be double those for Albanians, and the price of land to be purchased by Albanians would cost ten times the annual rent level of that land.

In the countryside, the privatisation of agricultural land coupled with the accumulation of capital from new marketing opportunities, petty cross-border trading and the receipt of remittances from emigrant workers, has seen a building boom. Lax reinforcement of local planning regulations coupled to the need to break away from previous cooperative and state farm settlement structures has seen the rapid erection of many single family dwellings on the newly acquired agricultural holdings. This has occurred most notably on the fertile lowland arable lands of the coastal plain where a diffusion of dwellings across the agrarian landscape will pose manifold problems for future infrastructure provision and for coherent planning and rural management. A major constraint on such construction, however, has been the limited availability of building materials.

Adding to these new rural development pressures are the activities of wealthier urban dwellers, who, seeking better housing standards than their former state apartments could offer, are also erecting rural or urban fringe dwellings of sometimes substantial proportions. Rapidly increasing private motor vehicle ownership is encouraging such centrifugal forces.

In many rural and urban fringe areas of the country frenetic house construction activity has thus taken hold, with extended families acting as the nucleus of this informal and often illicit sector.

3.5.8 Local government change

July 1992 saw a new decentralised system of local administration introduced in tandem with local government elections. Thirty-seven districts replacing the previous 27 were subdivided into 310 communes and 43 municipalities. Splitting up some of the districts was primarily in the electoral interests of the Democratic Party, as in the case of Kavajë, the Democrats' leading stronghold in the country, which became independent from the district of Durrës (see also section 6.1.3 below).

In the past, local authorities had been merely the executors of policies dictated by Tirana. Following the collapse of the communist government – which had controlled the provinces through powerful district party secretaries – the status of local government had been placed in limbo, and representatives of various political parties subsequently governed collectively on a temporary basis. Under the 1992 system, municipalities and communes were to enjoy far greater material, financial and executive rights at the expense of the centre. The position of mayor (formerly, executive committee chairman) also became much more important, with the post-holder empowered to make decisions in the critical housing sector. Local authorities also became responsible for distributing state payments to poor families following the liberalisation of basic foodstuffs' prices. The commune, as the smallest unit of local authority, would have its own administrative apparatus, including specialists such as doctors, veterinarians and policemen, but such plans depended upon securing adequate funding and developing a local tax base (Zanga, 1992b). The relative success of the former communists in the 1992 local elections did leave the political landscape of the new local government system in rather ambiguous and potentially confrontational circumstances.

4

The economic legacy

4.1 Changing circumstances

4.1.1 Inter-war development

As a small state, Albania found itself party to 'client' relationships for much of the first 30 years after its 'independence' in 1912. During the turbulent years up to 1918, several foreign interests carried out exploration work for natural resource exploitation: Italians for petroleum and coal, Austrians seeking copper and coal, and the French searching out pyrites and ferro-chromium. Following the First World War, a recovery in the world economy stimulated an increased demand for the country's minerals, and further West European and American economic interests entered the country (Fishta, 1992). As a long prelude to their invasion on Good Friday 1939, however, it was the Italians who increasingly benefited from the country's oil and other natural resource wealth. Although transport was easily effected across the Adriatic, internal movement of largely unprocessed primary materials was more of a problem. Crude oil was piped to Vlorë, where rail consignments of bitumen and rock salt were also sent. Chrome, iron, lignite and agricultural products went by road to Durrës (Figure 4.1). The quantity and quality of these products became increasingly erratic, however, and with growing Italian dominance

of the economy, other export markets withered away; any hope of establishing pre-export industrial processing facilities similarly waned.

The overall level of foreign trade was low, with a persistent deficit. Imports invariably outweighed exports by a value ratio of two or three to one. In August 1937, ostensibly to redress this balance, a restriction was placed on all goods from countries whose imports from Albania fell below 70 per cent of their exports to it. This left only Italy, Greece and the United States, and effectively excluded Yugoslavia, Romania, Germany, Czechoslovakia, Britain and Japan, thereby further acting to strengthen Italian control over the country. Trade volume per head of population in 1936 was about 3 per cent of the level of Britain, 12 per cent of that of Greece, and 44 per cent of Yugoslavia. By that time Italy was receiving some 80 per cent of Albanian exports and providing 25 per cent of imports. Increasing imports from Italy reflected that country's capital investment in Albania, and the continued accumulation of wealth by a handful of families centred around the king.

There existed a low level of urbanisation, a lack of indigenous social and cultural development and only the minimum of infrastructural facilities needed to permit foreign economic exploitation. An April 1926 agreement concluded between Zogu and the Italian Society

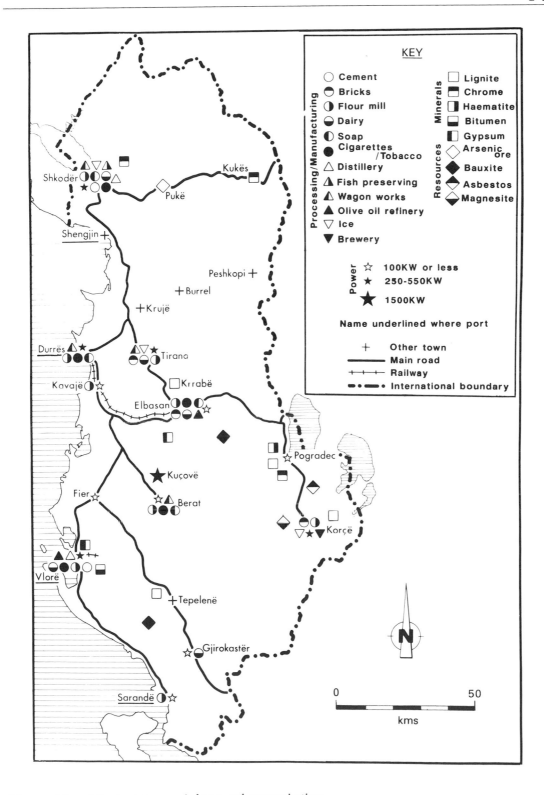

Figure 4.1 *Albania: inter-war industry and communications*

for the Economic Development of Albania secured 9.5 million gold francs for port construction at Durrës, Vlorë, Shëngjin and Sarandë, and for the draining of Durrës lagoon, with 6.19 million gold francs earmarked for the construction of 965 km of new road. But only improvements at Durrës, including what appeared to observers at the time as an excessive enlargement of the harbour, and, at a cost of 19.5 million gold francs, the construction of 275 km of road, were ever realised. Meanwhile, to govern a population of one million, Zogu saw the need to maintain three palaces.

Between 1925 and 1939, Italian loans, largely for the improvement of Albania's infrastructure, amounted to 130 million gold francs. On the eve of the Italian occupation, there were some 250 Italians employed in the Albanian civil service to manage and service the loans. Italians held monopolies over the exploitation of petroleum, copper and electricity supply as well as agricultural and forestry concessions.

After the 1939 invasion and Zogu's rapid flight, the country's economic base was rapidly consolidated (Table 4.1). Communications and basic infrastructure were selectively improved to meet new military demands. For example, the port of Shëngjin, with a local population of no more than 200 in 1943, and with no local industries, had its daily capacity increased fourfold, from 300 tonnes throughput in 1940 to 1,200 tonnes by 1943. Its jetties were increased in number from two to five to facilitate both the export of now scarce mineral resources from the northern highlands, and a continuous movement of military traffic (Mason *et al.*, 1945).

As suggested in Figure 4.1, by the early 1940s Albanian manufacturing activity was still severely limited and concentrated in a handful of small towns. The lack of good communications restricted trade and industry. All towns had bazaars, often protected by a fortress, which dealt in local pastoral and agricultural products, weapons and metal work, woodwork, leather, silk, embroideries and textiles. Periodic fairs and markets supplemented these centres of activity. But no large industrial establishments existed: processing and manufacturing was little

more than a cottage industry. Nine out of every ten industrial enterprises employed fewer than 15 workers, and even by 1943 less than 80 firms employed more than ten people (Mury, 1973, p. 23). Industrial output represented just 4.4 per cent of national income (Borchert, 1975, p. 181).

Not surprisingly, a significant proportion of industries was related to agricultural pursuits. While small, primitive water mills were ubiquitous, by 1943 'modern' mills powered by internal combustion engines could be found in the major settlements. Olive oil refineries at Elbasan and Vlorë complemented the localised oil presses. Oil residues were exported to Italy and Greece for further extraction (2,000 tonnes in 1938). Within Albania, one of the many applications of olive oil was in the few factories manufacturing soap. Locally grown and cured tobacco was processed into cigarettes in a further five factories, while five raki distilleries and an Italian-built brewery provided the Albanian population with further diversions.

Although 36 per cent of the country was forested, timber exploitation was hampered by internal transport problems: the numerous rivers flowed too swiftly through deep rocky gorges to be of much use for either floating or carriage by vessel. Nevertheless, some furniture production was carried on by cabinet-makers in most towns, as was small-scale coachbuilding. Hardwoods, particularly walnut, were increasingly being exported to Italy. A thousand tonnes of wool was produced in 1938–39, but subsequent Italian seizures, guerrilla destruction and the increased slaughter of sheep for food by the local population during the war, reduced the industry considerably.

The production of building materials, dominated by the use of local stone and masonry, was essentially small scale and localised. Lime kilns were ubiquitous: the working of brick clays took place in Tirana, Elbasan and Korçë, while, most notably, cement production was undertaken in Shkodër and Vlorë using local marls. Cement production in 1937, at 14,000 tonnes, appeared sufficient for the country's needs. In 1940, however, the Italians began the construction of a larger and more modern plant.

Table 4.1 *Italian control of Albanian resource interests*

Resource	Production	Location	Exploiter	Comments
Chromite	36,000t (1942) 1938–42 7-fold increase	Mëmlisht Kukës Klos Pogradec	Azienda Minerali Metallici Italiana	1940 estimate of 500,000t of workable reserves, enough to meet Italy's needs for more than a decade. Asphalted road built from Shkodër to Kukës
Copper	6,000t (1939)	Pukë Rubik	Montecatini Society	Production began 1939. Italian concessions in Mirditë since 1926 had yielded little.
Haematite	1.5 mn t (1939–40)	Pogradec Drin Valley	Ferralba	Estimated 20 mn t reserves. Plant for the fabrication of special steels to meet Italian needs was to have been built at Durrës. Rail transport had been planned.
Bitumen	20,000t (1940)	Selenicë	SIMSA	Exploited since classical times. Ironically, the country's lack of hard surfaced roads inhibited the exploitation of other minerals.
Petroleum	300,000t (1940) 1935–8 18-fold increase	Devoll Valley	Azienda Italiana de Petroli	Anglo-Persian concessions were gradually taken over in the 1930s. By 1938 445 wells had been sunk. A 74km pipeline was built from Kucovë to Vlorë for export to Bari and Livorno refineries (for aviation fuel for Reggia Aeronautica): vital in the face of League of Nations sanctions against Italy. Reserves estimated at 15 mn t. In 1944 the Germans began exploiting natural gas.
Lignite	7,000t (1939)	Krrabë, Korçë Basin, Memaliaj	ACAI	Small-scale workings for domestic fuel, brick-making and lime-burning.

Sources: Prampolini, 1941; von Luckwald, 1942; Zavalani, 1944; Mason *et al.*, 1945; Schnytzer, 1982, pp. 4–5; Fishta, 1992.

After the Italian capitulation and subsequent German occupation, all the concessions which had been granted to the Italians by pro-fascist quislings were rescinded and a new trade agreement was signed such that chromite and magnesite would be exported to Nazi Germany in return for consumer goods.

4.1.2 A satellite's satellite, 1944–48

The pre-war presence and then dominance of Italian interests in the economic exploitation of Albanian resources was of threefold significance for post-war development: (a) extensive geological exploration across the country had revealed the presence of a substantial range of mineral resources which could be exploited for the establishment of an industrial base; (b) a willing ally would be necessary to finance capital formation and capital goods imports; and (c) it emphasised the vulnerability of a small state for which economic penetration by a neighbour could ultimately result in political and military domination (Schnytzer, 1982, pp. 126–7).

The least developed European country by any yardstick, Albania in 1944 appeared a most unlikely society to fit classical Marxist precepts. That a uniquely Albanian form of communism evolved during the subsequent decades reflected the strong influence that external circumstances exerted upon the country to mould its domestic development path.

Having seen off both Italians and Germans from their national territories, Yugoslav and Albanian communist ruling groups proceeded to work closely together, albeit in a very unequal relationship: the Albanian party was little more than an extension of the Yugoslav (Lendvai, 1969, p. 183).

Economic resources were initally commanded both to make good war damage and then to consolidate the communist state. During the war some 61,000 buildings, 5.5 km of bridges and 2.5 km of docks had been destroyed, as had much of the country's 2,230 km of road, but Albania was largely without the financial resources to make good such damage. Reflecting the country's evolving political destiny, diverse and swiftly successive sources of aid arrived in the early post-war period from the United Nations Relief and Reconstruction Agency (UNRRA) ($27 million), Yugoslavia ($33 million) and the USSR ($150 million). By 1950, indicating the narrowness of the country's pre-war industrial base, industrial production was said to be more than four times the 1938 level.

After difficult negotiations, Hoxha's government accepted material and financial aid from UNRRA, for which it qualified by virtue of its guerrilla operations against the Italians and Germans. Of the $27 million received, a quarter was designated for food, and about an eighth for agricultural rehabilitation. One

hundred and fifty tractors and a number of lorries were supplied and assistance from a range of UN advisors was given for such necessary projects as marshland drainage and malaria eradication. Certainly UNRRA aid was at least partly responsible for staving off famine in Albania during this early period of reconstruction.

Increasingly, however, it was Yugoslavia which was to act as protector of the newly-spawned Albanian communist state. Just as Rome had outbid Belgrade in the pre-war period with its loans, assistance and ultimately dominating financial and administrative institutions, so Yugoslavia, under the guise of a fellow socialist ally within the penumbra of the Soviet bloc, began establishing binding economic and administrative treaties with Albania. Emblematic of this were two agreements signed in 1946: the Treaty of Friendship and Mutual Assistance; and the Treaty on the Co-ordination of Economic Plans, the Customs Union and Equalisation of Currencies. Just as the Soviet Union was establishing exploitative joint companies with its much smaller East European satellites in order to control them and benefit from their natural resources, so Yugoslavia pursued a similar policy with its much smaller neighbour, thereby rendering Albania a satellite's satellite. The Yugoslavs claimed that they did not themselves favour this form of development aid, but that Albanian backwardness made it essential (Wolff, 1956, p. 339).

Joint companies were set up for the exploitation of Albania's oil and metallic ores, for railway construction, electrification and foreign trade. To support such developments a joint Albanian-Yugoslav bank was established; credits amounted to two and three million dinars in 1947 and 1948, representing 56 per cent and 48 per cent of Albania's revenue for those two years respectively. Belgrade argued that Albania received 88 per cent of the net profits accrued from oil developments and 65 per cent from the railway (the 1947 Durrës–Peqin line for which the Yugoslavs supplied all finance and technical assistance). Yugoslavia also completed the 'Velika Selita' HEP plant (later renamed 'Lenin'), begun by the Italians.

During this period the elimination of

Table 4.2 *Albania: early post-war development policy*

(a) 1944–47: reconstruction of war damage and the development and consolidation of public ownership
Three main objectives:
(i) to draw the country out of its traditional backwardness;
(ii) to destroy the economic power of the bourgeoisie and foreign capital;
(iii) to consolidate the power of the communist party by giving the state the control of the country's economy.

1944: public control of all industry, banks, motorised transport, trade and mineral resources.
1945: all Italian and German properties were confiscated and all foreign concessions were revoked.
1947: total public control was completed; no private enterprises were now permitted.

(b) 1946–50: inauguration of co-ordinated national economic planning strategies based on Soviet lines
Essential objective: to establish a centralised 'command economy' planning system for setting priorities to concentrate resources in specific economic sectors.

1946: the State Planning Commission was given autonomy from the National Economic Council and made directly subordinate to the Council of Ministers. It began to compile the country's first national economic plan. This was applied over nine months of 1947.
1947: the 'Khozraschet' Soviet autonomous accounting system was introduced at enterprise level to allow planners to compile a more sophisticated plan for 1948.
1948: one-year plan to closely align Albania's economy with that of Yugoslavia.
1949–50: two-year plan to do the exact opposite.

Sources: Skendi, 1956a; Prifti, 1978; Schnytzer, 1982.

capitalist industrial production had been undertaken ruthlessly and without compensation (Table 4.2). Low levels of economic development, however, meant that this was no major feat.

Exploration and exploitation undertaken by the Yugoslavs increased oil production from the Kuçovë area and discovered new sources at Patos. Copper and chrome mines were re-opened. Some 27 bilateral treaties bound the two countries together; over 1,500 Albanian students were studying in Yugoslavia and almost 600 Yugoslav experts were placed in Albanian industry alone.

By 1947, however, strains were beginning to reveal themselves in the Albanian-Yugoslav relationship. Within the Albanian party the pro-Yugoslav faction was consolidating its position in preparation for the incorporation of Albania into Yugoslavia as its seventh federal state, thereby resolving the Kosovo problem:

If the national problem within Yugoslavia was to be solved by a federal state structure, nothing could be

more natural – and, of course, more advantageous for a highly ambitious communist leader – than to resolve the tangled issue of a large and compact Albanian minority in Yugoslavia by the unification of the entire Albanian nation as a member state of the Yugoslav federation. (Lendvai, 1969, pp. 184–5)

This aspiration, however, was cut short by Yugoslavia's expulsion from the Cominform. Ironically, this was partly a reflection of Tito's unwillingness to undertake bilateral projects with the Soviet Union through the medium of just the kind of joint companies that Yugoslavia had constituted for its economic relations with Albania.

Within 72 hours of the Cominform announcement in June 1948, the Albanian Central Committee was denouncing its own 'traitors and Trotskyites'. The Cominform break occurred at a timely moment, as Hoxha was barely holding on to office. He now had a prime excuse for purging all possible opposition. In July, Albania denounced all its economic agreements with Yugoslavia, declaring that

Belgrade had attempted to control Albania's economy and administration, and refusing to accept that it owed two and a half billion dinars worth of credits. Koci Xoxe, leader of the pro-Yugoslav faction, potential rival to Hoxha and one of the few high-ranking members of the party and government to actually come from a proletarian background, was sentenced to be shot.

4.1.3 CMEA partner: 1948–61

The brutal rupture in relations with Yugoslavia both prevented Albania's absorption into a far larger neighbour and opened up new and wider channels of assistance. Initially at least Albania was now to be a model ally of the Soviet Union. The break with Yugoslavia had necessitated a 20 per cent reduction in the investment plan for 1949, and some 6,000 comrades, representing about 8 per cent of total membership, had been expelled from the Albanian party, a purge which did much to dislocate the Albanian economy and jolt the morale of its workforce.

The Soviet Union stepped in to cover 40 per cent of Albania's state revenues. Advisors from other East European states, notably Czechoslovakia and the German Democratic Republic, supplanted Yugoslavs in the exploration for, and exploitation of, Albania's mineral resources. Before long the pattern of client relationship was repeating itself. Between 1948 and 1951 Albania traded exclusively with members of the CMEA, an economic constraint that none of the other European partners imposed upon themselves. During the 1950s the Soviet Union alone accounted for more than half of the country's foreign trade. By the end of that decade it was receiving 95 per cent of Albania's oil exports, 76 per cent of its tobacco and 38 per cent of its bitumen.

Albanian economic policies now appeared to follow a literal application of the strategy set out in Stalin's *Economic problems of socialism in the USSR*, his last published work (Schnytzer, 1982), which was never actually implemented as policy in the Soviet Union itself. A centralised form of control and planning appeared almost inevitable for post-war Albania, since for this small, albeit rugged country, central commands would be relatively easy to impose and monitor. It also suited a country previously characterised by autocracy and intense localism. Stringent application of the Stalinist model was, however, severely constrained in the early post-war period by (i) the low educational level of the population and an inadequate range of qualified personnel to administer a strong central bureaucracy; (ii) the need to maintain popular support rather than to restructure a society only recently devastated by five years of war; and (iii) the almost total absence of any industry to plan.

The country's first five-year plan (1951–55), embraced the Soviet model of development: 43 per cent of funds was earmarked for industry and mining compared to only 14 per cent for agriculture. No economic statistics were published, and considerable downward revision of the plan took place after Stalin's death in 1953. By this time however, the relative value of industrial as opposed to agricultural output was 60:40 compared to a ratio of 18:82 in 1938. For a society supposedly based upon the ideological principle of the revolutionary force of the urban proletariat, it was an outstanding structural irony that at the end of the plan period 70 per cent of the population remained employed in agriculture.

While the Soviet Union and its allies provided significant financial sums for the plan's enactment, as in Bulgaria, with few consumer goods upon which to spend their meagre incomes, the citizens of the People's Republic of Albania were compulsorily obliged to subscribe to state loan schemes: the first for 250 million leks in 1949 was said to be oversubscribed by one million leks, while the second for 300 million leks in 1952 was 35 per cent oversubscribed.

The second five-year plan period, 1956–60, the zenith of Albanian-Soviet co-operation, saw a long-range plan for 1961–75 promulgated with the aim of significantly changing the economic face of Albania. From February 1958, Soviet economic assistance was increased in the face of the Chinese 'Great Leap Forward'. Soviet, East German and Czechoslovak technicians in particular aided new mineral developments (ferrous-nickel, copper, chromium, oil refining), and the construction of HEP schemes to elaborate industrial and domestic electricity supplies. Albania's chromium production reached a level permitting this small country to claim highest world per capita production. In 1960 the 'construction of the economic basis of socialism' was declared to have been completed.

Following several years of apparent harmony, however, this plan period coincided with a wind of change blowing through Eastern Europe; 1956 in particular was a critical year. Khrushchev's denunciation of Stalin in the infamous 'secret speech' in Moscow filled the Albanian leadership with foreboding, a fear all too quickly justified with events in Hungary and Poland. China's 'Great Leap Forward', emphasising local self-sufficiency and diverging from Soviet advice, was soon to follow, setting forth aspects of a model of development which appealed to the still underdeveloped Albania (Logoreci, 1961; Tretiak, 1962).

Khrushchev visited Tirana in May 1959 and proceeded to commit two heinous crimes in the eyes of the Albanian leadership. Moscow was now pursuing a rapprochement with Belgrade, and the Soviet leader suggested that the Albanians did likewise. Further, Khrushchev advised the Albanians to abandon heavy industrialisation and convert their country into a 'flowering garden', growing semi-tropical crops and market-gardening produce for which the environmental conditions were more suited. Albania could receive all the necessary machinery it required from CMEA partners. The Albanian leadership thought otherwise (Zavalani, 1961). Khrushchev then made an equally unsuccessful trip to Beijing, and as the Sino-Soviet rift grew in intensity, Tirana increasingly voiced its support for the Chinese:

Faced with the choice between Soviet aid, which amounted to an estimated $600 million during the post-war period, and their survival in power relying on a distant protector, the Albanian leaders predictably opted for the latter course. (Lendvai, 1969, p. 194)

During a severe drought and serious food shortages in the summer of 1960, a shipment of 50,000 tonnes of Soviet wheat failed to arrive, at a point when the Albanians were down to their last 15 days' supply (Freedman, 1970). Within one month of the Twenty-second Soviet Party Congress in October 1961, when the Sino-Soviet dispute was finally brought out into the open, diplomatic relations between Albania and the USSR were broken off, Soviet, East German and Czechoslovak credits for the 1961–65 five-year plan were cancelled, and experts were withdrawn. Albania was again faced with a major political and economic reorientation even greater than that of 1948 (Logoreci, 1961; Skendi, 1962; Griffith, 1963; Hamm, 1963).

4.1.4 China's voice in Europe: 1961–76

While trade with the Soviet Union ceased completely in 1963, other CMEA members still accounted for about a quarter of Albania's foreign trade. But that is not to diminish the traumatic importance of this second major post-war rift. Albanian planners claimed that these events delayed the completion of some 250 projects within the country's third five-year plan (1961-5) by three years, with a 'knock-on' effect for subsequent plan periods (40 of the projects being incomplete by 1965) (Klosi, 1969, p. 17). Although China stepped in to provide some 90 per cent of the financial and technical aid which had been promised by Soviet-bloc members, an initial emphasis upon continuing the industrialisation programme had to be substantially modified.

That Albania was able to survive a transition away from Soviet hegemony has been ascribed to three basic pre-conditions: (a) the relative unity of Albania's top leadership (twenty of the 61 members of the Central Committee of the time were related, including five married couples and up to seven representatives of one clan); (b) Albania's relative geographical position, lacking contiguity with a Soviet-bloc country to preclude direct land-borne Soviet military intervention; and (c) the reality of a growing polycentrism within the international communist movement. The latter development in particular tended to draw Soviet attention away from Albania while also giving the small country moral (if not ideological) support in its confrontation with the first socialist nation.

Relations with China had been developing since the mid-1950s, and from 1955 significant annual trade deficits with Beijing began to be accrued, with grants and loans being extended to help cover the imbalance. Some degree of bilaterality was expressed, however symbolic it may have been in practice. For example, the November 1956 technical co-operation protocol between the two countries specified that Chinese information on the use of by-products of rice, the prevention of alkaline deposits in rice fields, and the production of plant seeds, would be exchanged for Albanian advice on social insurance, public health, the construction of small hydro-electric power stations in upland areas and the cultivation of tobacco, olive plants and cereal seeds (Prybyla, 1967, pp. 10–11).

Nevertheless, the fact remained that China could not compensate for the loss of Soviet support. Although during the 1961–5 economic plan period between 130,000 and 140,000 tonnes of wheat were shipped annually from China, that five-year plan had been geared specifically to Soviet and East European deliveries of machinery and equipment. Indeed, by October 1967 production bottlenecks had reached such a critical stage in Albania that all its major engineering enterprises had to concentrate on the production of spare parts.

Two significant trends emerged from this dislocated plan period: (a) a reorientation towards aspirations of self-sufficiency – pragmatically necessary in the face of uncertain external assistance, and dogmatically convenient to emphasise the need for unstinting efforts in home production and suspicion of external influences; and (b) greater emphasis laid upon agricultural development, interpreted by some observers as representing the influence of Chinese advisors.

Paradoxically, however, from 1961 heavy industry was particularly emphasised, as a response to: (i) the requirement to firmly establish the means of production in order to consolidate the socialist economic base within a framework of 'self-reliance'; and (ii) defence requirements, which in their turn took into consideration: (a) the economic and military vulnerability of the country before the war; (b) continued hostility towards the capitalist world; and (c) hostility towards the post-Stalin Soviet leadership.

With Chinese aid, the Albanian leadership began to emphasise production specialisation and economies of scale in order to rationalise economic and productive links between the various enterprises and branches of the economy. It argued that the basis of this approach had been established in the 1940s and 1950s in two stages as follows: (i) after liberation, with the revival of what little industry had previously existed, small enterprises were grouped into larger units, particularly oil presses, weaving mills, small hosiery workshops and engineering workshops; and (ii) during 1954–55, direct concentrations or transfers of activities between enterprises took place to assist the structural concentration of production and rational administrative control – in particular, small industrial enterprises such as printing shops and mechanical repair workshops were grouped into larger units.

Subsequent industrial location policy emphasised three dimensions (Banja, 1981):

(i) the 'rational utilisation of natural resources', through raising the level of processing close to the source of the raw material. Clearly, in a small, yet topographically difficult country, processing at or near source reduces transport costs, while the size of country suggests that the internal market distribution points are never too far away;

(ii) the 'harmonious and proportional distribution of industry to all the districts of the country' (Anon, 1982b, p. 256). Pointing to the pre-war situation, official literature emphasised the need to develop industry with a 'judicious distribution over the whole country' as essential in developing the well-being of all the people;

(iii) narrowing the distinction between town and country, largely implicit in the first two considerations. This was articulated in (a) the growth of the urban population and of new towns associated with new industrial and employment centres established since 1944; (b) raising the degree of mechanisation, electrification and labour productivity in the countryside; (c) raising the level of socialist relations in the countryside by transforming co-operative into state property and with it, an increased 'industrialisation' of rural production through the development of auxiliary activities such as the production of construction materials and food processing; and (d) raising the level of cultural, educational and welfare facilities and achievements in the countryside to make them comparable with the towns.

Electrification of the country was officially completed in November 1970, and exports began two years later (Gurney, 1978). The most notable feature of energy development was progress in establishing a 'cascade' of HEP stations on the Drin river in the north of the country (Çuedari, 1983; Paloka, 1981), which geographically complemented the exploitation of lignite, in the centre and south-east of the country, and of petroleum and gas in the south (Figure 4.2).

Inauguration of the fifth five-year plan in 1971 (Hall, 1975), emphasised metallurgical development and chemicals, planned completion of the country's then largest hydro-electric power station – the 250 megawatt complex at the Vau i Dëjes site – and commencement of building on a still larger plant. The latter, a 400 MW complex situated at Fierzë in the remote north-east of the country (Figure 4.2) reflected the need to closely integrate industrial development. Much of the power produced – projected at 17,000 million kilowatt hours a year – was to be used specifically for the country's developing metallurgical industry. Twelve kilometres to the north-east, a new town at Bajram Curri was built. Initially to provide residential and social facilities for Fierzë's construction workers, this urban implantation into an otherwise sparsely populated area was to eventually house 8,000 people. Acceleration of the rate of electricity production was notable, characterised by the concentration of generation capacity in rela-

tively large units and the elimination of uneconomic small-scale production, the re-grouping of power stations to effectively supply a national grid system, and the harmonisation of hydro-electric and thermal stations to compensate for seasonal fluctuations in water flow and to ensure uninterrupted power supplies.

Chinese influence on Albania tended to be over-emphasised by Western observers. Although Albania's very own 'cultural revolution' (1966–69) (Prifti, 1968; Pano, 1974) saw the official elimination of all religion in 1967 (Prifti, 1975a) (see section 2.4.2), abolition of direct taxation (1969), a reduction in wage differentials and an emphasis on rural projects through Chinese-inspired 'open schooling' for students, bureaucrats and other urban dwellers, this 'revolution' was far more tightly controlled than the Chinese prototype, and hardly penetrated the upper echelons of party and governmental activity.

Chinese economic assistance had been accepted in Albania since 1954, but Albanian dissatisfaction with both the quality and quantity of goods, finance and specialist advice was evident from about mid-1966, not least in the exhortations for 'self-reliance'. By this time, 60 per cent–70 per cent of Albania's trade had been switched to China, estimates putting the value of Chinese loans granted to Albania between 1954 and 1975 as amounting to almost $500 million (Prybyla, 1967, pp. 9–14; Bourne, 1972; Fontana, 1975; Marmullaku, 1975, p. 96; Prifti, 1978, p. 81):

Chinese aid allowed Albania to develop its economy, particularly its extractive industry, at a faster pace than would otherwise have been possible, while externally it helped Albania to withstand Soviet pressure and to defy the rest of the world. (Larrabee, 1978, p. 62)

China also needed Albania's support, however. For several years Albania acted as China's mouthpiece at the United Nations (before Beijing gained its own place there in October 1971); in Europe through Radio Tirana (for which the Chinese built a powerful transmitter near Durrës); and in Albania's written propaganda. However, despite the inauguration

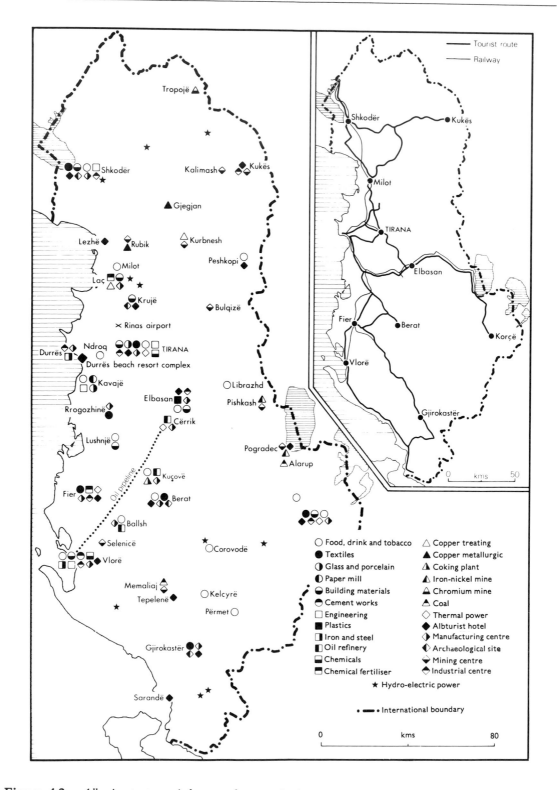

Figure 4.2 *Albania: post-war industry and communications*

of a weekly air service between Tirana and Beijing in November 1974, and the signing of a five-year pact to cover the 1976–80 sixth five-year plan period, disagreements not only of an economic kind were emerging. One difference was essentially ideological. According to 'Mao Zedong thought', there existed 'three worlds': the socialist, the capitalist, and that of developing nations, to whom the socialists should show friendship and give aid (Hinton, 1972). For Albania, there was only black and white: socialism and capitalism, two irreconcilable forces which, through the dictates of Marxism-Leninism, would ultimately witness the defeat of the latter by the former through dialectical inevitability. Neither did Albania subscribe to the 'enemy's enemy' theory, such that when Kissinger and then Nixon were invited to Beijing in the early 1970s, Albania began reviewing its stance towards China. Further perceived heresies were committed by the Chinese in showing approval of the EEC as a potential counterbalance against Soviet power, and in establishing relations with Britain, West Germany and NATO (Pano, 1977c).

As early as the November 1971 sixth Party congress, at which the Chinese were conspicuous by their absence, it was clear that all was not cordiale in the Sino-Albanian entente (Wohl, 1972; Fontana, 1975). Hoxha was openly declaring that, with one eye on Beijing, the struggle against imperialism was 'indivisible', and that it was wrong to make compromises with either of the two superpowers or their lackeys (Dobbs, 1977). Thereafter, numbers of Chinese advisors in Albania noticeably decreased (Anon, 1971b; Friendly, 1971), although the Chinese did begin to provide the country with MIG-21 fighter planes (Fontana, 1975).

The post-Mao change of ideological direction in China from late 1976, however, allowed both parties to disengage without losing too much face. The final nail in the relationship's coffin was Albania's June 1978 announcement of full support for Vietnam's position in its dispute with Beijing: in July China formally terminated all economic and military co-operation with Albania, although diplomatic relations were maintained.

Just as the Yugoslavs in 1948 and Soviet partners in 1961, Chinese advisors were finally pulled out of Albania in July 1978 (Kaser, 1979) to leave a small Balkan country, strong on rhetoric but weak on subtlety, needing to put flesh on its exhortations of self-reliance and self-sufficiency (Larrabee, 1978). Indeed, in December 1976 Albania had gone so far as to adopt a new constitution referring to itself as the People's *Socialist* Republic of Albania, the additional adjective symbolising the self-perceived role as the only remaining ideologically pure socialist society. By the end of the Sino-Albanian relationship, an estimated $850 million had passed from China to Albania in various forms of aid (Abecor, 1979). In summary, Albanian criticisms of Chinese policy are enumerated in Box 4.1.

Box 4.1 *Albanian criticisms of Chinese policy*

1. China exaggerated the role and value of its economic assistance to Albania.
2. The Chinese leadership deviated from Leninist norms of inter-Party relations.
3. The Chinese Party had a wavering attitude in the struggle against revisionism.
4. It was dangerous and counter-productive for the Chinese to maintain claims to Soviet territory.
5. Rather than providing Albania with appropriate and sufficient defensive hardware, Beijing had advised Tirana to conclude a military alliance with Yugoslavia and Romania.
6. 'Maoist thought' was confused and at times anti-Leninist.
7. The 'three worlds' theory negated the teachings of Marx, Engels, Lenin and Stalin.
8. The underlying aim of Chinese foreign policy was to establish that country as an imperialist superpower.
9. Chinese aggression against Vietnam was 'barbarous' and 'fascist'.

Source: Réti, 1983, pp. 192–4.

4.1.5 'Self-reliance': 1976–90

The break with China hastened a downward spiral of: lack of modern technology, domestic innovation and import substitution, unsaleable manufactures for export, lack of hard currency for imports. This was to take Albania all the way down to its political-economic crisis turning point of the early 1990s (Schnytzer, 1981, 1982; Wildermuth, 1989; Pashko. 1991; Sjöberg, 1991b).

With Albanian accusations of sabotage, none of the three major projects undertaken with Chinese guidance – Fierzë HEP scheme, Ballsh oil refinery and Elbasan metallurgical complex – were completed on time. Industrial and agricultural production goals were significantly reduced from 1976, and an all-round financial tightening, clothed in ideological rhetoric, was manifest: exhortations to save electricity; 30 per cent–40 per cent reduction in spare parts imports; another mass movement (of some 14,000 students and 'working youth') to the countryside to spur agricultural production; and a further narrowing of wage differentials.

Article 28 of the 1976 constitution (section 2.3.4 above) did not appear to leave a great deal of scope for international trade. Nevertheless, by the mid-1980s, estimates put annual Albanian trade with the rest of the world at a level of $550 million, mostly on a counter-trade basis, to retain national solvency in the absence of major foreign currency stocks.

Despite apparent self-imposed isolation, Albania embarked upon a process of quietly consolidating economic links with its traditionally hostile enemies, beginning with a trade agreement with Greece as early as 1970. 'Safe' trading partners in Western Europe were also sought: Italy, Scandinavia, France, Belgium, the Netherlands, Austria and Switzerland (Kaser, 1979). The United States remained beyond the pale: Britain and West Germany had outstanding debts owing, which, according to the Albanians, represented $30 million of Albanian gold and $1 billion in war reparations respectively. These 'obligations', the Albanians argued, would, until rectified, stand in the way of any re-establishment of mutual relations (section 6.2.4 below). Nevertheless, following the rift with China,

Albania began searching out Western markets for offshore drilling, hydro-electric and metallurgical technology, all areas of high West German expertise.

Despite the lack of diplomatic relations, both the USA and Britain received chromium exports from Albania. Indeed, as the world's third largest source of the ore, Albanian production was stepped up to 1.5 million tonnes by 1980, with exports to a wide range of Western markets.

Improving relations with Yugoslavia throughout the 1970s, prior to the riots in Kosovo from spring 1981, encouraged trade agreements, a defence alliance and co-operation in energy development. For 1980, trade was agreed between the two countries to be set at $135 million, and for the 1981–85 plan period it was projected at $720 million. While a majority of Albania's exports continued to go to Yugoslavia, imports covered ferrous metals, chemicals and such consumer goods as televisions. Some factories in Albania were to be built by Yugoslav enterprises (shades of 1945–48?), and Albania was to open a commercial office in Rijeka. Despite setbacks in relations, for the first time in its history Albania established a railway link with the outside world via Yugoslavia.

Given subsequent events, did the rhetoric of self-reliance ever have any substance? In 1976 the country claimed to have become self-sufficient in cereal grains and 85 per cent self-supporting in other food requirements. The same applied to (the extremely meagre level of) consumer goods production; while the country was a net exporter of oil and electricity. At the height of the alliance with Beijing, however, Albania was running an import deficit to China of about 30 per cent, and it is difficult to see how this could have been made up subsequently. Article 28 of the 1976 constitution may well have been drafted specifically to preclude Chinese and Soviet financial claims.

With industrial output for 1978 said to be 4.6 times greater than in 1960 (Anon, 1979), and a net export of oil and electricity, some economic progress had been made, but perhaps despite, rather than because of, Albania's policies and their method of execution. In particular, a series of vicious purges and an added wave of

Plate 4.1 *The 'social revisionist' Chinese leadership, symbolised by Deng Xiaoping, being droppped into the dustbin of history (by a vividly red hand) to join capitalism, fascism and Soviet revisionism. Adding pertinence to the hoarding is its location — in the grounds of Tirana's 'Enver Hoxha' tractor factory, which had been tooled up by the Chinese in the 1960s. By the time the photograph was taken in 1982, the plant was confined to producing spare parts, and the only tractor to be seen was on a concrete plinth at the factory gates*

Table 4.3   *Albania: estimated production growth, 1981–88*

	1981	1982	1983	1984	1985	1986	1987	1988
	Percentage growth over previous year							
Sandström and Sjöberg:								
Industrial production	6.2	4.7	1.0	3.3	−1.4	6.4	0.2	2.0
Agricultural production	3.7	4.0	9.4	−3.5	1.6	4.2	−0.4	−6.4
Industry and agriculture	5.4	4.5	3.7	1.0	−0.4	5.7	0.3	−0.8
Wildermuth:								
Agricultural production								
total	−1.0	3.0	6.3	0.0	0.2	−0.6	2.0	–
per capita	−3.2	0.8	3.9	−2.2	−2.0	−2.7	−0.1	–

Sources: Wildermuth, 1989, p.23; Sandström and Sjöberg, 1991, p. 938.

xenophobic paranoia in the mid-1970s seemed to indicate that there were calls within higher echelons of party and government for some degree of economic reform. The break with China and the inevitable requirement to turn to other, more diverse, trade and aid partners, would have appeared to be an appropriate point for structural rethinking. But rather than question the structure and organisation of the economic system, the party leadership blamed the malfunctioning of the system and the failures of the plan on the managers of the economy and the technocratic intelligentsia (Prifti, 1978, p. 87), who were thus removed, thereby fuelling further disruption.

Under these circumstances, the rhetoric of self-reliance continued within the 1981–85 plan period, and Albania's economy was set on an inexorable downward path for the rest of the decade. Emphasis on higher productivity and expansion of existing facilities, import substitution and export capacity growth was paramount. The introduction of new technologies from abroad, such as electronics, was reduced to a minimum.

Critical for post-China developments was a trend initiated just before the break with Beijing. In 1978 economic planning was reorganised to heighten the degree of economic centralisation (Schnytzer, 1981; Wildermuth, 1989; Pashko, 1991, Sjöberg, 1991b). This was particularly aimed at achieving autarky in food production and for tightening control over the rural population in order to achieve that aim

(Lange, 1981; Sjöberg, 1991a) (see sections 3.2.4 above, 4.2 below).

A compelling interpretation of Albanian development policy during the 1980s is that of a combination of medium-term attempts at rectifying the problems brought about by over-centralisation, and of short-term responses to poor annual peformance (Sjöberg, 1991a, 1991b, pp. 118–22). Such responses included:

(a) the April 1985 decision to use wage policy to encourage production, thereby re-emphasising material incentives and encouraging widening income differentiation (Xhaja and Metohu, 1988; Gjyzari, 1989);

(b) a reduction of the number of plan indicators for some enterprises and farms which were to be granted more discretion in planning, finance and pricing (Konini, 1989; Wildermuth, 1989);

(c) the establishment in March 1987 of a state commission on economic and financial control to oversee changes in the planning system;

(d) the issuing of a decree by the Council of Ministers in July 1987 granting districts a more active role in planning (Sjöberg, 1991a);

(e) in this way there appeared an upsurge of 'reform' proposals following years of poor economic performance (1984–85, 1987–88), and relative inactivity after relatively good years (1981, 1983, 1986) (Sjöberg, 1991b, pp. 120–22) (Table 4.3).

Table 4.4 *Albania: energy and mineral production, 1980–88*

	1980	1984	1985	1986	1987	1988
Energy						
Coal*	1,418	2,010	2,100	2,230	2,130	2,184
Crude oil*	1,900[‡]	1,300[‡]	1,200[‡]	1,400[‡]	1,200[‡]	1,200[‡]
Electricity[≠]	3,717	3,800	3,147	5,070	4,200[‡]	3,984
Ores						
Chrome*	1,004	960	1,111	1,207	1,080	1,109
Copper*	769	1,007	989	1,024	1,160	1,087
Iron-nickel*	597	1,080	905	–	970	1,067

Notes: * thousand tonnes; ‡ estimates; ≠ GWh

Source: Sandström and Sjöberg, 1991, p. 941.

Table 4.5 *Albania: major industrial development plans for 1990 and beyond*

1. Completion of:
   (a) Banja HEP scheme to provide an extra 40 million cubic metres of water for agriculture;
   (b) a nickel-iron mine in the Librazhd district, which would be capable of producing 500,000 tonnes a year;
   (c) two new chromite mines in Tropojë and Mat districts;
   (d) a new copper mine in Pukë;
   (e) new brown coal mines in Pogradec, Korçë and Tepelenë districts.

2. Expansion of:
   (a) ferrochrome unit at Burrell with two more furnaces;
   (b) chromite mine at Bulqizë;
   (c) urea unit at Fier;
   (d) copper wire mill, Shkodër;
   (e) spinning mill, Berat;
   (f) flour mill, Shkodër;
   (g) refrigerator factory, Lushnjë.

3. Inauguration of the construction of:
   (a) a coal concentrator at Korçë;
   (b) a coal brickette factory at Ballsh;
   (c) two further chromite mines in Librazhd and Pogradec districts to supply Elbasan's new ferrochrome processing unit

4. New shafts in the coal mines at Dibër, Kukës and Tropojë.

Sources: various: BBC SWB EE; BEE; EEM; EEN.

Within a decade characterised by 'an unambiguous trend of decline' (Sjöberg, 1991b, p. 121; see also Höpken, 1989; Wildermuth, 1989; Pashko, 1991; Sandström and Sjöberg, 1991), there was a significant shift in both capital investment and labour resources away from the spiralling inefficiency of heavy manufacturing to the mining sector, which had noticeably failed to take advantage of favourable world market prices, particularly in chromium, because of low productivity and poor quality of output (Table 4.4). This trend was to have been emphasised for 1990 and beyond (Table 4.5), and prior to the country's upheavals, new natural gas deposits in the Durrës and Delvinë areas encouraged a stepping up of onshore exploration work.

The year 1985 was particularly inauspicious for Albanian communists. Not only was it the final year of a less than inspiring five-year plan period, but in April, the country's only post-war leader, fountainhead and source of one of the world's last major personality cults, Enver Hoxha, died (Ascherson, 1985; Chamberlain, 1985; Colitt, 1985; Halliday, 1985; Modiano, 1985; Petrovic, 1985; Reuter, 1985; Smiley, 1985; Tifft, 1985). He had been ill for some time, and his successor, Ramiz Alia, had been effectively running the country for the past three years (Godwin, 1984). The year also saw the rise to power in Moscow of Mikhail Gorbachev, soon to be introducing notions of *glasnost* and *perestroika* to a bemused Soviet Union. Albania, Eastern Europe and the whole world order would never be quite the same again.

4.2   Agriculture and food

4.2.1   Inter-war development

With two-thirds of the country mountainous, Albanian agricultural potential would appear to possess strict limitations, exacerbated by man's environmental mishandling. Much of the country's forest land has been degraded, with generations of slash and burn clearance for pasture extension often resulting in bad soil erosion. This position has been worsened by the prevalence of goats feeding on young trees in regenerating areas, deforming them sufficiently to render the wood useless for timber production.

In the lowlands, as east—west flowing rivers slow down from their plunging upland courses, sufficient silt has been deposited to provide extremely fertile plains. Under Ottoman rule, however, these rivers were not regulated, such that bars developed at river mouths, entrances silted up, and inland lagoons and marshes developed. Such waterlogged land provided ideal breeding conditions for mosquitoes with the result that malaria became endemic, heavily constraining the physical ability of the population to undertake agricultural activities to their fullest extent.

An Italian report of 1922 emphasised that in combination with a warm Mediterranean climate and abundant water, the potential fertility of the then malarial coastal plains would be suitable for the cultivation of the most valuable industrial and oil-bearing crops, tobacco, linen, cotton and soya, as well as fruits and early vegetables (Zavalani, 1944). But agricultural methods were generally primitive. Arable land was only planted in spring, and seasonal employment caused many to search for casual work in forestry, fishing or town occupations, or to emigrate. Jealously guarded communal ownership of land persisted for forests, pastures and fisheries. Much of the cultivable land, however, had long been in the freehold ownership of a family, each member of which would have specific tasks under the headman's direction. Most houses had a garden plot.

In the more fertile and populous districts, farms averaged three to seven hectares in size. Poorer freeholders often became dependent upon richer landowners or town-dwelling merchants and money lenders, eventually selling their freehold to become tenant farmers. By the late 1930s some 40 per cent of the farming community had come to this position. The landed gentry tended to intermarry and form a compact aristocracy. Religious institutions also held large estates, although they had a better reputation as landlords.

Zogu's 1930 attempt at agrarian reform, to redistribute land to the landless peasantry, and to limit ownership to 40 hectares plus five hectares for each family member, was ineffective. Arable land, which comprised just over 11 per cent of the total land area, was mainly in the hands of the state, religious bodies and a few relatively wealthy families. The reform plan was to redistribute to landless workers one-third of all state lands plus a third of the remaining two-thirds larger than 40 hectares. An agrarian bank was set up to aid the plan's enactment, but the overall effect of the reform was limited. It included too many exemptions – vines, olives, fruit plantations and model farms – with the result that loopholes were easily found and excuses made for not handing over land. Further, no agricultural register existed to verify ownership and to facilitate redistribution (RIIA, 1939). Capital was also severely limited: in 1938 only 32 tractors existed within the country. Zogu's apparent aim had been to frighten the wealthy beys who opposed him, rather than necessarily to redistribute agricultural resources for purely altruistic motives. However, this threat of reform was sufficient to inhibit agricultural investment, particularly in the mechanisation of larger holdings (Schnytzer, 1982). This technical insufficiency was buttressed by illiteracy and a part-tribally organised peasantry often debilitated by endemic disease, particularly malaria.

During the 1930s the government attempted to increase the quantity and improve the quality of the country's agriculture by encouraging co-operative credit societies, seed innovations, technical agricultural schools and new breeds of animals, particularly Swiss cattle and Hungarian horses, to improve the country's stock. Yet by 1938 only 11 per cent of Albanian land was under cultivation. In 1943, when 87 per cent of the population was still engaged in agriculture, 96.5 per cent of arable land was devoted to food grains – predominantly maize for the staple porridge – and only 1.3 per cent was sown for cash crops. The year of 1942 was a drought year and food had to be imported, while in 1944 all essential foodstuffs except maize were rationed: the sale of agricultural produce was prohibited, as was the transport of foodstuffs between provinces.

The one agricultural success, although it operated largely outside of the Albanian economy, was a concession farmed by Italian colonists at Sukth, just outside Durrës. Output here was allowed to be directly exported to Italy without any tax imposition. After the war, this area, with extensions, became the country's first state farm, and the showpiece of Albanian socialist agriculture for impressionable visiting foreigners.

The combination of a 320 km coastline, great variety of high quality fish offshore, and clear freshwater lakes, provided considerable natural resources for an Albanian fishing industry. However, a lack of capital and technical equipment saw limited exploitation of this potential. Export rather than home consumption characterised the industry, with pre-war consignments of fresh, salted and smoked fish varying between a low of 183 tonnes in 1936 and a high of 523 tonnes in 1934. These levels were raised during wartime Italian exploitation. Coastal mullet, bass, dory and eels were complemented by sturgeon retrieved from fish traps on the longer rivers, trout, carp and eels caught with heavy fishing boats on Lake Ohrid, and sardines netted in Lake Shkodër, where a preserving factory was established.

With wartime destruction of Italian efforts at reclamation and mosquito control, between 60 per cent and 70 per cent of the population were affected by malaria by 1946, compared to only 16.5 per cent in 1939 (Borchert, 1975, p. 178).

4.2.2 Post-war collectivisation

As elsewhere in socialist Eastern Europe, a three-stage pattern was imposed upon post-war agricultural developments. The first, undertaken in Albania from August 1945, saw the expropriation of lands formerly held by 'foreigners', private institutions, banks, religious bodies and other large landowners. Previously about a hundred such landowners had owned a third of all Albania's fertile land. All holdings above 20 hectares were confiscated unless the owners were deemed to be employing 'advanced methods' of cultivation, in which case 40 hectares could be kept. By May 1946 Albanian leaders could declare that a landlord class had been destroyed.

Stage two was based upon a combination of Marxist rhetoric and the pragmatism of Machiavelli: land redistribution to the landless peasantry was seen not only as a basic plank of egalitarian socialism, redistributing resources in a more equitable fashion among the poorest social groups, but it was also a means of gaining peasant support for a still insecure communist regime. It was seen as (transient) compensation for the demise of peasant political parties. Invariably it preceded collectivisation and a socialisation of rural lifestyles. In particular, a redistribution of some 320,000 hectares to 60,000 peasant families substituted numerous dwarf holdings for large estates, with existing tenant farmers having first priority of allocation and second priority going to the families of partisans killed in the war. Holding sizes were restricted to about five hectares.

As the economically and technically least developed society in Europe, Albania's situation was exacerbated by an absence of any tradition of scientific agriculture. UNRRA aid was employed to assist the peasants with supplies, technical aid and instruction on the maintenance of newly imported equipment (Wolff, 1956, p. 340). An agricultural school was also established on a former Italian model farm at Lushnjë.

As elsewhere in Central and Eastern Europe, the third stage of agrarian transformation saw measures to bring about collective control of the means of agricultural production – co-operative and state farms – even though Albania's physical conditions were far removed from those of the Russian wheatlands. Many of the former church, foreign and state-owned lands, large estates, flocks, olive plantations, forests and water bodies were immediately transformed into (or simply retitled as) socialist state property. The state sector in agriculture thus comprised state farms, machine tractor stations (MTSs), district branches of the national seeds enterprise, the managing body of the irrigation system, forest enterprises and the scientific research institutes, stations and former Italian concessions. Much of the newly reclaimed and irrigated land of the coastal plains and in the Korçë Basin was turned into state farms which subsequently increased steadily in size. Although essentially located on the lowlands, state farms were also planned for the hilly and mountainous regions of the country as part of the long-term process of transforming rural property relations. The role of state farms reached its peak in 1988 when the sector produced 30.3 per cent by value of all agricultural output (DeS, 1991, p. 175).

Under Article 18 of the 1976 constitution all land was made state property, and was merely granted to agricultural co-operatives for their use. Article 19 did, however, provide reassurance that the use of such land was granted free of charge.

In the face of unpopular and often unsuitable forms of collectivisation, the euphemistic 'class struggle' brought to the fore an agrarian problem which Albania had managed to avoid during wartime. With the prospect of collectivised livestock ownership, many peasants chose to slaughter their animals rather than relinquish them. Thus the number of cattle per head of population in the country diminished, becoming lower by 1957 than it had been in 1938. At the same time, however, a new emphasis on the production of such cash crops as cotton, tobacco and sugar beet reduced the land area available for pasturing animals from 30.8 per cent of the total land surface in 1938 to 21.5 per cent by 1971. Such a reorientation of agricultural production, while not meeting Albania's food grain requirements until at least the mid-1970s, was coupled with an expansion of total arable land through marshland reclamation and hillslope terracing (292,000 ha in 1938 to 636,000 ha in 1973). Primarily, however, collectivisation and closer state control permitted an intensification of production through more and improved irrigation, mechanisation, increased use of fertilisers, improvements in seed strains and breeds of cattle, and electrification of farms and villages.

Officially acknowledged disparities between production objectives and levels of development encouraged the early introduction of agricultural technology. Ten MTSs were established on the plains in 1947 to provide, on a contractual basis, tractors, harvester-threshers and other machinery for agricultural co-operatives. Three aims were sought: (i) promotion of the mechanisation of agricultural work, since the co-operatives themselves could not be expected to cover the high cost of purchasing such machines; (ii) the rapid and continuous growth of agricultural production; and (iii) an increase in labour productivity with an overall reduction in production costs.

The MTSs were crucial instruments for agricultural procurement, assisting collectivisation drives and propagating the socialist message in the countryside amongst those least

Table 4.6 *Albania: changing composition of agrarian structures, 1950–90*

	1950 a	1950 b	1960 a	1960 b	1970 a	1970 b	1980 a	1980 b	1990 a	1990 b
Private sector	92.1	} 91.3	18.3	} 13.6	0	0	0	0	0	0
Family plots	1.9		27.4		23.0	3.5	19.2	2.7	20.9	4.3
Co-operative sector	1.9	5.4	41.6	72.2	55.1	75.8	55.5	75.8	49.9	71.6
State sector	4.1	3.3	12.7	14.2	21.9	20.7	25.3	21.5	29.2	24.1
Total	100.0	100.0	100.0	100.0	100.0	100.0	100.0	100.0	100.0	100.0
mn leks	1865		2702		4835		6987		8171	
thousand hectares		391		457		599		702		704

Notes:

a. % by value of production (at 1986 prices)

b. % of total arable land

Sources: KPS, 1989, pp. 80–81; DeS, 1991 pp. 175, 178–9; author's additional calculations.

inclined to be sympathetic. But whereas in the Soviet bloc equipment from MTSs was sold off to the co-operatives following Stalin's death, in Albania not only were MTSs not disbanded, but they were strengthened both in terms of increased numbers and scope of work. By the 1980s they numbered over 30, located in all districts of the country, and their range of mechanised tasks had been extended from ten to over 70 activities. They came to the aid of co-operatives when breaking in new land, and dominated the work of planting new vineyards, and digging irrigation and drainage channels and reservoirs. MTSs could incur heavy expenditure and investment in the development of agricultural equipment which co-operatives were incapable of undertaking. Because of regional differences in topography, soils and climate, it was argued that the consequent varying economic strength of co-operatives could only be compensated for by the state, through the MTSs paying the economically weaker farms especial attention (Anon, 1982b, pp. 291–2).

4.2.3 Towards total collectivisation

With food shortages and meagre resources in the early post-war years, top priority was given initially to increasing yields and cultivable area.

By 1954 the collectivised sector accounted for only 12.8 per cent of total agricultural output, and the pace of agrarian socialisation needed to be speeded up if ideals were ever to be realised. In December 1955 a directive to do just this was issued. This was forcibly pursued over the following four years to the extent that by 1960 over 86 per cent of the agricultural sector had been collectivised, incorporating the lowland plains and upland basins. This was complemented by the development of more than 20 plants for the processing or refrigeration of agricultural products. With improving peripheral communications, these were meant to enhance rural self-sufficiency in employment and to raise income levels and living standards. A party decision to fully extend collectivisation to the highlands was fulfilled in 1967 (Table 4.6). Increased collectivisation in itself reflected, on the one hand, the confidence gained from extending agricultural land by marshland drainage and hillside terracing, while on the other revealing the need to politicise a still conservative and often isolated rural peasantry.

In the meantime, under the influence of the apparent success of China's peoples communes, from 1959 a rationalisation process saw a merging of small co-operatives. Their number fell from 1,915 in 1959 to 423 by 1978, while the average number of families in a co-operative rose from 114 to 235. As in the earlier 'concentration' of industry, the regrouping of agricultural co-operatives was justified on the grounds of creating the conditions for better concentration, specialisation and co-operation in production. A spatially more significant dimension was the 'uniting' of co-operatives in adjacent plains and upland areas, with the aim of diminishing differences in socio-cultural development, incomes and standards of living of the inhabitants of both types of area (Baçi, 1981).

In 1971, however, a new form of agricultural co-operative was established as an interim means of advancing the transition from co-operative to complete state farming: the 'higher-type agricultural co-operative' (HTC), with exclusive access to one MTS, thereby representing a structural transition between the co-operative farm's sharing of an MTS's equipment with other co-operatives and the state farm's ownership of its own machinery. The state maintained control and ownership of the MTS but the higher co-operative enjoyed exclusive use. Methods of payment to the members of HTCs more closely resembled those of state farms than of other co-operatives: they entailed payment of 90 per cent of the planned salary every two weeks. At the end of the year, if the plan had been realised, the remaining 10 per cent was paid. If the plan was overfulfilled, members received an extra 10 per cent. Thirty per cent of salary was paid when bad weather made work in the fields impossible, and while each member was guaranteed a minimum wage, its level was determined on the basis of the economic capacity of each HTC. This meant that variations occurred across the country, being particularly evident between the plains and the upland areas. By 1981, 41 of the country's agricultural co-operatives had been transformed into HTCs, encompassing 23 per cent of the country's arable land, and Hoxha stressed the need for HTCs to be transformed into state farms during the 1981–85 plan period (Bollano and Dari, 1984).

Albanian agriculture was extolled as offering a unique contribution to Marxist-Leninist theory in two other ways (Anon, 1984a; Xhuveli, 1984): firstly, through the establishment of joint herds of privately owned livestock, which were previously scattered and kept for personal requirements; and secondly, through the aim of eliminating co-operativist families' agricultural family plots as part of the transition to complete state farming. Needless to say, both were highly unpopular amongst the peasantry, and the first, carried through to its illogical conclusion, proved to be an unmitigated disaster, and was reversed before the end of the decade. In contrast to 'revisionist' Eastern Europe, personal plots in Albania had been progressively reduced in size (Madhi, 1982). In compensation, increases in agricultural procurement prices, reductions in the prices of goods bought by farmers from the state, and state pensions for co-operativists had been introduced. It was argued that personal plots were incompatible with social ownership, and that anyway the farmer could buy products at lower prices in the co-operative shop than they would cost to grow on the plot.

The observable consequences of agricultural collectivisation could be summarised as:

(i) the development of much larger units of production, application of mechanical aids, regularised fields, the elimination of signs of property boundaries, effective access roads, appropriate buildings and locational relationships between the MTSs and the co-operatives they served;

(ii) the elimination of the former monocultural aspect of Albanian agriculture. In 1938 bread grains occupied 83.5 per cent of the country's sown area; by 1990 they represented 48.3 per cent (DeS, 1991 p. 183). Industrial crops were particularly important in diversifying and raising the level of agricultural production;

(iii) regional specialisation, exploiting comparative advantage of physical conditions within the framework of a planned 'national balance of production'. An important step along this path was the completion in 1973 of a national agricultural land survey, entailing soil and agrochemical analyses in all state farms and co-operatives. Thus while the structural balance of agricultural crops took on a more polycultural character, emphasis upon

Plate 4.2 *A shepherd shares the main road with his flock, south of Vlorë*

comparative advantage produced a degree of apparent regional specialisation, such as a concentration on cotton in the central coastal districts of Fier, Lushnjë and Durrës, sugar beet in the Korçë Basin, in the reclaimed Lake Maliq area, and vegetables particularly in the districts surrounding the main urban centres – Tirana, Durrës, Shkodër and Vlorë; and

(iv) land reclamation and irrigation, permitting a much greater area of cultivated land to be used for both food and industrial crops. By 1990, 423,000 ha were under irrigation, representing 60 per cent of the total cultivated area. A dense network of drainage channels was extended over 200,000 ha of land, comprising over 90 per cent of the plains area of the country.

Between 1946 and 1990 52,200 hectares of new land were brought into agricultural use, and 200,500 hectares were improved (DeS, 1991 p. 245). After the draining of the coastal lowlands, the greatest reserves of reclaimable land were in the upland regions of the country, and with this in mind, the widely employed slogan of the fourth five-year plan period was 'let us take to the mountains and the hills and make them as beautiful and as fertile as the plains'. This heralded the launching of a vigorous mobilisation of youth and agricultural workers to terrace hill slopes and plant fruit trees on them. From the mid-1970s, however, with the potential for expanding the cultivable land area diminishing, emphasis was placed more upon intensive use and amelioration of existing cultivated land to raise yields and further locationally rationalise production. Even so, by the later 1980s the area under crops came to represent only 40 per cent of the total land area of the country (see Table 1.3).

4.3 Transport and communications

4.3.1 Inter-war development

The area covered by Albania acted as part of an important through route in Roman times when the Via Egnatia bifurcated the country on its passage between Eastern and Western capitals (O'Sullivan, 1972; Raven, 1993). Modern road building, however, was only introduced into Albania during the First World War by the Austrians and Italians, and this was largely for strategic reasons. Between the wars, the Italians provided increasing financial assistance and technical aid for such development. After the 1939 occupation, the Azienda Strada Albania (ASA) was established, somewhat belatedly, to develop and maintain the road system. In the earlier 1930s, every Albanian over the age of 16 had been bound by law to give ten days' free labour to the state every year, largely entailing road construction (the corvée system). If a person did not wish to do the work, they could pay someone else to do it for them. The Italians inherited and exploited this tradition of free Albanian labour and put it to work for the ASA. By 1944 Albania had some 2,230 km of road, 1,500 km of which had been built for or by the Italians. Ironically, for a country which had been exploiting and exporting its high quality asphalt bitumen reserves for centuries, only 400 km of road had a permanent surface (see Figure 1.2), and much of that was subsequently damaged or destroyed during the war. Indeed, by the end of 1945 only one significant bridge was left standing (over the Mat river on the Tirana–Shkodër road).

The only pre-war railway in the country was the narrow-gauge line linking the Selenicë asphalt bitumen mines to Skele, Vlorë's export port, a distance of 31 km (Figure 4.1). The Italians had plans to establish electric railway links with the Yugoslav, Bulgarian and Greek systems, from Durrës to Elbasan and Ohrid to Vlorë, and from Vlorë to Korçë and Florina in Greece. Indeed, 83 km of track bed from Durrës to Elbasan via Kavajë was completed during the war, but the Italians removed the lines and bricked up the tunnels six months before they left the country. Surveys for the other routes had also been in progress (Mason *et al.*, 1945, pp. 337–9).

Internal air transport in this difficult country had developed to the extent that by 1939 services linked Tirana with Shkodër, Durrës, Vlorë, Gjirokastër, Korçë and Kukës, each of which had a relatively permanent airfield or landing ground. A further seven landing strips and three seaplane alighting areas also existed, although wartime damage took a heavy toll of these.

Of the country's four seaports, Durrës handled half of the country's imports, with 25,000 tonnes of cotton and woollen goods, timber, cement, petroleum products, iron and steel, and food coming into the port in 1937. Exports accounted for 32,500 tonnes of olives, hides, skins, eggs and 24,000 head of cattle. No more than 2,000 tonnes could be cleared in a day by road from the port, and no docks, slipways or repair facilities were available (Mason *et al*, 1945, p. 269). Vlorë, as the second port, exported 58,000 tonnes and 9,000 head of cattle in 1937. A significant proportion of this comprised crude oil and asphalt bitumen. Its sheltered bay was capable of accommodating some 20 10,000 tonne vessels. Both Durrës and Vlorë were relatively well served by inland roads. This was less the case with the smaller southern port of Sarandë, whose hinterland extended beyond the country's borders to Ioannina and Bitolj as well as to Korçë. Indeed, during the Greek advance into Albania in 1940 the port was used as a forward base. Both Sarandë and the northern port of Shëngjin were largely concerned with coastwise traffic, the latter, however, had good access to Lezhë and the Tirana–Shkodër road. In all Albanian port statistics of the time coastwise trade between the country's ports, doubtless adding considerably to the total trade figures, was not recorded.

4.3.2 Road transport

The communists claimed to have inherited just 2,800 km of roads, with large areas of the northern highlands completely devoid of such links. By 1990, total road length had increased to 7,450 km, having more than doubled since 1960 (Table 4.7): several new roads had been opened up in the mountains to previously remote villages. But although the extent of asphalted roads had increased by over six times in 30 years, such roads still made up less than 40 per cent of the total. One hundred and forty-two vehicles survived the war with a total

freight capacity of just 456 tonnes (Bërxholi and Qiriazi, 1986, pp. 131–2). Despite the development of a rail network, about two-thirds of both freight and passenger traffic has continued to be carried on the country's road network since the mid-1980s (Tables 4.8, and 4.9).

Inter-urban and rural public transport tended to be somewhat basic, given the relative lack of personal mobility under the communists. Most buses were Skodas of 1940s–60s vintage, many with more recent bodywork built by the Albanians to Chinese designs. However, the late 1980s witnessed a large influx of second-hand buses and coaches from France, Switzerland, West Germany, Italy and the Netherlands which improved immeasurably the standard of comfort on a number of urban services, with a trickle-down effect for inter-urban and rural routes. By 1985 seven times as many urban passenger journeys were being made compared to 1960, and by 1990, on the eve of private car use, the figure appeared to have stabilised (Table 4.9).

4.3.3 Developing the rail system

Topographic conditions in the country are far from ideal for railway development, with upland barriers and steep gradients in the centre and east of the country and formerly swampy lowlands in the west. Unfortunately, Albania's hydro-electric power resources have yet to see any electrification of the system, diesel power having monopolised traction for most of the railways' existence (although some steam locomotives came from Poznan in the 1940s). Czechoslovakia has provided Albanian Railways (HSH) with the bulk of its diesel-electric fleet, made up of three different classes of locomotive for shunting and main line duties (T435, T458 and T669s).

The first post-war railway, the 42 km Durrës–Peqin line, was opened in 1947 with Yugoslav assistance; the following year saw completion of the 37 km Durrës–Tirana link. Railway construction gained pace in the 1960s, with extensions south-, east- and northwards (Figure 4.2), such that by 1990 there were 720 km of railways (Table 4.7). One of the major

Table 4.7 *Albanian transport network lengths, 1950–90*

	1950	1960	1970	In kilometres 1980	1985	1989	1990
Roads							
Asphalted	181	446	1,213	2,254	2,457	2,800	2,850
	5.8	**12.8**	**22.9**	**36.0**	**35.5**	**38.6**	**38.3**
Not asphalted	2,919	3,024	4,091	4,002	4,472	4,450	4,600
	94.2	**87.2**	**77.1**	**64.0**	**64.5**	**61.4**	**61.7**
Total	3,100	3,470	5,304	6,256	6,929	7,250	7,450
	100.0	**100.0**	**100.0**	**100.0**	**100.0**	**100.0**	**100.0**
Railways	121	1211	203	337	608	684	720

Note: figures in bold denote % of total road length.

Source: KPS, 1989, p. 108; DeS, 1991, p. 269; author's additional calculations.

Table 4.8 *Albanian freight transport: the modal split, 1950–90*

	1950	1960	1970	1980	1985	1989	1990
Road	1,499	10,278	34,269	62,021	75,796	82,815	75,744
	57	**329**	**776**	**1,302**	**1,221**	**1,304**	**1,195**
	75	*81*	*81*	*72*	*65*	*65*	*66*
Rail	239	875	2,324	5,806	8,114	8,048	6,646
	9	**55**	**160**	**477**	**605**	**674**	**584**
	11	*14*	*17*	*26*	*34*	*33*	*32*
Coastwise/inland shipping	101	124	97	225	237	411	377
	11	**20**	**17**	**34**	**30**	**36**	**34**
	14	*5*	*2*	*2*	*2*	*2*	*2*
Totals	1,839	11,277	36,690	68,052	84,147	91,274	82,767
	76	**404**	**953**	**1,813**	**1,856**	**2,014**	**1,813**
	100	*100*	*100*	*100*	*100*	*100*	*100*
International shipping	–	157	470	715	781	668	613
	–	**277**	**1,895**	**1,537**	**2,134**	**1,657**	**1,657**

Notes:

1,499 in thousand tonnes.

  57 in million tonne/kilometres.

  75 % of goods transported domestically in tonne/kilomctres.

Source: KPS, 1989, pp. 105–6; DeS, 1991, pp. 264–7; author's additional calculations.

projects pursued in the 1970s was the construction of a railway network extending from the central Tirana–Durrës–Kavajë 'core area', linking the metallurgical complex at Elbasan with its ore sources to the west of Lake Ohrid, and pushing northwards through the chemical fertiliser centre at Laç to the northern city of Shkodër, for the eventual linking up with the Yugoslav rail system. The 1981–85 economic plan gave priority to doubling the capacity of the rail network, including an international link from Shkodër to Titograd (Podgorica) and a

Table 4.9 *Albanian passenger transport: the modal split, 1950–90**

	1950	1960	1970	1980	1985	1989	1990
Rail	830	2,498	6,047	5,840	8,885	11,724	11,908
	29.9	**90.3**	**252.9**	**368.6**	**563.7**	**752.7**	**779.2**
	44.5	*38.0*	*46.6*	*32.6*	*37.0*	*34.5*	*37.8*
Inter-urban road	232	2,973	9,577	39,815	47,207	72,625	54,124
	37.3	**147.5**	**289.8**	**761.9**	**960.7**	**1,427.8**	**1,280.3**
	55.5	*62.0*	*53.4*	*67.4*	*63.0*	*65.5*	*62.2*
Intra-urban road	113	16,535	67,694	93,233	118,478	116,530	117,600
	0.3	**82.7**	**486.1**	**659.3**	**973.6**	**885.6**	**893.7**
Inland waterway	–	–	–	–	29	170	203
	–	–	–	–	**0.6**	**4.0**	**5.3**
Total	1,175	22,006	83,318	138,888	174,599	201,049	183,835
	67.5	**320.5**	**1,028.8**	**1,789.8**	**2,498.6**	**3,070.1**	**2,958.5**
	100.0	*100.0*	*100.0*	*100.0*	*100.0*	*100.0*	*100.0*

Notes:
* by means of Ministry of Transport operations only.
830 in thousands of passengers.
29.9 in million passenger/kilometres.
44.5 % of inter-urban passengers.

Source: KPS, 1988, p. 115; 1989, p. 107; DeS, 1991, pp. 263, 268–9; author's additional calculations.

southwards extension to Vlorë (Kromidha and Konduri, 1984).

After much controversy between the two partners, the international rail link was inaugurated in 1986 (Hall, 1984a, 1985, 1987b). It was initially utilised at a minimal level, with Yugoslav sources quoting a 15 per cent load factor. However, traffic picked up during 1989, partly due to the movement of 10,000 tonnes of Albanian ferrous-nickel ore to Czechoslovakia, such that the Yugoslav income was $10 million for the year, sufficient to stave off demands for the line's closure. Indeed, Yugoslav Railways were willing to provide sufficient freight wagons to enable 150,000 tonnes of Albanian ore annually to be carried if necessary. During the first half of 1990, the volume of traffic on the line rose considerably, with 174,300 tonnes of Albanian goods being transported on Yugoslav railways (not necessarily via their mutual rail link), an increase of 19.4 per cent over the same period for 1989. The possibility was even raised of introducing a passenger service between Titograd and Shkodër (EIU, 1990e, p. 43).

In the post-Hoxha era, Albania continued to expand its railway network, employing substantial amounts of 'volunteer' labour. In the second half of the 1980s the system carried around a third of both the country's freight and passenger traffic (Tables 4.8, 4.9), although the latter figure is inflated as official data ignored the substantial 'hitch-hiking' undertaken over much of the country's roads.

A 63 km branch line into the upland Mat region, extending from the main line at Milot to Rreshen and Klos, a major project of the 8th five-year plan, 1986–90, was incomplete when processes of change began to overtake the country. It was to have provided key links for the movement of copper and chromite from the major extracting centres (Figure 4.2) of Rubik and Bulqizë respectively.

Average rail speeds of just 30 kph reflected much single line working and the fact that the nature of the system's track construction left a great deal to be desired. Following the establishment of diplomatic relations with West Germany, five second-hand diesel-hydraulic locomotives, more powerful than diesel-electrics operating in Albania, were delivered

Table 4.10 *Goods handled by Albanian seaports, 1960–90*

	1960	1970	In thousand tonnes 1980	1985	1989	1990
Durrës	1,107	2,069	2,227	2,181	2,773	2,336
	77.5	**87.7**	**81.2**	**84.2**	**84.4**	**82.9**
Vlorë	167	192	273	232	260	241
	11.7	**8.1**	**10.0**	**9.0**	**7.9**	**8.5**
Sarandë	99	50	149	133	179	150
	6.9	**2.1**	**5.4**	**5.1**	**5.4**	**5.3**
Shëngjin	55	48	93	44	75	92
	3.9	**2.0**	**3.4**	**1.7**	**2.3**	**3.3**
Total	1,428	2,359	2,742	2,590	3,287	2,819
	100.0	**100.0**	**100.0**	**100.0**	**100.0**	**100.0**

Note: figures in bold denote % of total.

Source: KPS, 1989, p. 108; DeS, 1991, pp. 270–71; author's additional calculations.

to the country in 1989 together with a number of surplus freight wagons. More locomotives were to follow. In their waning months the communists signed a protocol with the Italian government which included the provision for investment in the electrification of the railway line between Elbasan and Prenjas, linking the metallurgical plant of the former with the iron-nickel mines in the region of the latter. By 1993 nothing had come of this.

Durrës is the focal point of the rail system, with the main workshops, marshalling yards and a small port railway. The city's terminal station acts as the apex of the passenger network: services operate on three main routes via Durrës from Tirana to Shkodër in the north, Pogradec in the south-east and Vlorë in the south-west (Figure 4.2). For the communists' aborted 1991–95 ninth five-year plan, an extension of the railway system to the Greek border had been proposed.

4.3.4   Ports and maritime transport

Of the country's four ports, the role of Durrës has been dominant, handling over 80 per cent of the country's seaborne freight (Table 4.10). Vlorë has acted as the country's major naval military base, with its offshore former Soviet submarine base on Sazan island. The port was

in the process of reconstruction when change overtook the country. Both Sarandë in the extreme south, and Shëngjin in the north are concerned with coastwise traffic only and their port infrastructures are extremely limited.

Albania's first post-war international passenger ferry service, between Durrës and Trieste, was inaugurated in 1984, although functioning essentially to transport mail and other freight (Hall, 1987b). In May 1989, a passenger ferry was inaugurated between Corfu and the southern Albanian town of Sarandë, largely for the purpose of day excursions to Albania, at a frequency of two sailings per week during the summer months. Operated by Corfiote entrepreneurs, this venture re-introduced the concept of 'day trippers' into Albania, and represented the first link between Albania and the nearby Greek island for 40 years.

4.3.5   Air links

In contrast to pre-war conditions, when internal services were operated from half a dozen landing strips located close to major centres (Mason *et al.*, 1945), no domestic flights were operated for public use under the communists. Air rescue operations using helicopters and crop spraying with Antonov bi-planes were undertaken, however.

Plate 4.3 *The port and resort of Sarandë, the country's southern-most town. Because (rather than in spite) of its proximity to the island of Corfu, the north-east coast of which it faces, and because of passing Greek and Italian ferry and cruise ships, pleasure craft were notable by their absence here during the communist period, and strong searchlights would sweep the bay at night*

Up to the end of the 1980s, there were just six airlines operating nine round trips into Albania's only commercial airport, at Rinas, 20 km north of Tirana (Figure 4.2) every week. Indeed, for much of the post-war period few if any non-communist states' airlines bothered to call at this small isolated country with its jealously guarded airspace and lack of air transport infrastructure. The country had no airline of its own. While some East European airlines (INTERFLUG, JAT, MALÉV, TAROM) continued to serve the country, if only to provide transport for diplomatic bags. Alitalia curtailed its service in the 1970s. In the early 1980s Olympic began a service from nearby Ioannina, and Swissair inaugurated weekly flights from Zurich in 1986, considerably improving the convenience and quality of service from Western Europe. The following year, with Tirana's establishment of diplomatic relations with Bonn, Lufthansa established a service from Frankfurt.

In May 1989 JAT flights were cancelled. This was officially due to a shortage of aircraft, although with worsening Yugoslav-Albanian relations over the Kosovo question for some time there had been calls in Belgrade for the curtailment of the service. As change in Eastern Europe began to stir the Balkans, Western airlines began viewing Albania in a somewhat different light: in November 1989 a weekly service from Paris was re-introduced by Air France.

4.4   International tourism

4.4.1   Inter-war evolution

Economic and social retardation under the Ottoman Empire and the area's isolation from Western Europe meant that little 'tourism' development took place before the 1920s. By the middle of that decade, a report on an interview with the then President Zogu noted that:

. . . he discussed affairs in Albania, the improvements he wants to carry out to attract the tourist, and the ups and downs in his country, all of which must be attended to before Albania can be converted into another of Europe's playgrounds as he plans to do . . . he was a strong believer in road development. He asked our opinion of the hotels, and when we told him that the country must equip itself with better ones, decided to inspect them and endeavour to provide amenities for tourists. (Etherton and Allen, 1928, p. 195)

In the late 1920s and through the 1930s, however, facilities for travellers were minimal, and leisure opportunities for the domestic population − apart from the small political and social élite − were virtually nil. A limited number of hotels gradually developed in the major towns, largely for business travellers. The picture of other types of accommodation is sketchy. Albanians were renowned as ready hosts for any stranger, as famous earlier travellers in the country such as Edward Lear (1851; and Hyman, 1988) and Edith Durham (1909) have testified. By the inter-war period this hospitality was exemplified by the Bektashi Islamic sect, whose monastery near Krujë became a well-known source of accommodation for Western travellers (McCulloch, 1936, pp. 170−1; Hamsher, 1937, pp. 88−90; Matthews, 1937, pp. 71−84). Recent foreign implants, in addition to Italian hoteliers, included the Albanian-American Institute, near Kavajë. This was an agricultural school operated by the Near East Foundation which a number of travellers sought out (McCulloch, 1936, pp. 164−6; Hamsher, 1937, p. 92). Modern tourism in inter-war Albania is certainly poorly documented, although at Durrës Beach, now the country's main tourist centre, some development was noted in the 1930s (Diack and Mackenzie, 1935, p. 188), and by the 1940s one hotel and 15 villas could be found here to support recreational activities (Bërxholi, 1986, p. 30).

Access to the country was variable. An overnight boat service from Bari, on the Italian coast, was available, and there existed the opportunity of chartering small motor boats across the Ionian Sea between Sarandë and Corfu (McCulloch, 1936, p. 135). Lyall (1930, pp. 148−9) had earlier travelled by Lake Shkodër steamer from the Montenegrin village of Rjeka via Virpazar to Shiroka, the southern lakeside village which acted as the outport for Shkodër when the water level was too low to travel further. More recent times have seen Shiroka favoured by Albanian day trippers from Shkodër and Lezhë. In the mid-1930s, one could fly from Thessaloniki to Tirana, a comfortable two-hour journey in an Italian plane, or even travel on the twice-weekly Italian flight to Shkodër. By 1939, a thrice-weekly service connected Tirana with Rome, Thessaloniki, Sofia and Bucharest. With internal civil aviation centred on Tirana, a daily flight linked the capital with Shkodër, Podgorica and Cetinje in Montenegro. Further connections were provided to Durrës, Vlorë, Gjirokastër, Korçë and Kukës.

Road access into Albania was northwards from Ioannina, or south or westwards from Yugoslavia by one of several routes. The most infamous of these was at Han i Hotit, in the extreme north of country, used by travellers entering from Podgorica. At this frontier, in more recent times the foreign tourist's inaugural trudge across the hundred metres of no-man's land, laden with luggage and foreboding, towards an armed border guard, has become firmly entrenched in the pantheon of post-war European travel writers' clichés (e.g. Newby, 1984, pp. 111–12). Lyall (1930, p. 167) could write of the spot in the late 1920s:

Soon we came to an extraordinary country, where great grey rocks stood up like statues out of the scrub-oak, anything up to 20 feet high. A perfect place for an ambush . . . we crossed a stream; on the opposite hill a stone marked the actual frontier . . . . Next we had to cross a river flanked by a broad, reedy swamp, over which ran a crazy wooden bridge about a quarter of a mile in length . . . . It was, I think, the worst bridge I have ever seen. . . .

Thus the nature of pre-war access to and travel within Albania, coupled with generally impoverished economic conditions and potentially unstable political circumstances, severely constrained any significant tourism development.

During the Italian occupation, the then opulent Dajti Hotel was built in Tirana, and remains today as the capital's hotel for businessmen and diplomats, contrasting with the much brasher and more recent 14-storey Hotel Tirana.

4.4.2 Tourism under state socialism

The early post-war period, as in much of the rest of Eastern Europe (Hall, 1991), saw national priorities lying elsewhere, although organised recreation – 'social tourism' – began to develop for the domestic population, sponsored by enterprises and trades unions. In 1956 a state tourism organisation, Albturist, was established with Soviet assistance, following the Intourist model. An international tourist industry based largely on visitors from the socialist world began to develop, but this process was cut short by the Sino-Soviet rupture and the end of Soviet influence in 1961. Albania's tourism potential had been recognised by Czechs and Russians in the 1950s (Albturist, 1969; Ward, 1983), both groups taking a particular interest in the 'riviera' coast between Vlorë and Sarandë. The Czechs had hoped to develop Dhërmi on the Ionian coast as a holiday complex for their own workers. To the north, Soviet aid had helped to establish the five-hotel complex at Durrës Beach, which today remains the largest concentration of international standard tourist accommodation in the country. Khrushchev is said to have looked upon Albania as the potential Mediterranean playground for the rest of the Soviet bloc. According to one informant of Jan Myrdal's,

'Khrushchev came here and had a look. "Don't spoil the landscape with industries", he said. "Let's have a socialist division of labour. We'll industrialise ourselves, and you can grow lemons. Then we'll come here to you to swim". But then our government said, "Comrade Khrushchev, we've no intention of becoming a spa for Soviet functionaries. We've in mind to follow Comrade Stalin's advice and industrialise our country"'. (Myrdal and Kessle, 1978, p. 14)

With deteriorating Sino-Albanian relations in the early 1970s, a hotel-building programme was begun. Eleven were constructed between

1973 and 1982, providing approximately 1500 beds – almost doubling Albanian international standard accommodation capacity. The country's premier hotel, however, remained the Dajti in Tirana. That superb journalist, James Cameron, stayed there briefly in 1963:

The hotel in Tirana stood off the main boulevard behind a belt of evergreens. It was unexpectedly grand. Like almost everything else of any pretension in town, it had clearly been built by the Italians in an expansive mood, but it had long, long ago acquired the colourless antiseptic cheerlessness of all Popular Democratic hotels. This is very difficult to define; it has something to do with a dim economy of underpowered electric bulbs, an immobility of elevators, a dusty emptiness of showcases, a greyness of table linen, an absence of servants, and a superfluity of unidentifiable shadowy functionaries who are clearly neither staff nor guests. These characteristics are, in my experience, shared by all hotels in the Communist economy, and are explicable in the simple fact that, as befits their function in societies where people circulate only on specific instructions, they have long since changed from hotels to institutions. (Cameron, 1969, p. 256)

Following the loss of client relations with the Soviet Union and then China, tourism could have been employed as one means of attempting to overcome an economic introspection reinforced by the country's 'puritanical' 1976 constitution. But the Albanian leadership thought otherwise, and the limited nature of international tourism was certainly inadequate to help clear any hard currency bottlenecks.

The pursuit of an international tourism industry by a developing country or region can have considerable social, cultural, environmental, economic and political consequences (de Kadt, 1979; Lea, 1988; Bird, 1989; Pearce, 1989; Craik, 1991; Mercer, 1991). Within the framework of Albania's enclosed and strongly ideological political economy, the organisation of tourism was restricted by, and subordinated to, strategic considerations. This expressed itself in two ways. First was the continued sensitivity of border areas – arguably some of the most beautiful parts of the country – which constrained movement on land. Offshore, at the coastal resorts of Sarandë and

Durrës Beach, and on Lakes Ohrid and Shkodër (shared with Macedonia and Montenegro respectively) active patrol vessels served to remind potential long distance swimmers of patriotic obligations. The mid-1970s, with the Sino-Albanian entente in retreat, saw defensive pillboxes emplaced in most parts of the country, not least along the coastal beaches, and for a time, tourist resorts were completely closed to allow these 'magic mushrooms' to be planted.

Indeed, the author happened to be a member of a party visiting the country during December 1975 which was to be based in the Durrës Beach hotel complex with the possibility of optional excursions. Despite the UK tour operator's explicit warnings in its publicity material emphasising the distinctive aspects of a visit to Albania, at least one couple in the group were expecting nothing more or less than a languorous Adriatic beach holiday providing a Christmas tan. They, and the rest of the group, were somewhat bemused and not a little out of pocket as a consequence of being informed on arrival at Rinas airport that Durrës Beach was closed and that they would have to pay a supplement for a compulsory tour of the country which would last for the whole of their visit. A passing glimpse of Durrës Beach during that tour confirmed that pillboxes were being installed along the Adriatic coast and on the very beach where the group was supposed to have been based.

The second impact of strategic considerations was reflected in fears of alien influences and 'contagion' likely to be contracted by host populations coming into direct contact with foreign tourists. In response, the country's 'prescriptive' approach to tourism development incorporated a number of distinctive characteristics not least of which was a form of tourism apartheid (Box 4.2, Figure 4.3). By the eve of its demise in the early 1990s, this approach was shared only with such countries as North Korea (Hall, 1990f).

Such a prescriptive approach attempted to overcome, or at least ameliorate, three tensions which appeared to be inherent in the promotion of international tourism development within a Stalinist political economy:

Plate 4.4 *Durrës Beach: the country' most important focus of both domestic and international tourism*

Box 4.2   Major characteristics of Albanian 'prescriptive' tourism development, 1956–91

1. Employment of the group visa system, requiring potential visitors to subscribe to a group tour at least two months before the planned visit, and acting to screen out those considered to be undesirable.
2. The requirement for foreign tourists to enter the country and move around within it as a permanent, coherent group, of usually a minimum of 15 members. Such groups' conspicuousness contributed to the ease of their 'policing' by Albturist guides, drivers and others. Contact with the local population was kept to a minimum, reinforced by Albanians' requirement to report any personal contact with foreigners.
3. Itineraries, official guides, transport and accommodation were all prescribed, being provided specifically and exclusively by Albturist. Visitors in groups stayed in Albturist hotels, on a full-board basis.
4. Up to the early 1980s the country rigidly adhered to the notion that tourists should conform to a particular dress sense. Albania's points of entry thus had resident barbers and tailors whose role was to 'assist' new arrivals in appreciating Albanian notions of sartorial appropriateness.
5. Much Western literature was proscribed, particularly if of a political, religious or vaguely titillating nature.

Sources: Hall, 1984b, 1991.

(i) tourism as a major service industry requires flexibility and the ability to respond to changing consumer demands. Such concepts did not sit easily within the Stalinist organisational model. Pre-planned, limited-scale prescriptive tourism minimised the need for such flexibility;

(ii) as a service industry, requiring both initial capital and human resources, tourism might have appeared to be an irrelevant diversion from the major socio-economic priorities of state socialism. However, by promoting the role of Albanian culture and ideology for tourist consumption, foreign tourists could be presented with a 'good face' of the country and be imbued with a sense of the superiority of Albania's development path, thereby conferring on tourism an ideological role; and

(iii) the attraction of foreign, especially Western visitors, might have appeared to be serving just those people against whom the indigenous society had been galvanised. Through the delicate supervision of foreign visitors and the preclusion of any meaningful interaction with the host population, the validity of the state's xenophobic rhetoric for the host population could be preserved, and the actual protection of foreign guests secured.

As a consequence, with its other marginal attributes and severely limited scope within the Stalinist organisational framework, international tourism as a vehicle for strictly economic development received a very low priority, despite the country's natural assets. Apart from very brief and superficial reviews (Mandi, 1980; Anon, 1982b, 1989c), one guide-book long out of print (Albturist, 1969), and a handful of hotel pamphlets, very little effort was put into publicising and marketing the Albanian international tourist industry under the communists. Unlike the situation in neighbouring states, the activity never featured in the country's annual statistical handbooks, and had been either explicitly ignored or referred to in pejorative terms in political leaders' speeches and writings. Albturist's role up to the end of the 1980s had tended to be passive rather than active, responding to requests from foreign countries to despatch tourists to the People's Socialist Republic rather than explicitly promoting Albania abroad for tourism purposes. Overall, tourist numbers had never been large. During the late 1970s, annual averages were no

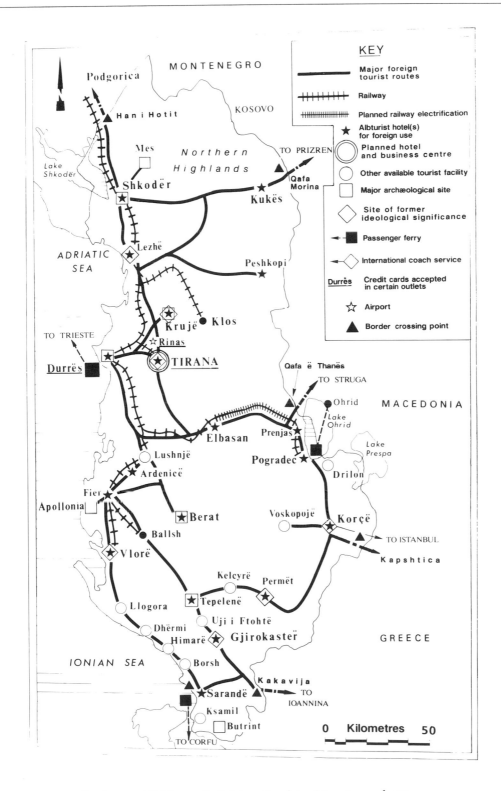

Figure 4.3 *Albania: pre-1991 'prescribed' international tourist centres and routes*

more than 2,500 (Hall, 1984b, p. 549). During the 1980s, numbers were clearly increasing, reaching around 10,000 by 1988, originating from more than 20 countries in Europe and Latin America (Shilegu, 1987).

With communism beginning to falter, the establishment of a Promotion Department within Albturist saw a more pro-active role beginning to be pursued: towards the end of 1989 a promotional pamphlet (Albturist, 1989) and tourist map (Albturist, nd) were produced, some postcards and hotel pamphlets were updated and improved, and a colour documentary film 'Tourist spots in Albania' was shown at the First International Festival of Films on Tourism held at Gudalajara, Mexico. Further, in February 1990, the daily *Zëri i Popullit* published the first ever Albanian tourism statistics: in 1989, 14,435 tourists were admitted to the country, including 3,830 Greeks and 633 Yugoslavs. In addition, 744 Greeks entered purely for the purpose of visiting relatives, while 643 Albanians travelled to Greece for the same purpose. Ninety-four Albanians travelled to Yugoslavia, although much was made of the fact that a further 610 had their applications for visas rejected by the Belgrade authorities. In all, some 1,400 Albanians were said to have travelled abroad during 1989 (a meagre 0.04 per cent of the total population).

4.4.3   The role of 'heritage' in tourism development

Although not explicitly promoted as such, 'heritage' has been a central focus of international tourism in Albania: pre-historic, classical, medieval and recent historical assemblages and artefacts have presented a range of 'heritage' experiences for both international and domestic tourists alike. Stalinist tourism – the complete control and chanelling of tourists' information and experience and of their economic and social impacts – was best exemplified on the ground when tourist groups were virtually compulsorily taken – segregated, ironically, from the host population – to see and hear declarations of ideological infallibility articulated through 'heritage' objects

and sites. Table 4.11 presents in summary the way in which these elements have been employed in support of the country's tourism development programme, and the following five brief examples will illustrate this further.

4.4.3.1 Interlinking heritage, nationalism and ideology. The country's 'museum cities' (Berat and Gjirokastër), acted as focal points on tourist itineraries, and were the recipients of two of the country's earlier post-war hotels. Formally recognised as 'national monuments' in 1961 and 1962, all buildings and activities within prescribed areas were placed under the state's protection. This entailed the conservation of existing buildings and the preclusion of new development, and in 1965 an Institute of Monuments of Culture was set up specifically to administer the restoration of buildings in such areas. Both cities are dominated by a castle. In the case of Gjirokastër, wealthy merchants' two-storey dwellings splay out along five ridges – 'like the fingers of a hand' (as Albturist guides would have it) – down from the fortified hilltop to the Drin valley below. But Gjirokastër's importance – indeed primacy as a state-protected assemblage – was assured by its being the home town of Enver Hoxha. Visitors were taken to his supposed birthplace, a well-appointed two-storey merchant's house which also acted as a Museum of the National Liberation War. From shortly after his death in 1985 until 1991, a monumental white marble statue of Hoxha dominated one of the town's five finger ridges, thereby interweaving cultural heritage with political 'inspiration'.

4.4.3.2 Reinforcing continuity. The 'hero city' of Krujë, situated halfway up a mountainside, has also been a key location on tourist itineraries. Here are the ruins of the fifteenth-century fortress from which the national hero Skanderbeg kept the Turks at bay for a quarter of a century, before they finally overran the country. An imaginative museum, in 'medieval' style designed by Hoxha's architect daughter Pranvera ('Spring'), in the early 1980s, now stands on the same prominent site as the original fortress. Its strikingly bright limestone walls dominate Krujë and explicitly symbolise a sense

Table 4.11 *The role of 'heritage' in Albanian tourism development*

Material culture	Tourism role						
	A	B	C	D	E	F	G
Domestic architecture	*	*	*		*	*	
Museum city assemblages							
Berat/Gjirokastër	*				*	*	
Hero city assemblage: Krujë	*				*	*	
Costume	*	*		*		*	
Dance	*						*
Music	*						
Musical instruments	*	*		*		*	
Copper working		*	*	*	*	*	
Woodworking		*	*	*	*	*	
Silverworking		*	*	*	*	*	
Carpets	*	*	*	*	*	*	
Pottery		*	*	*	*	*	
Literature		*			*		
Painting and sculpture	*	*	*	*	*		
Icons	*	*			*	*	

Notes:

A: prescribed tourist group visits.

B: present in museums.

C: represented in hotel architecture/furnishings and fittings.

D: available for tourist hard currency purchase.

E: available for tourist purchase in book/pamphlet form.

F: available for tourist purchase in postcard form.

G: available for tourist purchase in videotape form.

Source: author's field observations, 1974–93.

of national continuity by buttressing the common identity and lineage between past and communist national heroic leadership.

Other heritage experiences for tourists employed to reinforce past and present 'glories' included 'museum zones' covering sections of cities such as Durrës and Shkodër, and the important archaeological sites of Apollonia and Butrint.

4.4.3.3 Reflecting the country's stance on religion. From 1973 until the mid-1980s, the country's 'atheist' museum, situated in the northern centre of Shkodër – just around the corner from the (then closed) Roman Catholic cathedral – was often included in tourist itineraries. Within the museum, religion in general and Roman Catholicism in particular was portrayed as dividing, undermining and subverting the economic and social development of the Albanian state and people. Religion was seen as the Trojan Horse for imperialistic and irredentist neighbours (Catholic Italy, Orthodox Serbia and Greece, and Islamic Turkey), although the 'evidence' used to portray this claim was often crude and simplistic and embarrassing for relatively sophisticated Albturist guides to have to explain.

After Hoxha's death in 1985, a loosening of official attitudes towards religion became apparent. Not only was Shkodër's infamous tourist attraction closed, but museums dedicated in a positive way to religious artefacts began to be opened; that in Korçë, the 'Museum of Medieval Art', having a superb walnut iconostasis as its focal point. The eighteenth-century former Orthodox cathedral of Shën-Mëri (Saint

Plate 4.5 *Roman amphitheatre, Durrës: cavernous entry way into the open-air auditorium. At least one former householder of the city rues the day he decided to dig his garden: when Roman remains were unearthed and the huge subterranean site was discovered, the houses above began to be systematically demolished*

Plate 4.6 *Part of the refurbished Rruga Enver Hoxha in Shkodër prior to the social unrest in that city*

Mary), with its spectacular early nineteenth-century gold-plated wooden fretwork iconostasis, became a museum dedicated to the sixteenth-century icon painter Onufri, who helped establish a Berat 'school' of iconography. Located within the city's hilltop walled citadel, the museum even had its own illustrated foreign language guidebook (Nallbani, 1989): a rare event in Albania, and its young curator, Fatos Dingo, soon became a well-known character. Until 1991, any visit to such museums continued to be prefaced and justified by quotations from Enver Hoxha emphasising the need to treasure and learn from past Albanian material culture (even that of banned religion) and to understand its strong nationalistic value. Onufri, for example, was linked with the 'anti-Ottoman resistance of the Albanian people' (Nallbani, 1989, p. 3). Religious artefacts, including reproductions of twelfth-, fourteenth-, and sixteenth-century icons, also began to appear on postcards produced under the auspices of Albturist. In December 1990, when religion was finally reinstated, a number of mosques and churches were quickly reopened and made freely accessible to visitors.

4.4.3.4 Expressing cultural and ideological 'purity'.

The communists' cultural and ideological puritanism was brought home to foreign visitors on arrival at Albanian customs. Any document containing aspects of religion was regarded as anti-state propaganda and banned. If found on the person or in the luggage of tourists entering the country, it would be confiscated by customs, wrapped and sealed, and then required to be carried around with the group by the guide/minder, to be handed back on leaving the country. This applied to any material of a political or in any way titillating nature, and to most foreign guidebooks which unsuspecting visitors might bring with them, such as that by Ward (1983),

confiscated on the grounds of its 'misrepresentations'.

On the question of dress and demeanour Hoxha argued:

'Why should we turn our country into an inn with doors flung open to pigs and sows, to people with pants on or no pants at all, to the hirsuite and long-haired hippies to supplant with their wild orgies the graceful dances of our people?' (quoted in Gardiner, 1976, pp. 15–16; Doder, 1992, p. 74)

As a consequence, until the early 1980s, proscriptions included short skirts, extra long skirts, 'decolleté' necklines, flared trousers, extra narrow trousers, wedge heels, 'hot pants', males with 'long' hair and/or with full beards. The latter in particular reflected a desire to preclude any semblance of Orthodox priesthood and/or 'hippies'.

4.4.3.5 Encouraging skill enhancement.

The continued encouragement of traditional skills and crafts was certainly one positive aspect of the state's emphasis upon Albanian 'heritage'. Prior to Hoxha's death, for example, a number of streets in central Shkodër were refurbished, and a series of buildings was equipped to comprise a new National Exhibition of Material Culture. Opened in October 1981, the exhibition engaged some 800 folk craftsmen, artists and specialists across the country in the production of 'artistic objects of daily use, based on the styles and technique traditionally used by our creative people' (Senja and Kekezi, 1982, p. 8). Indeed, in conjunction with this venture, new workshops were set up for fine work in olive wood and sea shells at Krujë, Vlorë and Sarandë, for ornamental bottles at Shijak, and for the production of musical instruments at Pukë. Unfortunately, the main street within which this exhibition is set, Rruga Enver Hoxha (Plate 4.6), was seriously damaged during periods of social unrest in 1991. The street has since been renamed.

5

Environmental dilemmas

5.1 The environmental legacy

Albania's low level of economic development, limited motor transport, regulated tourism and continued economy of shortage helped to contain environmental degradation. None the less, half a century of 'Stalinism' brought substantial change to Albania's fragile environments in a number of specific locations, both in terms of the nature of land reclamation and industrial activity, and the lack of adequate pollution technology to cope with the deleterious effects of these and of rapid population growth. The country's major pollution problems have thus emanated from industrial effluent, agricultural run-off and domestic sewage (Çullaj, 1992, p.5).

5.1.1 Pre-industrial conditions

At the turn of the century, it was claimed that game-shooting in Albania was much easier than in other areas of the Balkans, not least because rifles and cartridges could be more easily smuggled in, being landed opposite Corfu, or off a yacht at any point between Shëngjin and northern Greece (Aflalo, 1901, p. 438). Mixed shooting along the whole coast was reported as being available – partridges, pheasant, snipe, duck, quail, hare – with the best of woodcock, boar and roe deer being available between October and December. Lezhë (where later Count Ciano was to set up a hunting lodge during the Italian occupation) and Butrint were seen as the best areas for such activity, although the whole seaboard and river mouths offered 'splendid chances'. Trout was abundant in all streams running into the Shkodër and Ohrid lakes.

While pre-war Albania was far from being the totally undeveloped malarial swamp that post-war communist histories would have had the world believe, environmental pressures from economic exploitation and development had been relatively low. Manufacturing was limited to domestic requirements, and was concentrated in a handful of towns. Power was usually provided by internal-combustion diesel engines, except for a small hydro-electric plant serving Korçë. Two Italian companies provided electric lighting for Tirana and Durrës. Deforestation, particularly for wood fuel, was already a major problem, however.

A public health service was first created in 1922, although it was hampered by a lack of funds and personnel. At that time tuberculosis was widespread, with a particularly strong incidence of adolescent pulmonary tuberculosis among Muslim women. High mortality levels were experienced in the Gjirokastër, Shkodër and Krujë districts. Syphilis was common in rural areas, as were intestinal parasites, and undernourishment was everywhere apparent. By contrast, cancer and cardiovascular diseases were reported to be rare. Anthrax was the major epizootic affecting humans, being widespread in the coastal plain. Most notably, malaria was endemic in all areas below 1,200 metres, and hyper-endemic in parts of the coastal plain and in the river valleys. In December 1933 the Director-General of Health reported 250,000 cases of malaria (McKinley, 1935) – equivalent to one-quarter of the total population. Under the auspices of the Health Committee of the League of Nations, surveys had been undertaken in 1923 and 1924 to prepare plans for the eradication or control of malaria (Haigh, 1925). While the inaccessibility of many of the country's villages hampered the spread of infectious diseases, this isolation was gradually being broken down during the inter-war period, with increasing seasonal and more regular migrations and movement between upland and lowland regions. Methods of recruitment for the army also contributed to this process (Mason *et al.*, 1945, pp. 119–22). Average expectation of life at birth in 1938 was just 38.3 years (KPS, 1989, p. 37).

Marshland drainage, begun in an organised fashion by the Rockefeller Institute, was said to have reduced the incidence of malaria; however, it did begin to destroy a number of wetland habitats. After their invasion in 1939, the Italians had grandiose plans for reclamation schemes, involving much of the coastal plain, Lake Maliq and the Vjosë valley. Of the country's total land area in 1938 only 11 per cent was given over to arable farming or fruit growing: this was largely confined to upper courses of rivers, upland plateaux and basins. Thirty-one per cent was pasture, 36 per cent woodland, 11 per cent was potentially productive but uncultivated, and the remaining 11 per cent of land stayed barren and unproductive.

It was recognised, however, that the malarial lowlands were potentially very fertile. Indeed, an Italian company obtained a concession of 3,000 ha for agricultural development at Sukth, near Durrës. Italian settlers drained and irrigated the land for arable cultivation to produce a model farm (which was to become a model state farm for visitors after the war). This enclave flourished virtually outside of the Albanian domestic economy. Albanian sources claimed that after the Italian invasion of 1939, plans were laid for 'tens of thousands' of settlers to establish themselves on the coastal plains, and Albania was to have absorbed more than a million settlers from southern Italy (Pollo and Puto, 1981, p. 225). During 1933–34, when the Albanian government had entered into secret negotiations with France in an effort to circumvent economic subservience to Italy, the French government had demanded exclusive rights to exploit the Albanian subsoil and sought control of much of the coastal plain for French settlers (Pollo and Puto, 1981, pp. 207–8). Neither colonisation plan ultimately bore fruit.

Upland erosional problems were exacerbated by deforestation for fuel and the widespread herding of sheep and goats. In 1938 wool was the most valuable export commodity; cheese was also significant. Goats were bred for mohair and milk. In the inter-war period it was already acknowledged that many forest areas, containing all of the best European hardwoods as well as conifers, had been devastated by reckless cutting for fuel or charcoal burning. Walnut had almost disappeared. In addition to domestic and ecclesiastical decorative uses, about 390,000 cubic feet were annually exported, mostly to Italy. Preservation and planting had not yet been considered (Mason *et al.*, 1945, pp. 246–7). Reflecting this problem, an Austrian botanist travelling in northern Albania in the mid-1930s noted, on arrival from Yugoslavia, the 'ridiculous' nature of the country's telegraph poles:

There is never a straight one, such as we are accustomed to in other parts of the world, but crooked and contorted monstrosities stuck into the soil at any angle and at varying distances. This is due to the serious lack of wood in Albania. They therefore use the trunks of *Quercus Cerris* just as it grows in the low country instead of importing foreign timber. One notices also how hard this pitiless deforestation makes the outlines of the hills, as if they had been cut out of cardboard .... The Government is busy constructing new roads into remote districts, but the native Malzors [highland dwellers] use them chiefly to aid them in their deforestation. (Lemperg, 1935, pp. 79, 81)

5.1.2 The Stalinist framework

Rapid industrialization, in order to liquidate the technical and economic backwardness, was considered as the main link for successful accomplishment of the major tasks of socialist construction ... it was decided that by the end of 1955 the volume of industrial production would be more than three times greater than in 1950 and 12 times greater than before the war. (Omari and Pollo, 1988, pp. 133–4)

As elsewhere in communist post-war Europe, heavy industry was seen as the driving force of the means of production, oriented towards the profligate exploitation of such natural resources as minerals and fossil fuels, which offered an immediate source of income. Manufacturing industry concentrated on mineral and metal processing and later on chemical production (Pashko, 1991, pp. 128, 133). Environmental degradation followed in the wake of such policies. Minimal pollution control technology, poor quality solid fuels, the glorification of belching chimneys as symbols of modernisation, and a managerial lack of interest in environmental protection were only partly mitigated by the indirect consequences of a very weak consumer society: a low consumption level coupled with an emphasis upon import substitution and recycling resulted in relatively low levels of material waste. The individual ownership of motor vehicles, for example, remained forbidden from the 1950s until 1991. Examples of substitution within an economy of shortage included the use of recycled strips of pneumatic tyre as bindings in hot houses, potentially lethal multiple sections of glass to replace broken windows in buses (particularly after the closure of Kavajë glass factory because of raw material shortages), and the use of rubber tyres for fuel in small bitumen plants (Hall, 1993a).

5.2 Environmental problems

5.2.1 Atmospheric pollution

Until recently there had been no effective atmospheric emission control. Officially, the Institutes of Hygiene and Epidemiology and of Hydrometeorology monitored air quality, but sampling frequency was inadequate, equipment was outdated and there was no possibility to measure vertical profiles (Çullaj, 1992, p. 13). Most industrial plant failed to use even elementary flue filters (Ellenburg and Damm, 1989). Yet official pronouncements claimed that constant attention coupled with the clear separation between industrial and residential zones guaranteed minimal atmospheric problems in Albania's major settlements. This was 'confirmed' by analyses of air quality in 12 centres (Karadimov, 1989). At the same time, however, researchers investigating the climatic factors influencing the content and transport of atmospheric pollutants urged that levels of soot and sulphur dioxide concentrations receive particular attention (Çobani, 1988). Carbon dioxide and nitrogen oxide are also problematic. Recent evidence suggests that in full operation, the country's metallurgical and chemical plants and thermal power stations emitted about 267,000 tonnes of SO_2 per year, and solid particles annually emitted amounted to 174,000 tonnes, over half of which was from the country's three cement plants (Çullaj, 1992, p. 13).

From 1988 there was a requirement for new industrial developments to be constructed at least four or five kilometres from residential areas. But pre-existing industrial concentrations within the built-up areas of such major settlements as Tirana, Shkodër and Korçë continued to pose major pollution problems. Technological assistance may help to address this deficiency with, for example, the installation of flue gas desulphurisation plant in whatever Albanian industry may survive the country's economic transition. Table 5.1 and Figure 5.1 indicate the nature and location of the country's major atmospheric polluters, exemplified in Box 5.1 and Plate 5.1.

A number of major settlements are situated in

Table 5.1 *Albania: major sources of pollution*

Location	Activity	Pollution
1. Elbasan	Metallurgical complex	See Box 5.1
2. Kukës, Rubik, Laç	Copper smelting	a. 38,420t pa SO_2 emissions from Kukës alone. b. Solid residues and chemicals
3. Shkodër	Copper-wire factory 3000t production in 1970 increased to 12,000t by 1989	SO_2 atmospheric emissions
4. Vlorë	Soda and PVC plants	Mercury, chlorine, vynilchloride, solid discharges
5. Fier	Nitrate and urea plants	Ammonia, arsenic, phosphates, nitrogen oxide
6. Laç	Sulphuric acid and superphosphate plant	SO_2 atmospheric emissions
7. Berat, Gramsh	Battery production	Lead
8. Durrës	Pesticide and chromate production	
9. Tirana	Dye and other chemical production	
10. Ballsh, Fier, Cërrik	Oil refineries	50 million m^3 pa discharged polluted water containing oil products, chemicals, sulphur, phenols
11. Oilfields	Oil extraction	1.4 million m^3 pa polluted water
12. Tirana, Korçë	Oil and lignite-burning power stations (lignite production increased 55-fold from 40,000t in 1950 to 2.19 million t in 1989)	SO_2 (68,000t pa) and ash emissions (high sulphur and ash content of both indigenous oil and coal)
13. Elbasan, Krujë, Vlorë	Cement plants: 15,000 tonnes production in 1950 increased 50-fold to 753,000t by 1989	
14. Tirana, Shkodër, Kavajë, Lezhë, Lushnjë	Paper and cellulose plants	
15. Tirana, Berat, Gjirokastër, Korçë	Textile and leather plants	
16. Rrogozhinë, Sarandë, Tepelenë.	Bitumen plants	Locally heavy emissions of hydrocarbons

Sources: DeS, 1991, pp. 156–9, 162–3; Çullaj, 1992, pp. 6–7, 13; author's personal observations, 1974–93.

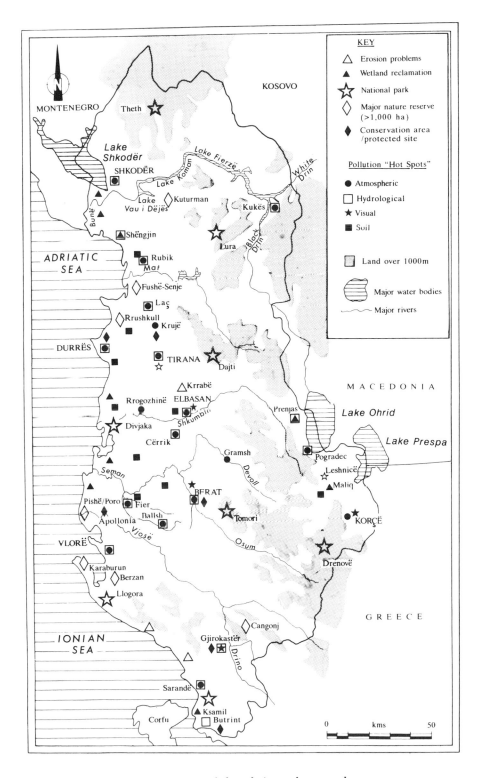

Figure 5.1 *Albania: sources of environmental degradation and protected areas*

Box 5.1 *Elbasan case study*

The combined emphasis upon Stalinist heavy industrialisation and dogmatic notions of 'self-reliance' reached its zenith in the late-1970s with the construction of the Elbasan metallurgical complex, the country's largest industrial plant. Begun by the Chinese, it was abandoned by them when Sino-Albanian political relations were broken off in 1978. Apparently denied access to the original plans and to pollution control technology, the Albanians laboured over a number of years to complete the project.

The plant has produced iron, steel, coke, ferro-chrome, nickel, cobalt, brick and oxygen. In 1989 a ferrochrome unit was completed. The second in the country, this was to process 100,000 tonnes of chromite annually in three smelting furnaces, to produce carbonic ferrochrome for export requirements. Completion of the works was speeded up for 29 November 1989, the 45th. anniversary of the communists' 'liberation': production was inaugurated a year after building began compared to the 4½ years taken over the construction of the similar plant at Burrel a decade earlier. Emphasising 'self-reliance', but also revealing the installation of obsolete technology and lack of environmental provision, official proclamations boasted that most of the machinery and other equipment was produced in the plant's own engineering works.

Atmospheric pollution is poured into the surrounding Bradashesh valley, encompassing forests with 'huge quantities' of carbon monoxide, sulphur anhydrite, sulphur dioxide, cyanic acid, ammonia, phenol, cyanuric acid, dusts and soot ashes produced. Thirty-five million cubic metres of effluent have been discharged into the Shkumbin river annually, including 180t of ammonia, 1.2t phenols, 450t sulphates, 6t cobalt, 3t copper, 1.2t magnesium, 1.6t cyanide and 1.5t zinc. Most of the river's water is used for irrigation in the Elbasan and Durrës districts, causing contamination of land and of the food produced.

The plant has directly employed a workforce of up to 12,000, who, with their families constitute more than half Elbasan's population. Some 300 other enterprises have been dependent upon it. It has been estimated that the plant costs the Albanian exchequer the equivalent of $40 million a year. Renovation to bring it up to an acceptable standard would cost $100 million. Possible links with a Czech enterprise could help save the nickel-cobalt section of the complex which employs 2,300: but only 300 of those would retain their jobs. The plant's fate will act to symbolise changing attitudes to the Stalinist past and to its environmental legacy.

As late as March 1991, Fatos Nano, then Chairman of the Council of Ministers was publicly discussing the potential closure of Elbasan not on environmental grounds but because it was wasting scarce hard currency reserves by requiring imported iron ore. Later in the year the plant was brought to a halt through a lack of raw materials.

Sources: Gurashi and Ziri, 1982; Hall, 1987a, pp. 52–4; Anon, 1989c, p. 6; Atkinson *et al.*, 1991, p. 24; BBC SWB EE/W0175 A/4 18 April 1991, EE/W0237 A/9 2 July 1992; Çullaj, 1992, pp. 6–7, 9–10; EIU, 1992c, p. 45.

basins and valleys, or are located adjacent to high ground, such that pollutants tend to become trapped. This is exacerbated by temperature inversions, as experienced, for example, in the country's highest city Korçë (at 800 metres) on calm evenings, when the centre and major residential areas of the town may become enveloped in the sulphurous outpourings of the lignite-burning power station.

In rural areas and some urban backstreets, poor road maintenance or lack of hard core produces high levels of atmospheric dust, especially through the long dry summer. The domestic burning of wood and low-grade coal adds to urban pollution problems, particularly in winter and under conditions of temperature inversions. While natural gas is piped to a number of urban homes (Hall, 1990a), wood-burning ovens are produced in quantity within the country and are domestically ubiquitous (see section 3.5.4 above).

Plate 5.1 *The heavily polluting Elbasan metallurgical combine*

Although no accurate data are available on the incidence and consequences of acid rain, degradation of vegetation around Kukës and Rubik is ascribed to copper smelting activity, while problems with olive trees near Ballsh are blamed on the emissions of the local petrochemical complex (Çullaj, 1992, p. 8).

5.2.2 Working environments

Health and safety legislation in factories and other employment centres appears to have been consistently flouted, in relation to protection from airborne pollution, noise, potentially dangerous open machinery, wet floor surfaces and inadequate lifting and other mechanical aids, ventilation and lighting. Idiographic evidence of noise pollution within workplaces, for example, has revealed employees of both sexes working excessively noisy machinery in textile mills, engineering workshops and other industrial enterprises, rarely using ear protection equipment. Outdoors, poorly constructed scaffolding, a lack of safety harnessing and an absence of hard hats have been commonplace on construction sites. The improvisation necessary to keep agricultural machinery and equipment working in the absence of appropriate replacement parts has also posed safety hazards.

In the Berat textile mills, the largest in the country, several visits over a number of years revealed lax use of face masks despite high and very visible levels of airborne fibres. Extractor facilities appeared ineffective, judging from accumulated deposits on machinery, window sills and other surfaces. Although economic restructuring may not see the survival of such plants (that at Berat having been designed by the Chinese in the 1960s), problems of the working environment have been barely addressed (although the EBRD has been looking at this problem), with female workers appearing to take the brunt of health hazards.

Many safety considerations have been flouted by transport undertakings, particularly in the difficult months of the early 1990s when, because of a shortage of glass and a spate of vandalism, buses and railway carriages operated with cracked, broken or missing windows. Rail services were eventually suspended because of theft and vandalism, rendering operations unsafe (section 8.3.7). Even under 'normal' circumstances, both major modes of public transport were seriously overloaded with passengers. The latter has often also applied to the many road freight vehicles which carry large numbers of 'hitch-hikers' in open and often potentially lethal conditions (see Plate 6.1). Road lighting is at best poor at night; most bicycles and many motorised vehicles also fail to be illuminated after dark. The substantial use of slow, unlit animal transport is an additional road safety hazard at all times of the day, but particularly at night. Due to the great age and nature of upkeep of road vehicles, buses and trucks regularly spew out clouds of thick diesel fumes.

Social security provision under the communists implicitly recognised the nature of working conditions. Miners, metallurgical workers and airmen were eligible for pensions at 50 after 20 years service. Workers in oil, cement, glass and rubber industries (together with teachers) could retire at 55 after 25 years service. Other workers were eligible for a pension at 60 after 25 years service. In all employment categories women were entitled to pensions five years earlier than men and with five years less service (Cikuli, 1984, p. 43). Invalidity pensions ranged from 40 to 85 per cent of the normal wage. Such provisions were being re-evaluated by the post-communist government.

5.2.3 Rural technology

From the 1960s, the use of Chinese-designed crawler tractors reduced some problems of soil compaction on the alluvial arable lands of the reclaimed coastal plain. But seed-bed preparation and drilling has tended to be poor: heavy equipment produced uneven surfaces, such that drills failed to seed up to 25 per cent of the ground (Atkinson *et al.*, 1991). Recent German aid in this area has been ameliorating the problem. Many tasks are still labour intensive, however, undertaken by human hand and

Table 5.2 *Albania: production and use of chemical fertilisers 1950–90*

Type of chemical fertiliser				Thousand tonnes			
	1950	1960	1970	1980	1985	1989	1990
Production							
Phosphate fertilisers	–	–	110	150	157	165	141
Ammonium nitrate	–	–	75	108	94	109	93
Insecticides	–	–	3	8	11	11	9
Use							
Nitrogenous	0.6	13	66	175	174	206	185
Phosphate	4.0	13	109	150	154	167	148
Potash	0.7	2	2	12	2	6	6
Total fertilisers used	5.3	28	177	337	330	379	340
Kg of 'active substance' per ha of tilled land	3.4	17	75	133	127	158	135

Source: DeS, 1991, pp. 158–9, 244.

animal power, often using improvised implements and vehicles. Privatisation and a reversion to smaller holdings will exacerbate this situation, at least for the short term.

The debris of non-biodegradable polythene used for hothouses, vehicle coverings and other purposes has had pervasive presence in the Albanian countryside in recent years. Destruction through high winds and lack of maintenance has seen such polythene covers ripped away from hothouse supports and scattered over increasing distances, with such adverse effects as the clogging of irrigation channels, the littering of fields and beaches, and the potential choking of livestock. In the early 1990s this was particularly apparent in several areas of the coastal plain, in the vicinity of Lake Ohrid and in a number of upland basins.

Problems resulting from the increased use of chemical pesticides and fertilisers in agriculture brought a recognition of the need for control late in the communist period (Hoxha, 1988). Insecticides have been used on an increasingly large scale: about 800 tonnes in 1960, 5,900 tonnes in 1970, and 10,200 tonnes in 1980 (Papajorgji, 1989, p. 43). Application of chemical fertilisers has grown considerably in the post-war period (Table 5.2), rising overall from just 5,300 tonnes in 1950 to 340,000 tonnes in 1990. This represents an increase from 3.4 to 135 kg per hectare of tilled land (DeS, 1991, p. 244). The use of ammonium nitrates and the highly toxic pesticide lindane (banned in Western Europe) (Anon, 1989a, p. 6) will have posed considerable water contamination problems with run-off from fields and the lack of water purification facilities to treat urban supplies.

Environmental activists have complained of the lack of systematic and reliable monitoring of soil pollution and of agricultural produce grown in the plains areas where the heaviest concentrations of pesticides and chemical fertilisers have been used (Çullaj, 1992, p. 12).

5.2.4 Erosion problems

Partly to meet increasing food demands for a rapidly growing population, vast areas of hillside were dogmatically terraced in the 1960s and 1970s (Skarço, 1984; Anagnosti, 1985). The characteristic slogan of the 1966–70 fourth five-year plan was 'let us take to the hills and mountains and make them as beautiful and fertile as the plains' (Skarço, 1984, pp. 63–4). Over 100,000 ha of virgin land were broken in for cultivation during that plan period, and a further 92,000 ha were so treated between 1971 and 1975. However, many of the hillsides should never have been terraced, the top soil being too shallow and the scrub too fragile for working. In many cases bedrock has appeared. Terracing may have been more effective had the terraces been properly built up with stones and then planted immediately. Fruit trees were often planted in areas too high and dry. Olive planting has had better results, but ground vegetation has been too sparse to prevent soil erosion, rapidly leading to gullies between the trees (Atkinson *et al.*, 1991). A number of problems resulted from the deployment of mass mobilisation, particularly the involvement of untrained 'volunteer' urban youth, in the terracing work.

Forests in Albania cover just over one million hectares (1,045,010 ha): 38 per cent of the country's territory (DeS, 1991, p. 238). Some evidence of acid rain has been observed, particularly in the country's northern forests (Atkinson *et al.*, 1991) but of more significance is deforestation, which, while historically rooted, has continued on an official and unofficial basis. The timber industry certainly has a strong vested interest: by the early 1990s there were 42 enterprises employing 13,000 people. In addition to demand for timber for building purposes, however, there has continued to be a substantial requirement for wood fuel, not least to meet the large demands of domestic wood-burning ovens. All upland families and the majority of those living in ten towns use wood for domestic fuel (*ATA*, 3 August 1992). The crisis of the early 1990s witnessed a desperate and disastrous period with families taking the law into their own hands, often for sheer survival, felling trees en masse, in 'protected' areas, in regions prone to erosion and flooding, and in urban parklands. Perhaps most immediately striking of all has been the decimation of century-old roadside poplars which gave many straight rural roads a strong Gallic flavour.

By contrast, afforestation was said to have taken place on almost 200,000 ha between 1951 and 1988, with a further 467,000 ha of forestry improvement during that period (KPS, 1989, p. 90). This programme helped to stabilise some areas of hitherto fragile conditions. The planting up of susceptible areas with stabilising trees usually involved *Pinus pinea* and *P. radiata*. The districts of Pukë, Shkodër, Librazhd, Kukës and Fier were the main focus of this activity. In the Vlorë district, for example, by the mid-1980s 4,500 ha of forest had been improved and 4,000 ha of denuded land re-afforested (Bërxholi, 1985b, pp. 31–2). A national programme to prevent soil erosion entailed the reported planting of nine million saplings during the 1987–88 winter (Anon, 1989a, p. 6). Fruit and olive tree planting had latterly involved individual rather than contour terracing, and this policy could be seen being implemented in such districts as Sarandë and Pogradec. The need for international collaboration, which has long been recognised (e.g. Bouvier and Kempf, 1987) is now vital. Latest estimates suggest that more than 10 per cent of land annually cropped (57,900 ha) requires increased soil protection work and about 10,000 ha on the coastal plains have salinity problems (Çullaj, 1992, p. 8).

5.2.5 The impacts of irrigation and reclamation

Since 1940 major programmes of wetland drainage have been undertaken as part of the drive against malaria, with most marshes being converted to agricultural lands irrigated through a series of reservoirs. Rivers, especially in the coastal belt, have been regulated and canalised. Between 1946 and 1983 some 9 per cent of the country was drained, and between 1966 and 1970 at the height of the programme 20 per cent of all capital investment was devoted to major hydrological projects. Inland, drainage of the Maliq lake and marshes, which started in 1946, had resulted in a loss of some 60,000 ha of wetlands by 1974 and the improvement of a further 170,000 ha for agricultural production. The area is now Albania's main sugar-beet source.

With rainfall unevenly distributed throughout the year – Albanian agriculture often suffers from a shortage of water between April and September – water improvement projects have been closely associated with irrigation, which by 1990 had been extended to some 60 per cent of all cultivable land (compared to 47.4 per cent in 1970 and 10.5 per cent in 1950), representing an irrigation capacity of 423,000 ha, the figure for 1970 being 283,800 ha and for 1950 39,300 ha (KPS, 1989, p. 89; Papajorgji, 1989, p. 43; DeS, 1991, p. 242). Irrigated flood plains provide important habitats for wetland birds and other fauna (Grimmett and Jones, 1989). The most recent multipurpose water scheme, Banja, on the Devoll river between Elbasan and Gramsh, like the schemes on the Drin before it, has entailed valley flooding, village relocation and communications reorientation. The environmental impacts of such schemes are as yet little known.

5.2.6 Water pollution

No urban settlement has sewage treatment facilities, such that solids and liquids are discharged into rivers and the sea (Selfo, 1993).

In the coastal plains, the more important rivers are visibly polluted by industrial wastes. The Seman receives ammonia, arsenic and nitrates from the Fier fertiliser plant, as well as an estimated 14 barrels per day of petroleum seepage from the poorly maintained oil wells scattered across arable cultivation (Çullaj, 1992). A full picture of toxicity from metals is not yet available, but with little waste treatment, untreated discharges pose threats to both aquatic life and human health. Run-off from increasing use of chemical fertilisers noted above (section 5.2.3) is also a contributory factor. The lower reaches of many streams and rivers in the central part of the country already appear to be organically dead. In upland areas careless mining activity has heavily polluted water bodies, such as the Shkumbin which runs red downstream from the ferro-nickel workings of the Librazhd and Prenjas areas; and the Mat, contaminated with wastewater from copper,

chrome and metallurgical workings (Çullaj, 1992). It had been acknowledged for some time that waste from paper mills (such as near Lezhë) and industrial plants associated with non-ferrous metals had damaged aquatic flora and fauna along a number of rivers and estuarine areas, and for several years apparently fruitless calls were made to find more suitable ways of protecting ecological balance in such areas (Tartari, 1988).

Most Albanian rivers are characterised by a high content of solid particles, mostly due to erosion processes. Estimates suggest that a mean annual volume of 65.7 million tonnes of solid alluvial material reaches the sea, equivalent to 1,498 tonnes per square kilometre per year (Çullaj, 1992, p. 10).

Albania's 247 freshwater lakes, with a surface area of 461 sq km, are recognised as wetlands of international importance. They have acted as breeding and feeding areas for White and Dalmatian Pelicans (with 11 pairs of the latter being located in 1985 and five birds at Divjakë in 1989), the Pygmy Cormorant (a large colony of which is thought to be at Lake Shkodër), various herons (see Karadimov, 1989), and several other waterfowl species. The precarious position of some of these has been a matter of concern: wetland modifications are thought to have caused recent decline. Lake Ohrid, a UNESCO-recognised 'natural monument', has particular interest due to a rich endemic and relict fish and aquatic fauna (Carp, 1980): for example, 24 varieties of carp are unique to the lake (Bërxholi, 1986, p. 30; Vickers, 1992a).

The country's four major natural lakes are shared with Montenegro (Shkodër, 368.0 sq km), Macedonia (Ohrid, 362.6 sq km), Greece (Little Prespa, 23.5 sq km), and, in the case of Lake Prespa (285.0 sq km) with both Macedonia and Greece. While this raises questions of transboundary pollution, such as the discharge of industrial waste from the aluminium smelter at Podgorica in Montenegro reaching Lake Shkodër, it also provides an opportunity for possible regional co-operation. This will be particularly necessary following a 1991 Albanian-Macedonian agreement to build a road around Lake Ohrid to link the towns of Ohrid, Pogradec and Struga, and to further develop hotels and shops in the Albanian town. Increased pollution from visitor use can be expected to result.

The smaller lakes of the northern mountains, such as Lurë, appear to have largely retained their character, although domestic tourism pressures have been increasing. In the extreme south-west of the country, the larger Lake Butrint (16.3 sq km) has been developed in recent years for mussel cultivation. However, diversion of some of the lake's freshwater sources for irrigation purposes has increased the lake's salinity to the detriment of its fauna. Indeed, the over-exploitation of fresh water for irrigation purposes has resulted in notable ecological damage in a number of the country's smaller lakes (Çullaj, 1992, p. 11).

By the early 1980s only 56 per cent of the country's villages were supplied with drinking water (Shkodra and Ganiu, 1984, p. 36). In 1986 it was resolved that by 1990 sufficient quantities of pure water would be available for all the country's settlements. Subsequently, particular attention was centred on the construction of aqueducts to supply towns and villages (Frashëri, 1988). This programme was severely disrupted by subsequent events, and water quantity remains insufficient in most urban areas. Tirana, for example, with 300,000 residents and major industrial enterprises, has a total supply of between 1,300 and 2,000 litres per second (Çullaj, 1992, p. 12). As a consequence, running water has been limited in the capital for domestic purposes to less than eight hours in every 24.

Little detailed literature is yet available to indicate how far substantial spillages in the oilfields, run-off of pesticides and leaching of livestock and human manure has polluted water tables and wells. There are, however, some considerable localised problems (Trojani, 1991). Poor domestic and industrial plumbing and maintenance of water and sewage pipes, aqueducts, irrigation canals, village taps and standpipes, permits bacteria and other harmful additions to enter domestic water supplies. Critically, in view of recent near drought conditions, it also results in an enormous inadvertent waste of water. Such problems have appeared to be widespread in recent years, as spare parts have become scarcer and public services run down.

Although no major algal bloom problems have yet been reported along the Albanian coast, the impact of untreated urban domestic and industrial waste, offshore discharges, and pollution originating in neighbouring countries, including radioactive contamination (Çullaj, 1992, p. 11), have begun to take their toll on Albania's marine environment. The polluted nature of water adjacent to the ports of Shëngjin, Durrës, Vlorë and Sarandë, where waste and spillages from vessels is locally problematic, has been impacting upon nearby tourist resorts. This has been exacerbated by the discharge of polluted rivers reaching the Adriatic coast, notably the Bunë on the Montenegrin border, the Mat south of Lezhë, and the Shkumbin, Seman and Vjosë between Durrës and Vlorë. Water pollution has certainly adversely affected fisheries and doubtless other fauna and flora (PADU, 1990). Major lagoons — Butrint near Sarandë, Karavastë near Divjakë and Nartë near Vlorë — are particularly vulnerable.

Tourism along Albania's varied Ionian and Adriatic coasts has been concentrated in and around Durrës Beach (sections 3.2.3, 4.4.2), which has accommodated up to 60,000, mostly domestic, holidaymakers per month in summer (Bërxholi, 1986, p. 30), and in a handful of other centres such as Vlorë and Sarandë. Increasing tourism pressures, particularly along the relatively unspoilt Ionian coast, will bring environmental deterioration in their wake. Sewage, solid waste and other refuse disposal, degradation of habitats through recreational pressures, substantially increased traffic and the need for improved transport infrastructures and other utilities, will all take their toll, imposing adverse impacts upon the very marine and landward environments which can provide the basis for such tourism expansion.

In the extreme south of the country, careless local recreational activity, coupled with flotsam from the many Greek and Italian vessels passing through the Corfu Straits, has already contributed to a substantial littering of the coast with waste material at such locations as Ksamil. However, as noted above, the country has shown a willingness in recent years to undertake more active participation in international approaches to combating pollution problems in the Mediterranean basin (Pano, 1990). New political and economic conditions within the country, involving Western assistance, should permit the application of waste treatment and other anti-pollution technologies.

In early July 1991, the country's first ever 'National symposium on the coastal space' was held in Tirana, with Italian attendance (Anon, 1991b). Later that month, alongside Italian, Greek, Yugoslav and EC representatives, Albania became a signatory to the 'Declaration on the Adriatic Sea' in Ancona. An initiative was launched to clean up the northern stretch of the Sea and to keep the Albanian coast pollution-free, establishing guidelines for 'environmentally-friendly' tourism development (Anon, 1991a).

With industrial closures in the early 1990s, monitored rivers and coasts were revealing by the end of 1993 a noticeable improvement in water quality. To the north of Durrës, for example, identification of the first hermit crab was a significant indicator of improving biodiversity (Vaso, 1993).

5.2.7   Visual pollution

Enver Hoxha . . . was the most tragic figure in our history. You cannot stand anywhere in Albania without seeing bunkers. He buried us in bunkers. (Sali Berisha, quoted by Sullivan, 1992, pp. 18–19)

From the period of worsening relations with China in the mid-1970s, national defensive measures were increased and included the installation of pillboxes, shelters and other visual intrusions (Plate 5.2). Air-raid shelters were built into urban residential and industrial areas. They are often distinguished by heavy metal doors above small elevations at ground level, although they tend to be unobtrusive. Defensive concrete pillboxes, however, numbering 300,000, were scattered throughout the country following the Warsaw Pact invasion of Czechoslovakia, and were elaborated when the relationship with China went into decline. Visually scarring the landscape and encroaching

on valuable agricultural land, they were particularly numerous in 'strategic' areas: near borders, ports and along the key Durrës–Tirana trunk road. Before coming to power, the Democratic Party pledged to dismantle them at the earliest opportunity, and German interests have been recruited for the purpose (Kalo, 1993). Suggestions for alternative uses have included bat homes, mushroom-growing sheds and beach huts.

One result of the housing shortage in both urban and rural areas, has been that families have often been moved into apartments and houses before the external decor is finished. In particular, completion of the outer facing of urban apartments has often considerably lagged behind their occupation, and in many cases low-rise brick-built flats have never been faced. This has reflected a shortage of materials and distribution problems (Hall, 1990a) and presents a very shoddy outward impression of such residential units.

Insensitively located rural apartment blocks, usually associated with the administrative centres of state farms, can often be found in otherwise harmonious landscapes, as in the coastal village of Lukovë, where three four-storey units dominate a ridge some 200 metres above the Ionian Sea. Slightly less prominent are the 11 four-storey blocks of the nearby coastal village of Piqeras.

As a postscript to the lifetime personality cult, some particularly hideous large statues of Enver Hoxha were erected after his death in 1985, most notably in the centre of Tirana (toppled and broken up by rioting crowds in February 1991) and on a dominant bluff in his home town of Gjirokastër (protected by special armed units until later removed in 1991). During December 1990 the remaining statues and busts of Stalin were removed, including that in central Tirana facing Lenin – who met the same fate the following year – across the Boulevard of the Nation's Martyrs. Large posters and other political exhortations have been largely abandoned since the communists' loss of power in June 1991. In rural areas they had symbolised an interesting continuity by taking the place of religious roadside shrines on mountain passes.

Plate 5.2 *Artillery silos in the foothills of Mt. Dajt, overlooking Tirana*

Table 5.3 *Albania: major examples of visual pollution*

1. Industrial areas with disused parts, obsolete equipment and unusable machinery left lying around, as in the Elbasan metallurgical complex.
2. Hideously patched up industrial plant, as at Laç superphosphate works.
3. Badly constructed and designed industrial buildings, such as the iron-nickel mine at Prenjas and copper smelters at Fushë Arrëz.
4. Poorly repaired or unsurfaced roads and open areas in towns and cities which turn virtually into lakes after heavy rain, such as the centre of Fushë Krujë, where the open bus station becomes a desultory quagmire.
5. Ugly, prefabricated concrete irrigation canals, such as those near Kavajë, and poorly constructed railway viaducts, as between Elbasan and Prenjas. Indeed, constructed with the aid of 'volunteer youth', much of the railway system now needs to be overhauled to render it physically capable of supporting a modern transport system.
6. As well as polluting nearby rivers, the ferro-nickel mining activity of the Prenjas-Pishkash area has left red trails along most of the roads of the area, as well as open-cast scars.

Sources: author's personal observations, 1974–93; Dede, 1986.

A greater visual blight was imposed by officially sponsored hillside 'graffiti', often marked out in bare limestone, extolling the virtues of the party and 'Comrade Enver'. It appears that these confections were usually put together by members of the armed forces (Gardiner, 1976, pp. 61–2) and were often etched in acid to ensure their permanence (Flint, 1993). Although by no means unique to Albania, one of the most grotesque examples was an enormous 'ENVER' prominently splayed across five ridges facing the town of Berat and extending to a height of some 30 metres. Other examples included the huge 'PARTI ENVER's on the mountainside facing Gjirokastër and overlooking the village of Borsh on the Ionian coast, and a pervasive 'POPULL PARTI ENVER' spread over three ridges by the village of Lin next to Lake Ohrid (Plate 5.3).

Most such exclamations had been removed, damaged or allowed to be overgrown even before the communists finally lost power, to be gradually replaced by motifs of a more universal design. In April 1991, following anti-government rioting, in the town of Kavajë the still almost sacrilegious grafitto 'ENVER=HITLER' was prominently painted onto a wall. In the same month, however, the 'hero' town of Përmet still sported a range of the old ideological tapestry, ranging from '1908'

(Hoxha's birth year) etched into the surrounding hillside, to a large floral display of 'PARTI ENVER' embellishing the town centre. Other aspects of visual pollution are noted in Table 5.3.

5.3 Protection and conservation policies

5.3.1 Organisational framework

While 'Stalinist' policies emphasised socialist man's triumph over nature, they also provided some protective window dressing, with legal enactments, on paper at least, suggesting that environmental matters would be brought under control. Early examples of Albanian environmental legislation included those concerning control of hunting (November 1951) and forestry protection (October 1963) (IUCN, 1967; Borisov *et al.*, 1985; IUCN-EEP, 1990). National parks were created under the auspices of these laws. Until the early 1970s, however, most ecological effort was concentrated on the protection of rare animals and plants. Article 20 of the 1976(–1990) Constitution pointed to environmental protection as being a duty of the state, all institutions and citizens (PSR of Albania, 1977, p. 14).

A Central Commission for the Protection of

Plate 5.3   *The People's tapestry: part of a large three-word slogan ('People – Party – Enver') overseeing the village of Lin, on the western shore of Lake Obrid. The train is travelling north from Pogradec, passing strip family agricultural plots*

Table 5.4 *Albanian participation in international environment-related meetings*

April 1985: International Congress of Infectious Diseases, Cairo: attended by Albanian viral disease experts: the first sign of a more outgoing approach in the same month as Hoxha's death.

1987: Balkan Seismology Working Group Conference, Tirana: the hosting of this session was a sign of Albania's willingness not merely to participate in international gatherings.

December 1987: International Conference on Balkan Ecology, Sofia: concern expressed over the negative impact of industrialisation, urban development and intensified agriculture, on the condition of air, water and soil. It stressed the need for co-ordinated efforts for the conservation of nature. A weak joint statement (signed by Albania, Bulgaria, Greece, Romania and Yugoslavia) merely noted that participants had exchanged information on the state of the environment, on their respective national programmes of environmental protection and on ways and means of co-operation within the Balkans, and that they had discussed specific ideas and proposals.

February 1988: Balkan Foreign Ministers' Conference, Belgrade: communiqué on tourism, transport and protection of the environment.

September 1988: Balkan Scientific Conference on Environmental Protection, Varna: included nine papers presented by Albanian representatives.

July 1989: Albania signed the World Heritage Convention.

May 1990: First Balkan Energy Ministers' Conference, Tirana: agreed to establish working groups for environmental protection.

June 1990: Albania became the last Mediterranean country to be a party to the UNEP Regional Seas Programme (Barcelona Convention), when it became a signatory to the Mediterranean Action Plan (MAP). The country had refused previously to participate, failing to attend the initial Barcelona conference in February 1975 and refusing to be a signatory to the February 1976 Convention for the Protection of the Mediterranean Sea against Pollution (then signed by 12 states). On accession, Albania proposed the inclusion of six sites under the Convention.

July 1991: National Symposium on the Coastal Space, Tirana: with Italian participation.

May 1992: International Seminar on Environment and Development, Tirana: jointly sponsored by the Society and government Committee for the Preservation and Protection of the Environment. Major international funding bodies were in attendance.

1992–94 Albanian Coastal Area Management Programme as part of the MAP.

Sources: BBC SWB EE/W0008 A/1 14 Jan 1988; Atkinson *et al.*, 1991, p. 27; Pastor, 1991, pp. 103, 112; Çullaj, 1992, p. 13; Murphy, 1992.

the Environment existed at Council of Ministers level. Such commissions were said to have been set up in every ministry and central institution and in the executive committees of the district people's councils. Groups for the protection of the environment should have been constituted at every enterprise, agricultural co-operative and institution in the country. No industrial project or major construction was supposed to be built without an environmental impact study first being carried out on its potential implications. Such studies should have incorporated measures on: the distance of industrial projects from residential areas; methods of transporting and disposing of industrial wastes; steam and dust; protection of water and vegetation; and the nature of raw materials used and the technological processes to be applied.

In practice, this structure counted for little given the overriding need for plan fulfilment and heavy industrial development coupled with a general lack of environmental awareness and absence of appropriate pollution control technologies. However, the country was characterised by continuing low levels of consumerism; programmes against waste; and the need for recycling materials within an economy of shortage, albeit not necessarily resulting from environmental considerations. Official concern was obliged to be more explicit as a consequence of Albania's growing participation in international forums during the later 1980s (Table 5.4). For example, the Central Commission for the Protection of the Environment was reorganised in 1988 to more effectively combat pollution problems.

Until Hoxha's death in April 1985, the country tended not to participate in any international gatherings or treaties, including environmental agreements and conventions, justifying this on the grounds that each was dominated by at least one of the superpowers. However, attendance by viral disease experts at an international congress in Cairo almost immediately after the leader's death apparently indicated an abrupt change of direction and a new desire to enter the world scientific community. Indeed, subsequently Tirana acted as host to a number of international conventions, such as the 1987 inaugural meeting of the Balkan seismology working group, and in May 1990 the first gathering of Balkan energy ministers, which agreed to establish working groups for environmental protection (Table 5.4).

Most notably for environmental matters, Albania was a party to the February 1988 Belgrade foreign ministers' communiqué on tourism, transport and protection of the environment, and there was significant Albanian participation at the Balkan Scientific Conference on environmental protection in the area, held in Varna, Bulgaria in September of that year (Çobani, 1988; Dinga, 1988; Dollani, 1988; Frashëri, 1988; Gjiknuri, 1988; Hoxha, 1988; Mara, 1988; Puka, 1988; Tartari, 1988). In July 1989 the country signed the World Heritage Convention, although no Albanian sites were listed in a subsequent United Nations inventory (IUCN, 1990, p. 227). This was followed, in 1990, by Albania becoming the last Mediterranean country to be a party to the UNEP Regional Seas Programme (Barcelona Convention), proposing the inclusion of six

coastal sites under the convention. However, at the time of writing no Albanian biosphere reserves had been notified under the UNESCO Man and the Biosphere (MAB) Programme, nor was the country yet a signatory to the 1971 Convention on Wetlands of International Importance (Ramsar Convention). Indeed participation in international gatherings did not necessary indicate an immediate broadening of horizons, as the following extract from a paper presented at Varna in 1988 by the vice-president of the Albanian Academy of Sciences might suggest:

. . . in spite of the priority given to the development of the chemical, non-ferrous metals industries and agricultural intensification, we can confirm that the natural environment in Albania is in a genuinely pure condition with no great problems. (Mara, 1988, quoted in Atkinson *et al.*, 1991, p. 24)

The last communist government was said to have been favourably disposed towards preserving the country's remaining wetlands (Atkinson *et al.*, 1991), although concern had been expressed over three projects for soil improvement and land reclamation which overlapped or adjoined coastal wetlands considered to be of international importance (IUCN-EEP, 1990, p. 7; Kusse and Winkels, 1990).

A broader dimension to Albanian environmental concern nevertheless emerged after the 1989 upheavals in Eastern Europe (Hall, 1990b, 1990c, 1990e). Divisions within the ruling élite saw younger, more 'reformist' leaders beginning to express criticism of previous practice. The health minister saw 'impetuous' development policies as the cause of substantial deforestation and atmospheric pollution, and in May 1990, in one of the then most explicit official comments on the country's environmental situation, *Zëri i Popullit* (16 May 1990) carried an article by the chairman of the Foreign Economic Co-operation Committee, Farudin Hoxha (no relation), arguing that the coal industry, mining 2.4 million tonnes annually, was both uneconomic and environmentally harmful, and that it was unacceptable and irresponsible for the country's leadership to permit the industry to continue in its present manner; such 'primitiveness' would not be forgiven by future generations. This was just the tip of an iceberg of increasing unease. Ironically, however, just as in agriculture the poor production level of the mining industry had recently stimulated increased state subsidies – whereby prices paid would be a function of production costs – which, while attempting to boost production, could only be a recipe for further state-sanctioned environmental degradation as more difficult and sometimes fragile environments were more intensively worked.

The participation of some 30,000 athletes in the May 1990 inaugural Tirana marathon preceded a rather hollow mass environmental protection campaign instigated under the title of 'Week of the Mediterranean Environment', with lectures held in the capital on anti-pollution measures. People in the rest of the country were mobilised for 'cleaning and restoration' activities. However, the hastening of political and economic change from the end of 1990 (AMC, 1991), and the drafting of a new constitution provided the impetus for a much wider public debate of environmental concerns than had been possible hitherto, although this was overtaken by the near anarchic condition of the country during the second half of 1991 (McDowall, 1991a, 1991b, 1991c).

The legalisation of opposition political parties in December 1990 saw an Albanian Ecology Party established. In the run-up to the country's first post-war multi-party elections in March 1991, its three manifesto pledges were environmental improvement, national unity, and peace. The party failed to win any seats in the new parliament, and its specific environmental policies remained unclear. Unlike the major opposition Democratic Party, however, which appeared to alienate the collectivised rural peasantry by declaring a wish to privatise the land, the Ecology Party opposed rural land sales. In the political arena, the Ecology Party was later, in 1991, to be joined by the Green Party, while an Association for the Preservation and Protection of the Natural Environment (PPNEA) was established largely by members of the scientific establishment (section 5.4.1 below). It was the latter which jointly sponsored, with the government Committee for the Preservation and Protection of the Environment, a seminar on Environment and

Development in Albania, held in Tirana in May 1992 and attended by representatives of the major international funding banks. Albania had gained access to the World Bank and the IMF in October 1991, and in the following month an environment and energy mission of the European Bank for Reconstruction and Development (EBRD) had visited the country after its admission to that body (Dyvik, 1991; Murphy, 1991).

Following the upheaval brought about by successive changes of government, the administrative framework for enforcing and overseeing environmental protection was in flux during 1992. A Central Environmental Protection Commission, established in 1979, operated from within the Council of Ministers, and included representatives of ministries and research institutes. Its major role was to monitor the work undertaken by ministries, local authorities, institutions and farms. Later reorganisation saw the establishment of a Ministry of Public Economy and Protection of the Environment, which, in May 1991, was actually demoted, for reasons of streamlining governmental structure, to committee status, although its chairman was to be of ministerial level. A watchdog role has also been undertaken supposedly by the Ministry of Health's Department of Hygiene and Environmental Protection, particularly in relation to the workplace environment. A number of ministries have had their own sections for environmental protection, although a major responsibility for nature conservation has fallen within the purview of the Ministry of Forest and Water Economy. Hitherto, each administrative district's executive committee had one person responsible for environmental matters, although they were rarely trained for the purpose.

Several scientific institutions have directly and indirectly contributed to environmental protection work. The leadership of the Association for the Preservation and Protection of the Natural Environment (PPNEA) largely hails from the Natural Sciences Faculty of Tirana University, which was established in 1957 (Anon, 1985b). Other bodies contributing to environmental protection work have included the Natural History Museum, which belongs to the University, the 14 hectare Botanical Gardens (containing some 2,000 endemic species) which are jointly supported by the University and Tirana city authorities, and the Institute of Scientific Research in Hygiene and Epidemiology in Tirana, whose work includes analysis of the physical and chemical properties of drinking water, protection from environmental pollution, the study of noise and vibration, dietary nutrition and occupational diseases (Cikuli, 1984, p. 77).

During 1991 higher education was reorganised. The former 'Enver Hoxha' State University in Tirana was divided into two institutions – Tirana University and the Polytechnic University – and a Tirana Agricultural University was carved out of existing institutions (section 3.3.3.4 above).

The Academy of Sciences, established in 1972 and derived from the Committee for Science and other university institutes located in Tirana, has been made up of three sections: Social Sciences (humanities), Natural Sciences, and Technical Sciences, the latter comprising the Institute of Hydrometeorology, Seismological Centre, Centre for Geographical Study and Laboratory for Hydrological Research. The Academy held a conference on environmental protection in 1978 (Lloshi, 1990, pp. 14–15). At the time of writing the Academy was being restructured.

5.3.2   Rural protection and conservation

The close juxtaposition of diverse and relatively unmodified habitats, ranging from Mediterranean to Alpine, has maintained a diversity of flora, fauna and land-forms. The country's rich flora, for example, boasts some 3,200 species, resulting from the conjunction of:

(a) location in the midst of the most important routes of plant migration;
(b) the presence of an old flora, which includes many species which survived glaciation;
(c) a varied topography, matched by few European countries, and dominated by high mountains; and
(d) a dense hydrographic network.

Three types of protected 'natural' areas have been designated in Albania (Bogliani, 1987; IUCN-EEP, 1990; Atkinson *et al.*, 1991). These are:

(i) National parks. Providing areas for public access, recreation and education, a total protection regime is imposed within them, with no permanent human occupation or exploitation. Hunting and ancient grazing rights are prohibited, although villagers from neighbouring settlements are permitted to gather dead wood. Tourism is encouraged, with limited motor access, and each park has a forest lodge for accommodation. There are seven national parks (Figure 5.1), ranging in size up to 4,500 hectares (Table 5.5).

(ii) 'Integral' reserves. These are strictly protected for nature conservation: public entry is prohibited.

(iii) 'Orientated' reserves. Providing areas for education, they also act to protect landscape and wildlife. Traditional human activities such as fishing can be pursued.

Additionally, some 12,200 ha are designated as game reserves (Çobani, 1989). Protected animals include the brown bear, lynx and chamois. Artificial winter feeding is organised for roe deer, chamois and wild boar (Bërxholi and Qiriazi, 1986, pp. 39–41). Bird colonies on the islands of Kunë (in Lezhë district) and Adë (Shkodër district), as well as the pelican colony in Divjakë, are also protected. In the latter case, only 45–50 pairs now survive (Hoda, 1993b) yet in the mid-nineteenth century, Edward Lear was inspired by the sight of several hundred pelicans on the salt flats of Vlorë:

As we skirted these salt lagoons, I observed an infinite number of what appeared to be large white stones, arranged in rows with great regularity. . . . I resolved to examine these mysterious white stones forthwith . . . when-lo! . . . many great pelicans . . . rose up into the air in a body of five or six hundred, and soared slowly away to the cliffs north of the gulf. . . . The birds frequent the coast around Avlóna in great numbers, breeding in the rocky inlets beyond the bay, and living on fish and refuse in the salt lagunes. (Lear, 1851, pp. 294–5; Noakes, 1985, p. 190)

Table 5.5 *Albania: protected 'natural' areas*

1. National parks

Name	Category*	Size (ha)†	Designated	Characteristics
Dajt	II	− /4,000	1966	Between 400 and 1612m asl. Beech, Bosnian pine, sycamore, maple and white fir mixed woodland flora with Mediterranean maquis; some open meadows.
Divjakë	II	1,194/4,000	1966	Aleppo and stone pine forest, salt marsh and dune flora on the Adriatic coast; endemic orchids; pheasantry.
Llogora	II	1,040/3,500	1966	Black pine and deciduous forests; rich shrubby flora; Mediterranean pastures above 2000m.
Lurë	II	1,300/4,000	1966	Bosnian, Macedonian, Scots and Black pine, beech and spruce; Alpine meadows; glacial lakes.
Theth	II	2,700/4,500	1966	Beech forest; some pines; rich herbaceous flora.
Tomor	II	− /3,000	1956	Beech forests and Bosnian pine; Alpine meadows.
Bosdovec		1,350/ −		Black pine and beech forests.

2. Major nature reserves (1,000 ha or larger)

Name	Category	Size
Berzan	IV	1,000
Cangonj	IV	3,000
Fushë-Senje	IV	4,200
Karaburun	IV	12,000
Kuturman	IV	4,000
Pishë/Poro	IV	5,500
Rrushkull	IV	1,800

3. Specially protected areas

Name	Category	Size	Designated	Characteristics
Divjakë (Karavastë Lagoon)	SPA	1,000	1956	Pelican reserve within the coastal national park

Notes:
Additionally, there are a further 11 category IV protected areas of less than 1,000 ha and six category VIII areas.

* See IUCN, 1990, pp. 9–14 for definitions of conservation management categories.

† sizes are taken from Bërxholi and Qiriazi ('national parks') and IUCN/IUCN-EEP respectively. Çobani refers to 'about 8,400 ha of national parks', Bërxholi and Qiriazi cite 18,000 ha. For Dajt, Hoda (1993b) refers to 'nearly 2,200 ha'.

Sources: Polunin, 1980, pp. 108–11; Basha, 1986, p. 22; Bërxholi and Qiriazi, 1986, pp. 37–8, 1990; Çobani, 1989, p. 49; IUCN, 1990, p. 23; IUCN-EEP, 1990; PADU, 1990; Atkinson *et al.*, 1991, pp. 11–14; Hoda, 1991, 1993b; author's field observations, 1974–93.

Overall, some 350 types of bird are found within the country, and a number of eliminated species have been re-introduced. Albanian fauna is rich and varied, with both Mediterranean and European characteristics. Officially, hunting is severely restricted but may gain greater significance as a means of accruing hard currency; in practice, on the other hand, it appears to have been widespread and locally safeguarded, continuing long traditions. With increasing

Plate 5.4   *A wooded section of the protected Karavastë marshes, Divjakë, on the Adriatic coast south of Durrës*

human and economic pressures, deforestation may threaten the habitats of such rare animals as the brown bear, of which there were an estimated 500–800 in the northern mountains in 1987 (Atkinson *et al.*, 1991).

Some 260 kinds of fish can be found in Albanian waters. Sardines are caught in the Bay of Vlorë, at Durrës and Shëngjin; grey mullet is caught in coastal lagoons and other varieties fished include white perch, barbel, cod and tuna (Bërxholi and Qiriazi, 1986, p. 43). But Albanians have never been notable fish-eaters, and under communism the need to secure the country's maritime and lake borders severely constrained the development of a fishing industry. However, frogs have been exported in large numbers to France for culinary purposes.

5.3.3 Urban conservation policies

Although still an essentially rural society (Sjöberg, 1991a), Albania's erstwhile penchant for scarring the landscape with hastily constructed polluting factories and poorly finished apartment blocks has been only marginally offset by positive attitudes towards urban conservation and protection.

Many religious buildings were destroyed or rebuilt for non-religious functions during and after the 'cultural revolution' of 1967, and many old town centres have been destroyed through comprehensive redevelopment based on structure plans of the 1970s (Hall, 1987a, p. 51). Selective urban conservation, however, has been pursued through the designation of protective zones in much of the old residential districts of Berat and Gjirokastër ('museum cities') (Plate 5.5) (Riza, 1971, 1978, 1981a; Anon, 1973a; Adhami and Zheku, 1981; Çavolli, 1987b; Strazimiri, 1987), and in the historic parts of Durrës and Krujë (Toçi, 1971; Karaiskaj and Baçe, 1975; Riza, 1975), while restoration has been carried out on an individual site or street basis in a number of other urban centres such as Korçë, Shkodër, Tirana, Vlorë and Elbasan (Anon, 1973b, 1977; Muka, 1978; Bërxholi, 1985b, p. 27; Miho, 1987; Thomo, 1988).

Early in the country's post-war development,

legislation on the protection of monuments of culture and the environment was particularly aimed at ending the plunder and degradation to which the country's ancient monuments had been subjected. As noted earlier, the towns of Gjirokastër and Berat, received the official accolade of 'museum city' on account of their rich architectural and archaeological heritage. This status was bestowed in 1961 and 1962 by a 'special decision' of Albania's Council of Ministers, to bring all buildings and activities within a prescribed area under the protection of the state. The conservation of existing buildings, particularly in groups, and avoidance of new development, were central to this philosophy.

The Roman amphitheatre at Durrës, still being excavated, is the central focus of several classical sites within the city. Krujë was declared a 'heroic city' on account of its historic role against Turkish incursions: somewhat ironically, a Turkish bazaar has been the subject of considerable restoration work here.

All four cities were focal points on the prescribed itineraries of foreign tourists (Hall and Howlett, 1976; Hall, 1984a, 1984b), and as national monuments they attracted considerable attention from the state, representing an indirect investment in the tourist industry and a more direct investment in housing. One of the embracing arms of such state activity has been represented by the Institute for the Restoration of Monuments of Culture, established in 1965 specifically to administer the protection, preservation and restoration of buildings in protected areas, with powers which were further elaborated in 1972 (Anon, 1972b, 1972c; Papa, 1972 for general guidelines; and Anon 1973b, 1973c, 1977 for applications in Gjirokastër, Korçë and Elbasan). This body has major branches in Tirana, Berat, Gjirokastër, Korçë, Shkodër, Vlorë, and Peshkopi. Of the Institute's five major sections, that for Traditional Buildings has been chiefly concerned with dwelling houses in traditional urban and rural styles.

In Berat, three of the city's districts are regarded as conservation areas – 'museum quarters' – and have received special attention from the Institute. The Mangalem district, for

Plate 5.5   *Gjirokastër, one of two 'museum cities', with its fortress rising above distinctive domestic architecture*

example, adjacent to the city's fortress, contains many typical two-storey dwellings with slightly protruding wooden balconies on their upper floors, and many finely decorated arched windows and pantiled roofs. Such dwellings have been built on terraces, lining the lower hill slopes leading up to the fortress. With their appearance of many windows facing outwards, they have contributed to Berat's characterisation as the 'city of a thousand windows'. Open landings are also typical of such dwellings, presenting broad views out for their occupants, and are often partly or completely encircled with skilfully carved stones. The city was hit by an earthquake in 1851, and although much subsequent rebuilding has taken place in the old quarters, the distinctive character of these essentially privately owned family dwellings is still much in evidence.

In Gjirokastër three zones were recognised. Within the historic centre a 'museum zone' of highest merit would be restored and enhanced. A second 'protected zone' of less merit, though still important, would be protected from new development. Outside of these zones, the remaining built-up area of Gjirokastër – largely post-war residential and industrial growth below the historic city's hill slopes – was declared a 'free zone' in permitting new, planned development to take place (Riza, 1971, 1978; Anon, 1973a).

Major archaeological sites, notably at Apollonia and Butrint, were put under the protection of the state (Zarshati, 1982; Baçe and Çondi, 1987; Adhami, 1988). Even under the communists, debate and activity among Albanian archaeologists, architects and historians was lively in the realms of conservation and restoration (Anon, 1981b). The country's Democratic Party prime minister at the time of writing, Aleksander Meksi, is himself a leading expert on historic building restoration (e.g. Meksi, 1983).

Green and open spaces have been emphasised in urban development and redevelopment programmes. The southern city of Vlorë, for example, had over 50 hectares of such space by the mid-1980s, with an aim to provide ten square metres of greenery for each of the city's 65,000 inhabitants by 1990 (Bërxholi, 1985b,

p. 41). Such green spaces provide important lungs for humans and wildlife alike. In the open spaces of central Tirana, for example, nightingales and scops owls can regularly be heard.

5.4 Post-communist priorities and problems

5.4.1 The environmental lobby

Environmental movements were at the forefront of opposition groups calling for *glasnost* and democracy in other Central and East European societies (Baumgartl, 1993), but this was not the case in Albania. Perhaps three factors accounted for this: (a) the questions of rectifying human rights abuses and seeking political and economic freedoms were far more fundamental and pressing in Albania than in neighbouring countries, and by comparison, although acknowledged to be important, environmental concerns took on a relatively low priority; (b) this also partly reflected the fact that the degree and scale of environmental degradation in Albania had not been as great as in other Central and East European societies, although there were clearly significant pockets of ecological devastation; and (c) independent movements had simply not been allowed to develop within the country, and any environmental debate had been strictly confined to scientific, party and governmental forums.

It was not until opposition parties were legalised in December 1990 that environmental pressure groups and political parties were able to represent 'green' interests. Both an Ecology and a Green party were established, although they made little impression on the electorate (section 5.3.1 above). However, the Association for the Preservation and Protection of the Natural Environment (PPNEA), established by academics and nature lovers in June 1991, has gained some recognition, and, together with and through the government's Committee for Environmental Preservation and Protection (CEPP), has been able to pursue three main goals: (a) raising general environmental awareness within the country; (b) providing practical solutions to environmental problems; and (c) encouraging and supporting environmental education, especially among the young (Gjiknuri and Çullaj, 1993).

With a claimed membership of 400, the Association is based in Tirana but has branches in Elbasan, Shkodër and Vlorë and an associated youth wing – *Pearl* – with 70 members. Although it has no central office or infrastructure, PPNEA has been undertaking voluntary work in three fields of activity: stimulating mass activities, convening scientific meetings, and developing international links.

One element of recent concern involving all three of these dimensions has been the growth of illegal hunting by foreigners. With the loss of access to their Croatian habitats, some 500 mostly Italian hunters came to Albania during 1991–92 and allegedly entered nature reserves and other protected areas and killed thousands of birds, including six pelicans. The association subsequently petitioned the government on this matter, organised protests and invited Greenpeace to Albania to address the problem and place it within the international arena (Malltezi, 1993).

5.4.2   Evaluation

Even environmentalists from Tirana University's Natural Science Department argued that it was difficult to provide a comprehensive evaluation of the Albanian environmental situation in the early 1990s (Çullaj, 1992). This resulted from three sets of major shortcomings:

(a) lack of pollution monitoring and analyses undertaken by the country's scientific community, preventing the appropriate identification of problems and setting of priorities. Only a few rivers and certain locations have been monitored since 1970 by the Institute of Hygiene and Epidemiology and the Hydrometeorological Institute in Tirana;

(b) a similar lack of official information on environmental problems during the near half-century of communist rule; and

(c) the unprecedented disruption to economic life coupled with substantial uncontrolled environmental interference experienced during the early 1990s, such that while industrial pollution and use of agricultural chemicals rapidly diminished, illegal tree-cutting and land degradation increased.

In the short term, the most important environmental problems facing the country and needing to be addressed, were seen to be: (a) soil erosion; (b) deforestation; (c) contamination of soil and groundwater in some agricultural areas from fertiliser and pesticide run-off; (d) pollution of surface water from the discharge of industrial effluents and liquid sewage in urban areas; (e) pollution of soil and groundwater by solid wastes and liquid effluents from mining activities; (f) localised air pollution from industrial plants and urban discharges; (g) preservation of biodiversity and virgin natural areas; and (h) the likely growth of tourism (Çullaj, 1992, p. 6).

5.4.3   Consequences of social upheaval

Additionally, consequences of the social upheaval which took place in the early 1990s, and the dramatic change in social, economic and political values faced by the Albanian people, brought about several aspects of at least short-term environmental concern:

(a) as noted above, in the grab for land which took place ahead of an orderly privatisation process of agricultural co-operatives, buildings on land sought by its previous owners were destroyed. These included much needed primary schools in rural areas and the installation of oil wells, causing further spillages and toxic run-off;

(b) physical protection has been required for the country's only botanical gardens following illegal attempts to restitute previous land rights which threatened the gardens with fragmentation and building development. Subsequently, the gardens' director suffered an arson attack on her flat;

(c) the cutting and felling of trees and shrubs in both urban and rural areas in a desperate attempt by families to maintain domestic fuel supplies in the face of all-round shortages;

(d) despite supposed protection, much destruction and looting of state property took place, including the theft of 15 third-century BC sculptures from the Apollonia archaeological site during November 1991 (McDowall, 1991d); as noted above (section 5.4.1), overseas hunting groups posed particular problems in the interregnum period of 1991/2 when environmental protection measures were poorly enforced; and

(e) imitating urban western practice and, in an *ad hoc* way, echoing previous communist eyesores, elements of Albania's youth have taken to graffiti (Plate 5.6).

5.4.4 Motor vehicles

While the country reasonably claimed that it had maintained a relatively 'pure' environment in many districts because so few motorised vehicles had existed up to the 1991 legalisation of private motor transport, none the less, the use of low grade, sulphurous fuel, coupled with poor maintenance of often long time-expired Chinese and Soviet-bloc machines, produced relatively high local concentrations of vehicle emissions. Since 1991, however, the number of cars has risen rapidly (from 5,000 to 20,000 by mid-1992). Many of these vehicles have been far from safe, aged, fuel-hungry second-hand models secured by expatriates for a population with little experience of driving motorised vehicles or of being pedestrians in a motorised age – a fatal combination, particularly when mixed with much animal-powered transport, bad roads and poor lighting. In the seven months from March to September 1992, for example, 208 people from the Tirana district alone were killed in road accidents. Age of vehicles, lack of spare parts, and lack of experience in both driving and repair led to many being abandoned within a relatively short time, thereby adding visual pollution and disposal problems to those of substantially increased vehicle emissions produced by usable cars (Plate 5.7). At the end of 1992 proposals were being put forward for Tirana's first motor-car scrapyard.

5.4.5 International toxic waste dumping

According to the German federal Criminal Bureau, illegal toxic waste dumping in Central and Eastern Europe by West European firms increased tenfold over the decade to the early 1990s, with German interests leading the field of offenders. Greenpeace estimated that only 5 per cent of the perpetrators of such offences were apprehended (Hall, 1992f). Ironically, rules approved by EC environment ministers in October 1992 permit EC countries to refuse to accept toxic waste from their neighbours, but leave them free to dump such material on Central and Eastern Europe and the developing world.

Between November 1991 and February 1992 over 600 tonnes of pesticides were shipped to Albania by Schmidt-Cretan, a joint venture between a waste contractor in Hannover and an Albanian toy company. The shipments, which were labelled 'humanitarian aid for use in agriculture', contained pesticides made in the former East Germany that were either banned or past their sell-by date. According to the German environment ministry, the pesticides included formulations containing lindane and other organo-chlorines, and herbicides with high concentrations of dioxins. They would have cost at least DM8,000 per tonne to dispose of in Germany. The shipment had been approved by the Albanian agriculture ministry, but in March 1991 the Albanian state firm Agroimport asked Schmidt-Cretan to stop the shipments because the barrels that had arrived were old and leaking. A subsequent rail shipment then arrived at the border, was sent back, but returned repackaged. Subsequent disquieting reports talked of local people stealing the drums from storage areas in Durrës port and the military camp at Milot, emptying them and using them to store water and food (Mackenzie, 1992).

Although the international Basel Convention of 1989 on hazardous waste precludes use of the

Plate 5.6 *The 1970s imagery of Pink Floyd seems to have belatedly caught the imagination of the youth of Central and Eastern Europe. Until 1991 a full-size statue of Lenin stood on this plinth in front of the National Art Gallery, central Tirana. The plinth too was removed soon after this March 1993 scene was recorded*

Plate 5.7 *Substantially increased numbers of motor vehicles since 1991 and the lack of facilities to deal with their disposal are causing growing problems. In this case the burnt out bulk of a car has been abandoned by the roadside along with the stripped remains of three former state-owned Tirana buses, acquired second-hand from Lyons in the late 1980s. On the eastern fringe of Tirana, March 1993*

much abused export category of 'industrial material' and insists that toxic waste can only be exported to countries which use advanced disposal methods, under European Community regulations any type of waste can be shipped to third countries for 'recycling' or 'recovery'. Under these rules the shipments to Albania would be legal because the pesticide was to be used.

The Albanian experience followed hard on the heels of German toxic waste dumping in Romania (Ciulache and Ionac, 1993), the outcry against which necessitated a two-day visit by the German environment minister to Sibiu and Bucharest, a public apology, and the signing of an environmental accord between those two countries. At the time of writing, the Albanian Committee for Environmental Protection and Preservation, while responsbile for the safe disposal of the toxic substances on Albanian soil, was unable to do so because of the high cost involved (*ATA*, 16 July 1993).

Part III

Albania joins the new world disorder

6

Responding to change

6.1 Domestic change and upheaval

6.1.1 Perspective

With Hoxha's apparent lifelong reverence of Stalin (Hoxha, 1980b), Albania remained outwardly hostile to the 'capitalist' world (e.g. Hoxha, 1980a, 1982a). Following the Albanian leader's death in 1985, the country continued to condemn developments taking place in the rest of Eastern Europe, denouncing Gorbachev's *perestroika* as a restoration of capitalism. Emphasising this stance, a special issue of the journal *Probleme Ekonomike*, published for the 45th anniversary of People's Albania, devoted a section to a hostile critique of *perestroika* as 'bourgeois-revisionist economics' (Bozdo, 1989; Daci, 1989; Hana, 1989; Shyti, 1989; Xhuvani, 1989).

As the country's leader put it:

'Perestroyka' (sic) means reforming the whole of Soviet society, not in order to strengthen the positions of the working class and socialism, but in order to strike them the final blow. 'Glasnost' means to open the way once and for all to the bourgeois ideology, to enable opportunists and the partisans of pluralism to determine what is good and what is bad. . . . Our Party will march consistently on the road of irreconcilable struggle against modern revisionism of whatever kind and whatever name it assumes. As Enver Hoxha advised us, socialist Albania will work persistently for the building of socialism, with complete faith in an unwavering following of the teachings of Marx, Engels, Lenin and Stalin, which have displayed and are displaying their vitality and universal value day by day. The fact is that, guided by these teachings, by implementing them in a creative manner in our concrete conditions, socialist Albania is forging ahead, developing and becoming more beautiful (Alia, 1988, pp. 304–5).

In contrast to this rhetoric, however, the Party began to unveil a range of economic, political and social readjustments designed to defuse the growing unrest which was being fuelled by events elsewhere in the region. Indeed, with both Albanian and neighbouring countries' television services broadcasting those events, the demonstration effect of the December 1989 Romanian 'coup' on the Albanian people was particularly telling. From the first weeks of 1990, Albania was set on an inexorable course of massive political and economic change: each minor step fuelling even greater demands and aspirations for change. Major economic, political, social and developmental shifts took place within a telescoping effect of events which overturned most of the central tenets of the previous half-century. This snowballing process culminated in a grudging acceptance of political plurality, a subsequent succession of weakened governments and the

173

eventual removal of the communists from national political power, through the ballot box, in March 1992.

6.1.2 Measured responses

With a growing internal power struggle and a long-term drought crippling agricultural and industrial production, the Albanian leadership's outward reaction to political change in the rest of Eastern Europe was a series of policy statements during the first half of 1990 which tinkered with the economic, political and judicial system in the hope of forestalling major unrest. Measures aimed at improving democracy at the grass roots, reducing bureaucracy (a recurrent theme), and emphasising a commitment to the provision of foodstuffs would be phased in:

(a) multiple candidates in elections for National Assembly representatives were introduced, but with no provision for opposition parties, the official line being that there was no (post-war) history of opposition within the country and therefore no merit in its artificial creation;

(b) between January and April 1990, 266 directors and officials in Tirana were changed following the removal of the necessity of Party membership for appointment to middle- and high-ranking administrative positions. As a result, non-Party members soon made up two-thirds of employees in ministries and central state departments;

(c) as a means of improving the economic mechanism, elements of self-financing for enterprises were introduced;

(d) the possibility of establishing 'friendly' relations not only with the European Community — something which the Albanians had been working up to for some time — but also with the two 'superpowers', was mooted, confounding a central tenet of the previous 30 years' foreign policy (Zanga, 1990c);

(e) further inroads into the country's diplomatic isolation were indicated by a desire to

participate in the CSCE process: Albania had been the only European country not to sign the Helsinki Final Act in 1975.

Alia now attempted to present himself as a reformer, only two years after the publication of his sycophantic contribution to the posthumous Hoxha personality cult, *Our Enver* (Alia, 1988). He complained that reactionary elements within the party were blocking reform. Wittingly or otherwise, by obstructing some of the reform policies, the hardliners precipitated unrest which grew to a scale unprecedented in post-war Albania. The conservatives also thereby provided Alia and the reformers with an excuse to remove them from positions of power. Four Hoxha supporters, including the interior and defence ministers, were replaced. But it was clear that Alia was willing to tolerate the discussion of issues only while debate took place within the confines of the Party-controlled media and did not challenge the PLA's supremacy (Biberaj, 1991).

The *Sigurimi* not-so-secret internal security police (who had had two postage stamps issued to honour their thirtieth anniversary back in 1973), and a recently-formed and somewhat shadowy anti-terrorist para-military unit, the *Sampist*, continued to represent strong arms of the reactionary forces, and were left untouched. Despite this, inevitably the people's aspirations were raised. When these were dashed, social unrest dramatically increased, as when passports, which were to be the right of every Albanian citizen, were not made readily available. Crowds of Albanians responded by pressing themselves into Western embassies in Tirana to seek safe passage out of the country, and 10,000 others staged a public demonstration in the capital in support.

Alia responded somewhat ambivalently to these events. He called the refugees hooligans and misguided, claiming that they had been manipulated by forces from outside of the country. He was, however, unwilling to commit the military. Ultimately, the refugees were allowed to emigrate, thereby ridding the country of many malcontents, and Alia came to be seen as a hesitant reformer seeking compromise solutions to retain power. His brief popularity suffered a notable downturn (Biberaj, 1991).

A commission was set up to revise the 1976 constitution, particularly in relation to the nature of the 'leading role' of the party, to endorse direct foreign investment (forbidden by Article 28), and to amend or scrap Articles 37 and 55 which broadly prohibited religion. But this was too little too late. Piecemeal reform and gentle evolution began to appear increasingly inadequate. The country had a much longer journey to make than its Balkan and East European neighbours in terms of economic, social and political restructuring and modernisation, and time was running out as events began to take on a momentum of their own.

Was there any alternative to a total restructuring of the political system, in order to permit these processes to follow their due course? At this time the recent experience of other Balkan societies suggested ambiguity. Despite the despatching of the Ceauşescus, the new Romanian National Salvation Front government appeared to be communist in all but name with many old faces remaining. Bulgaria returned the (renamed) communists in the country's 1990 elections, and Serbia under Milosević, while nationalistic, was clearly holding onto old political and centralist dogmas. There still appeared to be manoeuvring room to enable the Albanian communists to cling onto political power. But would the underlying tribal nature of Albanian society re-surface? One line of argument suggested that if the Party continued to hang onto power for too long it would provoke bloody revolution in which thousands of Party functionaries and officials could die in a mass of revenge killings, as old scores were settled in the traditional way (EEN, 1990c).

In December 1990 discontent focused on student demands for better working and living conditions in Tirana, the removal of Hoxha's name from the University's title, and their own political party. These in their turn appeared to encourage riots in Shkodër (where attempts were made to dynamite a statue of Hoxha and to take the local radio station), Durrës, Kavajë, Sarandë and, worst of all, in the industrial centre of Elbasan, where shops and vehicles were ransacked and set ablaze. No longer were the people to be cowed: in the second half of 1990, young people in particular began to reveal a genuine loss of fear of the internal security apparatus.

Following the student-inspired mass demonstrations, non-communist political parties were legalised. The Democratic Party, led by two English speaking, former PLA intellectuals, Sali Berisha, a heart specialist, and Gramoz Pashko, a university economist, was established on 12 December 1990. Some half a dozen other parties soon followed, including the Christian Democratic Party, established by Father Simon Jubani, Albania's leading Catholic activist, who had only recently been released from over two decades of imprisonment.

With an opening of the mass media, on 5 January 1991 the first edition of the Democratic Party's newspaper *Democratic Revival* (*Rilindja Demokratike*) was published. All 50,000 first edition copies were said to be sold out within two hours of reaching the news stands.

When it finally came, however, a year later than in the rest of the region, Albania's December 1990 anti-communist 'revolution' only partly removed the existing political leadership. But during 1991 Albanian state structures collapsed as four successive governments struggled with an economic impasse between forces attempting to establish the beginnings of a market economy and the old guard attempting to sabotage such efforts. Growing social unrest and food shortages were the result.

The toppling of Hoxha's statue by protesting crowds in Skanderbeg Square in February 1991 was broadcast live on national television. Similar spontaneous demolitions soon followed elsewhere including, eventually, at his birthplace, Gjirokastër. Alia responded by setting up a presidential council and assuming personal charge, thereby probably averting a bloody confrontation, although it was later claimed that he had given the Ministry of Internal Affairs orders to fire on the Tirana demonstrators if necessary.

Alia now presented himself as the only person capable of guiding the country through a difficult transitional period, although exactly

175

Plate 6.1 *Precarious rural transport, south of Pogradec. It is spring 1991: the victory salute represents new-found freedoms in general, and support for the Democratic Party in particular*

what would be at the end of the transition, and how long it would take, were unanswerable questions. Clashes between pro- and anti-Hoxha forces in the Tirana Military Academy resulted in four deaths, and were viewed as a possible prelude to a military coup (Zanga, 1992b). In March another exodus of refugees, to Italy, took place (section 6.2.3 below).

6.1.3 Multi-party democracy

Initially, the first post-war multi-party general election was to have been held on 10 February 1991. But the communist leadership eventually gave in to pressure from the opposition parties to postpone the date by two or three months in order to give them time to organise: the date was re-set for 31 March.

With a turnout of around 95 per cent, Western observers confirmed that voting for the 250-seat legislature was mostly fair, despite reports of intimidation by the communists in rural areas, and the presence of their still tight grip on most of the country's media. The opposition were successful in towns and cities: Alia's reputation was further dented with his rejection by the Tirana electorate. Berisha won a landslide victory in Kavajë, an anti-communist stronghold. It was here that the country's major glass factory had seen production halted and where the first, unprecedented 'ENVER = HITLER' wall slogan had appeared (see section 5.2.7). The major source of employment for local young women was a Dickensian carpet factory, while perennial food shortages were blamed on the fact of Kavajë being placed within Durrës local authority district with that port city enjoying preferential treatment for food supplies.

Winning the rural areas and two-thirds of the seats in the new parliament, the PLA's success was partly due to peasants' fear of the Democratic Party selling off land to foreigners. The elections thus polarised Albanian society along political–geographical lines. Renewed clashes in response to the election results, which many anti-communists claimed were rigged, saw protestors in Shkodër fired upon, with the result that four people were killed,

including a local Democratic Party leader. For a number of days the city was out of control: the local PLA headquarters and police vehicles were burnt out.

On re-election as president, a post he had held since 1982, Alia formally resigned his PLA offices, a requirement of the new draft constitution, which separated party and state posts. He had been a Party member since 1943 and first Party secretary since 1985.

But only a month in post, the new government was toppled by a general strike, with newly formed trades unions demanding faster and more radical change. Less than a week later, on 10 June 1991, the PLA held its tenth and last congress. For the first time Hoxha was openly attacked. Hitherto, the Party had studiously avoided addressing the question of the personality cult. At the Congress it also voted to change its name to the Socialist Party of Albania (SPA), and instituted internal structural changes in an attempt to achieve a new image. The PLA would have celebrated its fiftieth anniversary in the following November.

A reformist party leadership was now elected with Nano, the previous, short-lived prime minister, as its president and minister for foreign economic relations in a new 'government of national salvation'. This was headed by Ylli Bufi, the previous food minister, and included, for the first time, members of the opposition. The SPA's leadership now supported the switch to a market economy and sought to take the party into the mainstream European democratic left. The ADP dismissed the new party's programme and claimed that its members were still crypto-communists.

Within the coalition government, an interim body of 25 members pending elections in May or June 1992, the SPA was given 12 portfolios: seven went to the ADP, and the rest to smaller parties and independents. At best it could only muddle through. But as the country's economic problems deepened, a series of strikes brought the country to a virtual standstill. The Democratic Party demanded that general elections be brought forward to February 1992, and that former communist leaders be arrested. Divisions began to show within its ranks, however, and led by Berisha the ADP eventually withdrew from the coalition government in December 1991.

The general elections, subsequently held in March 1992, saw the demise of the vestiges of political power to which the communists had been clinging for a year. In the first round of ballots on 22 March the Democratic Party (ADP) won 92 seats against the SPA's 38, the Social Democratic Party's (SDP) seven, the Union of Human Rights' (UHR) two, and the Republican Party's (RP) single seat.

Victory would have been more overwhelming under the old first-past-the-post electoral system as the ADP gained 90 of 100 constituency seats. But with a further 40 seats distributed on the basis of proportional representation, the extent of the ADP's landslide was somewhat tempered, depriving it by a small margin of the two-thirds majority required by the People's Assembly for major constitutional legislation. This was overcome by keeping a pre-election pledge to form a coalition with the SDP and RP. The International Republican Institute, representing the US Republican Party, claimed it had given Albania's Democratic Party more than $500,000 worth of equipment and aid (Simmons, 1992). The Socialist Party, on the other hand, had to settle for what help it could gather from its Greek and Italian counterparts.

Ramiz Alia, heir to the country's die-hard Stalinist leader Enver Hoxha, now resigned as Albania's president, even though he had a further four years' term of office to run. Sali Berisha, leader of the Democratic Party, was the sole candidate as his successor, and members of parliament voted for his accession by 96 to 35. Although himself a former communist, Berisha enjoyed general respect as an early proponent of multi-party democracy, even though he did not hand in his Party card until December 1990. One of the first actions of the new government was to extend presidential powers.

Four months after its defeat in the parliamentary elections, however, Albania's Socialist Party made substantial gains in the country's first democratic local elections on 26 July (Table 6.1).

Comparing these results with those of the

Table 6.1   *Albanian local government election results, 26 July 1992*

Voter turnout: 70.5 per cent
Elections for: offices in 37 districts, 43 municipalities and 310 communes.
Voting by party nationwide (%):

Party	% of votes	
Democratic Party	43.16	(65.7*)
Socialist Party	41.32	(27.1*)
Union of Human Rights (surrogate for Omonia)	4.34	
Republican Party	3.43	
Party of Democratic Union (Balli Kombëtar: National Front)	0.90	
Agrarian Party	0.86	
Christian Democratic Party	0.83	

Note: * results of 22 March 1992 parliamentary elections.

Sources: *ATA*, 8 August 1992; Zanga, 1992b.

March elections, it appeared that a chasm had formed between central and local government. The significantly lower voter turnout (down from 95 per cent) suggested that many who voted for the Democrats in the March elections stayed at home in July. The 70.5 per cent poll certainly represented a traumatic shift from the official version of previous voting practice (Tables 6.2 and 6.3; although it should be noted that the official term used, 'participation in elections', is somewhat ambiguous). Complacency, disillusionment and searing summer heat were all seen to contribute to this, while a significant number of those who voted for the Socialists had a great deal to lose from the fall of communism.

The outcome of the elections tended to heighten the political polarisation between urban and rural and north and south. Socialists scored heavily in the south, both in the provinces and in the cities, although they also made some surprising inroads in the north, including Berisha's birthplace, Tropojë. In the oil city of Kuçovë (formerly Stalin City) the Socialists won more than 75 per cent of the vote; in Skrapar (Albania's communist bastion), nearly 80 per cent; and in Berat, Vlorë, Fier and Elbasan somewhat smaller percentages. The

Table 6.2 *Participation in elections for deputies to Albania's People's Assembly, 1945–87*

Election date	Participation in elections (% of electors)	Votes for the candidates of the (communist dominated) Democratic Front (% of votes cast)
2 December 1945	89.91	93.16
28 May 1950	99.43	98.28
30 May 1954	99.92	99.86
1 June 1958	99.98	99.96
3 June 1962	99.99	99.99
10 July 1966	99.99	99.99
20 September 1970	100.00	100.00
6 October 1974	100.00	100.00
12 November 1978	99.99	100.00
14 November 1982	100.00	99.99
1 February 1987	100.00	100.00

Source: KPS, 1989, p. 29.

Table 6.3 *Participation in elections to Albania's people's councils, 1949–89*

Election date	Participation in elections (% of electors)*				
	Villages	*United villages*	*City quarters*	*Towns and cities*	*Districts*
June 1949	94.10	–	–	–	95.80
September 1952	99.49	–	–	–	99.91
March–April 1954	–	–	–	99.96	99.87
November 1955	99.56	–	–	–	–
December 1956	99.83	–	99.95	99.88	99.84
April 1960	99.98	–	99.98	99.98	99.99
May 1964	99.99	–	99.99	99.99	99.99
June 1967	99.99	–	99.99	99.99	99.99
September 1970	100.00	100.00	100.00	100.00	100.00
December 1973	100.00	100.00	100.00	100.00	100.00
April 1977	100.00	100.00	100.00	100.00	100.00
April 1980	100.00	100.00	100.00	100.00	100.00
April 1983	100.00	100.00	100.00	100.00	100.00
April 1986	100.00	100.00	100.00	100.00	100.00
May 1989	99.99	99.99	99.99	99.99	99.99

Note: * % vote for Democratic Front candidates ranged from 96.50 in villages in 1949 to 99.96 in districts in 1960. Thereafter the figure is 99.99 or 100.00 for all councils apart from a lapse in villages in 1970 for which it is 99.98.

Source: KPS, 1989, pp. 31–3.

Plate 6.2   *A partisan veteran acting as guardian for the Kukës martyrs' cemetery, July 1991*

Democrats won convincingly in their traditional strongholds of Tirana, Shkodër, Durrës and Kavajë (Zanga, 1992b).

The Socialists would have won even more had not the Democrats changed the method of seat allocation to a more proportional system four days after polling. On 29 July parliament rushed through a new electoral law altering the proportional allocation of seats in town and city councils. The new law resulted in the transfer of control of a number of councils from Socialist (according to the original electoral law) to Democratic.

A second round of local elections took place on 2 August. The SPA complained of widespread electoral abuse by ADP supporters. The Electoral Commission ordered a third round of voting after the revelation that in the district of Fier names had been removed from the electoral register and voters had been intimidated outside polling stations. This decision was later overruled by the Constitutional Court and the district was awarded to the ADP. These final stages of the country's first post-war multi-party local elections were not auspicious.

Soon after (13 August 1992), five MPs from the ruling Democratic Party set up the Democratic Alliance Party. These were led by Gramoz Pashko, one of the two co-founders of the ADP, who had been recently expelled from that party, along with seven other leading figures, for criticising the apparently increasingly autocratic nature of presidential rule.

6.1.4 The role of the military

Albania joined the Warsaw Pact in 1955, but finally withdrew in 1968 (although in practice in 1961) following the Soviet-led invasion of Czechoslovakia. Since the break in relations with China in the mid-1970s the Albanian army had received very little new equipment apart from light weapons produced at armaments plants in Berat and Gramsh. There was claimed to be a lack of both radar and anti-aircraft artillery (Pettifer, 1992). Ammunition had been in particularly short supply. In 1992 Albanian armed forces personnel totalled 40,000, of whom 22,000 were conscripts.

Military service had been reduced to 18 months' duration for the air force, army and navy and three years for special units. Paramilitary forces included 12,000 frontier guards and 5,000 internal security troops. The system of ranks, abolished in 1965, had been restored (EIU, 1992a, p. 33).

The Democratic Party-led government did little to restore the officer corps' morale after years of neglect when it took the decision in 1992 to retire all officers over the age of 50, and to replace the Chief of Staff Kostas Karolli by an inexperienced political appointee and friend of Berisha's, Ilir Vasho. The defence minister Safet Zhulali, was a former schoolteacher from Dibër. Many officers felt that while they had done nothing to obstruct democratisation, they had been constantly attacked subsequently as ex-communists (*EEN*, 4 January, 1993, p. 3).

Some success was, however, accomplished in gaining foreign assistance from a number of diverse sources to help modernise and retrain the military. This, it was hoped, would raise the military's efficiency and self-esteem in the face of increasing tension in the Balkans. Following the re-establishment of diplomatic relations with the USA (section 6.2.4.3 below), both government and armed forces had hoped, unrealistically, that foreign exchange and other benefits could be earned by leasing the former Soviet naval facilities on Sazan island off Vlorë to the Americans. Although nothing came of this, with an increasing likelihood of the spread of the Yugoslav wars of succession, in December 1992 Albania became the first former Warsaw Pact member state to formally apply for NATO membership. In quietly rejecting this application the following month, NATO advised Albania to pursue closer links through the North Atlantic Consultative Council, which was set up to foster links with former Warsaw Pact countries. Indeed, military agreements were subsequently undertaken with Hungary and Bulgaria. Budapest would help train Albanian officers and share its experience in reforming the military for post-communist conditions, and a five-year agreement on scientific and technical co-operation in the sphere of military affairs was signed with Sofia for mutual protection against potential Balkan conflagration.

Plate 6.3 *An off-duty army conscript taking the Ionian Sea air at Himarë, April 1991*

Following its rejection of Tirana's application, NATO began to take an active interest in Albania, and a flurry of high-level contacts followed during the spring of 1993. The NATO Secretary-General, Manfred Wörner, visited Tirana and promised to broaden technical co-operation. This would include assistance in the reorganisation of the Albanian general staff, advice on drafting Albania's new defence policy, inviting Albanian officers on board NATO ships in the Adriatic and supplying communications equipment to the Albanian army. His visit was followed by that of General James Davis, chief of staff of SHAPE, NATO's central command. At much the same time, Albania sent its defence minister to participate in the NATO Co-operation Council meeting in Brussels, and in an important symbolic gesture, the US Navy frigate *USS Kaufmann* paid a courtesy visit to Durrës (EIU, 1993c, p. 42).

Potentially the most fruitful military agreement, as part of a package of wider co-operation, was reached with Turkey during the second half of 1992 covering co-operation in military education and technology, following a series of meetings inaugurated a year earlier. Subsequently, the Turkish destroyer *Fevzi Cakmak* paid a visit to the port of Durrës in August of that year. It was the first Turkish warship to visit Albania since at least the Ottoman era (Zanga, 1993a). Under the agreements, scores of Albanian military cadets would be trained in Turkey, military delegations would be exchanged and each country's military would take part in manoeuvres on the other's soil. Although the impression was given that NATO was fully supportive of this venture, some degree of ambiguity lingered, particularly in relation to the position of Greece.

The prospect of hostilities breaking out in Kosovo had focused attention on Albania's lack of military preparedness. In the event of conflict, Albania would at best be faced with a crippling refugee problem, at worst a slide into war all along its northern and eastern frontiers. As a number of Kosovar Albanians (perhaps 200) had been living in old army camps such as at Labinot, east of Elbasan, and in Tropojë

district in the north-east, Serbia was suggesting that these were being trained militarily. However, as most of them had served as conscripts in the former Yugoslav armed forces, they were already trained, probably to a higher level than the Albanian army (*EEN*, 4 January, 1993, p. 3).

6.1.5 Continuing uncertainty

6.1.5.1 Delicate democracy. Critics of the Democratic Party-led government claimed that the relative stability which was being experienced by mid-1993 had been achieved at the cost of an increasingly autocratic presidential rule, including attempts to muzzle the media, which although now free were not necessarily independent. For example, the authorities charged the editor of *Koha e Jone*, one of the country's few newspapers not affiliated to a political party, after he published a report that armoured units of the Albanian army had been sent near the Kosovo border. Although the government denied the report, it brought a charge of causing panic, punishable by up to five years' imprisonment. *Koha e Jone* was considered to be the most independent newspaper in Albania. Published twice weekly, at the time it had the second largest circulation within the country after the Socialists' organ *Zëri i Popullit*. Indeed, both *ZiP* and the ruling Democratic Party's mouthpiece *Rilindja Demokratike* had experienced a sharp drop in circulation to 10,000 and 7,000 respectively. It appeared that readers were tiring of the two main parties' confrontational polemics, and the price of the four-page newspapers had more than doubled. In order to meet rising costs, newspapers were selling increasing amounts of advertising space, leaving little room for news (Zanga, 1993f). When surveyed early in 1993, only 25 per cent of Albanians polled said they trusted the press.

President Berisha's authoritarian tendencies were likely to be contained by two factors: (a) Albania could not afford to alienate its Western aid donors by violations of human rights; and (b) Berisha needed to hold together the DP's fractious parliamentary group. In particular, he needed to take care not to alienate the right-wing *Balli Kombëtar-Legaliteti* faction of his own party, which had the allegiance of nearly half of the DP deputies in the People's Assembly. The *Balli Kombëtar* were fulfilling the function of opposition to the government (EIU, 1993c, pp. 39, 42).

6.1.5.2 Awaiting a constitution. The prime minister, Aleksander Meksi, had promised to submit the long-awaited new constitution to the People's Assembly by 16 June 1993. The Democratic Party (DP), under president Berisha, had 92 MPs in the 140-seat parliament – two votes short of the two-thirds majority needed to approve constitutional amendments. The DP could usually call upon the support of the Republican Party's one MP, leaving it dependent upon the small Social Democratic Party's (SDP) six MPs, who threatened to walk out of parliament when the new constitution failed to appear by the appointed time. The government then produced a hurried draft, which was promptly attacked by the Socialist Party, the SDP and the ex-DP splinter group the Democratic Alliance (DA). As a result, a parliamentary drafting commission was to start work on a new version (*EEN*, 22 June 1993). This continuing lack of a post-communist constitutional framework for the country's development exerted a severe handicap on the provision of assurances and guarantees for potential investors.

6.1.5.3 High level corruption? Amid talk of growing mafia links and vast fortunes being made on the black market, the Albanian press began to question the nature of profiteering from the resale of foreign aid. In one short piece (Topia, 1992) for example, it was pointed out that between September 1991 and June 1992 food aid to the value of $300 million arrived in the country, to be sold to the people at a third of its value. Yet the foreign economic relations ministry had admitted to collecting only 70 per cent of the revenue due, leaving three billion leks unaccounted for. The Italian judiciary subsequently opened investigations into a number of Rome politicians, including the former foreign minister Gianni de Michelis, concerning irregularities in food

and medicine aid to Albania (*EEN*, 28 May 1993, p. 12).

Early in 1993 the prime minister of the the post-communist caretaker government in Tirana, Vilson Ahmeti, was arrested on corruption charges along with two officials of the Albanian Trade Bank. The arrests followed claims that $1.6 million had been secretly paid to a French citizen to act as a mediator in renegotiating Albania's foreign debt. This allegedly took place at the time when Albania had the former Italian finance minister, Senator Beniamino Andreatta as its official negotiator. The alleged corruption was said to have taken place while Mr Ahmeti's government was guiding the country towards the March 1992 elections (EIU, 1993c, p. 41).

The last socialist prime minister and leader of the main opposition party, Fatos Nano, was arrested in July 1993 after being charged with abuse of power and costing the state 8.4 billion leks (roughly $8 million) by insisting that foreign aid in 1991 be handled by a single Italian company, which overcharged (*The Independent*, 31 July 1993). When allegations were first made against Nano in parliament earlier in the year, fighting broke out in the chamber amongst MPs and sittings were suspended for over a week. When Nano was not allowed to defend himself,

Within 10 minutes expensive suits were hanging in threads from their portly owners, fists and flower pots were flying in every direction (*EEN*, 11 May 1993, p. 8).

A party rally in his support called the same evening in Tirana's main football stadium was sabotaged when the electricity supply was switched off. Shortly afterwards, Ramiz Alia, who had been under house arrest on related corruption charges for nearly a year, was moved to prison.

Both Alia and Nano had been implicated by government spokesmen in the dubious affairs of Illiria Holdings, the Swiss-registered company run by Kosovar Albanian Hajdin Sejdija, who appears to have been the first person in recent history to have driven the streets of Tirana in a Rolls Royce. Allegedly, Illiria Holdings declared bankruptcy, leaving an enormous hole (known locally as 'the grave') in a central Tirana park where a luxury Sheraton hotel was to have been developed, and a similar hole in the savings of many small Albanian investors. Sejdija fled at the cost to Albania of as much as $40 million, and at a stroke the reputation of Kosovar businessmen was undermined. This added to the disenchantment in Albania with the general hesitance which the Albanian diaspora had maintained over investing in the country, despite previous promises of support (*EEN*, 27 April 1993, p. 8).

Much was made by the Albanian media of financial and military aid previously provided in the form of a 'Solidarity Fund' to Marxist-Leninist movements. Communists from Indonesia, Sudan, Sri Lanka, Brazil, Peru and Ecuador were said to have received military training in Albania during the 1960s, and the practice was thought to have continued well into the 1980s (EIU, 1993e, pp. 41–2).

Enver Hoxha's widow Nexhmije, was sentenced to nine years imprisonment for misappropriating 750,000 leks, and this was extended to eleven years on appeal.

6.1.5.4 Monarchs. Although the number of true pro-monarchists might be counted on the fingers of one hand (Luxner, 1993b), the political base to 'restore' a monarchy under Leka, son of Zogu, has been competed for by two 'Legality' parties. The Legality Movement Party (or *Legaliteti*), which claims to be the country's oldest political party, dating back to 1923, has been led by Nderim Kupi – the nephew of Abbas Kupi, holding dual US-Albanian citizenship, from Queens, New York – who played a key role in the abortive US-British attempt in the 1950s to destablilise Hoxha's regime. Nderim Kupi fled Albania in 1957 with his mother after two terms of imprisonment. The second party, the National Organisation of the Legality Movement was established during the Second World War, and managed a relatively high profile first post-communist congress in Tirana's palace of congresses in May 1993.

Meanwhile, Leka lives on a farm near Johannesburg, where he fled in 1975 after being kicked out of Spain for illegal political activities and gun-running. He briefly set foot in Albania in November 1993, but was hurriedly deported when he refused to renounce his monarchic aspirations.

6.2 New outlooks

6.2.1 *Tirana looks out*

The pace of improving foreign relations noticeably increased after Hoxha's death in April 1985 (Biberaj, 1985; Zanga, 1988a, 1988c). This included the establishment of diplomatic relations with West Germany, promotion of foreign language teaching and literature and an improvement in relations with the country's neighbours, Yugoslavia aside. By 1990, Albania's attitude to foreign relations had changed from that of isolationist dogma to relatively flexible pragmatism. This arose from:

(a) the desperate need for economic and technological assistance to begin to drag the country out of the slough it had dug for itself through its past attitudes to the outside world. An immediate aim was to boost exports, to gain hard currency, and to considerably increase the availability of consumer goods as one means of placating domestic frustration; and

(b) the desire to be acceptable to the world community, not least within the common European home, at a time when world events were moving quickly, and when Europe in particular appeared to be moving towards an all-embracing form of mutual support.

The establishment of diplomatic relations with the Federal Republic of Germany in 1987 was most notable, considering previous apparently insurmountable obstacles. A protocol was signed covering co-operation in mining, energy, the chemical and food industries. Trade between the two countries improved dramatically during 1988, with Albanian exports increasing by over 80 per cent (raw materials by 160 per cent) and imports by nearly a quarter. Under a further agreement signed in March 1989, Bonn was to provide Albania with DM10 million in 1989 for financial co-operation, and a similar total in 1990 for technical co-operation, covering mining, iron and steel, oil production and livestock breeding. Some debate surrounded the nature and conditions of these financial sums: to avoid compromising the constitution it seemed at one point that the Albanians were trying to pass them off as war reparations.

In 1987 Albania and Greece terminated the theoretical state of war which had existed between them since Italy attacked Greece from Albanian territory in 1940. In the following year they agreed to encourage local trade and travel across their difficult 250 km land frontier and across the narrow channel between Corfu and the Albanian coast. Tirana decentralised foreign trade activities by setting up seven district-based enterprises (in Durrës, Shkodër, Gjirokastër, Kukës, Pogradec, Korçë and Sarandë districts) aimed at promoting border trade. By the end of 1989, they were said to be conducting large-scale business with Greek, Yugoslav and Italian companies dealing in cement, building stone and marble, medicinal herbs, seafood, agricultural produce, brandy and craft goods (EIU, 1990b, p. 38).

But it was the newly found relationship with West Germany which was to act as an economic Trojan Horse for a country whose stance of relative self-reliance had restricted its access to modern technology and thus had considerably limited its capacity to more effectively exploit and process its natural riches. In particular, oil, chrome and copper posed productivity problems throughout the second half of the 1980s. During 1990 oil production was reduced by more than half to just 1.5 million tonnes, largely due to the obsolescence of the Soviet and Chinese technology being used, producing a recovery factor of only 12 per cent (Anon, 1991b). Indeed, virtually all industrial plant, dating either from the pre-1961 Soviet period or from China up to the mid-1970s was obsolete, being usually copies of earlier, often already outdated Western technology. By 1991, estimates of the sum required to modernise the country's textile, steel, chrome, oil and other mining industries and transport infrastructure over the next decade were being put at $10

billion (*EEM*, 11 January 1991), representing $3,000 for every Albanian man, woman and child. The West German injection had given the Albanians a taste for Western aid and technological support.

In its waning months, the ruling communist regime created the People's Assembly's Foreign Economic Co-operation Committee, which soon reported what had been painfully obvious to the rest of the world: that the country needed to increase its economic and industrial co-operation with other countries in order to gain access to essential modern technology. It also noted Albania's rich mineral resources and favourable natural conditions for further developing the tourist industry. The report put a final nail into the coffin of Article 28 of the Constitution, and shortly afterwards several major economic reform decisions were announced. Notwithstanding its constitutional position, the country had already increased significantly its level of borrowing from Western banks: the extent of which had crept up since 1985 to $268 million by the second quarter of 1989, and by the end of that year to $392 million, with the country's liabilities exceeding its assets by $85 million. By September 1991, that gap had increased dramatically to $257 million (Table 6.4).

6.2.2 Regional co-operation

Following the re-establishment of diplomatic relations in 1987, Greece was instrumental in persuading Albanian representatives to abandon their distaste for international gatherings and attend the February 1988 Balkan foreign ministers meeting in Belgrade. In a joint communiqué, the meeting's participants expressed a commitment to economic co-operation in a number of fields including tourism, transport and protection of the environment (Anon, 1987a, 1988a). This was followed by a three-day conference of Balkan deputy foreign ministers in Tirana, in January 1989, the first international meeting at such a level ever to be held in the Albanian capital. Reflecting this gathering's success, a full foreign ministers' conference was convened in Tirana in October 1990.

Table 6.4 *Albania's position in relation to Bank for International Settlement (BIS) members, 1980–91*

| | US$ million, end of year position | | | | | | | |
	1980	1985	1986	1987	1988	1989	1990	1991*
Assets	68	16	15	100	139	307	222	30
Liabilities	–	7	42	83	113	392	412	287
Net assets	–	9	–27	17	26	–85	–190	–257

Note: the BIS bank reporting area has grown over the period covered in the above figures: the data are thus not strictly comparable from year to year.

* January–September

Source: EIU, 1992a, p. 51.

Political relations with neighbouring Yugoslavia, however, remained bad. Mutual hostility continued to be focused on Kosovo, although the Albanian government insisted that it held no irredentist claims to the region. Indeed, differences in living standards, personal mobility and religious freedom acted as a major barrier to any potential closer relationship between Kosovo and Albania while the communists remained in power in the latter. Albania's new-found desire to participate in the CSCE process might have calmed Yugoslav fears of potential Albanian irredentism in Kosovo, but rising Serbian nationalism was causing considerable alarm in Tirana, as it was in much of Yugoslavia itself.

The October 1990 Balkan Foreign Ministers' conference in Tirana marked only the second time in 60 years that the Balkan governments had held such a high-level meeting, and lofty declarations of co-operation emerged. Alia called for a 'new vision' in the Balkans, but rejected any idea that borders might be changed. Yet a 'Balkanisation' of the region – disintegration along ethnic lines – appeared a more real danger than for many decades. The process of Balkan co-operation which had begun in 1988 at the previous meeting in Belgrade had been seriously compromised: the political landscape was now very different from that of two years previously. Greece and Turkey had been unable to establish a rapport, environmental issues interceded between Romania and Bulgaria, the Macedonian question clouded relations between Yugoslavia,

Greece and Bulgaria, and squabbles between Greece and Albania had resurfaced since the conservative New Democratic Party had assumed power in Athens. The latter problem concerned the Greek minority in Albania and the irredentist claims of church-led conservative groups to areas of southern Albania. And of course the governments of Tirana and Belgrade agreed to disagree over the Kosovo question. Relations between Bulgaria and Turkey had improved since the forced Bulgarisation of ethnic Turks had been ended by Sofia (Zanga, 1990f). The disintegration of Yugoslavia was yet to get underway.

Some important proposals were made in the final document, including the setting up of a permanent body with its own secretariat, which would mediate in Balkan disputes, ethnic or otherwise, and would represent the six states in meetings with other European regional groups. It was also proposed that a Balkan summit of heads of state be held and that the foreign ministers convene annually instead of once every two years. A working group was put in charge of preparations for the next meeting, which could be held within two years. The Albanians proposed that 'the principles of good neighbourliness' be set down in a separate document. The Romanians suggested the setting up of a direct telephone link between the Balkan foreign ministers, the Turks the establishment of a Balkan development bank, and the Bulgarians a conference of Balkan defence ministers. With hindsight, such proposals appear more than a little hollow.

Indeed, overall the summit yielded few immediate results, the final document simply reiterating the fundamental principles of co-operation in the Balkans that had been adopted in Belgrade two-and-a-half years previously. Concerted efforts to achieve integration with the rest of democratic Europe were called for, and Western Europe was asked not to continue ignoring the Balkan states.

6.2.3 Migration and neighbourly tensions

From mid-1990, when the country's internal security and control mechanisms began to falter, means began to be found to circumvent the previous Draconian controls on movement into and out of the country. In the first three years of the 1990s, some 300,000 people – almost 10 per cent of the total population – succeeded in leaving Albania. Subsequently, many were forced to return, notably from Italy and Greece. Since the Second World War, Western Europe had hardly been touched by what was a perpetual global refugee crisis. The Albanian migrations, combining elements both of 'east–west' and 'south–north' migration, suggested both a real and symbolic end to this aloofness.

The exodus which followed the embassy crisis of June 1990 replicated events in Central Europe a year before, when thousands of East Germans had sought asylum in Western embassies in Hungary and Czechoslovakia. In this instance, Western governments exploited the political value of granting asylum as communist regimes disintegrated before their eyes.

From January 1991, however, the nature of Albanian emigration began to deviate from other patterns of European migration (Collinson, 1992). An increasing proportion of those crossing into Greece were ethnic Albanians rather than Greeks from southern Albania. The pressure to emigrate stemmed both from a lack of faith in the promise of reform and from the general sense of insecurity and potential for violence which pervaded the country in the lead-up to its first multi-party general elections. The direct contribution of successive Albanian governments to emigration

is debatable: charges were made that Tirana's security services encouraged asylum-seekers in their 1991 attempts to reach Italy, in order to put pressure on Rome and its EC partners to recognise Albania's problems and assist the country.

Subsequently, Tirana argued that Western governments should agree to take a quota of Albanian migrant workers – both to relieve pressure within the country and to stimulate desperately needed hard currency remissions. Given Western Europe's biting economic recession, the problems for Germany posed by unification, and the threat of mass refugee movements from Central and Eastern Europe, these suggestions fell on less than sympathetic ears. Nonetheless, in the second half of 1992 1,070 Albanians found work abroad through official channels, the host countries being Italy, Germany, Croatia, Austria and Switzerland. The target figures for such planned labour migration in 1993 were 1,500–2,000 Albanians for Italy, up to 1,000 for Germany and 300–500 in the other countries (EIU, 1993e, p. 45).

None the less, through reinvigorated links with the Albanian diaspora (section 2.5 above), and an estimated 300,000 Albanian emigrants in work or seeking it outside of the country, the value of remittances to the country for 1992 was estimated at $400 million (*ATA*, 7 October 1992; EIU, 1993b, p. 32), equivalent to more than four times the value of Albania's exports for the year.

6.2.3.1 With Italy. The first major migratory wave to Italy after the 1990 embassy siege exodus, took place in March 1991, following a series of urban demonstrations, including the toppling of Hoxha's statue in Skanderbeg Square and subsequent widespread arrests. Riots in Durrës and attempts to storm the harbour area in the second week of February preceded the commandeering of several ships, the first of which reached Brindisi on 1 March. Within a week, some 15,000 Albanian refugees had reached Italy and thousands more had converged on Albania's ports hoping to make the journey.

For whatever reasons, the Italian government was slow to organise emergency aid at its east-coast ports. Under considerable UNHCR pressure, after two weeks Rome announced that all Albanians who had arrived (by now some 20,000) would be exempt from the strict application of Italy's new immigration law, and the majority of Albanians who reached Italy at this time were allowed to stay.

A second refugee flood to Italy followed the June 1991 collapse of the communist government at a time of rapidly deteriorating economic circumstances and increasing food shortages in Albania. As had been the case with the efforts to resolve the embassy crisis in 1990, success in eventually curtailing the March exodus had been largely due to the harsh measures taken by the Albanian authorities – under pressure from Italy – to stop anyone leaving the country (Collinson, 1992). Military blockades had been set up at all ports, and any crowds trying to board ships were forcibly dispersed. That would-be emigrants managed to overcome such constraints for a third time, in August 1991, seemed to indicate the continued desperation of many Albanians. By now, Tirana had a new interim government, and with the partial removal of the communists, Italy or any other potential host country was less likely to take seriously emigrants' pleas of fear of persecution. It was now argued – and this also applied to refugees trying to enter Western Europe from other Central and East European countries – that accepting large numbers of asylum-seekers was not in the interests of promoting democracy and stability under the new political circumstances. Any subsequent migration was therefore to be defined as economic and was to be prevented.

Yet on 8 August 1991 the dangerously overloaded MV *Vlora* carrying, in appalling conditions, some 10,000–15,000 tightly packed Albanians, forced its way through an Italian naval blockade to the small port of Bari. The vivid media images of the scene will persist for a very long time. Most of those who arrived in Bari were taken to a football stadium in preparation for mass repatriation. With a minimum of even the most basic assistance, many collapsed from hunger and heat exhaustion in the port and in the stadium; in the desperate circumstances, clashes with the Italian security forces were inevitable, adding further to the confusion and brutality of the situation. By various means, all the Albanians were repatriated.

These events had perhaps two immediate implications: (a) Albania's uncomfortably close geographical proximity to richer Western European countries was suddenly, and traumatically brought home to a West which had thought of Albania, if at all, as a small, obscure country tucked away in a far corner of Europe, or even beyond; and (b) the Albanian exodus literally brought home to the West the increasing volatility and unpredictability of European population movements in the wake of the collapse of communism.

The longer-term implication saw the EC, and principally Italy, jolted into providing large amounts of emergency food and other aid to Albania. Initially, responses to Albania's increasingly desperate plight had been slow and *ad hoc*. By mid-1993, as the country's economic condition showed signs of improvement, the EC aid programme had been placed on a much more systematic footing (section 6.2.5 below). However, hundreds of would-be refugees continued, intermittently, to attempt to commandeer ships out of the country. They were forcibly deterred in Durrës in February 1992, at Vlorë in June of that year, in both Durrës and Vlorë again in July 1992 (triggered by the ending of unemployment benefits for state workers), and in Shëngjin in the following January (after severe flooding in the region had brought further hardship).

6.2.3.2 With Greece. Between 1990 and 1993 some 150,000 Albanians travelled to Greece to find work. Many more simply crossed the border in order to obtain much sought after consumer goods, often in exchange for critically needed food resources such as sheep or cattle. Albanians in Albania, had after all, suffered the lowest standard of living in Europe and the most prescriptive laws on the ownership of private property anywhere in the world. Consumer goods were minimal, and the recent break-up of collective agrarian structures provided some families with farm animals surplus to their immediate individual requirements which they used to redress past material deprivations. This short-sighted, if understandable position, saw Albanian agriculture limping along almost at a subsistence level while food aid continued to be needed in large quantities to feed the urban population.

In January 1991, more than 10,000 Albanians, many of them ethnic Greek, took the opportunity of political confusion within the country to trudge through difficult wintry mountainous conditions across the border into Greece. This prompted Athens to send an official delegation to Tirana – the first high-level government group to visit Albania since World War II – headed by prime minister Constantinos Mitsotakis. Agreement was reached to stop the flow and for Athens to send back the refugees 'without adverse consequences' for them when they returned to Albania. In turn, Albania was promised an immediate credit of $20 million. Yet this did not deter desperate Albanians who continued to take the difficult escape route throughout 1991.

In December 1991 the Greek government began mass expulsions of illegal immigrants, and through 'operation Scoopa' 100,000 Albanians were deported. Greece had several reasons for removing Albanians (*EEN*, 6 July 1993): (a) they were exacerbating the unemployment situation in Greece by saturating the casual labour market; (b) they appeared to have a worse than average record of lawbreaking, a factor seized upon and emphasised by Greek politicans; and (c) Greeks were becoming particularly concerned about the post-communist resurgence of Islam in Albania and how it could 'infect' the Orthodox Greek state. On the one hand, the expulsions appeared to be indirectly beneficial to the EC since the Community was substantially underpinning funding for Greek unemployment support, but on the other hand, with an increasing interest in Albanian affairs, the EC had no wish to see potentially destabilising acts taking place in the region.

As a legacy of the Turkish empire and its destructive disintegration earlier this century, there are large numbers of ethnic Greeks living in southern Albania and long-settled Albanians in north-western Greece. Known to Albanians as Çamëri, this area became part of Greece in 1913, although it was briefly under the nominal control of Albania in 1941 during the Italian occupation. The Greeks in Albania are concentrated in the southern towns of Gjirokastër and Sarandë and in adjacent rural areas, in often difficult terrain. In this region of enormous tourism potential can be found archaeological sites of classic antiquity, emphasising the area's important past role within the Mediterranean basin's major civilisations, situated close to long stretches of sandy beaches little more than a flat stone's throw from Corfu. Picturesque, if often abandoned hillside villages look down upon poorly finished post-war apartment blocks and half-abandoned industrial sites in valley bottoms – stark witnesses to past misguided development policies.

With some justification, the Greeks in Albania claim to have suffered persecution during the country's half-century of Stalinism (section 3.1, above). The Greek government has argued that the minority numbers 300,000 or 9 per cent of the total population of Albania, and lives in what Greeks refer to as 'northern (Vorio) Epirus'. The use of this geographical term is no less implicitly irredentist than the use of the name 'Macedonia' by the former Yugoslav republic at which Greeks themselves take so much offence: 'Epirus' in both ancient and modern Greek means 'solid land', as distinct from the islands (Tachtsis, nd, p. 190).

This region was part of the Greek territories that were hived off when the imperial powers drew the borders of Albania in 1912 in London. According to the 1914 Protocol of Corfu, which was later annulled by the 1921 Paris Conference, virtually the whole southern half of Albania, below the Shkumbin river, was to have become Greek territory.

According to the last national census in Albania, undertaken in 1989, there were 58,758 ethnic Greeks in the country (section 2.1 above). An independent estimate might suggest a community of about 120,000, based on an extrapolation from the 1992 general election results in which the ethnic Greek party polled 54,000 votes. The discrepancy in numbers, a not unfamiliar theme in the Balkans, partly arises from the Greek practice of counting all Albanians with Orthodox leanings as Greek, thereby imposing a cultural imperialism over Albanian and Serbian Orthodox Church adherents within the country. This is something from which the consecration of the first Albanian Orthodox Church in the 1920s, in Boston, Massachussetts was meant to signal an escape. Indeed, members of the Greek Orthodox Church appeared to be most vehement in their irredentist leanings towards southern Albania. Orthodox Metropolitan Sevastianos, based in the northern Greek town of Konitsa, whose diocese theoretically encompasses much of southern Albania, appears to be a strong proponent of the cause of the Greek Movement for the Recovery of *Vorio Epirus*.

With the rehabilitation of religion in Albania since 1990, religious argument has been increasingly interwoven with political and territorial considerations. Greek clerics, allowed into the country to help rebuild the churches, were subsequently viewed by some Albanians as a Greek nationalist fifth column, preaching division and secession. The Greek minority has its own-language primary schools but also wants its own secondary schools and university education, economic 'decentralisation', and full representation in the police, judiciary, military and civil service.

Ironically, the Albanian Stalinist leadership largely came from the south of the country, and Enver Hoxha was actually born in the part-Greek town of Gjirokastër (Argyrokastro). Under the communists this was designated as one of two 'museum cities' on account of its architectural heritage and, as a backcloth to the Hoxha personality cult, Gjirokastër acted as a focus for Albania's limited tourism industry. Latterly, the country's leaders have tended to come from the north. President Sali Berisha, a member of a powerful Islamic clan, hails from Tropojë district adjacent to the border with Kosovo in the north-east. Despite the government's democratic pretensions, this implicit religio-regionalism has only fanned Greek fears of unfair treatment.

Greek-Albanian relations at both local and national levels were soured in June 1993 when Tirana deported Greek Orthodox priest or *archimandrite* ('abbot') Chrysostomos ('Golden-tongued') Maidonis for allegedly preaching secessionism and distributing pro-Hellenic literature. The Greek consul in Gjirokastër was informed of the deportation prior to its taking place, but his attempts to physically prevent it were to no effect.

When some 300 Albanian ethnic Greeks sought to travel to Gjirokastër to protest, they were forcibly stopped by Albanian riot police. Athens responded by reinvigorating its policy of expelling illegal Albanian immigrants, some 30,000 of whom were removed within days (Smith, 1993a). While relatively minor by recent Balkan standards, these incidents are indicative of a wider malaise within the region, compounded by the fact that while the Greek media rallied to the defence of the Orthodox church, the Albanian media ignored the Gjirokastër problems and carried round-the-clock reports on the plight of the Albanian expellees returning from Greece.

The Greek expulsion of the Albanians was viewed in a context whereby ethnic Greeks in Albania for some time had been able to acquire a Greek visa and work permit – by invitation of the Greek government. Greek officials in Albania and in the border customs and police units were claimed to have been corruptly selling Greek visas to Albanians in large numbers. In May 1993, the going rate for a visa corruptly obtained through Greek officials in Tirana was said to be $300–$350. For longer-term stability, the Greek government could have set a quota for the number of Albanians it was prepared to accept, and as Albania itself presented substantial business opportunities for Greek entrepreneurs, Athens could have done more to encourage mercantile interest in its north-western neighbour (*EEN*, 6 July, 1993, p. 5). For its part, the Albanian government could have shown a little more sensitivity to the fears both of its own Greek minority and of Greek public opinion fanned by vested interests in Athens, Ioannina and Konitsa.

Albanian president Berisha appealed to Secretary-General Boutros Boutros-Ghali for UN intervention to put an end to the Greek government's deportations. He argued that the migrants had been indiscriminately seized, maltreated and beaten, a claim later reiterated by the Albanian foreign ministry. Berisha asserted that the expelled Greek cleric had openly expressed territorial claims (*ATA*, 28 June, 1 July 1993). Albania recalled its ambassador to Greece for 'consultations', and Greece cancelled three planned official visits to Albania, making it clear that the expulsions would continue until all illegal Albanian immigrants had been returned. For their part, the Greek government sent dispatches to the UN, to the Conference on Security and Co-operation in Europe and to the World Council of Churches, complaining about the deportation of the cleric.

Albanians made the point that if a Turkish *imam* in Thrace had been caught distributing literature advocating Turkish irridentism of parts of Greece, he would have been jailed. Indeed, in July, shortly after the Greek prime minister, Constantinos Mitsotakis, had argued that the Greek minority in Albania should have the same autonomous rights as Tirana was demanding for Albanians in Kosovo, two ethnic Turkish-Greek parliamentary deputies from Thrace argued that if Greece was demanding autonomy for the Greek minority in Albania, then why should the ethnic Turks in Greece not demand the same? (*EEN*, 20 July, 1993.)

With a Balkan 'civil' war on their doorsteps, neither Greece nor Albania could afford to sacrifice regional co-operation and good neighbourliness at a time when Greece, the only Balkan EC member, was left with few friends in the region, and when Albania required all the EC assistance that could be offered to it. By the end of 1993 a joint commission had been set up between the two countries to oversee the problems of Albanians in Greece.

6.2.3.3 With Turkey. At the time of writing, no tensions existed in relations with Turkey, but tensions within Albania existed over those relations. Seeking allies within the region and citing the presence of a sizeable ethnic Albanian community in Turkey and historic ties as the basis for friendship, the Tirana leadership came to view Albania's international role as a bridge between east and west. Critics argued that rather than a bridge, the country could

become a bridgehead for Turkish aspirations in Europe. The Socialists in particular portrayed the relationship as part of a wider rapprochement with the Islamic world which would prejudice Albania's relations with Europe.

Under civil and military agreements undertaken during 1991 and 1992, scholarships were granted to Albanian students to follow higher education courses in Turkey. With such places numbering up to a hundred, this represented a provision twice as great as the combined number of Albanian students despatched to Western Europe and North America (Zanga, 1993a).

6.2.4 Global relations

Alia announced a major shift in the country's foreign policy in his closing speech to the 10th Plenum on 17 April 1990 (Zanga, 1990c), in which he signalled Albania's interest in establishing diplomatic relations with the two superpowers and the EC and a desire to join the CSCE (Zanga, 1990b). Justifying such changes, the Albanian leader argued that he was simply carrying on his predecessor's tradition of diplomatic manoeuvring in order to guide Albania through the new political conditions prevailing in Europe, thereby attempting to present a major turn-around in Albanian foreign policy in terms of natural continuity (Zanga, 1990c).

6.2.4.1 With the UN. The United Nations Organisation, which Albania had largely ignored in the past, regarding it as a tool of the superpowers, began to receive friendly overtures during 1990. Tirana began to praise the organisation for its important role in international affairs, particularly after UN Secretary-General Javier Pérez de Cuéllar visited the country in May 1990. Tirana's new attitude was influenced by UN economic support received in 1990 by Albania as a developing country. Pérez de Cuéllar encouraged the Albanian leadership to increase the pace of democratisation and reminded his hosts that economic and political relations were closely intertwined, and stressing that economic and social rights were inseparable from individual rights. Appreciating that some countries remained sceptical about Tirana's human rights record, the Albanian leadership later insisted on having the UN, rather than individual West European countries, help organise the orderly departure of the Albanian refugees in the aftermath of the storming of embassies in July 1990. The UN complied with the request.

In late September 1990, Alia flew to New York for the UN's 45th. anniversary celebration, the first time an Albanian head of state had attended an official meeting in the West. Its purpose was to demonstrate his desire to continue a pragmatic foreign policy and to attract support for Albania's membership of the CSCE. Alia's wide-ranging UN address criticised the Yugoslav position on Kosovo, and raised the question of the historical injustice Europe had perpetrated against Albania's territorial integrity in 1913. The international community was told that it should not be indifferent to the matter of Kosovo, particularly since Europe, having redrawn the map of the Balkans earlier this century, had not only a moral but an historical responsibility for the Albanians in Yugoslavia (Zanga, 1990d).

Since the Albanians wanted to be reintegrated into global affairs, to join Europe and be part of the Helsinki (CSCE) process, it was only appropriate to establish relations with both superpowers.

6.2.4.2 *With Moscow*.

Diplomatic agreements on the expansion of political, economic, scientific and cultural contacts with the Soviet Union in July 1990 ended almost three decades of estrangement. Since 1985, the year both Hoxha died and Mikhail Gorbachev assumed the Soviet leadership, the Kremlin had called for a healing of the rift (Traynor, 1990). Previously, Hoxha had railed against:

... the Khrushchevites who, in their superpower greed, wanted to turn our People's Republic into a vassal state, a part of the Russian empire! ... We told them to their faces: we would rather eat grass

than submit to you or anyone else. (Hoxha, 1984a, pp. 579, 580)

6.2.4.3 *With Washington*.

In December 1990, leaders of the newly established opposition Democratic Party urged that the United States immediately open diplomatic relations with Tirana (Binder, 1990). Despite the Albanian communists' outward dismissal of the US as the imperialist superpower bent on world domination, the countries' longer historic relationship was far from anatagonistic. Many southern Albanians migrated to, or sought work in, the United States in the early decades of the century, Hoxha's father among them. The USA had helped to preserve Albania's identity when, at the Paris Peace Conference in 1919, President Woodrow Wilson had firmly opposed the division of Albania between Italy, Yugoslavia and Greece. When fascist Italy occupied Albania in 1939, the United States alone of the major powers denounced the attack. After its post-war liberation, Tirana requested recognition by the West. In November 1945 the US government expressed its readiness to establish diplomatic relations, requesting assurances of free and fair elections in accordance with the Declaration of Yalta.

But post-war relations soon began to deteriorate, and the American mission (along with that of Britain) complained of Tirana's repressive internal policies. In November 1946 the United States withdrew its mission, six months after Britain had done so, on the grounds that diplomatic relations between the two countries had become impossible. The lowest point in relations came in the early 1950s when the United States and other Western countries planned and organised uprisings in some of the communist countries of Eastern Europe. Albania was selected as the most suitable country to test the merits of a clandestine operation. The British intelligence officer Kim Philby, a Soviet agent, betrayed the plot, which then turned into a disaster (Cookridge, 1968; Page *et al.*, 1968; Philby, 1968; Amery, 1973). Somewhat cynically, in 1955, President Eisenhower offered $850,000 in food aid, which the Hoxha government firmly rejected.

The US government's overtures to normalise relations with Tirana date back to the early 1970s and the time of Nixon's visit to Beijing. For its part, Tirana had been displaying a far less belligerent attitude to the United States since Washington had expressed unease over Belgrade's handling of ethnic unrest in Kosovo. Although discussions on re-establishing relations began in the summer of 1990, culminating in complete agreement in September, reservations concerning Albania's human rights record restrained moves on the US side. Following the December 1990 legalisation of non-communist political parties, however, objections eased, and despite lingering reservations from the office of the US Secretary of State, diplomatic relations were resumed in March 1991. A bilateral economic agreement was eventually signed on 10 June 1992.

6.2.4.4 With London. After four decades of refusing to talk to one another, Britain and Albania reopened diplomatic channels in May 1991. The rift with Britain in 1946 was triggered when two British destroyers hit mines in the Corfu Straits, with the loss of 45 seamen. In 1949 the International Court of Justice in the Hague awarded compensation to Britain amounting to $1.45 million (£843,000) (plus interest), which Albania refused to recognise. Britain in its turn refused to hand over 2,399 kg of Albanian gold bullion until Albania accepted blame. The gold, which the Nazis had plundered in both Rome and Tirana during the Second World War, had belonged to the pre-war National Bank of Albania. Recovered by the allies, it was held in the Bank of England on behalf of the Tripartite Commission for the Restitution of Monetary Gold. The Commission comprised Britain, France and the United States, and was established at the 1947 Paris Peace Conference, which Hoxha attended (Milivojevic, 1992, p. 33). Until the Corfu Straits incident the allies had been intent on returning the ingots to Albania (Wright, 1949; Chung, 1959; Halliday, 1986).

As late as 1990, Alia was arguing that Britain still had the outdated mentality of the 1940s: 'it is high time for it to give up this position' (*Zëri i Popullit*, 19 April 1990). But

during the year, for the first time, Albania accepted liability for the Corfu Straits incident, although insisting that the gold (estimated at £18 million) would have to be returned at the time of normalisation of ties with Britain. Under a proposed arrangement, this thorny issue would be shelved until after diplomatic relations were established. The situation was complicated by the fact that the Tripartite Commission required unanimous agreement before any gold deal could be made. Certainly, prior to the establishment of Albanian–US relations, the Americans would have vetoed any such deal unless it encompassed compensation for expropriated US assets. On 22 May 1991 the UK Foreign Office announced that it had agreed in principle to establish diplomatic relations, and that representatives of the two countries would be meeting in the next two weeks to finalise arrangements. Agreement to return the gold was reached in Rome the following year.

Reflecting the UK's belated recognition of the significance of the Albanian-speaking world, on 28 February 1993 the BBC relaunched its Albanian Service broadcasts on medium wave, using Radio Tirana's 500 kW transmitters at Lushnjë, in addition to short-wave broadcasts from London. Previous broadcasting to Albania had only lasted from 1940 to 1967 when Foreign Office spending cuts took it off the air (Culf, 1993).

6.2.5 Aid programmes

Following the multi-party elections of March and April 1991, the subsequent collapse of the new communist government and the establishment of a coalition in June, Albania was formally admitted to the 34-nation CSCE. In foreshadowing this development, the then Italian foreign minister Gianni de Michelis promised the country £30 million in aid and talked of Italy's 'special duty for historical and geographical reasons' towards Albania. The German foreign minister Hans-Dietrich Genscher was about to visit the country, and the US Secretary of State, James Baker, the highest American official to visit Albania, was to arrive in the following month. Relations were formalised with the EC. Prime Minister Ylli Bufi met with Pope John Paul II in July 1991, and from the Vatican they announced that Albania and the Holy See would re-establish diplomatic relations after a break of 45 years.

One major consequence of the grim economic situation was the dangerous breakdown of law and order. Lawlessness reached alarming proportions and threatened to turn into organised crime. Some foreign relief organisations decided to leave the country following mob attacks.

The mass escape of thousands of Albanian refugees on a ship commandeered to Italy forced events. Following the horrendous scenes at Bari after arrival (section 6.2.3.1 above), Italy came to the forefront among Western countries trying to rescue Albania from economic disaster and the threat of mass hunger. The country began to resume its pre-war role of protector towards its eastern neighbour: the sudden arrival of thousands of refugees on Italy's east coast left Rome with little choice. In September 1991, Italian troops were sent to Albania for the first time since 1943, to take part in 'Operation Pelikan'. Some 800 Italian soldiers supported by helicopters and truck convoys were stationed at Durrës and Vlorë ports and in 27 other locations throughout the country, in order to distribute, over a period of three months, emergency food aid amounting to $70 million. Francesco Cossiga visited the country, the first Italian president ever to do so.

A three-year plan for economic co-operation involving some $800 million was agreed in principle. Italian officials estimated that Albanian industry required a minimum of $200 million a year in economic aid. Operation Pelikan was extended to the end of the year. Once the Italians had completed their operation, the G-24 Western industrialised nations would supply substantial food aid in the form of 50,000 tonnes of wheat a month until June 1992. Indeed, agricultural aid for 1993 was likely to amount to $100 million, mostly from the G-24 countries, but also including a $15 million credit negotiated with the World Bank. Operation Pelikan was further extended to 1994, with up to 140 billion lira earmarked to this end.

In the wake of these events, Italy gained a very high profile as the neighbour most willing to provide practical support for an ailing Albania (Table 6.5). This reinforced that country's position as a major source of Albania's joint venture partners (Table 8.3 below).

Reflecting new world order relationships in Eastern Europe, whereby Italy and Germany were competing to extend their spheres of interest, Germany also promised DM75 million in financial and technical aid to the end of 1991. Part was being given in the form of long-term credits to ensure a regular flow of food and medical supplies and to help rebuild the country's infrastructure. At the third meeting of the German-Albanian economic commission held in Tirana in November 1991, the Germans urged Albanian officials to abandon the policy of state control over the economy in order to eliminate inefficient bureaucracy and needless ideologically motivated constraint. German State Secretary Erich Riedl was quoted as having bluntly told the Albanians to roll up their sleeves and stop acting like beggars on the world stage.

Indeed, in October 1991, the country was finally admitted to the global capitalist economy: it joined the IMF and the World Bank and became a participating member of the EBRD. In response to the reform programme initiated by Gramoz Pashko, the EBRD announced an 'initial strategy' for the country, including assistance for banking, foreign investment and privatisation. Three economic priority areas required urgent addressing if Albania was not to remain dependent upon aid for the forseeable future: these were agriculture and food, energy and minerals, and tourism. An assessment of these sectors is undertaken in Chapter 9.

Desperately needed foreign aid thus started to become a reality during 1991 for a country that had begun to experience belatedly the difficult transition from command to market economy. Its predicament was in many ways worse than that of Romania or Bulgaria. Economic ignorance, ideological single-mindedness and

Table 6.5 *Italian aid to Albania*

Nature of assistance	Italian organisation	Cost (billion lire)
Emergency grants		
Heating materials	AGIP	8.5
Electricity distribution network in Tirana	ENEL	5.0
Integrated project for agriculture	AGROTEC	12.0
Silos at Durrës	COGIUAL	7.8
Total		**13.8**
Grants		
Milk processing	TECNAL	13.0
Food centre	BONIFICA	14.0
Provincial master plan project	CNEL	4.0
Merlon Foundation	Merlon	0.3
Total		**31.3**
Project AID 91		
Urban electricity distribution system	ENEL	11.0
Hydraulic network	ASTALDI/BONIFICA	13.0
Bovilla HEP station	ASTALDI/BONIFICA	25.0
Total		**49.0**
Aid credit 1992–94		
Bushati HEP station	ANSALDO	25.0
Railway reconstruction	RIC	14.0
Kavajë glass factory etc.	I. ASSUNZIONE	5.0
Oil industry infrastructure	SISA/BERTOLLI	7.5
Integrated telecomms project	BERD	20.0
Italy–Albania water pipe	IRITECNA	14.0
Development of hydrogeological reserves		4.0
Prefabricated materials for housing		5.0
Apartments for the homeless		10.0
Total		**104.5**
Grand total		**198.6**

Source: Berisha, 1992, p. 10.

years of relative isolation had rendered the country traumatised and virtually inert in the face of necessary change. The enormous task of re-establishing national self-confidence and rebuilding society from the inside now faced the Albanian people. It was clear that foreign aid would remain of critical importance for several years.

In July 1992 a G-24 meeting was held in Tirana to take stock of the aid programme to the country and to co-ordinate future assistance. The Albanian government had earlier submitted a six-point plan highlighting areas of greatest need: (a) balance of payments support to ensure food supplies for the winter and the purchase of raw materials and spare parts; (b) support for health, education and social welfare; (c) assistance in restructuring selected industries; (d) help to improve management and administration; (e) investment in modernising infrastructure; and (f) approval for an annual meeting of aid donors to review the country's requirements.

These requests were accepted in broad outline including an endorsement of the action plan for agriculture prepared under the EC's PHARE Programme. Total aid disbursed or pledged by the G-24 amounted to $900 million,

Table 6.6 *PHARE and EC humanitarian assistance to Albania, 1992*

	Assistance agreed for 1992		Contracted by end of 1992	
	(million Ecu)			
1. National EC PHARE programme	25.0		17.5	
Agriculture	15.0		9.7	
Agricultural and livestock inputs		9.0		8.0
Mechanisation		3.5		0.0
Technical assistance and training		2.5		1.7
Technical assistance	10.0		7.8	
Transport, spare parts and technical assistance		4.4		4.0
Liquidation, restructuring and privatisation of large industry		0.8		0.1
Small and medium enterprise support, including credit delivery		1.3		1.1
Promotion of financial, banking and investment services		0.5		0.2
Support for training in, and environmental implications of, tourism		0.2		0.0
Trans European Mobility for University Studies (TEMPUS)		1.2		1.2
Support for public administration, including customs		0.9		0.9
Support for medical aid and hospital restructuring		0.7		0.3
2. Humanitarian aid	50.0		41.0	
Total	75.0		58.5	
%	100.0		78.0	

Source: PHARE, 1993, Annex 1.

80 per cent of which was being provided by the EC (EIU, 1992d, pp. 44–5). The IMF gave the green light for aid donors to begin or to consolidate their assistance programmes for Albania, and a stand-by short-term stabilisation programme covering a credit of $40 million for critical emergency imports was negotiated with the Fund (Ruli, 1992). An 18-month study would be undertaken to assist Albania's longer-term needs, a period which, to some Albanian commentators at least, seemed like a lifetime, given the country's crisis position (Pepo, 1992).

Albania was first included in the EC PHARE programme in 1992. The national indicative programme for that year amounted to 25 million Ecu (Table 6.6). This was part of total EC funding for the country which amounted to 188 million Ecu for the year, including humanitarian, balance of payments and food assistance. Of the 15 million ECU allocated to agriculture, nine million were directed to agricultural and livestock inputs, 3.5 million to mechanisation, and 2.5 million ECU to technical assistance and training. This assistance supported the establishment of the Project Implementation and Co-ordination Unit (PICU) within the Ministry of Agriculture and Food, the use of short-term technical assistance, and the establishment of six regional PICU teams

(PHARE, 1993). Of the 4.4 million ECU for the transport sector, buses, spare parts and technical assistance were receiving priority. Technical assistance amounting to 2.6 million ECU was provided to help in the development of private sector enterprise restructuring and development of the financial and banking sector. Within the TEMPUS higher education training programme, eight joint European projects (JEPs) were being implemented. Medical aid and a study for a reorganisation of the hospital sector were being focused on the needs of Tirana maternity hospital.

PHARE programmes were implemented through the Aid Co-ordination Unit installed within the Ministry of Finance and Economy, and in future they would take account of the need for priority change, likely emergencies and the changing pace of economic and democratic reform. Every sector in Albania was seen to have a high priority, but with an emphasis on economic reform aimed at sustainable growth, the European Commission emphasised the need to agree an ordering of priorities and to concentrate efforts in specific areas while aiming to complement other aid programmes and aspects of economic development such as agreements on trade and co-operation.

Criticism of Western assistance for environmental improvement in Central and Eastern Europe generally has been severe (Jenkins, 1992; Baumgartl, 1993; see also Haigh *et al.*, 1992). An EC overview (G-24 Co-ordination Unit, 1993) revealed that between 1990 and 1992 such assistance amounted to just 6.8 per cent of total aid. Of this 1,048m ECU sum, Poland, Hungary and Czechoslovakia took the lion's share, leaving just 70.7m ECU or 7.4 per cent for the other countries of the region. Representing most of Albania's share, the World Bank commissioned an environmental strategy study (World Bank, 1993) which recommended: (a) a restructuring of economic incentives to encourage more efficient resource use; (b) an overhaul of environmental legislation; and (c) a strengthening of the government's Committee for Environmental Protection and Preservation and other agencies with environmental responsibilities. Support funding

would be sought from the Mediterranean Technical Assistance Programme (METAP) and the Global Environment Facility (GEF) (Kosmo, 1993).

6.2.6 Growing links with the Islamic world

Albania's successful application to join the Islamic Conference Organisation (ICO) rendered the country eligible for Islamic Development Bank (IDB) credits, which, in the wake of the Bosnian war, were expected to be comparatively generous. It did, however, emphasise continuing political division within the country, with the newly formed (November 1992) Democratic Alliance Party (DAPA) arguing that such membership detracted from Albania's European orientation and that it lent credibility to Serbian propaganda about the emergence of Islamic fundamentalism in the country.

Albania's drive towards a market economy received a boost from the signing of a memorandum of understanding with the Gulf Co-operation Council (GCC) in Jeddah in September 1992. It established the Arab Albanian Islamic Bank (AAIB), the country's first Islamic bank, with an authorised capital sum of $100 million, provided by investors from Saudia Arabia, Bahrain and other GCC states. The Bank of Albania was to hold 60 per cent of the stock, with the Arab Islamic Bank (AIB) holding the remainder. The AIB was expected to provide technical and management assistance to the new bank. If successful, it was hoped that the bank would open the way for greater foreign investment. As an Islamic bank, the AAIB would have to conform to Sharia law: interest payments replaced with profit sharing, with no investments in trade considered bad for health or moral standards permitted. The hoarding of goods and the creation of monopolies are also prohibited under Sharia law, and the AAIB would also discourage trading in luxury goods.

Against the background of an intense debate within the country, Albania openly appealed to Arabs and Muslims to increase investments in the country. As the Governor of the Bank of

Albania noted, Albania was part of Europe geographically, but spiritually the country was looking toward closer ties with the Arab world (Savvides, 1992). Subsequently, a delegation from the Islamic Development Bank concluded an agreement with the Ministry of Education on establishing printing houses, supplying laboratory equipment and setting up an institute of Arabic language and five schools. The delegation discussed the introduction of Islamic capital into the infrastructure, telecommunications, agriculture, oil industry, transport and other fields of the national economy.

The Yugoslav vortex

7.1 Kosovo disputed

7.1.1 Kosovo in a Slav state

While today some 3.3 million people live in Albania, up to a further three million Albanians live in adjacent areas of the former Yugoslavia. Of these, about two million are in Kosovo (Albanian Kosovë/Kosova), and 400–700 thousand are in neighbouring western Macedonia and in the Macedonian capital Skopje. Smaller groups inhabit contiguous districts of southern Serbia and Montenegro. With the violent disintegration of Yugoslavia, the nature and disputed role of Kosovo and other Albanian-inhabited lands brings into sharp focus the inextricably complicated and potentially calamitous relationship between the Albanian state and adjacent territories in this least developed and most volatile corner of Europe.

Yugoslavia, initially the Kingdom of Serbs, Croats and Slovenes, a country carved out of two former empires after the First World War, was, literally, the land of the south Slavs, of whom Serbs numbered the largest. As a federal country after the Second World War, it was divided into six republics, each based on a Slav 'nation' (Figure 7.1). Its two non-Slav 'nationalities' – Albanians in Kosovo and Magyars in Vojvodina – could not, almost by definition, be given republican status, although under Tito, their inhabited areas were given 'autonomous region' status within the republic of Serbia (Box 7.1, Table 7.1).

In the ruins of the Ottoman Empire, the Treaty of London of 1913, while recognising for the first time an independent Albanian state, also ceded Turkish territory to Greece, Croatia, Bulgaria, Montenegro and Serbia. It was the latter state which incorporated the region of Kosovo, as well as Albanian territories in western Macedonia and a portion of Albanian territory that had been appropriated by Montenegro after the 1878 Congress of Berlin (Pipa and Repishti, 1984; Pipa, 1989). The Paris Peace Conference, which began in January 1919, set permanent boundaries between the newly established Kingdom of Serbs, Croats and Slovenes, and surrounding countries, although as noted earlier, the final demarcation of Albania's eastern boundary was only made in July 1926 (Hondius, 1968).

Kosovo was not easily won by the Serbs. In 1913, Kosovar Albanians had risen against the invading Serbian and Montenegrin armies, but the resistance was quelled by force, and the first Serbian and Montenegrin settlers were sent to claim the newly 'liberated' lands (Banac, 1984).

By the end of Ottoman rule, education among the Kosovar Albanians was conducted in both religious and secular schools. But all

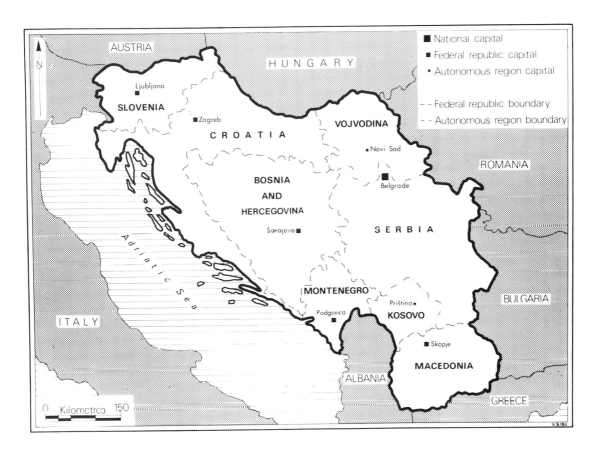

Figure 7.1 *Post-war Yugoslavia*

existing schools were shut down by the Serbs in 1913. Between 1916 and 1918, however, Kosovo was occupied by Austro-Hungarian forces and nearly 300 Albanian schools were re-opened in Albanian inhabited territories. Albanians were also permitted to fly the flag of the newly created Albanian state, with the Austrians seeking to win Albanian support against the Serbs.

Following the peace, Serbian impositions were reintroduced, and all Albanian language schools in Kosovo, Macedonia and Montenegro were closed. Official Serbian policy of assimilation or expulsion of Albanians led to the Ministry of Foreign Affairs stating in 1929 that there were no national minorities in the southern regions (Banac, 1984, p. 298).

The inter-war period thus saw a Serbian dominated nationalist Yugoslav state denying its non-Slav minorities cultural equality and the rights guaranteed to minorities under international law, as formulated by the League of Nations and to which Yugoslavia had given formal recognition (Claude, 1969). Albanian schools and language materials remained suppressed, Albanian intellectuals, clergy and civic leaders were persecuted, and census figures were manipulated, with Albanians designated as Turks or Muslims (Prifti, 1978, p. 225).

The dispute over Kosovo was one reason that Albania did not settle its final borders with Yugoslavia until 1926 (Wolff, 1956, p. 139). By the Treaty of Tirana of that year, Italy and Albania acknowledged that any infringement of Albania's political, administrative or territorial integrity was contrary to their mutual political interest (RIIA, 1939, 89). In an annexed note to this treaty, Italy acquired the right to intevene

Box 7.1   *Kosovo: major characteristics*

Within the former Yugoslavia, Kosovo:

(a) was the least economically advanced region;
(b) had the highest rates of unemployment;
(c) enjoyed the lowest per capita incomes;
(d) suffered the highest illiteracy rates; and
(e) maintained the highest birth rates.

Indeed, Albanians in Kosovo enjoy the highest birth rate in Europe. Statistics derived from the only partially published 1991 census would be incomplete since the Albanians in both Kosovo and Macedonia boycotted the survey. The 1981 Yugoslav census figure of 1,730,879 ethnic Albanians is long out of date. The Albanians and other minorities in Yugoslavia long believed that official census figures systematically understated the true size of their respective groups. This problem has, however, been clouded further by the absence of tens of thousands of ethnic Albanian migrant workers away in Western Europe or further afield.

According to the 1981 census Serbs made up 13 per cent of the Kosovo population, a figure estimated to have been reduced to 10 per cent by the late 1980s due to both continuing emigration to Serbia proper and the much higher Albanian birth rate, which in 1987 was 27.4 per thousand compared to a figure of only 4.6 for Serbia proper and 7.1 for Yugoslavia as a whole. Local Albanians claimed that Serbs left due to the economic situation in Kosovo, with the unemployment rate having been approaching 50 per cent. Serbs claimed that emigration took place under Albanian pressure.

By 1987 the Serbian republic proper had a population of 5.57 million, compared to the next largest republic, Croatia with 4.44 million (see Table 7.1). 'Unitary' Serbia incorporating Kosovo and Vojvodina contained a population of 9.3 million, almost 42 per cent of the former Yugoslav total.

Albanians represented the third largest ethnic group in Yugoslavia at the point of that federation's disintegration, exceeded only by the Serbian and Croatian 'nations'. Yet Albanians were relegated to the legal status of 'nationality', even though they outnumbered four of the six official 'nations' (Slovenes, Montenegrins, Macedonians, Slavic Muslims). Thus, recognition as a 'nation' was an ethnic Albanian demand of the Belgrade authorities.

Unlike the Serbs, scattered around much of the former Yugoslav area, Albanians inhabit a compact region contiguous with Albania, albeit divided between three former republics. For Serbs, such contiguity has been a major factor inhibiting any significant devolution of power to the region: republican status was always seen as the thin end of a wedge ending in unification with Albania and the disintegration of Yugoslavia.

in the external or internal relations of Albania whenever the latter so requested. Four months later Yugoslavia broke off diplomatic relations with Albania and mobilisation took place on both sides of the border. As Albania became more dependent upon the Italians, so the Yugoslav state appeared to pursue more oppressive measures against its Albanian minority in Kosovo. Albanian landowners' estates were divided for Serb migrant settlers, an estimated 40,000 families of whom colonised the region in the wake of an agrarian reform programme. Written title deeds were demanded where tradition rather than documentation had previously

established possession of land for Albanians. In addition, many Albanians – as Muslims – were deported to Turkey: agreements between Yugoslavia and Turkey undertaken in 1926 and 1938 envisaged the transfer of up to 400,000 ethnic Albanians. Albania itself was too weak to respond.

The 1931 Yugoslav constitution reorganised the internal administrative structure of the country, dividing it into nine provinces (*banovine*), based on economic units and employing names of rivers, the stated purpose of which was to create a stronger sense of unity among the peoples of Yugoslavia by avoiding

Table 7.1 *Yugoslavia: regional differentiation, 1987*

	Population ('000s)	Per capita social product	Output per worker in social sector	Net personal income ('000 dinars)	Job-seekers as % of workforce in social sector
Kosovo	1,760	36	69	1,418	55.9
Slovenia	1,871	179	145	3,140	1.7
Croatia	4,437	117	106	2,208	7.7
Vojvodina	1,977	133	103	1,885	15.2
Bosnia and Hercegovina	4,155	80	85	1,736	23.9
Serbia*	5,574	94	93	1,846	17.7
Montenegro	604	80	90	1,522	24.5
Macedonia	1,954	75	75	1,399	27.0
Yugoslavia	22,332	100	100	2,045	16.2

Note: * Excluding Kosovo and Vojvodina.

Source: Magaš, 1993, p. 191, after Lydall, 1989.

distinctions based on ethnicity (Hondius, 1968, p. 106). But by trying to ignore the historic territorial divisions of national groups this policy merely stoked the fires of nationalist feeling, particularly amongst non-Serbs.

7.1.2 'Greater Albania'

Local Albanian beys countered Belgrade's policies by setting up the Kosovo Committee to promote the idea of a greater Albania and to encourage young men not to serve in the Yugoslav army. When Italy invaded Albania in April 1939 and established a protectorate in Tirana, the conquest placed the Italian dictator Benito Mussolini in a position to play godfather to a greater Albania when the Axis powers carved up Yugoslavia in the spring of 1941. He acquired not only Kosovo but Albanian inhabited parts of Montenegro and Macedonia, thus gaining for the new Albanian state considerable territory and about 700,000 new citizens (Wolff, 1956, p. 202). Significantly, the Italians opened a large number of Albanian language schools in Kosovo, the first since the end of Austrian occupation in 1918 (Logoreci, 1977, p. 70).

Although short-lived, this greater Albanian state left a lasting impression on nationally minded Albanians, establishing a precedent and inspiration, despite the unacceptable circumstances in which the union was undertaken (Figure 1.2). Following the Italian capitulation in September 1943, Germany took over Albania and gave 'ostentatious support' to Albanian nationalism and the cause of a greater Albania (Jelavich, 1983b, pp. 275, 298). The Germans also set up the Albanian SS Skanderbeg Division, which pursued a campaign for the expulsion and extermination of the Serbian population. At the same time, anti-communist forces in Kosovo met in Prizren and founded the Second League of Prizren for purposes of securing Kosovo's post-war union with Albania.

7.1.3 Mutual perfidy

Through the Jajce Declaration of 1943, under Tito's leadership, the Yugoslav communist partisans sought to assure Albanian nationals that after a communist victory, Yugoslavia would establish a federal constitution within which minorities would be granted full equality.

But over the new year period of 1943/4, at a local conference of the National Liberation Movement of Kosovo province, it was agreed that Kosovo could secede from Yugoslavia after liberation in order to join with Albania. Indeed, the Yugoslav Communist Party had made declarations to this effect previously in 1926 and 1940 (Pano, 1968, p. 40). However,

... it was only with the help of Albanian Partisans [on instructions from their leader Enver Hoxha] that Tito was able to 'pacify' Kosovo, killing in the process 'tens of thousands' of Kosovo Albanians. The emigres have called Hoxha's action a 'great betrayal' of the Albanians of Kosovo and contend that he and his coterie bear a heavy responsibility for the reversion of Kosovo to Yugoslav control at the end of the war. (Prifti, 1978, p. 229)

Thus, while both the pro- and anti-communist Kosovar Albanians wanted a union of their region with Albania, but were divided over the means of achieving that goal, the Albanian Communist Party revealed no visible interest in furthering these aims. The Yugoslav communist leaders were constrained by (Serb-led) nationalist feelings and the requirement to maintain Yugoslavia's pre-war boundaries (Shoup, 1968, pp. 75–7, 105; Jelavich, 1983b, p. 298). Hoxha later wrote that Tito had told him that 'Kosova and the other regions in Yugoslavia, inhabited by Albanians, belonged to Albania and should be returned to it', but that 'for the time being we cannot do this, because the Serbs would not understand us' (Hoxha, 1982b, pp. 284–6). Tito apparently had in mind some link between Kosovo and Albania within a larger Yugoslav-dominated Balkan federation.

On the Allied side, there was no recognised Albanian government-in-exile to plead the case for Kosovo (Zogu had been largely discredited by fleeing the country when the Italians invaded), and at their various conferences, the Allied leaders did not discuss the thorny question of redrawing political boundaries to better correspond to ethnic divisions. In Albania itself, the nationalist Balli Kombëtar resistance movement wanted to keep Kosovo, but by the end of the war it was Hoxha's partisans who controlled Albania.

7.1.4   Post-war Kosovo

The Yugoslav partisans took control of Kosovo after the German withdrawal from the area at the end of 1944. Massacres of Albanians by Serbs followed, apparently in reprisal for the earlier activities of the SS Skanderbeg Division (Jelavich, 1983b, p. 298). For the most part, minority groups throughout Yugoslavia had made a 'negligible' contribution to the partisan cause during the war, and it was especially difficult for Tito's representatives to recruit Albanians to their ranks. From December 1944 until the following summer Kosovo Albanians staged the only major example of an armed rebellion against Tito's government (Shoup, 1968, pp. 75–6, 104–5).

Under the federal constitution of post-war Yugoslavia, Kosovo was recognised as a separate administrative area within the Republic of Serbia, and was officially established as an autonomous region in September 1945. This represented, for the first time, the recognition of the Albanians within Yugoslavia as a distinct national group inhabiting a specific territory. Albanian schools were opened and the Albanian language was legally acknowleged; but Serbian remained supreme (King, 1973, pp. 134–6). Indeed, between 1945 and 1966, internal affairs minister and vice-president Aleksander Ranković exercised a ruthless control over Kosovo, viewing the Albanian minority as a political liability. This position was particularly heightened after Yugoslavia's expulsion from the Cominform in 1948, from which time the Tirana leadership could openly criticise the Yugoslav government, although Hoxha's call for an anti-Tito uprising and the union of Kosovo with Albania came to nothing.

With Stalin's backing (Artisien, 1984), the Albanian media now gave extensive coverage to the 'persecution' experienced by Albanians in Yugoslavia. While the arguments that were ranged against the Yugoslavs' treatment of their Albanian nationals were similar to those of the inter-war period, the territorial significance was that the federal Yugoslav state had divided its largest non-Slav group, and third largest ethnic group in the whole of country, into three separate administrative units, reminiscent of Ottoman practice. Despite inhabiting a geographically contiguous and relatively compact area, the country's Albanian minority was divided between the Kosovo region within Serbia, the republic of Montenegro to the north-west, and Macedonia to the south (Figure 1.1). Albanians within Kosovo were themselves politically divided, with officials following the Yugoslav line. This heightened the Tirana government's fear that Kosovo was being employed by the Yugoslavs as a centre for subversion against the Albanian state.

Rankovic's fall in 1966, and the demolition of his police state apparatus in Kosovo, was followed in 1968 by ethnic Albanian demonstrations in Kosovo and in the Tetovo area of Macedonia in favour of establishing an Albanian republic on an equal footing with the six South Slav republics in the Yugoslav federation (King, 1973, p. 140). The Belgrade government recognised the need to respond positively to such a situation. Ironically, these developments coincided with an improvement in Albanian-Yugoslav relations following the Warsaw Pact intervention in Czechoslovakia. As a consequence, by 1971, when full diplomatic relations had been restored, Kosovo had been converted 'from an ideological battleground to a bridge of co-operation' (Prifti, 1978, p. 233). Constitutional amendments in 1969 and 1971 provided for a greater degree of self-rule for Kosovo, and symbolically saw the official name for the region changed from the Serbian term Kosmet (Kosovo-Metohija). The 1969 constitutional amendments were particularly significant in two ways: (a) the birth of Kosovo was now described as 'the result of the common struggle of the peoples and nationalities of Yugoslavia during the National Liberation War', rather than the previous 'decision of the People's Assembly of the Republic of Serbia'; and, (b) the right of a republic under the 1963 Constitution to alter its boundaries – and by definition those of the autonomous regions within it – could no longer be undertaken without its citizens' consent (Artisien, 1984, p. 268).

In 1969 the essentially Albanian University of Priština was opened; and much wider opportunities in the arts and entertainment were given to the Albanian language and culture. A series of protocols were inaugurated in 1970 between the universities of Priština and Tirana, and large numbers of text books and substantial amounts of teaching materials found their way to Kosovo from Albania. Most notable in cementing cultural relations, in April 1968 a conference on language held in Priština resolved to abandon the use of the Geg dialect in literature in favour of the standardised Albanian adopted as the uniform mode by the Tirana government. The most important development took place in 1974, when the new Yugoslav constitution gave Kosovo a degree of autonomy *vis-à-vis* Serbia that was virtually equivalent to full independence as a separate republic, although the region fell short of republican status in name.

Despite the substantial development funds which were now flowing into the region from other parts of Yugoslavia, Kosovo remained the most backward component part of the federation, with the highest rates of unemployment, illiteracy and natural growth, and lowest per capita incomes. Albanians clearly lagged behind Serbs in competition for skilled jobs and top positions in industry and commerce. As the global oil crisis made itself felt, *Gastarbeiter* began returning home from Western Europe, reducing the flow of workers' remittances and placing further pressures on the local employment situation. From 1974 such tensions began to express themselves in more demonstrations and counter-imprisonments.

7.1.5 Post-Tito Yugoslavia

Tito's death in 1980 was a turning point: the departure of the great unifier and balancer of ethnic particularism also removed what many Kosovar Albanians saw as an insurance against Serb hegemonic aspirations. Serbian communist leaders now began to be more outspoken in their criticism of previous policies, with implicit emphasis being laid on the need for a stronger, more nationally important Serbia (Artisien, 1984). The following March saw ethnic Albanian demonstrations – initially localised in Priština over university conditions in student halls of residence and canteens. These soon escalated into ethnic riots and demands for the secession of Kosovo from Serbia. Yugoslav counter-measures were severely enforced, mostly by army units.

When the university was established, it had been envisaged that it would undertake teaching in both Albanian and Serbo-Croat on an equal basis, but with positive discrimination in admissions policy in favour of Albanians at a ratio of 34:1. With unemployment up to 20 per cent, and per capita funding from central government, the university roll had soon swollen to almost three times its planned size. After the 1981 disturbances some attempts to slim down the institution were made by gradually reducing admissions, but a decline in applications from non-Albanians was compensated for by Albanian school-leavers from Macedonia, despite the fact that Macedonia had two universities of its own (Anon, 1987b). The imbalance in favour of Albanians thereby became more marked.

Talks held between Albania and Yugoslavia on cultural agreements over the 1981–84 period floundered: Tirana argued that cultural exchanges should be limited to Kosovo, Montenegro and Macedonia. The Yugoslavs insisted that any co-operation should also benefit Slav minority groups in Albania. Tirana responded to this by claiming that Yugoslavia had suddenly created a 'Macedonian problem', given that the Albanian government was loath to admit to the need for any special treatment or recognition for its small ethnic Macedonian, Montenegrin and Serb populations.

From 1981 onwards there was a marked deterioration in the nature of Albanian-Yugoslav political relations, as the Yugoslav authorities reacted heavy-handedly to the Kosovo situation. Economic relations were, however, maintained, with Yugoslavia remaining Albania's most important trading partner, being responsible for about 17 per cent of the smaller country's trade.

Kosovo Albanian demands grew to that of republic status. The population size of the province was, after all, two-and-a-half times larger than that of the republic of Montenegro, and such status would represent the fulfilment of the commitment made during the war by the Yugoslav communist leadership. However, such demands were thwarted both by Serbian opposition – said to have persuaded Tito against such a move in 1968 – and by Kosovo's contiguity with Albania, suggesting that republican status would be merely the first step towards integration with Albania, and, ultimately, the disintegration of Yugoslavia.

The Tirana government's claimed position on Kosovo, was, despite Yugoslav accusations to the contrary: (a) not motivated by any irredentist claims on Kosovo or on any other part of Yugoslav territory (Alia, 1983); (b) as a defender of Albanian nationals from real or alleged discrimination and persecution by the Slav majority in Yugoslavia; and (c) to support (peacefully) the struggle of the Albanian minority in Yugoslavia for full national equality. As such, the Albanian government declared its wish to maintain normal relations with Yugoslavia, and did not, for example, raise the Kosovo issue at the United Nations or at any other international forum (Biberaj, 1985, p. 42). By contrast, the essentially anti-communist emigré community, regularly referring to 'enslaved Kossovo' (as in their *Albanian Resistance* news sheet), used the regional term to include those Albanians in adjacent Macedonia and Montenegro, and, arguing that Kosovo represented the 'other half' of Albania, contended that without Kosovo Albania could not be a viable nation (Prifti, 1978, p. 239).

Any notion of enlarging Albania would have been ideologically unacceptable to the communist Tirana government (Wiles, 1982), tinged with the memory of the fascist-inspired greater Albania of 1941–43. A union with Kosovo would have brought Albania more problems than it could have handled. Albanians in Yugoslavia represented the equivalent of almost two-thirds of the population of the Albanian state; they enjoyed higher standards of living, relative freedoms of movement and religious practice, and would have soon become dissatisfied and an uncomfortable source of unrest and instability.

In the wake of the 1981 riots and Yugoslav accusations of Albanian meddling in a neighbouring country's internal affairs, cultural ties between Kosovo and Tirana were cut by Belgrade; school and university text books from Albania were supplanted by Serbo-Croat works in Albanian translation (Artisien, 1984). Albania later claimed that the Yugoslavs had also deliberately delayed building their part of the railway line between Shkodër and Titograd (Podgorica) which was to provide the first fixed transport link between Albania and the outside world (Hall, 1984a, 1985, 1987b).

7.1.6 Post-Hoxha circumstances

Following Hoxha's death in 1985 and Tirana's gradual reversal of its isolationist stance, it was the Yugoslavs who began to feel that they were being misunderstood in the wider world. A key element, not only in Kosovo's future but in the subsequent rise of Serb nationalism and the eruption of the Yugoslav wars of succession, was the publication of a draft Memorandum prepared in 1985 by a working group of the Serbian Academy of Arts and Sciences. In setting out a nationalistic Serb attack on the nature of Yugoslavia, this Memorandum argued that: (a) the federal government had discriminated against Serbia in the economic field, and this had arisen from the fact that, following the fall of Ranković, Yugoslavia had been run by two non-Serbs — Tito, a Croat, and the Slovene Edvard Kardelj — to the economic benefit of their respective republics; (b) the partition of Serbia into three parts under Tito's 1974 constitutuion — Serbia proper and the autonomous provinces of Vojvodina and Kosovo — had to be reversed; and (c) Kosovar Albanians were pursuing anti-Serb policies which had to be terminated (Cviic, 1991, p. 65; Magaš, 1993, p. 199). Published just as Slobodan Milošević was consolidating power, the Memorandum found the Serbian Communist Party split on how to cope with domestic nationalism: an absence of condemnation from the highest political circles implied tacit support and also stifled internal discussion.

Serb officials now argued that Albanian propaganda and 'misinformation' had encouraged a distorted foreign media coverage of events in Kosovo (Zanga, 1987). Belgrade appeared to be particularly upset by an editorial in the Tirana Party daily, defending Tito's legacy and name from what it claimed to be 'the Serbian unitarist lobby'. But Albania continued to declare that destabilisation of Yugoslavia was not its aim:

As Yugoslavia's neighbours, and also very much interested not only in the fate of our Albanian brothers but also in the peace and security in the Balkans, we do not want under any circumstances a deterioration of the situation in Yugoslavia and its destabilisation. (*Zëri i Popullit*, 27 October 1987)

At the February 1988 Belgrade Balkan Foreign Ministers Conference, Albania's Reis Malile rejected any foreign intervention in Kosovo and dismissed the need for boundary changes (Steen, 1988). Indeed, prior to the conference a cultural agreement had been signed between the two parties in Tirana, such that state relations between Albania and Yugoslavia now actually appeared to be better than relations between Albanians and Serbs within Yugoslavia.

While Islamic fundamentalism had not yet posed major problems within Yugoslavia, the Kosovo Albanian daily *Rilindja* criticised the pro-Albanian irredentist stand taken by a number of Iranian newspapers, most notably the *Teheran Times* and *Kejhan International*. The majority of Kosovo's two million Albanians are Muslim (with about 60,000 Roman Catholic) and had enjoyed relative religious freedom, with substantial numbers making the annual pilgrimage to Mecca. Iranian papers argued that the Albanians were under permanent police 'oppression' and that hundreds were jailed. They did, however, rely on Amnesty International reports, which, the Yugoslav press was quick to point out, the Iranians themselves had rejected when 'Iranian crimes against human rights' had been spotlighted. Iran's support for Albanian nationalism was, of course, motivated by religious rather than any ideological considerations. Indeed, it was particularly ironic given that Tirana's policies on religion at the time would have found little sympathy in Teheran, although both countries appeared to be in 'revolutionary solidarity' in their opposition to the activities of the superpowers (Zanga 1986b).

As noted in section 1.1.3 above, the crucial historic-cultural role played by Kosovo for both Albanians and Serbs renders this piece of Balkan territory an irreconcilably contested source of national identities and a potentially explosive source of conflict in a region of upheaval. Until the end of 1989, Albanian national identity had been perceived and expressed rather differently by: (a) the Albanian state; (b) Albanians in Yugoslavia; and (c) Albanian emigrés. With the coincidence of the violent disintegration of Yugoslavia, Serbian impositions on Kosovo, the democratisation and opening up of Albania, and general instability within the Balkans, the perceptions of all three have now largely converged.

7.2 Change and upheaval in Yugoslavia

7.2.1 Milošević

The meteoric rise to power in Serbia of Slobodan Milošević was based on his belligerent nationalism and the need to subjugate Kosovo to Serbian authority, although he was never too specific on detail:

If the Memorandum provided a theoretical basis for Serbian reassertion . . . action was provided by Slobodan Milosevic, who became Serbia's party leader in 1986 . . . . Within a year he was proclaimed as the right man to lead . . . the third Serbian uprising . . . . (Cviic, 1991, p. 66)

In a 1988 speech Milošević promised that the Serbs would 'win the battle' for Kosovo regardless of internal and external obstacles (Szulc, 1992). This was to be a watershed both for the ethnic Albanian role in Yugoslavia and for the very existence of Yugoslavia itself.

With growing crises in the country — runaway inflation, strikes (over a thousand in 1987), and financial scandals such as that surrounding the state-run Agrokomerc firm (caught issuing $1 billion worth of false promissory notes) — political diversions were required. Upon consolidating his power, Milošević began to whittle away the rights of both

of Serbia's autonomous provinces, Kosovo and Vojvodina. His placing both under closer Serbian control (initially in police, judicial and economic planning matters), stimulated major protests, including a general strike in Kosovo (February 1989) and mass desertions from the Yugoslav Communist Party there. Tirana found itself being drawn more intimately into the Kosovo problem in order to protect its brethren against 'greater Serb hegemony'.

Somewhat defensively, Belgrade officials pointed out that Kosovo's development had been a national priority: during the period 1983–87, for example, the public sector alone had created more than 27,000 jobs, mostly in newly built factories. But Kosovo had not sufficiently realised its own human and natural resources, such as investment in the region's irrigation systems. In 1988 Kosovo received the largest share — 48.1 per cent — of the Federal Development Fund, representing regional aid to Kosovo equivalent to approximately $1 million daily. Further, Kosovo had been released from the obligation of repaying some foreign loans, and had been granted additional aid to help insolvent banks and enterprises. Yet, according to *Tanjug*, Yugoslavia's central news agency, the structure of the Kosovo economy had changed little. The exceptionally high birth rate was seen as a major problem by Belgrade: here was a backward area — albeit a Serbian cultural hearth — now inhabited by alien people who could not, or would not, share Serb values and aspirations. Why, therefore, the Serbs argued, should the Albanian Kosovars be given privileges and be heavily subsidised for their fecklessness?

In mid-1990 Serbian authorities effectively abolished the Kosovo provincial government and legislature and introduced a series of amendments to the Serbian constitution that effectively removed the legal basis for Kosovo's autonomy. Substantial suppression followed (Box 7.2). The Albanians refuted the legality of the Serbian moves, and their democratically elected legislature and government went underground. In September 1990 the legislators met in secret in the town of Kacanik and approved a constitution that gave Kosovo republican status within the Yugoslav federation. Meanwhile,

Box 7.2 *Serbian impositions on Kosovo*

1. The police, local government, hospitals, higher education, hotels, newspapers and radio, and most state factories were placed in Serbian hands. In August 1990 the Serbian Parliament ordered the closure of Kosovo's leading daily newspaper *Rilindja* ('renewal'), on the grounds that it published anti-Serbian propaganda. This was followed by the closure of other Albanian language publications and the cessation of radio and television broadcasts in Albanian (apart from two ten-minute evening news bulletins), rendering 1,300 ethnic Albanian journalists unemployed. Radio and television broadcasts from Tirana were jammed. A revived *Rilindja* was subsequently published by emigrés in Switzerland and smuggled into Kosovo.
2. By autumn 1992 at least 100,000 Albanians had lost their public sector jobs over the past two years for political reasons (including 800 of Priština university's 900 academics), out of a total workforce of 240,000, throwing many families back onto dependence upon remittances from the diaspora.
3. Albanians were banned from holding public meetings and enjoyed no access to courts.
4. Most of the province's former parliamentary and government members fled abroad following the 1989 Serbian impositions.
5. The security forces heavily armed the Serbian and Montenegrin populations. Following Macedonia's declaration of independence in November 1991, Serbian troops were withdrawn from that republic and relocated in Kosovo. All major towns – Priština, Peć, Prizren, Djakovica and Kosovska Mitrovica – became garrisoned with a full range of armour and artillery which could be deployed swiftly.
6. Albanian monuments were torn down.
7. Serbian supplanted Albanian as the official language of Kosovo. Latin alphabet Albanian street names were replaced by Cyrillic Serbian ones. Priština university was renamed after Dositej Obradovic, a late eighteenth-century, early-nineteenth-century Serbian scholar.
8. Serbian and Albanian schools were segregated. A Serbian curriculum was introduced into the schools in 1991: at least 6,000 Albanian teachers were dismissed by the Serbian authorities for refusing to give up the Albanian curriculum. In turn, 450,000 pupils and students at all levels boycotted classes and started attending private schools set up by the unemployed teachers who were paid DM20 per month with contributions from Kosovar Albanians working in Germany and Switzerland. Attendance and good performance at these 'national' schools became a point of Albanian pride in the eyes of parents and pupils alike.
9. Albanians were encouraged to leave Kosovo. Some observers argued that the Serbian government had a long-term plan to deport 120,000 Kosovar Albanians who were considered to have settled there since the Second World War, in addition to any aspirations to undertake militarily inspired 'ethnic cleansing'.
10. By autumn 1992 the Serbian branch of the International Red Cross had confirmed that there were plans to settle 140,000 Serbian refugees in Kosovo; 3,000 had been moved there already in addition to about 4,000 Serb settlers organised by *Bozur*, the Serb organisation set up in the 1980s to oversee the resettlement of Kosovo by Serbs, with offers of subsidised employment and free housing. In practice, more Serbs had actually left than had settled in Kosovo in recent years.
11. In October 1992, UN human rights envoy Tadeusz Mazowiecki warned that the human rights of Kosovo's Albanian majority were being 'systematically violated' by the Serbian authorities. He called for the establishment of a 'joint Albanian-Serbian group under international auspices'. The Albanians agreed to his suggestion, but local Serbian officials said they had no authority to do so.

Sources: Vjesnik 21 December 1991, 2 January 1992; *East European Newsletter*, 21 September 1992, p. 3; *The Economist*, 1 August 1992; Moore, 1992a, 1992b; *RFE/RL Daily Report*, 24 September 1992, p. 4; *RFE/RL Research Report*, 30 October 1992, p. 70; *Reuter*, 10 August 1992; Tanner, 1992; Tihon, 1992; Zanga, 1992a.

Serbs crudely attempted to portray Albania as a Muslim country, detached from Europe, in an attempt to present the Albanian movement in Kosovo as fundamentalist.

7.2.2 Mutual fears

While ethnic Albanians had been reasonably successful in private business in Kosovo, most Serbs had been employed in the state sector by some 350 inefficient enterprises. These companies and the government itself were run by officials from Belgrade who had little intention of putting down roots in Kosovo. Anger against these 'carpetbaggers' was such that Kosovo Serbs themselves petitioned to demand more qualified and honest officials (*Frankfurter Allgemeine Zeitung*, 14 January 1992). This was exacerbated by the commonly felt belief amongst Kosovo Serbs that substantial numbers of Albanians were illegal immigrants from Albania, or their descendants, and should be deported.

For their part, Kosovo Albanians feared that the Serbian authorities wished to extend their 'ethnic cleansing' policy to make way for 300,000 refugee Serbs from Croatia and Bosnia. It was becoming increasingly unlikely that former autonomy could be restored or republican status achieved within a rump Yugoslavia, given events in Croatia and Bosnia. Following the September 1991 referendum, therefore, unification of all ethnic Albanian lands of the former Yugoslavia into a new, compact political entity, appeared an emerging possibility, with several likely alternative situations:

(a) within a confederal (rump) Yugoslavia, which appeared to be increasingly unlikely; or,

(b) outside a Yugoslav state, which would pose problems of vulnerability from an increasingly belligerent Serbia (and Montenegro). Ibrahim Rugova, chairman of the leading Albanian party in Kosovo, the Democratic Alliance, argued that the only solution was to establish an internationally recognised, neutral, independent, and democratic

republic that would guarantee the rights of minorities and strive for good neighbourly relations. A special 'extraterritorial' statute could be enacted to protect Serbian monuments and churches in Kosovo, and the region could be proclaimed a demilitarised zone (Zanga, 1992f); or,

(c) as part of a greater Albania, an option which, with political and economic change in Tirana, was looking a far less impossible proposition than hitherto. Albania had become a member of CSCE and would be in a position to argue the case for a greater Albania within that international forum if necessary. Prior to the Democrats' victory in the 1992 Albanian general election, the prime minister of the underground Kosovo government argued that a united Albanian state was unlikely before the year 2000, but that it was only natural for Albanians to want to live together. By contrast, the nationalist Albanian General Party, founded in Kosovo in 1991 and claiming 95,000 members, called for the unification of Kosovo with Albania and with other Albanian territories.

As one commentator has put it;

So what is it Albanians want? The answer, whether in Kosovo, Albania or Macedonia, rarely differs. They want to live as one people. However, they couch this ideal in obfuscating phraseology (McDowall, 1993, p. 12).

For their part, Serb arguments also varied. They included the following:

(a) Kosovo was an integral part of Serbia and the Kosovar question was strictly an internal affair of the republic;

(b) some Serbs suggested that Kosovo be split and that Serbia be allowed to hold onto a strip of land bordering Serbia where most Serbian churches and monasteries are located; and

(c) more extreme approaches, such as that of the Serbian Radical Party, called for the forcible removal of all Albanians to 'their mother country' (*Die Tageszeitung*, 11 May 1992).

Box 7.3 *Albanians in Macedonia*

The largest Albanian population outside Kosovo is in western Macedonia, part of a strategic area controlling north–south routes through the Balkan mountains, where the 1912 and 1913 Balkan wars began. Endless arguments surround the size of the minority: the boycotted census of 1991 recorded 429,562 Albanians or 21 per cent of the Macedonian population. Albanians themselves claim to make up between 35 per cent and 48 per cent of the population. The true figure has potentially crucial constitutional implications.

Albanians form an outright majority in the Tetovo and Gostivar communities, make up roughly half of the population in Kičevo and Debar (Dibër), and constitute a large minority in Struga and Kumanovo. These communities form a compact unit that borders on Kosovo and Albania. While they never enjoyed broad autonomy like the Kosovars, what rights Macedonia's Albanian community did have were placed in jeopardy by the rise of Macedonian nationalism in the late 1980s.

One of the first developments to receive widespread publicity was the Macedonian authorities' decision to pull down the walls that Albanians traditionally erect around their houses for protection and for drying tobacco. In later moves, teachers lost their jobs for using Albanian in class, and Albanian language television was limited to 20 minutes a day.

For their part, Macedonians have feared Albanian secession which would render Macedonia even smaller and poorer. Albanians, with the republic's highest birth rate, have felt that they have been treated unfairly. Although the Party for Democratic Prosperity took the Albanian vote in the 1990 elections, and Albanians were represented by 23 deputies in Macedonia's 120-seat parliament, the Macedonian authorities responded by imposing direct rule from Skopje in Tetovo and Gostivar. The Albanians boycotted the September 1991 referendum on Macedonian independence and campaigned against the new Macedonian draft constitution which rendered Albanians at best one of several tolerated minorities, alongside Turks, Bulgars, Greeks, Serbs, Jews and Gypsies. (This mix has led to both the French and Italians adopting the name *Macedonia* for their fruit salads) The Albanians demanded instead that their political, linguistic, and cultural rights be defined in an article explicitly recognising their status as a people equal to the Macedonian nation. The Macedonian authorities amended the final version of the new state's constitution by replacing the term 'national state of the Macedonian nation' with the more neutral 'civil state', and in April 1993 Albania followed the United Nations in formally recognising the *Former Yugoslav Republic of Macedonia*.

Controversy over the actual size of the Albanian population in Macedonia has been fuelled by the influx of large numbers of Kosovars fleeing Serbian oppression, at the same time as most of the 130,000 ethnic Albanian workers in Croatia, many from Macedonia, have returned home. An internationally monitored census was scheduled for April 1994.

Sources: Perry, 1992, 1993; Smith, 1992; Szulc, 1992; Poulton, 1993.

On 17 January 1992, Alia met with a delegation from the 'Republic of Kosova' and, arguing that Yugoslavia had now ceased to exist, claimed that Tirana was, therefore, interfering in nobody's affairs by demanding for ex-Yugoslav Albanians all national and human rights and freedoms which should belong to a large and homogenous national community. Coming from Hoxha's Communist successor, this was not a little ironic. The Democrats had already endorsed an eventual 'democratic' union with Kosovo in their initial 1990 programme. In July 1991 the Albanian parliament had passed a cross-party resolution warning that 'the whole Albanian nation' would respond to 'genocide' against the Kosovars. After coming to power in Tirana in 1992, the Democrats reiterated their position.

As in Bosnia, however, any conflict in Kosovo would see a massacre of the local Albanians, since they had so few arms in comparison with the Serbs. Albania itself would be able to offer little formal military assistance.

Box 7.4   *Albanians in 'Yugoslavia': political awakening*

Kosovar 'independence'
In September 1991, Kosovo Albanians voted in a referendum to endorse overwhelmingly the Kacanik constitution drafted a year earlier: 98 per cent of registered Albanian voters turned out, despite a heavy Serbian police presence, and backed a 'sovereign and independent' Kosovo with 99.7 per cent of the vote.

In the next month, the legislature met and declared Kosovo a 'sovereign and independent state'. This was recognised by Albania but by no other state. In December, Kosovo appealed to the EC to extend recognition, even though Brussels had made it clear that in its view Kosovo, unlike Slovenia, Croatia and Bosnia-Hercegovina, was not a Yugoslav republic and hence ineligible for consideration as an independent state. By February 1992 Albanian organisers claimed to have collected half-a-million signatures on a petition to the UN Commission on Human Rights protesting about the situation in Kosovo. Could it now be argued realistically that a six million-strong Albanian nation would provide for a more balanced Balkans?

On 24 May 1992 the Albanians of Kosovo took part in elections for a breakaway parliament and president. Serbian police intervention meant that voting was forced to take place in homes and mosques, with the support of a wide range of groups including the Prizren Women's Forum. The election headquarters in Priština was a tiny cabin in a car park. This was the only place in Kosovo where Albanians were legally permitted to meet.

Albanian referendum in Macedonia
Revisions to the new Macedonian constitution did not go far enough to appease most Albanians, who called a referendum on 'territorial and political autonomy' on 11 and 12 January 1992. While community leaders supported an independent Macedonia, they insisted the constitution be redrafted to grant Albanians the status of a nation (Box 7.3 above). Albanian organisers claimed a 75 per cent turn-out for the referendum, despite police attempts at intimidation, and a vote of over 90 per cent had approved the proposal. Some urban Albanians felt, however, not only that formal autonomy was unnecessary, and that disharmony between Macedonians and Albanians only helped the Serbs, but that Macedonia's Albanians should serve as a link between that republic and Kosovo. Further, Albanian entrepreneurs had much to gain from the Macedonian privatisation process, which a World Bank report in August had applauded as 'a well thought-out economic programme under most severe circumstances'.

Albanian referendum in southern Serbia
On 1 and 2 March 1992 a referendum was held in the Presevo, Bujanovac and Medvedja communities of southern Serbia bordering Kosovo. In this vote 99.94 per cent of the 'citizens' opted for political and territorial autonomy. The chairman of the electoral commission, Professor Ibrahim Kadriu said that the option for joining Kosovo was now on the agenda.

Albanians in Montenegro
Albanians in the Montenegrin communities of Ulcinj, Plavlje and Gusinje, which border on northern Albania, called for their own referendum in March 1992. A meeting of the Democratic Forum of Albanians (members of the republic's third largest political party, the Albanian Democratic Alliance) in August 1992 in Ulcinj reaffirmed the need to hold a referendum as soon as possible, but it was unclear as to whether the forum, seeking autonomy to preserve the national identity of the Albanians, was proposing cultural or political autonomy. Albanians represent about 8.5 per cent of the population of Montenegro.

Sources: EEN, 21 September 1992, p. 4; *Frankfurter Allgemeine Zeitung* 17 March 1992; Miljovski, 1992, p. 51; Tanner, 1992; Poulton, 1993.

7.3 The international imbroglio

7.3.1 Sanctions against Serbia

Two months after UN sanctions were imposed on Serbia and Montenegro in June 1992, the Serbian media were making much of the claim that the Kosovar economy had been particularly inconvenienced: more than half of the work-force in the province's 26 major enterprises had been laid off, with combines suffering from shortages of raw materials, fuel and components.

In November 1992, the White House, no doubt mindful of the increasingly vociferous ethnic Albanian lobby in America, decided that the United States must act to check any Serbian moves against Kosovo, fearing that as many as 1.5 million ethnic Albanians in the province would flee south through Macedonia and into Greece. Athens had privately warned that under such circumstances it would send troops north into Macedonia to block the flow of refugees, a decision that could trigger military intervention by Turkey, Bulgaria and Albania (Poot *et al.*, 1992). Prior to this, Washington and major European capitals had appeared to view the Kosovo question merely as a human rights or minority problem. But the emergence and spread of the Serbian initiated conflict in the former Yugoslavia had placed the issue of Serbian repression in Kosovo in a new light, with the result that both the EC and the US had begun to put diplomatic pressure on Kosovo and economic pressure on Albania to refrain from belligerent actions (Zanga, 1992f).

In early October, a joint congressional commission had already approved a $5 million aid package for Kosovo alongside one of $20 million for Bosnia-Hercegovina. By this action, Albania argued that the US was *de facto* recognising the independence of Kosovo.

Turkey was also favourably disposed towards the predominantly Muslim Kosovars, but refrained from taking an official position on the question of independence, wishing to avoid stoking the fires of an already volatile situation. Ankara was particularly concerned to prevent any conflict spilling over into Albania. In late July 1992, Turkey and Albania signed a defence co-operation agreement, which was promoted in September with an official visit to Turkey by the head of the Albanian general staff (*ATA*, 24 September 1992). Together with joint economic pacts, this agreement was signed at a time of increasing diplomatic and military rivalry between Athens and Ankara in the region, and allowed Albania to deploy newly trained infantry and armoured units along its northern and eastern border areas adjoining Montenegro and Kosovo, and potentially along its southern border with Greece.

Rome remained conspicuously silent on the Kosovar question, despite having expressed concern over the potentially explosive situation. Tirana tried to scare the Italians by alluding to the possible consequences of the conflict in Kosovo including triggering another mass exodus of Albanians to Italy. Conflict in Kosovo would see large numbers of Albanian Kosovars flooding Albania, exacerbating social tension there and possibly prompting more Albanians to flee across the Adriatic (Zanga, 1992f).

7.3.2 What's in a name?

In response to the perceived usurpation of an exclusively Greek name by the former Yugoslav republic, Greece joined Serbia in imposing an economic blockade on Macedonia. As early as September 1992, Macedonia's only oil refinery had been shut down as the result of 70,000 tonnes of crude oil being blocked at the Greek port of Thessaloniki, a vital lifeline for Macedonia. Greeks were increasingly apprehensive concerning the growth of Macedonian nationalist 'protection committees', which recalled the much feared pre-war IMRO terrorist organisation. If conflict developed in Macedonia it would devastate the Greek tourist industry, one of the country's economic mainstays, even if conflict did not stray across the border.

Albanian riots in Skopje in early November 1992, which ended in four dead and 35 wounded after police opened fire, were seen by many Macedonians as a dress rehearsal for an uprising. The demonstrations had developed

213

after news spread that an ethnic Albanian youth arrested for cigarette smuggling had been badly beaten by the police (*RFE/RL Daily Report*, 11 November 1992). Four days later, Nevsat Halili, leader of the Party for Democratic Prosperity (PDP), the main Albanian political party of Macedonia, addressed the EC and demanded it withhold recognition of Macedonian independence because of the human rights situation there. The Greeks made much of this, taking out full-page advertisements in the British broadsheet press and quoting the ethnic Albanian position to support their argument for not recognising Macedonia (Konstantinidis, 1992).

Given the dismal state of the Serbian economy, Milošević proposed in June 1992 a Serbian-Greek confederation. This included suggestions that they could share the partition of their common neighbour (*Frankfurter Allgemeine Zeitung*, 20 June 1992; *The Wall Street Journal*, 26 June 1992): certainly, with Serbia and Greece physically separated by Macedonia, closer ties between the two would be inevitably at their common neighbour's expense. Under these circumstances, the Macedonians appreciated that the main threat to their new state came not from Albanians, but from Serbia and Greece. As a consequence, the Macedonian leadership undertook to promote dialogue not only with its own Albanians, but also with those of Kosovo and Albania proper, which, for their part, largely shared the view that a Macedonian-Albanian conflict would benefit only Serbia and perhaps Greece. Certainly Kosovar Albanians were conscious of keeping the questions of Kosovo and Macedonia separate. Albania and Macedonia pledged in June 1992 to establish a 'model relationship' based on open borders and economic co-operation (*EEN*, 21 September 1992, p. 5).

7.3.3   Turkey and the Islamic world

Turkey's size, wealth, ties with Balkan Muslims, position *vis-à-vis* Greece and its political resurgence within the new world disorder provided it with a critical role in the region. Not least in

importance was the fact that over two million people of Bosnian Muslim origin were living in Turkey as the result of migrations which took place from 1878 until well after the end of World War II. However, Turkey was also faced with several other pressing concerns: its own Kurdish population, the Cyprus situation, and its rapidly growing role in former Soviet Central Asia, particularly in its attempts to offset Iranian influence there.

A special meeting of the foreign ministers of the Islamic Conference Organisation (ICO) was held in Istanbul in June 1992 to discuss the situation in Bosnia-Hercegovina. The ICO, founded in 1971, has limited practical possibilities as an organisation, but it does provide a forum within which 46 Islamic countries are able to air their views on issues of importance to the Muslim world. The conference blamed Belgrade for the massacres of Muslims in Bosnia and Hercegovina, and called on the UN Security Council to consider military intervention if sanctions did not work. It also urged ICO members to place troops at the UN's disposal for such an operation, and set up a 'development bank' to help the victims of the conflict and assist the reconstruction of towns and settlements (*Frankfurter Allgemeine Zeitung*, 20 June 1992).

Turkish diplomacy also brought leaders of 11 countries of the 'Black Sea region' to Istanbul to sign a general agreement on economic co-operation. The Black Sea regional concept placed Turkey firmly in the centre of a new post-Cold War grouping which, in the longer term, could go some way towards helping to stabilise the Balkans, although the group's initial aims were essentially economic. Clearly, here was a useful ally for Albania in a very uncertain Balkan climate.

7.3.4   Panic buttoned

In the lead up to the December 1992 Serbian presidential elections, in which the 'Yugoslav' prime minister, Milan Panic was challenging Slobodan Milošević, the former made a number of statements concerning Kosovo which he was subsequently unable to support in deeds. Panic visited Kosovo and spoke to Kosovar Albanian leaders while in London. He assured them that his government would restore the province's self-governing status, which it had lost in 1990. In talks with the Albanian prime minister in Tirana in August, Panic claimed that he would lift the state of emergency in Kosovo to coincide with a Greek-Yugoslav plan for an international conference on Kosovo. But Serbian political parties criticised him for not consulting with them and rejected the idea of a conference.

Following two days of demonstrations by ethnic Albanians in Kosovo in October 1992 calling for the restoration of Albanian language teaching, Panic agreed to open primary and secondary schools in early November, as he accompanied international mediators Cyrus Vance and David Owen through Kosovo. Panic admitted that Albanians had been 'locked out' of Serbian political life and stressed the need to remedy this situation, step by step. Owen argued that while Kosovar Albanians should not demand independence, they should receive back the autonomy that Milošević had removed from them.

Panic was heavily defeated in the subsequent elections, and was forced to resume his life in the United States. The Serb grip on Kosovo tightened.

PART IV

Albania into the twenty-first century

8

Economic restructuring

8.1 Framework for restructuring

8.1.1 Tinkering not restructuring

In the second half of the 1980s, the Albanian leadership began to tinker with the country's economic mechanisms in an attempt to render an anachronistic system less inefficient – just as the Soviet-bloc European states had done, to little effect, when their economies began to run out of steam in the 1960s.

In June 1989 financial organisations were instructed to undertake closer and more thorough audits at production centres in order to attain greater productivity and lower rates of raw material consumption. Included in this new emphasis were exhortations to reduce construction and lead-in times for new developments, and to extend import substitution. In fact, notions of recycling and import substitution had been prevalent for at least a decade and a half: 'no import without export' had become a familiar slogan on hoardings throughout the country. Responsibility for organising 43 per cent of plan requirements in agriculture now passed from central to district authorities, in order to encourage local initiative and attune planning more closely to local conditions. This development followed trial experiments in Elbasan, Përmet and Lushnjë districts, and was seen as an important step in establishing a better equilibrium within the economic planning system.

But the world was moving faster than Albania, and events in the rest of Eastern Europe shook the country's leadership out of its torpor: policy statements made during the first half of 1990 not only further tinkered with the economic system but, more dramatically, also promised changes in the political and judicial system. Ever since the mid-1970s, increased centralisation and loss of external support, following the rupture in relations with China, had exacerbated the inevitable decline in the country's economic circumstances. The social and political structure had become sclerotic, a condition reinforced by the hermetically sealed nature of Albanian life. Now, both international and domestic circumstances were to contrive to bring an unprecedented sense of urgency to the country's leadership:

1. The economic transition now being experienced by Albania's major Eastern European economic partners required those countries to begin trading for hard currency. Some 60 per cent of Albanian trade had been with CMEA member countries, and a considerable burden would now be placed upon the country's meagre financial resources, unless symmetrical counter-trade

arrangements could be continued, or certain imports curtailed.

2. There was an overriding need to forestall major unrest which was now being encouraged by the success of democracy movements elsewhere in Eastern Europe as transmitted daily into people's homes through the medium of their television sets (see section 8.3.3 below).

3. With well over 80 per cent of Albania's electricity normally being hydro-generated, several winters of virtual drought had brought half of the country's industry to a standstill. A 1990 decree permitting state employees to be paid 80 per cent of their wages if they were made unavoidably idle due to raw material or energy shortages only encouraged further plant closures. Irrigation for agriculture had also been disrupted such that food shortages began to affect urban areas. As early as 1988 a number of urban demonstrations had erupted in response to a disruption in food supplies.

4. Depressed world commodity prices had severely affected the country's main exports of chrome, copper and nickel, the output of which was already constrained by poor productivity and bad management.

5. Following the minor liberalisation of trade in 1988, an active management of foreign reserves became necessary. However, staff of the foreign exchange department of the State Bank became over-enthusiastic. They traded wildly on the spot money market and took positions of up to $2,000 million (with the country's annual export earnings at little more than $100 million). Inevitably, these inexperienced traders lost a disastrous $170 million during 1989 and 1990, forcing Albania to curtail all foreign payments in January 1991 (Åslund and Sjöberg, 1991, pp. 11–12; *Zëri i Popullit*, 25 June, 28 June, 1991; *Bashkimi*, 1 August 1991).

8.1.2   A new economic mechanism?

What was to become known as the New Economic Mechanism (NEM) was announced in May 1990. An emphasis was to be placed upon improving the existing economic system by introducing elements of self-financing to enterprises. Within the continuing framework of five-year and annual economic plans, changes would now include the provision of enhanced material incentives at the workplace, a gradual transition to enterprise self-sufficiency, greater freedom for agricultural enterprises to sell their surpluses, and improved provision for individual self-build housing, in a climate of persisting housing shortage. Initially this reform would be limited to 94 industrial and 100 agricultural enterprises, but would be extended to the rest of the economy in 1991 (EIU, 1990e, pp. 12, 40).

This was followed in July 1990 by the legalisation of private handicrafts and family trade businesses. Craftsmen and tradesmen would be allowed to set up private businesses at home, in the street or in shops. They would be able to set their own prices and seek their own suppliers, but would not be able to employ anyone outside of their own families. By the autumn some 150 small businesses had begun operating privately in the capital, and at year's end it was being claimed that there were some 1,500 private entrepreneurs operating in the country, with around 7,000 privatised service units including fruit and vegetable traders, butchers and restaurants as well as craftsmen (Haastad, 1990).

In March 1991, less than two weeks before Albania's first multi-party general election, prime minister Fatos Nano pronounced that he and other top officials of the PLA now saw private enterprise as the only salvation for the country's economy. The government passed a decree preparing the way for a privatisation programme in industry and agriculture. In the latter case it wanted farming in the fertile lowlands to be partly private and partly collective, but accepted that agriculture in Albania's highlands should be fully privatised.

Quickly brought down by strikes, the last communist government gave way to a coalition which proceeded to embark on market-led reforms. A land law was passed to distribute parcels of land to private farmers, and some prices were liberalised, immediately causing a sharp rise in inflation.

8.1.3 The parameters of restructuring

In Albania's planned economy, money, prices, costs, interest rates and microeconomic considerations had played a very minor role (Kornai, 1980, 1982; Kowalski, 1983, 1987; Funck and Kowalski, 1987). Enterprises' behaviour was influenced primarily by the existence of 'soft' budgets, permitting them to disregard both the financial aspects of their activities and the markets for their output. Restructuring needs to include the 'hardening' of these budget constraints, and a change in the ways in which economic actors perceive the role of financial levers in the functioning of the economy.

The major elements of economic restructuring are: (a) privatisation: removing predominant state ownership of fixed assets, formulating bankruptcy laws and establishing stock exchange activities (Kowalski, 1990; Lipton and Sachs, 1991; Milanovic, 1991); (b) eliminating the planning apparatus and institutions administering the traditional economic system; (c) introducing currency convertibility related to a market-based reform of the price system; (d) establishing a private banking system; (e) introducing a tax system commensurate with a market economy; and (f) reforming the laws governing the activities of foreign capital and of the regulations on foreign trade.

Across Central and Eastern Europe major impediments to restructuring were arising due to the attitudes of economic actors steeped in decades of central planning, and from the absence of the institutional and legal frameworks that formed the organic fabric of market economies in the West (Kowalski, 1991). While such constraints have been substantial in Central Europe, for the Balkans in general, and Albania in particular, long isolated from the West, insulated from the world economy and with significantly less advanced human skill resources, they have posed greater and more complicated problems.

As the most critical of economic restructuring processes, privatisation encompasses three processes: (a) the transfer of ownership of such enterprises as small shops, repair workshops and the like, from the state or local authorities to the private sector: small privatisation; (b) although a major issue in agricultural land redistribution, reprivatisation is of little significance in the Albanian industrial and service sectors as relatively few businesses existed in the 1930s and 1940s to be expropriated by the communists; and (c) large privatisation, transferring the ownership of large, mainly industrial, enterprises, presents major and sometimes insurmountable problems. Grossly inefficient throughout Central and Eastern Europe, in terms of both technology and manpower, plants such as the Elbasan metallurgical complex have been burdened with extremely high overhead costs. While theoretically providing a source of employment for large numbers of people, and dominating local employment structures, often working conditions for employees have been lamentable (section 5.2.2). Externally, enormous environmental damage has been caused by these combines, with often high levels of atmospheric emissions and water-borne waste discharges polluting the very residential and recreational environments in which the plants' workers and their families live, work and rest.

Gramoz Pashko (1991, 1993b), one of the first people in the country to have an appreciation of Western economics, as deputy leader of the Democratic Party and the architect of reform within the coalition government, looked to the Polish model for inspiration. Consequently, the June 1991 economic programme of the Albanian government set itself the task of following the conventional wisdom acquired from the experience of the stabilisation programmes of Poland, Czechoslovakia and Bulgaria (Åslund and Sjöberg, 1991; see also Lipton and Sachs, 1990; Blanchard *et al.*, 1991).

A National Privatisation Agency was established, with executive powers to assist and coordinate the process of transfer to private ownership. But plans to sell off enterprises in the service and trade sector by auction met with opposition from the employees of these units, and the Agency switched policy to the worker-participation model. Thus the country's 2,000 small enterprises were sold off to their employees by the end of 1991. Retail trade was privatised completely, while the large departments of wholesale trade and large hotels would remain under state control in the short term.

Plans for the privatisation of large industries were, however, to follow the Polish model. The enterprises would be divided into groups and a special fund was to be set up to be managed by a joint commission of foreign and Albanian specialists. The size of each fund would be based on estimates of the market demand for shares in the enterprises of each particular group. It was claimed that this process would ensure the natural transformation of the enterprises into share-holding entities and would create the conditions for the establishment of the necessary financial institutions for a market economy (Gajo, 1992). This mechanism would therefore disqualify those enterprises which would not appeal to the market. A widely held fear was that most manufacturing and processing plants would fall into this category. Certainly the view from outside of the country was that existing factories were hardly worth privatising. There was little likelihood of Western investors being interested in crumbling, palaeotechnic white elephants: it would be easier to scrap all existing plant and start again (Lindsay, 1992, pp. 13, 9). By the time of the spring 1992 elections, however, neither a strategy nor appropriate legislation was in place for large-scale privatisation.

Meanwhile, the country's economic crisis had grown steadily worse throughout 1991. By the end of the year the economy was on the verge of total collapse. Industrial and agricultural output had been halved during the first six months of 1991, and total industrial production for the year would be only 12 per cent–15 per cent of that for 1990. Severe shortages of spare parts and of raw materials crippled industry. Inflation, unknown under Hoxha, rose to over 100 per cent for the year.

8.1.4   Shock therapy?

Following the Democratic Party's victory in the March 1992 general elections, the new parliament approved the Meksi government's reform programme to restructure the collapsing economy and to turn back a rising tide of crime. In the first ten days of April 1992 alone 13 murders and 100 robberies were reported. Meksi asked for the support of the unions who had used a general strike to bring down the country's government the previous May. A major immediate task of the Democrats was to get people back to work: more than 50 per cent of workers were receiving the 80 per cent 'lay-off' payment.

A privatisation plan centred around three elements:

1. Complete land privatisation by amendments to the land law enabling a speed up of the privatisation of co-operatives and the provision of a legal framework for establishing a market in land and lease-holdings. A special commission was to be set up to review compensation for former land-owners.
2. A gradual but full privatisation of most state enterprises through a three-stage process:
    (a) a speeding up and completion of ongoing privatisation in retailing, services and transport;
    (b) a restructuring of food and light industry enterprises to prepare them for privatisation; and
    (c) a longer-term, four- to five-year privatisation programme for heavy industry, entailing a free distribution of shares to the adult population.
3. Encouraging the creation of new private firms, thereby eliminating the monopoly position enjoyed by state-owned enterprises (EIU, 1992c, pp. 43–4).

Some of these reforms were introduced during July and August 1992, not exactly amounting to a 'big bang', but none the less representing a radical package of measures. Most prices were freed and trade was liberalised, including the lifting of import restrictions on all goods except those representing a threat to the country's security or environment. Such liberalisation, however, was being hindered by difficulties in obtaining visas for Albanian businessmen travelling to the West, partly due to high levels of illegal Albanian immigration.

Albanian government recognition of this problem was only made apparent in March 1993 when 'business' passports began to be issued for businessmen, journalists and academics, who, it was hoped, would more easily obtain Western entry visas. Such a system did, however, raise the spectre of the travel restrictions and privileges of the communist era (EIU, 1993c, p. 41).

To get the country back to work there began a phasing out of the 80 per cent 'lay-off' payment and the gradual introduction of unemployment benefit of about 650 leks a month. The granting of freehold ownership of land to Albanian enterprises and individuals was legalised. Loans would be provided for families to enable them to buy their own state homes or other residential properties. For foreigners the maximum leasehold was extended from 49 to 99 years (section 3.5.7 above).

A two-tier banking system was established, although financial services remained rudimentary (*BEE*, 28 September 1992). The task of the state bank, now independent from the government, was to apply monetary policy, issue money and set the exchange rate. The National Bank of Albania, the Commercial Bank, the Savings Bank and the Bank of Agriculture and Development were now the country's commercial banks. The Commercial Bank would continue to be the sole bank dealing with foreign commercial operations, but it would accept only US dollars. Under the new banking law, joint venture banks, subsidiaries or branches of foreign banks could now operate in Albania. From January 1993 the National Bank and the Commercial Bank merged to become the National Commercial Bank, with branches in 37 areas. In partnership with the Banco di Roma and the Arab Islamic Bank, the Italian-Albanian Bank and the Arab Albanian Islamic Bank were set up (section 6.2.6 above).

The Bank of Albania introduced internal convertibility for the lek, the value of which was allowed to sink against the US dollar from 50 to 110 to bring it in line with the black market exchange rate. Financial policies were drastically tightened, with the aim of cutting the budget deficit from a level equivalent to half of the GDP over the previous 18 months to less than 20 per cent. Public sector pay increases would be limited and spending on the military and internal security would be reduced. With enormous overmanning in the state sector, soaking up considerable hidden unemployment and acting as a potent element of patronage at both national and local government levels, in early 1993 the government announced a cost-cutting exercise of a reduction in the state bureaucracy by 5 per cent. It was likely, however, that ways of subverting this requirement would be found by contracting labour which would be nominally private (EIU, 1993c, p. 44).

The main revenue sources would be customs duties and petroleum taxes. Tax revenues overall had declined from 42 per cent of GDP in 1990 to 28 per cent in 1991, and to just 16 per cent in the first half of 1992. A problem which continued through 1993 was that government control over tax collection remained tenuous. Approximately a half of all imports were expected to take the form of emergency food supplies. By January 1993 unemployment had reached 250,000 or almost 14 per cent of public sector employment (*Albanian Radio*, 21 January 1993). By that time it was being estimated that of the country's 2,657 enterprises and institutions, 1,482 (55.5 per cent) would need to reduce considerably the size of their work force, 142 (4.30 per cent) were likely to go bankrupt, and only 191 (7.18 per cent) were expected to increase their payroll (Stefani, 1993).

Nevertheless, EC support for small and medium-sized businesses was beginning to be taken up with enthusiasm. Assisted by a *Lancashire Enterprises* unit, based in an office within the Tirana University's Faculty of Economics and Business, the project disbursed or committed $1.32 million in loans between February 1992 and May 1993 to assist over 400 Albanian businessmen. At the end of that period a further 500 entrepreneurs were aiming to participate in the scheme. In December 1992 the private sector was employing an estimated 45,000 people nationally (Stefani, 1993). In the capital there were 8,321 private businesses (compared to just 398 in

Table 8.1   *Albania: economic results and forecasts, 1989–94*

	1989	1990	1991*	1992*	1993[†]	1994[†]
NMP[≠]	2.0	−6.0	−45.0	5.0	10.0	15.0
Industrial output[≠]	5.2	−6.0	−50.0	5.0	8.0	12.0
Agricultural output[≠]	9.0	−3.0	−35.0	10.0	12.0	10.0
Investment[≠]	1.5	−5.0	−60.0	–	10.0	12.0
% Inflation			104	220		
Budget deficit[‡]			5.5	9.0	23.3	
Hard currency trade $ million						
Exports fob	309	258	100	65	100	200
Imports cif	393	423	100	120	150	220
Production levels (in thousand tonnes)						
Crude oil		1,067	845	588	650	
Chromite concentrate		158	88	62	70	
Cement		645	304	200	300	
Sugar		15.3	3.0	1.4	2.0	
Cigarettes (millions)		4,947	1,703	1,076	1,500	

Notes:
[≠]   percentage change on previous year
*   estimate
[†]   forecast
[‡]   billion leks

Sources: BEE, 28 September 1992, p. 473; EIU, 1993c, pp. 40, 43–4.

March 1991), employing 13,000 (*ATA*, 23 November 1992). By this time Tirana District was accounting for 24 per cent of the national tax revenue, and this proportion was rising, with private sector sources increasing by 15 per cent over the year (*ATA*, 8 December 1992). By April 1993 the private sector was accounting for two-thirds of all exports and three-quarters of imports. Some economic indicators at least suggested that late 1992 and early 1993 were seeing the beginnings of a recovery (Table 8.1).

A much longer time-horizon was now being given to large-scale privatisation, with 1997 being suggested as the target date for completion (Fishta, 1992), but the government began to be criticised for leaving the process to apparent spontaneity. With World Bank support, however, in September 1993 an agency for the restructuring of enterprises was established within the Ministry of Industry, Mining and Energy Resources. Armed with a budget of 2,400 million leks, the agency was to prepare 30 weak state industrial enterprises for

privatisation and market conditions. It was not made clear at the time whether this included the option of immediate closure (*ATA*, 24 June, 7 September, 1993).

8.2   Encouraging inward investment

8.2.1   Joint venture laws for industry

Opening economic sectors to foreign interests, although exposing vulnerable economies to potential international monopolies held by transnational corporations, is intended to bring useful experience of foreign competition and investment. With this requirement in mind, in August 1990 a joint venture (JV) law was introduced, allowing a foreign partner to hold up to a 99 per cent share, freeing JVs from planning obligations and giving them foreign trade rights. They would also receive legal protection against expropriation and nationalisation. Materials imported for processing and

Plate 8.1 *One of the first examples of service industry private enterprise was the Struga cafe-bar, set up on a piece of Tirana parkland*

Table 8.2 *Albania and selected East European countries: tax incentives for foreign investment*

Country	a	b	c	d	e	Other incentives
Albania	None	None	To 1995	1996–8	50*	40% tax reduction for foreign investors reinvesting profits. 5% instead of 15% turnover tax for firms with more than 33% foreign capital
Bulgaria	$100K+	49	None	U/l	10‡	5-year CFL; other tax exemptions in high-tech, agriculture or food-processing industries
Estonia	$1m+ $50K –$1m	50 30	3 2–3‡	5 2	50 50	3-year CFL against taxable profits; exports for hard currency not subject to 18% VAT
Poland	≠Ecu 2m+	None	None	U/l	Ex	3-year CFL in equal instalments; since February 1992 loss may be offset against future income from any source
Romania	$10K+	None	2–5‡	To 5	To 50	2-year CFL. Annual deductions of 5% of profit before taxation
Slovakia	DM1m+	30	2‡	Nil	Nil	5-year CFL. Tax incentives for operating in cities in east Slovakia
Slovenia	None	None	1	2nd year 3rd year	66 33	Further reductions available to firms operating in free-trade zones, less developed or less-inhabited areas. Reinvested profits get up to a 15% tax reduction

Key

a	investment requirement for tax holiday or tax reduction
b	% minimum foreign participation
c	tax holiday in years
d	period of additional tax reductions in years
e	% tax reduction offered
*	for doing business for at least ten successive years
≠	in regions with high structural unemployment, introducing new technology or enabling export of at least 20% of total output
‡	reduction on profits
CFL	carried forward losses
Ex	exemption with conditions
U/l	unlimited

Source: Yee, 1993, pp. 6–7.

re-export could be considered duty free. Priority would be given to projects entailing modernisation and technology transfer, export promotion, import substitution and consumer goods production (Baker, 1990). The relatively cheap labour offered by Albania could encourage significant inward investment once stability had returned to the country (and indeed to the region).

Table 8.2 summarises the major tax incentives available to investors as at mid-1993, and compares them with those for other selected East European countries. Most offered some form of tax holiday, usually with a minimum threshold for Western investment – Albania and Slovenia being exceptions – along with an additional period in which investors were allowed to pay reduced taxes. Two major countries of the region no longer offered major tax incentives to foreign investors: the Czech Republic merely permitted a five-year loss carry-forward, and Russia abolished tax holidays in 1992. In mid-1993 both Hungary and Poland were also reportedly considering abolishing incentives.

This clearly raises the question as to the relevance and value of tax incentives for the attraction of foreign investment to a country such as Albania. Overall economic and political conditions are likely to be more important for long-term investors, and lengthy approval processes for tax breaks can anyway be counter-productive. On the other hand, with recession continuing in the West, several Central and East European countries feel that they need to be as attractive to investors as possible, and tax incentives could be a deciding factor for a company choosing between investment in Albania and a country such as Portugal (Yee, 1993).

In 1991 foreign trade was liberalised and a Foreign Investment Agency was established to act as a channel between potential investors and the Ministry of Foreign Trade. A Chamber of Commerce was also set up to provide a veneer of assurance for investment protection. Subsequently, five new foreign trade organisations were created to simplify procedures by allowing direct liaison with relevant ministers. To encourage proactive investment policy, commercial offices were established in countries where diplomatic relations had been restored recently, to generate interest in specific sectors (Keay, 1992).

While Western countries showed willingness to provide humanitarian aid, they were less willing to provide infusions of cash, for several reasons: (a) Albanians had been slow and inefficient in introducing the radical reforms needed to attract foreign investments; (b) continued political and social instability; (c) Albanians themselves had virtually no capital with which to support entrepreneurial aspirations; (d) only a limited degree of private

enterprise had been developed, in some cases with financial support from relatives abroad; and (e) the bureaucracy remained strong, and few Communist officials and managers had been replaced.

A major constraint on foreign investment – regional and domestic instability, a lack of infrastructure, excessive bureaucracy and collapsed economic structures aside – was a still largely absent legal and accounting framework for investment and joint ventures: no unified tax system for foreign investors was in place, nor was any company law. However, the country was aiming to adopt EC legislation on such issues as profit and capital repatriation and to adapt them to Albanian conditions. Before the March 1992 elections, perhaps only 50 foreign companies had expressed any serious interest in the country, but following the outright victory of the Democratic Party, enquiries increased substantially (Keay, 1992), and joint ventures began to be established in a number of fields. The new government expressed its aim to simplify the environment for foreign investors by streamlining departments and reaffirming the desire to bring relevant legislation into line with the rest of Europe. Initial declarations suggested, however, that the country would not permit large-scale foreign investments to the extent where they could overshadow the national economy. It was acknowledged that Albania was a potentially rich country, requiring appropriate technology, management skills and training to enable it to make the best of itself.

However, it was also recognised that securing realistic investors would not be easy as, for example, Albania's major minerals were currently experiencing depressed price levels on world markets, while incurring high extraction costs: in 1992 the chromium industry was only working at 40 per cent capacity, and copper at 50 per cent. Many mines and smelting plants were lying idle and those in production were wasteful of ore due to the inefficiency of crude processing equipment built in Albania by Chinese engineers in the 1960s (Bird, 1992a).

The Democratic Party government's early laws on taxation of profits and rules covering foreign investment appeared to suggest that

Albania was actually moving away from a genuine commitment to the development of a free market and towards the maintenance of a highly centralised economy dominated by institutional bureaucracy (Standish and Yates, 1992b). All foreign investment above $50,000 would now require authorisation from the Ministry of Trade and Foreign Economic Co-operation rather than from local authorities, and fears were raised that inevitably the centralised bureaucracy would act as a constraint on investment. Berisha had to go into print to 'guarantee' the security of foreign investments (Berisha, 1992). A possible solution was the establishment of a unitary privatisation and foreign investment agency, to replace the existing Privatisation Agency, Privatisation Commission and the Foreign Investment Agency.

Within the new tax laws, a 10 per cent transfer tax imposed on profits remitted abroad was seen as a further discouragement to inward investment. In their examination of the constraints on foreign investment, Standish and Yates (1992b) argued that there was now at best a hesitant attitude towards the development of capitalism, and an indication that rapidly introduced legislation could be equally quickly overturned if it proved inappropriate:

. . . a fundamentally unhealthy philosophy which has its roots in opportunism and desperation, rather than sound economic policy. (Standish and Yates, 1992b, p. 9)

In the context of (a) national and regional instability, (b) adverse publicity, (c) a poor competitive position in relation to the investment potential of other East European countries, and (d) a vast majority of state enterprises operating on a deficit basis, the lack of basic facilities to encourage investors to persevere through the country's bureaucratic nightmare was an insuperable handicap. Additionally, there still existed amongst key officials an 'invasion' mentality in relation to foreign investment (Standish and Yates, 1992a).

By the end of October 1992 licences for 76 JVs had been issued (Table 8.3). Of these 27 had been granted by the Council of Ministers during the unstable period from September 1990 to the end of August 1991. Forty-nine had been issued in the following 12 months, of which six had been subsequently invalidated. Thus licenses for 70 JVs remained valid. Fifty-five per cent of these were based in Tirana while several major cities, such as Pogradec, Krujë, Laç, Peshkopi and Përmet had yet to host such ventures. Thirty JVs had been established with Italian companies, 12 with Greek firms and the remaining 28 were with organisations from some 13 other countries. Albania's Deputy Minister of Trade argued that these figures – 65 per cent of all JVs were with immediately neighbouring countries and 43 per cent were with Italy alone – revealed the need to establish better relations with investors from the United States, Germany, Austria and other developed countries with advanced technology, as well as with businessmen from the Albanian diaspora who wished to invest in the country. Defects and delays in undertaking technical and economic feasiblility studies in a number of districts were criticised as inhibiting inward investment (*Bashkimi*, 28 October 1992).

Of the 70 authorised JVs, 27 per cent were in light industry, 20 per cent in agriculture and foodstuffs, and 17 per cent in the business sector. The capital invested amounted to $56 million, of which 60 per cent was from foreign sources. Investments in offshore hydrocarbon exploration and exploitation still dominated foreign capital expenditure, and agreements had been established on the mutual increase and protection of investments with Germany, Italy, Greece, Turkey and Switzerland (Hoxha, 1992). By the beginning of 1993, 55 JVs were actually in operation, the same number as twelve months previously (Afezolli, 1993).

In the service sector, Benetton was to open five shops by the spring of 1994, and a site for the first Coca Cola bottling factory had been established on the fringes of Tirana.

8.2.2 Frameworks for skills transfer

The Albanian education system (section 3.3.3) had managed to place a number of obstacles in

Table 8.3 *Albania's major joint ventures*

JV name	Location	Albanian partner	Foreign partner	Initial capital (US$ m)	Activity
Adelchi	Shkodër	Leather & shoe factory	Italian	‡	Shoe production
ADA	Tirana	Teknoimport	French	1.0	Commerce & transport (licence suspended)
AA Glina	Gjiro-kastër	Gjirokastër food enterprise	US	0.006	Packaging and sale of Glina mineral water
AGIP*	Durrës	Oil General Directorate	Italian	‡	Offshore oil and gas
AIDA	Durrës	Durrës fishing companies & Ihtimpeks Tirana.	Italian	0.007	Fishing
Alba	Sarandë	NPV	Greek	0.384	Clothing
Alba-Greek	Sarandë	NTSh	Greek	0.420	Shipping
Albamar	Durrës	Durrës fishing company	Italian	0.168	Fishing
Albanian Airlines	Tirana	Albtransport	Austrian	2.0	Air transport
Alban Interurban	Tirana	NT Interurban	German	0.31	Road transport
Albanuova	Durrës	Automobile service	Italian	0.6	Transport services
Alb-Ducros	Tirana		French	0.05	Medicinal plants
Albinfra-structure	Sarandë	Asphalting enterprise	Italian	3.0	Reasphalting
Albit-Agro	Durrës	Hamallaj state farm	Italian	2.05	Agriculture
Albital Servis	Tirana	General Directorate of Economic Informatics	Italian	0.01	Computer services
Albafredi	Tirana	Fuel distribution enterprise	Italian	0.01	Fuels
Albatros	Tirana	Albturist	French	0.1	Tourism
Albcam-Intertrade	Tirana	Transshqip	German	‡	Transport
Albitalia Bashtova	Kavajë	Bashtova state farm	Italian	3.0	Agriculture
Aliagri	Lushnjë	Lushnjë state farm	Italian	‡	Agriculture
Almak	Tirana	NNI	Macedonian	1.017	Construction
Almod	Durrës	Durrës rubber enterprise	Italian	‡	Shoe manufacture
Aulona	Tirana	NTI	Swiss	0.029	Commerce
Berup	Berat	Construction enterprise	Italian	‡	Marble

Continued

Table 8.3   *Continued*

JV name	Location	Albanian partner	Foreign partner	Initial capital (US$ m)	Activity
Bulo Larissa	Gjiro-kastër	Bulo state farm	Greek	0.418	Agriculture
Calcaturo-ficio	Tirana	Shoe enterprise	Italian	7.314	Shoe manufacture
Camo-Tirana	Tirana	Tirana plaster enterprise	Italian	0.8	Construction & maintenance
Cam-Toys	Tirana	Galanteria	Italian	0.003	Production & sale of toys
Chevron*	Durrës	Oil General Directorate	US	‡	Offshore oil and gas
Deminex*	Tirana	Oil General Directorate	German	‡	Offshore oil and gas
DIF	Durrës	Alburist	Italian	‡	Beach construction
Disko-Bar-Lux	Tirana	Palace of Culture	Italian	0.226	Culture (!)
Durrës Park OAS	Durrës	Durrës forest enterprise	Italian	0.02	Hunting
Edicom	Durrës	Apartment construction enterprise	Italian	1.0	Construction
Editoria Albacori	Tirana	Naim Frashëri publishing house	Italian	0.02	Publishing
Eldamak	Elbasan	Elbasan mechanical plant	Chinese	1.0	Metallurgy
Elfrigo	Tirana	Refrigeration enterprise of Tirana	German	0.009	Transport, import/export of refrigerated food
Emigrant, The	Tirana	NTUS no. 3	US-Alb	0.317	Commerce
Eurofoods	Sarandë	Vurg Agricl. Enterprise	Greek	2.450	Agriculture
Evalbel	Tirana		Greek	‡	Handicrafts
General Invest	Tirana	NTUS no. 3	US/Irish	0.6	Food, commerce
Gatic SA	Gjiro-kastër	Gjirokastër clothing enterprise	Greek	‡	Clothing
Global	Korçë	NRA Korçë	Greek	‡	Manufacture and marketing of fur and textile articles
Hamilton*	Durrës	Oil General Directorate	US	‡	Offshore oil and gas
Hojej	Tirana		UK	‡	Commerce
Iliria Holdings	Tirana		Swiss	‡	Commerce, tourism (licence suspended)
Inditer	Tirana	Tirana industrial enterprises	UK/Lebanon	‡	Finance

Continued

Table 8.3 *Continued*

JV name	Location	Albanian partner	Foreign partner	Initial capital (US$ m)	Activity
Inplastreg	Tirana	NTI industrial merchandise enterprise of Tirana	Italian	‡	Reconstruction of Tirana sales network
Inter-Alba	Tirana		Greek	‡	Commerce
Inter-Kinex	Tirana	Tirana film enterprise	Kosovar	‡	Distribution and screening of cinema films
ITS	Sarandë	Alpturist	Italian	‡	Tourism
Katel	Elbasan	Elbasan flattening plant	Kosovar	0.181	Heavy industry
Klub Shqiperia	Tirana	Tirana sports centre	Lichtenstein	1.489	Service to sport tours
Lake Mall, The	Tirana	NTUS no. 2	US-Alb	0.547	Retailing
Lorenso	Tirana	Tirana artisan enterprise	Italian	0.788	Smoking pipes
Megam Vlora	Vlorë	Vlorë oil-soap enterprise	US	0.586	Oil & soap production
Mikaberat	Berat	Tobacco enterprise	Greek	1.511	Tobacco
Minnav	Tirana	Minergoimpeks	Italian	0.138	Industry
Mobilieri Delvina	Delvinë	Woodworking enterprise	Greek	0.203	Furniture
Occidental*	Durrës	Oil General Directorate	US	‡	Offshore oil and gas
Perla	Sarandë	Artistic products enterprise	Greek	0.637	Artistic products
Prodent-alfarma	Tirana	Profarma	Italian	0.250	Medical equipment
Rehor Albania	Gjirokastër	Gjirokastër shoes enterprise	Greek	0.015	Shoes
Samanko	Tropojë	Ministry of Mining	South African	80.0	Exploitation & sale of chromium ore extracted in Kam, Tropojë district
Sport Club Partizani	Tirana	Partizani Club	Italian	0.1	Sport
S.T.S. Sarandë	Sarandë	Alpturist	Italian	0.02	Tourism
Tradex Torovica	Lezhë	Torovica state farm, Lezhë	Greek	0.957	Marketing of farm produce
Trans-albania	Tirana	Transshqip	German	0.1	International transport
U. Mek. Carmosini	Shkodër	Mechanical plant enterprise	Italian	2.96	Mechanical plant

Continued

Table 8.3   *Continued*

JV name	Location	Albanian partner	Foreign partner	Initial capital (US$ m)	Activity
UP	Dibër region	Muhuri mine	Italian	‡	Marble

Notes:

* not strictly joint ventures: the foreign owned enterprises operate on the basis of apportionment of production.

‡ sum undisclosed.

Sources: *Albanian Economic Tribune*, 1992, 3(7): 29; 4(8): 27; 7(11): 32; 8(12): 22; 1993, 1(13): 12.

the way of the potentially upwardly mobile: (a) there were substantial differences in the levels of schooling achieved between regions and between urban and rural areas; (b) skills taught in junior secondary and secondary schools were often geared to perceived local needs; and (c) where more widely applicable professional training was available locally, there was no guarantee that this would open up the scope for geographical and thus social mobility. Indeed, the practice of assigning graduates from tertiary education to specific employment in particular locations militated against such possibilities (Sjöberg, 1991a, pp. 65–73, 1993, p. 499).

As noted earlier (section 3.3.3), the nature and methods of the Albanian higher education system had not been intended for significant independent thought and an appreciation of 'Western' development processes. Five thousand economics graduates were being produced annually, but none had been prepared for a market economy and the transitional road to it (Permeti, 1991). Massive shortfalls in adequately trained and equipped personnel existed at all levels, but particularly in managerial and organisational roles. The country's petroleum industry, for example, was woefully short of appropriately trained managers and economists, placing the country's oil corporation Albpetrol at a distinct disadvantage when negotiating contracts with hard-headed Western multi-nationals.

However, in addition to the training and skills transfer opportunities afforded by the large-scale funding from the financial institutions, a number of the joint ventures undertaken have been notable for their transferable skills component. In developing the Albanian Airlines company (section 8.3.5 below), pilots were initially Canadian, but the venture partner Tyrolean Airways began recruiting young Albanian male engineering, chemistry, physics, mathematics and computer studies graduates for one year pilots' courses in the United States. Technical personnel also began to be recruited from the ranks of the country's graduates and sent on training courses in Austria. Initially cabin staff were a mix of Albanian and Canadian nationals, but the latter were to be phased out as experience and in-house training brought local recruits up to appropriate standards (Baçi, 1992).

Hewlett-Packard, the first Western computer company to establish a presence in Albania, embarked on a training programme for its Albanian managers at the International Management Development Institute in Lausanne. The company's Albanian engineers attend courses at its training centre in Vienna (Kemp, 1992).

While both examples represent the sophisticated end of the joint venture spectrum, they none the less provided the beginnings of means to raise the level of technical and managerial experience and expertise which was so vital both in practical and symbolic terms, for Albania's survival into the twenty-first century.

8.3 Providing the infrastructure

Although human resource development, economic restructuring, political realignment, legislative reform and new freedoms of social and spatial mobility represented the outward superstructure of change and development, major obstacles to the success of such processes were presented by the country's hopelessly inadequate infrastructure. Somewhat belatedly, upgrading became a major priority of the 1993 economic programme, assisted by an $80 million World Bank facility and additional assistance from the European Community and the EBRD. Generally, however, negotiations between the government, international financial institutions and possible private investors were moving at a very slow pace: even after the IMF green light in mid-1992, bureaucratic obstacles and the passing of inconsistent legislation had the effect of both slowing down, and dampening overseas enthusiasm for, investment opportunities. That this was attributable to the Albanian government's concern for its development policies to be sustainable was debatable. While investment in infrastructure would clearly be a long-term process, two elements which were being looked to for relatively quick results were the redevelopment of Durrës port (section 8.3.4) and Rinas airport (section 8.3.5) (Keay, 1993b).

8.3.1 Energy

Although the short-term prospect was for a reduction in the country's energy consumption, with the likely closure of inefficient and dangerous heavy manufacturing plant, the longer-term picture was inevitably one of increased consumption. The series of dry winters in the second half of the 1980s highlighted the country's high dependence upon hydro-powered electricity. Hydro capacity of 1,600 mW accounted for nearly 85 per cent of the country's total installed capacity and actually met 95 per cent of consumption (*EEM*, 2 October 1992, p. 7). Generation was dramatically reduced and electricity supplies became restricted and even more erratic,

causing much industry to close down. To claim that the Albanain 'revolution' was the first to result from global warming is more than a little rash, but the chain of events which culminated in social upheaval and political change in the early 1990s were heavily influenced by the country's economic vulnerability to climatic change.

Within a few years, much existing equipment, including Chinese generators dating from the 1960s and 1970s, would need to be replaced. The 400 kV transmission system, part of which was damaged by storms in 1992, also needed upgrading. Power lines were generally inadequate and often dangerous. In some areas, local people had illegally tapped into the existing distribution system and, as a consequence, transformers had quickly become burned out. In 1992 alone 2,000 new units were needed as replacements. As all consumers became connected properly to the grid, the electricity supply industry needed new meters and extra cabling, much of which came from Croatia, Macedonia, Italy and Greece. Upgrading the distribution system would cost more than $100 million for the pylons and cabling alone.

By the end of 1992 ambitious plans were being discussed to develop new generating stations using natural gas or hydro-electric power and financed by the World Bank. The bulk of generating capacity lies in three large hydro stations on the Drin river in the north of the country and two thermal stations in Tirana and Korçë. Discussion was taking place over the relative merits of developing small hydro schemes of up to 1mW serving villages and small towns, some of which already exist from the 1950s, alongside plans for much larger schemes such as a 1,000 mW Vlorë coastal power station using domestically produced natural gas. This latter development would permit the de-comissioning of the heavily polluting thermal plants, and had attracted the attention of the AGIP group since it would provide potential export capacity for the Italian market. Greece, a country which was already importing around $7 million worth of Albanian electricity annually, was also showing interest in the project.

8.3.2 Water supply

Uncertain supply, pollution and contamination of domestic supplies were a particular problem for urban householders as well as for agriculture and industry. In addressing these problems, the World Bank, German and Italian interests became involved in improving local water supply systems. For 1993 the World Bank provided a $40 million loan, one-quarter of which would be used to upgrade the existing system and the remaining $30 million would be employed in constructing a completely new system to guarantee continuous supplies. A particular focus would be placed on Tirana, Shkodër and Vlorë. The German government had previously granted aid worth DM 10 million to upgrade the systems of Kavajë and Kukës, the latter in particular being notoriously erratic, despite the country's largest reservoirs being located in the district!

8.3.3 Telecommunications

Arguably the most significant structural deficiency throughout Central and Eastern Europe at the end of the 1980s, the provision of a modern telecommunications system for such a small yet strategically positioned country as Albania could be fundamental for the pace and nature of future development. With a still predominantly rural population, the technological leap to telecottages and other decentralised forms of development strategy employing information technology, would not be such an unrealistic medium-term proposition given the younger generation's willingness and ability to respond to innovation.

It was as recently as 1971 that both the country's first electronic computer centre and television station were established, while only in 1973 was a national telephone system completed, all with Chinese assistance (Prifti, 1979, p. 197). Until the late 1980s, little change had been brought to these systems, apart from inevitable spare parts and technical shortcomings. By 1990, it was estimated that Albania had just five telephones per thousand population, compared to figures of 320 for Bulgaria, 170 for

Hungary and 200 for Yugoslavia (Hall, 1991, p. 77). Although facsimile machines were slowly increasing in number in the early 1990s, the most reliable way to communicate with offices in Tirana continued to be through the medium of a telex, as the very limited number of telephone lines were busy throughout the day, rendering fax communication difficult. Up to 1992, only piecemeal improvements had taken place in the telephone system, such as the cross-border connections between eastern Albania and Macedonia established at the end of 1991 (*Tanjug*, 11 December 1991).

Subsequently, upgrading the country's tele-communications systems became a major goal of EBRD assistance. During 1992 the Bank assisted the Albanian PTT in installing 3,000 automatic lines in Tirana, clearly with one eye on improving the infrastructure for business development. This included mobile phone booths set up in central Tirana (Plate 8.2) and other cities to alleviate pressure on the hotels and central post offices which previously provided the only access to public telephones. This was but the first step in a very necessary comprehensive upgrading and expansion of the national system, an immediate aim of which was to increase the country's telephone density by 30 per cent (Bismarck-Osten, 1992). A $10 million loan from the EBRD was made available for telecommunication modernisation and development during 1993.

As part of a wider package of agreements on co-operation in transport and communications with Croatia, the Albanian posts and Telecommunications Department signed a letter of intent to participate in a German-Croatian-Greek fibre optic cable project. A submarine cable would be laid from Dubrovnik to Durrës and then on to Corfu (*ATA*, 16 March 1993; Croatian Radio, 16 March 1993; EIU, 1993c, p. 47). Almost simultaneously, perhaps symbolically reflecting Albania's desire to act as a neutral east–west, north–south communications and cultural bridge, an agreement was reached with Bulgaria, FYR Macedonia, Italy and Turkey to establish the Trans Balkan line telecoms bridge. This would entail the construction and maintenance of a 1,000 km long digital system of optical fibre cables and digital

Plate 8.2 *As a short-term means of upgrading Tirana's telecommunication system, this mobile public telephone unit, provided by Italy, was being used in the centre of the capital in March 1993*

radio relay systems to connect the five participating countries to each other and to Western Europe (*EEM*, 11 June, 1993).

In a further EBRD-led project launched in mid-1992, an improvement in the television broadcasting facilities of 15 Central and East European countries was to be facilitated by a $15 million investment which would help link them to the Eurovision Network by satellite through the design, supply and installation of earth stations. Twelve countries, including Albania, would each borrow $1 million guaranteed by the European Broadcasting Union, membership of which the borrowers were taking up.

Under the communists, domestic television broadcasts had been limited to a few hours each evening. The attraction of Italian programmes in particular became insatiable. By 1986, 86 per cent of manual workers and 92 per cent of intellectuals in Tirana had a television set in the family, and television viewing took first place amongst recreational activities, according to a social survey of that year (Tarifa and Barjaba, 1990, pp. 14–15). With opening borders and the active role of remittances from expatriate workers, this trend would be intensified: 71,000 television sets were cleared through customs during 1992, compared to a total of 33,000 entering the country for the whole period between 1944 and 1990 (*ATA*, 5 January, 1993).

Through the early 1990s, the position of state-controlled Albanian Radio and Television had remained more stable than the largely political party-controlled press (section 6.1.5.1 above). Programming was expanded, professional standards were improved, and, in tandem with the EBRD, as noted above, plans were drawn up for satellite broadcasting. The radio's recently introduced programmes for Albanians abroad had become popular (Zanga, 1993f).

8.3.4   A major regional axis?

Albania once sat astride the major routeway from Rome to Byzantium – the Via Egnatia – and the site of its present major port, Durrës, was the landfall for the movement of goods and people eastwards across the Adriatic. With a population of 120,000 by the 1990s, Durrës had become the country's second largest city, focal point of Albania's rail system, and centre of commerce under the communists (Bërxholi, 1986). The port had retained a pre-eminence in external maritime trade (Table 4.10), but in international terms was very restricted in size, draft and technology: the port basin was only 67 hectares and quayside cranes had a maximum lifting capacity of 15 tonnes. Critically, the port was unable to handle container ships, and had the unenviable reputation of being the least efficient in Europe: in recent years several importers had opted to unload seaborne goods at Thessaloniki in northern Greece and bring them into Albania by road. Yet Durrës had the potential to be one of the busiest dual passenger and freight ports on the Adriatic.

The city's role would be enhanced considerably if a nineteenth-century dream was finally realised: a rail link from Bulgaria and Macedonia to the Albanian coast. The Skopje railway enterprise of Macedonia had begun working on plans for the construction of 121 km of track linking the Bulgarian, Macedonian and Albanian rail systems before the fall of Albania's communists. By improving communications, such a line would considerably shorten the distance for shipping goods from Italy to Eastern Europe and the Middle East. Durrës, the line's Adriatic terminus, would stand to gain considerable advantage from this, particularly if the Albanian authorities opened it up as a free port. The possibility that Albanian ports might be opened up as free trade zone areas in order to attract Western investment, was initially signalled in the summer of 1990 when the private export-import company Makimport of Skopje was offered talks on the use of the port facilities of Vlorë, Albania's main naval base and hitherto the subject of strict security (Bërxholi, 1985b).

In May 1993, Albanian, Bulgarian and FYR Macedonian transport ministries agreed to go ahead with Black Sea–Adriatic high speed road and rail links, air routes and a digital telecoms link (section 8.3.3). Italy and Turkey would join the project later. Financing from the EBRD was being envisaged. (*Bulgarian Telegraphic Agency*, 7, 10 May 1993; *EEM*, 11 June 1993).

A notable joint venture was undertaken when Transalbania was established in November 1992 as a partnership between 38 Albanian transport and communications enterprises and the German Kuhne Nagel International group with 10,200 collaborators in 66 countries. For their part, the Germans re-emphasised that Durrës was the best port linking (Western) Europe with the Ukraine, Romania and Bulgaria, and acknowledged the potential for overland transport requirements from Albania (*ATA*, 20 November 1992). An upgrading of Durrës port began in 1992 when the construction of a new 15,000 sq m ferry quay was begun which would permit three passenger vessels to be in port at any one time. Subsequently, a long-term low-interest credit of $8.7 million was secured from Kuwait to assist the port's redevelopment.

8.3.5 Improving air links

The Albanian administration viewed civil aviation as the transport sector offering the best opportunities for foreign investment (Llukani, 1993). There appeared to be four elements within this picture with varying degrees of attraction: (a) air traffic control and related technology; (b) improvement of the general infrastructure of Rinas and other potential airports; (c) freight handling and onward land transport; and (d) passenger airlines.

Apocryphal stories used to abound concerning the small, folksy, sheep grazing Rinas airport's lack of everything from radar to a stand-in air traffic controller. Situated 25 km to the north-west of the capital, it was built in 1948, with a strictly limited capacity and a concrete tiled runway extended to 2,700 metres. In 1990, newly installed technology enabled the Albanian government, for the first time in its post-war history, to permit overflying rights for international airlines, thereby helping to ease the air traffic bottleneck experienced in Central Europe and the Mediterranean area (and later to avoid the war zones and embargoed territories

of Bosnia and Serbia/Montenegro respectively). A British Airways flight from London to Athens was the first to achieve successfully the feat of overflying 'virgin' Albanian territory.

Passenger throughput increased substantially in the early 1990s: 35,000 in 1990 rising to 50,000 in the following year and to 80,000 in 1992. Following Albania's admission to the International Civil Aviation Organisation in that year, an innovative agreement was arrived at between the International Air Transport Association (IATA), International Airadio and the Albanian Air Traffic Agency to upgrade the Rinas air traffic control (ATC) system. In the first phase, from April 1993, up to $900,000-worth of communications equipment would be installed in the Tirana ATC centre to replace 1950s-vintage Russian and Chinese equipment. It would be paid for by airlines placing their hard-currency overflying fees into an IATA-administered account. Similar funding systems had worked successfully for some African countries. If the initiative proved successful, radar and infrastructure improvements could be funded similarly (*Flight*, 22 July 1992). In early 1993 Siemens of Germany drew up a master plan for the reconstruction and modernisation of Rinas which would cost DM400 million. Annual passenger capacity of 1.5 million and enlarged landing areas to accommodate such aircraft as B-757s and A-320s were planned. Given the pivotal role of Rinas in linking the country to the outside world and in being the gateway for incoming tourists, this work was seen to be of the highest priority.

Not since the 1930s had domestic civil flights operated, other than air rescue operations using helicopters and crop spraying from Antonov AN-2 bi-planes. But with the growth of tourism pressures, there existed the possibility of internal flights re-appearing. These might use airfields and landing strips, mostly current or former military bases, at some ten locations (Llukani, 1993), ranging from large operational runways at Lezhë and Kuçovë, to basic airfields with virtually no infrastructure, such as at Kukës, Korçë, Vlorë, Shkodër, Sarandë and Gjirokastër, several of which would be well-placed for the designated tourism development zones. During 1993 negotiations were under way with the Ministry of Defence to place these potential secondary civil airports under the jurisdiction of the Ministry of Transport, a process which had taken place elsewhere in Eastern Europe (Hall, 1993d, 1993e), although the minister envisaged nine domestic air routes for mail and freight (*ATA*, 4 October 1993). In the short to medium term the feasibility of using small planes would be questionable given the costs and probable low utilisation level. There was, however, some scope for the development of a second international airport in the relatively isolated south of the country, and the possible development of a 2,000 metre runway facility outside Sarandë was being examined, although existing traffic control considerations for movement into and out of Corfu were likely to be an inhibiting factor.

The name *Albanian Airlines* appeared in August 1992 as the result of a joint venture between Albtransport, the state enterprise dealing with air freight, aircraft handling and other non-ATC airport services, and Tyrolean Airways. Operating two Canadian Dash-8 aircraft, flights were inaugurated, under a ten-year agreement, between Tirana and Vienna, Rome, Munich, Zurich and Frankfurt, with the Austrian partner being responsible for the supply and upkeep of the aircraft (*BEE*, 7 December 1992). The venture's inaugural flight on 31 August 1992 brought to 50 the total number of flights to and from Tirana each week. Soon after, the Polish state airline, LOT, introduced regular flights from Warsaw. Of considerable interest was the inauguration in February 1993 of a weekly direct service to New York by Arberia Airlines, an Albanian-American organisation (*ATA*, 10 February 1993).

From 1991, international courier companies began to establish themselves within the country, aiding communications links with the outside world particularly for the growing business community. Reflecting the reduction in technological and political impediments to flights into and out of Tirana, DHL opened an office in Albania in July 1991. An exclusive representative agency agreement with Albtransport provided a staff of four and an office in the centre of Tirana. DHL supplied equipment and

a car, and provided staff training. On average, DHL was shipping 200–500 packages per month into Albania, and about 80 out of the country. The company operated at loss for the first year. Planning to open an independent office in January 1993, even though the company was ready to pay a rather higher monthly rent of about $10–$15 per square metre, it could not find a suitable site (Kobylka, 1992).

8.3.6   The road system

In the early 1990s, of the country's 18,000 km of roadway only about 40 per cent was usable by motorised vehicles. This was administered by the Ministry of Transport, whose 8,000 km comprised main national and secondary roads. The remainder, around 10,000 km, served mining areas, forestry and other areas of economic activity for access to, and the transport of, local products. All the main highways – Durrës–Shkodër, Durrës–Tirana, Durrës–Elbasan – were badly rutted, virtually unlit and bedevilled by slow moving erratic vehicles and animal transport. Virtually no dual carriageway existed, apart from short stretches in Tirana. Abandoned wrecks had also become a major driving hazard (McDowall, 1991a), and with vandalism a problem, provision of secure vehicle parking had become a notable growth area for private enterprise (Plate 8.3). With a rapid increase in mostly poorly maintained, ageing second-hand motor vehicles – 17,000 were imported in 1992 – substantial problems had been added to the already inadequate road system.

Road services also remained poor. With only 40 petrol filling stations in the whole country, the industry ministry announced in February 1993 that to distribute motor fuel private firms would need a government licence, as (black market) interest in this limited commodity was increasing rapidly. Secure car parking was also to become regulated, but roadside facilities and recovery provision remained minimal and prone to abuse.

During 1993 a regional enterprise was being established to maintain the national road

Plate 8.3 *Showing enterprise of which some Western educational institutions would be proud, the Centre for Geography in the Academy of Sciences has taken over part of the former Zogu royal complex in central Tirana. Restoration of the building is being partly financed by hiring out space in the grounds for secure vehicle parking. On the left is one of the vehicles of the Médecin Sans Frontières aid operation*

system. Funding for this and for new and improved roads within the country was in the form of World Bank credits, $18 million of which was coming from the International Development Association and $8 million from Kuwaiti sources (*ATA*, 26 June, 7 September, 1993).

For some time there had been plans to create a cross-border motorway network in Albania as part of the Trans-European Motorway Project, which would also require additional road-building by Albania's neighbours. The main routes would be east–west, Durrës to Pogradec and on into FYR Macedonia and Greece and the Black Sea (section 8.3.4 above), and north–south, from Shkodër to the Greek border, probably linking Tirana, Berat and Gjirokastër. The proposed 1,000km highway from Durrës to Istanbul would be planned to reduce the existing 30-hour journey to just ten hours. Again Albania was looking to international development aid programmes to fund the estimated $500 million cost of its stretch of the road, while neighbouring Macedonia was hoping to attract private investment for its likely $280 million commitment.

As the privatisation of road freight and passenger services proceeded in 1992, the first private transport co-operative – Albsped – was established in Tirana, with 300 joint owners having between them 150 vehicles in various states of repair and a number of workshops. Seven additional branches were established in the other main towns. The enterprise aimed to provide efficient domestic and international transport and storage operations (*ATA*, 24 November 1992). By mid-1992, the number of privately owned inter-urban buses had grown rapidly to 500, with the streets adjacent to Tirana's railway terminus developing as an *ad hoc* inter-urban and international bus station.

8.3.7   Constraints of the rail system

Albanian Railways' (Hekurudhë Shqipërisë – HSH) train movements met several constraints which reduced overall speeds, such that published timetables have shown passenger train averages of no more than 50 km per hour.

Speed restrictions were the result of relatively poor quality rails, sleepers and track bed, not helped by having been put together with the aid of 'volunteer' labour (section 2.3). Curves and gradients in this topographically difficult country, particularly on the central line to Pogradec, exacerbated such shortcomings. Relatively infrequent passing loops on this basically single track system served to reduce speeds further (Hall, 1985). By the late 1980s it was obvious that the system required a thorough overhaul and the introduction of electrification to raise speeds and tractive effort (Hall, 1987b).

During the spate of attempts to leave the country during 1990, angry crowds who had been turned away from Durrës port by the military after failing to commandeer vessels, vented their frustration by attacking the city's railway complex and setting fire to rolling stock. In 1991, with law and order deteriorating further, state property was considered fair game for theft and vandalism. Railway telegraph wires were taken for fencing and for their copper content; poles were taken for firewood and building materials; passenger carriages lost their seats, windows and other fittings; and locomotives were relieved of their headlamps. Eighty-three passenger coaches (75 per cent of the original fleet) were destroyed. During one local dispute over the redistribution of land, crowds stopped a train and ripped up the track in front of it to demand the return of the land they once owned (Sarbutt, 1992). By this time the railway system was already suffering severe shortages of most items, one of the most obvious being a lack of window glass, and in February 1992 all passenger services were suspended on safety grounds.

After a few months, the lines from Durrës to Tirana and Pogradec resumed operations, with two passenger-workings each day and a small amount of freight. But the workshops at Durrës were packed with unserviceable locomotives, wagons and carriages, and people could be seen quite openly stealing fuel from locomotive tanks. Of HSH's 70 T669 locomotives, about half were isolated on closed lines around the country, at the mercy of thieves and vandals, although all five diesel-hydraulics obtained from the German Federal Railway in 1989 could be accounted for. Sixty-three passenger coaches were donated subsequently by Italy, to be followed by rails and 50,000 sleepers, and the Tirana–Shkodër passenger service was restored later in 1992 with these. Radio signalling was to be installed where fixed equipment had been destroyed, and police surveillance of the railways was doubled. The Railway Directorate estimated that $200 million was needed to renovate the existing system, and plans for a 120 km link from Pogradec to Florina in Greece via Korçë, at a cost of $260 million, were again being discussed, with the possibility of finance from European Community development funds (Sarbutt, 1992). The latter agreed to finance a modernisation of the railway's telecommunications system and to provide funding for other vital supplies, while Italian State Railways would provide retraining programmes in Italy for Albanian rail officials.

The period 1993/4 was therefore likely to be critical in beginning to substantially upgrade the country's infrastructure, until then a major bottleneck in development processes. Without an adequate and modern infrastructure, investment in the country's three major economic prospects – agriculture and food, minerals, and tourism – would remain less than effective.

8.3.8 Land rights

Property compensation and restitution was given legal status in May 1993. Non-agricultural land and buildings confiscated by the communist regime after 29 November 1944 was to be returned or compensated in full to the former owners and their heirs up to an area of 10,000 sq metres, On land of between 10,000 and 100,000 sq metres the extent of restitution or compensation was to be 10 per cent, and above that size it would be one per cent. Restitution would be postponed for three years in the case of land and buildings being used for public needs.

The source of no little criticism was the provision that property privatised after 1991 would revert to its original owners, The existing owners would be compensated by the state for what they paid for the property. If the current owners had set up shops, restaurants or other economic units, they would be designated co-owners with the original owners. Over the following two years they would be required to pay rent to the original owners (at a rate of $2.15 per sq metre each month in Tirana and less in the rest of the country).

The separate law on agricultural land stipulated full compensation for land up to 15 ha. Between 15 ha and 100 ha, compensation was fixed at 10 per cent, and above 100 ha at two per cent. The monetary value of compensation was to be legally established within six months.

Property formerly owned by Zogu and foreigners would not be covered by the legislation. Additionally, collaborators with the wartime Italian and German occupiers, former senior communist officials and people sentenced for serious crimes against property were also excluded (EIU, 1993c, p. 44).

Former property owners who were dissatisfied with this legislation established the Property with Justice National Association, and claimed to represent 150,000 families. They staged a three week hunger strike in May and June 1993 objecting to the laws' failure to return property in full, to the co-ownership provisions, and to delays in compensation payments.

9

Sustaining the future

In a relatively short time, the Albanians have shown some flair for petty trade and commerce, and, with open borders, improved transport and communications systems, Albania could become the entrepôt of the Balkans (section 8.3.4 above). There are, however, three major areas of economic development upon which the country will largely depend for its short- to medium-term future: agriculture and food, energy and minerals, and tourism. The development of all three will be constrained both by past mistakes and by the need to rectify some of the consequences of those mistakes, particularly in the protection and conservation of the fragile Albanian physical and cultural environment. The thrust of this chapter is that for sustainable economic development to succeed, the needs and sensitivities of the physical and cultural environment must be respected and protected: this is no better exemplified than in the promotion of 'ecotourism' (section 9.3 below).

9.1 Agriculture and food

9.1.1 Tinkering with the rural economy

Between 1946 and the end of the 1980s cultivable land increased by about 240 per cent, but between 1950 and 1990 the population increased by 270 per cent. Overall, the amount of arable land per person decreased by 10 per cent, and this process accelerated during the 1980s. Arable land currently comprises 700,000 ha, 450,000 ha (64 per cent) of which is on sloping ground. Expansion of cultivable land entailed an improvement in desalination methods (although salination remains a problem), reclamation from coastal and lake-side lagoons, and an extension of cultivation in upland areas, often through extensive terracing (Hall, 1987a; Kusse and Winkels, 1990) (but see section 5.1 above). Collectivised agriculture absorbed a rapidly growing workforce during the 1970s and early 1980s. Today, however, with privatisation and uncertainty, the 70,000 young people entering the national job market every year can no longer be accommodated in the agrarian sector. Recent rural to urban migration and waves of emigration have partly reflected this problem, and such processes are unlikely to abate in the short term.

With mounting criticism of the sector's failings, a 'reformist' agriculture minister was appointed in 1988. Subsequent experiments in decentralising economic and administrative control to a few selected districts saw brigades of 30–60 peasants, corresponding to one or two extended families, given the right to 'own' small herds. By October 1989 it was being argued that this semi-privatisation of livestock had led to a fivefold increase in the number of cattle held. As a result of this 'success', from December 1989 co-operatives were permitted to sell their surplus at local markets, and in the following month they were encouraged to market their farm and livestock products in major urban areas – a significant departure from past practice, reflecting the need for a positive response to social unrest following urban food shortages (Plate 9.1). Wholesale prices fixed for co-operatives would also be freed to reflect efficiency (EIU, 1990c, p. 36), with the state willing to buy above-plan production at 50 per cent rather than the previous 10 per cent bonus rate.

Previous socio-economic policy had discriminated positively in favour of rural against urban and upland rather than lowland areas (Hall, 1987a). But with an increased urgency to stimulate food production, and the establishment of a new Agricultural Bank to sanction and monitor the viability and execution of rural projects, a fourfold locational designation was introduced for funding agriculture, whereby state subsidies for marginal, inefficient, farming areas were actually increased. The zones – 'lowland', 'hilly', 'mountainous', and 'the north-east' – were to receive successively higher prices for their produce by virtue of their higher production costs, a recipe for increasing inefficiency and hastening detrimental ecological consequences in marginal and fragile environments. National events soon overcame the implementation of this policy.

An FAO mission in December 1989 pointed to the need to strengthen the knowledge of specialists in the fields of saline soils improvement and land reclamation, through seminars, feasibility studies and pilot projects, and recommended extending the laboratory of the Institute of Pedology and the completion of a national soil survey at a scale of 1:10,000 (Kusse and Winkels, 1990).

9.1.2 *Agrarian restructuring and privatisation*

In July 1990, in stark contrast to previous policy, a programme of encouraging the development of private agricultural plots was begun, particularly aimed at stimulating meat and vegetable production and at raising rural incomes. Peasants were allowed to rear cattle on their own plots, and co-operatives were asked to transfer stock to their members for this purpose: in hilly and mountainous areas 2,000 sq m were to be given to each member, in addition to their private plots, and in lowland areas peasants were to be given up to 2,000 sq m including their plots (EIU, 1990d, p. 36). Persistent drought tended to undermine the programme, however.

None the less, the domesticated animal population again increased dramatically although a significant growth in the number of sheep and particularly goats was also evident, which, through indiscriminate grazing, was likely to exert adverse impacts on a number of fragile environments, creating conditions for renewed erosion in upland areas.

The coalition government's land and private property laws of July and August 1991 dissolved all co-operatives but forbade the purchase or sale of land. Anarchy in the countryside followed as co-operatives were broken up and land (230,000 ha out of a total of 531,000 ha) distributed among the peasants, some of whom also seized land and livestock. In the rush to regain lands held before the war, former rural landowning families were unilaterally claiming and fencing off territory, even destroying buildings such as schools (Zanga, 1991b) and installations such as oil wells (Kristo, 1991) in the process. Essential foodstuffs were rationed, and the country became almost totally dependent on foreign food supplies. There was widespread looting of warehouses as people went in search of food; and officials warned of the possibility of hunger in the provinces during the winter months. The quality of life in the country, already the lowest in Europe, plummeted even further. On taking office in the spring of 1992, the new Democratic Party government urgently needed to focus its attention on completing and consolidating land reform so that external aid could be switched away from food, as Albanians rediscovered their capacity for feeding themselves, and onto the transfer of skills and appropriate technology and information (Hall, 1992d).

As the country's economy has opened and

Plate 9.1   *A desultory private market, Vlorë*

personal mobility is enhanced, whole areas of upland agriculture, particularly the hillside terracing which enjoyed substantial investment of financial and labour resources in the 1960s and 1970s, have become vulnerable to abandonment, as rural to urban, and upland to lowland migration gains pace (Plate 9.2). While a shedding of surplus rural labour might appear to present an ideal opportunity for agricultural mechanisation, difficult topography coupled with capital shortages will severely constrain such developments. Inaccessibility, a poor infrastructure and generally harsh living conditions could generate mass depopulation in upland areas, particularly of young rural-dwellers seeking an easier life in lowland and urban areas. This would swell the ranks of the country's unemployed, and in turn exert pressures for emigration.

9.1.2.1 Co-operative associations. Out of the co-operative land redistribution process, official figures claim that over 400,000 family holdings emerged, ranging from 0.8 ha to 2 ha in size, with an average of 1.5 ha, and covering 75 per cent of the country's arable land. The problems confronted by such family farms have been immense: (a) a lack of capital and space to improve production techniques; (b) uncertainty of input supplies; (c) exposure to competition and risk for the first time; (d) primitive marketing and unstable markets; (e) poor access to information – particularly of a specialised economic and commercial nature – and to technical assistance; (f) lack of forward planning; (g) high rates of interest for credit and unpredictable rates of inflation; and (h) an inadequate legal system to permit the buying and selling of land (Leiby and Marra, 1993).

These circumstances have required the development of 'capitalist' farmers' co-operative associations, which began to emerge after the April 1992 electoral defeat of the communists. By mid-1993 some 90 associations, made up of 15–20 families joining voluntarily and electing a management board, had been established, with total land-holdings averaging 40 ha, but varying from 25 ha to 300 ha. Most have been developed in lowland arable areas and their formation was said to be stimulating market

response, increased productivity, greater use of machinery, a move away from subsistence and a lower use of female and child labour compared to those family units not involved in such associations. For example, land sown with grain was shown to be three times greater per family within the associations than in non-associated farms, while land devoted to water melons, which had experienced significant market price reductions, was ten times less (Anon, 1993b). However, one suspects that the more advanced farms and members of the farming community are more likely to join co-operative associations as the latter would begin their existence in an advantageous position, the joining of such associations subsequently reinforcing differences between farms.

From 1992, up to 300 trade centres were being set up by agricultural training centres to assist the newly private farmers.

9.1.2.2 External assistance. One obvious problem now confronting Albanian farming was the degree to which the huge amount of food aid being supplied to the country represented serious competition for, and an inhibiting influence on, domestic food producers. At the same time, farm animals were being smuggled across the border into Greece to pay for the increasing flow of consumer goods moving in the opposite direction (Dizdari, 1992). Although agricultural production rose by an estimated 13 per cent in 1992 (PHARE, 1993), by the end of that year, the Albanian government was arguing that it would be another three years before the country could re-attain 1989 living standards. With the extensive use of British seed, however, wheat production in 1993 was about 700,000 tonnes, and the speed of harvesting was generally twice that of the communist period, the task being accomplished in five rather than ten days (*EEN*, 21 September 1993, p. 7).

Early in the process of economic change, several agricultural missions, most notably of German, Italian and Dutch specialists, visited Albania to provide advice on a range of agrarian problems and to help establish a domestic fund of up-to-date technical know-how for agricultural recovery. Fiatagri became

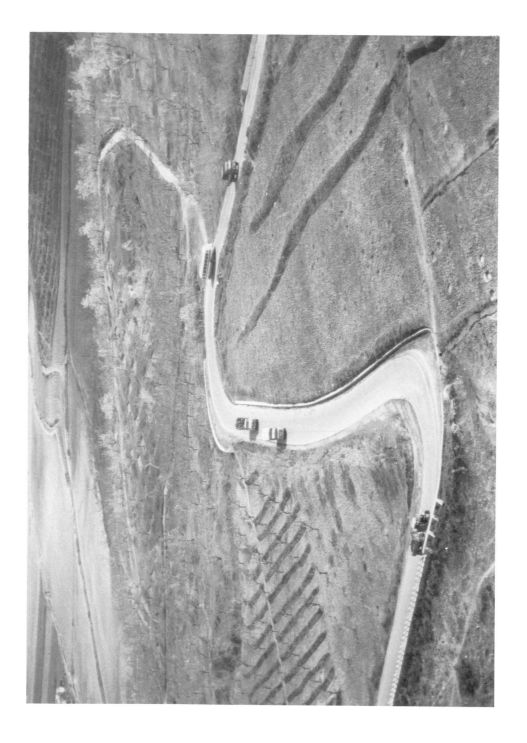

Plate 9.2   *A mountain road in the south-east winds through part-abandoned terracing*

involved in pilot projects in the north of the country for mechanising the sowing and harvesting of 300 ha each of maize and rice, employing machinery previously untried within the country. The Italian company later provided laser technology to aid soil levelling. Albanian reports of these projects were optimistic, quoting a 50 per cent increase in maize yields with a 50 per cent reduction in costs after the first year (Anon, 1990), and a doubled yield with costs reduced by 58 per cent, and in the case of rice by 75 per cent, at the end of the two-year trial period. In the autumn of 1991, a joint agribusiness venture with the French Ducros company, based in Durrës, secured a monopoly on processing all cultivated oleaginous crops and indigenous flora. This company would be able to operate tax-free for at least three years (Anon, 1991a). Italian, Greek, Turkish and German interests have all subsequently invested in the food industry, a sector which has substantial potential but which has laboured under severe under-capitalisation (Plate 9.3).

At an international conference on foreign support for agriculture, which met in Tirana in November 1992, there was clearly no shortage of interest in the sector, with representatives of the EC, World Bank, UNDP and FAO in attendance. Emphasising the importance of price liberalisation, privatisation and the development of private co-operatives, it was agreed to make available not less than $100 million to support Albanian agriculture, which was seen to have a promising future. The World Bank, the EC and the Phare Programme would draw up a development strategy emphasising the development of rural businesses, with an overall investment of $30 million, over two-thirds of which would be used in 1993. Most significantly, the International Development Agency subsequently established a rural development fund which would grant loans of $20–$500 to enable small farmers to buy implements or livestock in order to help establish small rural businesses. Communes in the country's ten poorest districts would also receive between $11,000 and $25,000 to improve rural infrastructures and aid employment generation (EIU, 1993c, p. 47).

Germany, Italy and Greece would provide a total of $20 million to renovate agricultural equipment and tractors, and the Phare Programme would offer $3.5 million. Irrigation would receive $40 million from a variety of sources including the World Bank. Investment support for animal husbandry, forestry, the privatisation of the food industry and upland development would also go ahead.

Finance Minister Genc Ruli reckoned that agriculture would account for half of the country's GDP in 1993. Lowland farming was showing promise by the end of 1992 while upland agriculture was aiming more or less for self-sufficiency. Loans from the agricultural bank at 2 per cent interest over 15 years, and the exemption of import tax on farm equipment had stimulated rural mechanisation. About 90 per cent of non-state farm land (412,000 ha) had been privatised, and 80 per cent of peasant families had become landowners. In the absence of significant foreign investment, private farming was being seen as the most critical factor for national economic recovery in 1993. The country's 225 state farms (now known as agricultural enterprises), covering 23 per cent of cultivated land, were to be privatised during the year.

9.1.2.3 Joint ventures. In August 1992, an Agency for the Restructuring and Privatisation of the Agricultural Enterprises was set up for the purpose within the Ministry of Agriculture. Aided by foreign consultants, a three-stage programme was devised: (a) provision of credit guarantees to cover autumn and winter investment requirements; (b) dissolution of some state farms, particularly those in upland areas, by distributing land and implements amongst their workers; and (c) a reorganisation of the state farms into joint-stock companies with joint participation of workers, managers and the state.

The district of Kavajë was in the forefront of transforming state farms into joint ventures. The fruit-growing farms of Kavajë and Rrogozhinë, with a total land area of 864 ha, established joint ventures ('Albitalia' and 'Agrifoods') with Italian-Romanian Adventure East Service SRI, employing a total of 600

Plate 9.3   Labour-intensive, all-female activity in the fruit bottling and processing plant of Peshkopi, close to the border with Macedonia

workers at an average daily rate of $2. Also in the Kavajë district, the Gosa state farm joined with the Italian company Manfredonia FG to employ 650 workers at a similar salary level (Anon, 1993b).

The Italian-Romanian group later set up a JV with the Spitalle Frutore Durrës agricultural enterprise with the intention of improving farming and agricultural processing industry and of stimulating tourism. The project also envisaged the development of 300 ha of heated glasshouses, not only to improve and diversify agricultural production, but also for the supply of hot water for Durrës residents (*ATA*, 15 June 1993).

Privatisation of agricultural mechanisation enterprises (formerly known as machine and tractor stations) began in October 1992 (*BEE*, 30 November 1992). Of the enterprises' 5,500 tractors, about 2,000 were sold to their drivers in time to prepare soil for autumn sowing. Five thousand requests for tractors had been submitted by the end of October. These were being processed slowly by the privatisation agencies. Thirty repair centres were also being sold off. Other measures were being taken to speed the pace of mechanisation, such as the purchase on credit of imported equipment. About 35 tractors had arrived from Italy and 75 from Germany. New private firms were also beginning to import agricultural equipment, as were some Albanian emigrés working abroad.

In autumn 1992 the government was claiming that thousands of people were being removed from the social assistance list as agricultural privatisation was beginning to regenerate rural employment. A decision to grant land to all former agricultural personnel brought benefits to thousands of urban families, who, because of their connections with nearby farms, would be eligible for the receipt of land, olive trees, vineyards and fruit trees. Land ownership problems persisted, however.

9.1.2.4 Land rights complications. The lack of incentive for Albania's private farmers to produce cash crops for the domestic market needed to be seriously addressed. It particularly arose out of the combination of small size of holdings – mostly between one and two hectares – and the legal inability to trade in land due to the absence of a proper record of land ownership. While such structural and legal obstacles to the development of an efficient agricultural sector have been evident throughout much of Eastern Europe, confronting this problem was particularly urgent in a country with potentially abundant resources yet unable to feed itself (EIU, 1993c, p. 40).

Early in 1993 the government was coming under mounting pressure from former property owners to abrogate the July 1991 land law which redistributed land formerly held by agricultural co-operatives to their former members rather than to the prior owners who lost their land during the communist era. The organisation representing these former owners, the Property with Justice National Association, heightened its campaign for the full restitution of confiscated property. The government responded by passing a restitution and compensation law (section 8.3.8 above) which provided for full compensation for those with land of no more than 15 hectares and a graduated compensation scheme for others. This would be paid in state bonds.

A problem surrounded the legal position of current farmers, who appeared to receive only vague status as tenants. The law forbade the further purchase of agricultural land in order to prevent these 'tenants' from causing additional confusion by selling the pre-1946 owners' land before compensation arrangements could be secured. Two problems followed from this (a) the tenant farmers would feel insecure until they knew for certain that they legally owned the land they tilled, thereby inhibiting investment in it; and (b) the (presumably temporary) prohibition on land purchases prevented good farmers from expanding their activities.

One possible way out of this dilemma surrounded the position of the 150,000 ha of former state farm land. This was now partially or wholly farmed by its former employees who lived in hope that they would receive full title to the land within three years. However, some of the former state farm land could be given to tenants of former landowners so that the latter could be given some of their land back if they wanted it, and some of the poor aspiring highland farmers could be offered lowland land (*EEN*, 21 September 1993, p. 8).

9.1.3   Priorities for an agrarian future

Few overviews of rural restructuring and privatisation in Eastern Europe have yet been published (Cochrane, 1992; Turnock, 1993a; being exceptions; see also, for example, Morgan, 1992). Yet within a regional framework, it is clear that in terms of national livelihood and past policy emphases, as well as the need to feed the population, agricultural activity in Albania has been relatively more important than in most other countries.

By 1993 there were five priorities within the agricultural sector (PHARE, 1993): (a) transformation of state farms; (b) development of rural credit and input/output marketing; (c) irrigation and road infrastructure; (d) issue of formal land titles; and (e) development of agro-industry.

As joint ventures were being established with former state farms on the fertile coastal lowlands – 30 had been formed by the end of January 1993 – the imminent intensification of agriculture raised a number of questions. Most notably:

(a) with two-thirds of the country's population having been retained in the countryside (Sjöberg, 1991a, 1992), major spatial readjustments would be required. The very substantial reduction in an agricultural labour force requirement would demand policy options for both providing alternative rural employment and appropriate urban occupations. If these were not in place and instability continued or intensified on the country's eastern borders (Pettifer, 1992), pressures for mass migration would increase;

(b) the extent to which an adequate national agricultural training and assistance system could be put in place. Attention was being focused on the role and character of the Tirana Agricultural University at Kamëz. Of $25 million US aid for Albanian agriculture, $6 million was allocated for the University's restructuring, and American teachers became a regular feature of the institution (Leiby and Marra, 1993). The University also formalised relations with universities in Italy and Germany, the government of the latter having allotted DM5 million to it for technical aid, specialist teachers and equipment (*ATA*, 22 May 1993). Overall, the EC was providing more than $100 million for the development of Albanian agriculture during 1993;

(c) the extent to which farm credit could be extended to small and middle-sized farms and farm associations and be coupled with training schemes to enable a rational use of mechanical and non-chemical agrarian aids. In 1992, for example, in one of the regions of most intensive agricultural activity, much of the 28.7 million leks in credit extended by Durrës branch of the Bank of Agriculture and Development was employed to buy fertilisers and erect buildings, including glasshouses and bakeries;

(d) the extent to which market mechanisms could establish a sectoral balance of production within the country. During 1992 annual agricultural output increased by 17 per cent, but while large increases were recorded in the production of green vegetables, pulses, potatoes, water melons and dairy produce, especially milk, the output of industrial crops decreased dramatically, reflecting the structural changes taking place within the agrarian sector. New private peasant farmers preferred to grow crops intended for consumption and for domestic markets, from which they could derive larger profits than from industrial crops, the processing of which had been disrupted, as had production from the previous major source, the state farms, because of structural transformation;

(e) the extent to which substantially increased use of chemical fertilisers and pesticides, as an inevitable concomitant of intensified agricultural activity, would damage Albania's vulnerable natural environment.

Thus far, the level of use of chemicals on the country's land has been relatively limited (although see section 5.2.3 above). Would it be too bold or naive (or both) to suggest that Albania could respond to the growing Western niche market demand for organically grown food by actually *reducing* levels of chemical use, at least in certain locations and agrarian sectors and targeting such markets for its produce (assuming EC co-operation)? Although perhaps presenting short-term problems of organisation and marketing, a significant segment of Albanian agriculture devoted to organic farming could provide an appropriate sustainable future for the rural population, complemented by small-scale 'green' tourism (section 9.3).

9.2 Mineral exploitation

9.2.1 Resource development

The country's poor infrastructure and its proximity to the wars of Yugoslav succession has continued to deter many potential investors. Further, emphasising the bureaucratic hurdles and inconsistent legal environment, the turn-over tax reform of 1990 rendered enterprises in the metals and machinery sector even more uncompetitive. The chrome industry, for example, was paying a total turnover tax of 105 per cent because its seven production stages were being carried out by seven separate companies, and individual enterprises were each obliged to pay the tax. This situation was somewhat ameliorated by a 1993 budget which lifted the liability to turnover tax from some of the hardest pressed sectors of industry.

A comprehensive upgrading of technology and technical efficiency both in processing capability and pollution minimisation, of skills training and management effectiveness, were urgently required to help realise Albania's not inconsiderable resource potential. This potential is enhanced by the availability of low cost domestic energy, mostly hydro-electric, for the major energy-intensive refining industries.

9.2.2 Oil and gas

By mid-1993, five Western oil companies (Agip (Italian), Deminex (German), OMN (Austrian), Occidental and Chevron (both US)), had made the only substantial foreign investments in the Albanian economy, all of which were for offshore exploration work, the seismic survey stage of which had been mostly completed by the end of 1992. As exploratory drilling was beginning in 1993, oil company representatives were pointing to the high expense of their operations due to the depth to be drilled – 4,500 to 5,000 metres. Global Marine (USA) subsequently established a 50:50 joint venture with Albpetrol to provide offshore drilling operations for other companies (*BEE*, 18 October 1993, pp. 9–10).

The onshore industry was restructured during 1992 with the Albpetrol National Oil Corporation, based at Patos. However, because of organisational disruption, a decrease in the number of wells – including destruction as a result of land grabs – strikes, and a shortage of funds, production for 1992 was a mere 5 per cent of the pre-1989 level. Nevertheless, in November 1992 geological data on prospecting for oil and gas were exhibited in London and Houston, and some 50 companies expressed an interest in the call for investment proposals for the sector (*ATA*, 12 February 1993). Albanian hopes were beginning to be raised (Kadia, 1993), and estimated production for 1993 was 600,000 t of petroleum and 100 million cubic metres of natural gas.

Following a regional evaluation of the country's potential, produced by a joint venture between the Geological Institute for oil and gas at Fier, the geology department at Tirana University and Simon Petroleum Technology of Wales, the government began to open up the possibilities for further onshore development. Six exploration blocks covering 700 sq km in the Vlorë, Durrës and Delvinë areas were offered, the bids for which were due to close in mid-June 1993. Twenty-five-year contracts would include provision for a five-year research and exploration period together with on-site training for Albanian technicians. A production-sharing agreement would see capital expenditure recoverable over five years, and up to 40 per cent of annual crude oil production would be payable for cost recovery. Natural gas would remain the property of the Albanian government which hoped that the country could be linked to a supply of Russian natural gas via pipelines through Macedonia and Greece.

International oil companies were also invited to submit bids for a $70 million recovery enhancement project for existing onshore fields, again to employ local staff and services and to spend $5 million on environmental improvement. Yet one estimate of the total cost of production modernisation was put at $750–$1,000 million (*ATA*, 5 July 1993).

A recurring theme in the public expressions regarding the multinational companies was the complaint that investment risks were too high and rewards too low to warrant a long-term presence in the country. By mid-1993 three major oil companies were planning on a significant scaling back of their operations. Prospects in Albania were claimed by them to be poor compared to the far more lucrative incentives being offered by the governments of Russia, Kazakhstan and Uzbekistan. As the opportunities for Western oil companies were far exceeding their strength, the companies could afford to be selective in their operations. Company representatives were claiming that Albania presented the worst deal available (Luxner, 1993a). Occidental's agreement, for example, gave the company a 13 per cent share of all potential oil revenues in its concession area, compared to 20 per cent or 30 per cent offered by some other countries. The Durrës Basin was seen to be high risk in that it was undrilled and there was no guarantee of hydrocarbon deposits there, the companies claimed.

A further argument used by the multi-nationals in their efforts to extract more concessions from the Albanian government, and a recurrent theme in this volume, was the incomplete and inconsistent legal environment for investment. Particular problems were set by laws which were passed and then within a few weeks were amended as the result of domestic political pressure. Local bureaucratic practices

and inevitable infrastructural shortcomings added to the companies' problems, which, in respect of onshore blocks, would be further complicated by unresolved questions of land ownership (Luxner, 1993a).

9.2.3   Coal

In addition to more common problems of mineral exploitation, Albanian lignite appeared to be a poor prospect for investment. Seams were thin, ash content was high, extensive beneficiation was required, a multiplicity of grades were found – reckoned at about 60 – and coal was placed in a poor domestic competitive position in relation to hydro-electric power. Given the abundance of lignite in neighbouring countries and the fuel's harmful environmental attributes, the prospect for the sector was not good.

9.2.4   Chromite

The country's chromite mines were grossly undercapitalised, and production had been gradually decreasing to 420,000 tonnes by 1992 (60 per cent of the 1991 level and little more than a third of the 1.2 million tonnes mined in 1986), with 70,000 tonnes of concentrate produced. If mines and processing plant were able to be brought up to recognised world standards of technological efficiency and organisational effectiveness, production could be trebled (*Mining Journal*, 1992, p. 4). Modern systematic exploration had not been undertaken to any great extent, and the area of potential chromite mineralisation was estimated to be greater than 3,000 sq km, almost 10 per cent of the country's total land area. With considerable potential for discovery and exploitation of highly profitable concentrations, foreign industrial groups, notably South African, were taking a close interest in developments in this field. The Samanko company was aiming to invest $80 million on exploitation and sale of chromite ore (*BEE*, 28 September 1992).

An 'arm's length' corporation, Albkrom, was set up to oversee the industry, and with World

Bank and EBRD encouragement, seven foreign companies submitted investment proposals for the industry in 1993. Two short-term problems were inhibiting investor enthusiasm, however: a 50 per cent decrease in world market prices during 1992, and continuing strikes at Bulqizë mine, which, with a third of the country's production, was working at only 15 per cent–20 per cent capacity. A longer-term problem for the processing industry was the development of a complex at Radusha in neighbouring FYR Macedonia, for the processing of imported Albanian ore, while Albania's own plant was languishing (Hido, 1993).

9.2.5 Nickel

In 1990 Albania produced 12,000 tonnes of nickel, almost 2 per cent of world production, ranking it amongst the top 15 producers. Annually around one million tonnes of ore has been mined, the majority of which has been processed at the smelters in the Elbasan combine. Around one-third of total output had been exported to Czechoslovakia in recent years: up to 1978, production was exclusively for that market. Known reserves, at about 60 million tonnes of iron with one million tonnes of contained nickel, were considered to be sufficient for 100 years. As a potential by-product, some 80,000 tonnes of cobalt, the equivalent of three years' world consumption and having an *in situ* value of more than $2,500 million, was reckoned to be exploitable (*Mining Journal*, 1992, p. 6). Exploration potential was seen as very good, particularly in the Kukës district and at Bitincka in the south, with most likely exploration targets being near-surface high tonnage nickel-silicate laterites with 2.6 per cent nickel content.

9.2.6 Copper

Known reserves of copper were estimated at around 50 million tonnes. Some 27 individual deposits have been worked in recent years, annual production capacities ranging from 30,000 to 200,000 tonnes. With value-added refining and fabrication, copper production was reckoned to be worth $170 million. The industry has employed a large workforce of 11,000, in the past supplemented by convict labour, and production reached a peak in 1985 at 989,000 tonnes. Again, exploration of potential mineralised areas was far from comprehensive, and inward investment was sought both to aid efficient prospecting in the Pukë and Mirditë regions, considered to have the greatest potential, and to upgrade technology and know-how at existing mining and processing locations. Although the 'arm's length' Albbaker corporation was set up in 1992, the industry's domestic debts were considerable, and a new financial mechanism was required to deal with them if the industry was to appeal to investors (*ATA*, 15 October 1992).

During 1992, ore output from the country's eight mines fell to just 256,000 tonnes. In March 1993, the smelters at Laç, Kukës and Rubik resumed operation, but the 1993 target production figure of 800,000 tonnes appeared excessively optimistic and a thinly veiled attempt to attract foreign investment. Two further impediments to such investment were presented by the poor quality of ore grades, ranging from 0.8 per cent to 3.0 per cent metal content, and the depressed domestic market for the copper wire and cable produced in Shkoder, the quality of which has been too poor for export markets. Some electrolytic copper, has, however, found overseas markets (EIU, 1993c, p. 46). During 1993, Saudi Arabian companies were showing interest in possible co-operation with the industry.

9.2.7 Other mineral and ore potential

Perhaps most interesting in terms of investment potential is the nature of building-stone within the country. Limestone, dolomite and marble quarries have been worked at Krujë, Vlorë and Elbasan, tied in to the cement industry, while large granite quarries can be found in the copper belts of Fushë-Arrëz. High quality decorative stone such as marble and alabaster has been in continual production for centuries, and with one of the world's leading centres of dimension stone processing just across the Adriatic, potential for the industry, particularly with Italian investment, is considered to be high.

9.2.8   Mineral future

Northern Albanians often complain that the Hoxha clique, originating from the south of the country, both discriminated against the north and doubly disadvantaged the region by extracting its mineral wealth for little regional gain while forcing the employees of extractive industries to endure appalling working conditions. There is both considerable known and likely unknown mineral wealth within the country. Policy decisions on how that potential is exploited and the wealth used for both local and national benefit will be no small political task. Investment returns for foreign collaborators could be very considerable given favourable world market conditions. With appropriate technology for an efficient value-added processing industry, the economic benefit for Albania could be immense. But in following the path of opening up and overhauling its minerals sector, the country and its investors have a strong obligation to (a) treat Albanian industrial workers with dignity and provide healthy working and living environments; and (b) minimise the potential environmental degradation associated with mineral extraction, transport and processing.

9.3   Sustainable tourism?

9.3.1   Selling Albania: tourism concern

As a key sector for Albania's future development, tourism has been identified as perhaps best meeting the objectives for assisting the country's medium-term regeneration. Within this perspective it has been argued that tourism could: (a) develop as a sustainable, environmentally sound industry; (b) promote Albania as an attractive destination; (c) optimise foreign exchange earnings; (d) generate employ-

ment opportunities for Albanians; (e) encourage and facilitate profitable investment; (f) contribute to a refurbishment and enhancement of the national infrastructure; and (g) generate optimum economic benefits for all regions of the country (Touche Ross and EuroPrincipals Limited, 1992, p. 2). Crucial to the unleashing of this cornucopia is the 'selling' of Albania (Box 9.1): a country where the concept of marketing tourism, or indeed marketing of any sort, had not been viewed as a priority skill acquisition.

Albania's prime attraction rests in the country's natural and cultural heritages. But while these are critical resources and important marketing assets for the tourism industry (section 4.4.3 above; Hall, 1992a), they are also both extremely vulnerable and vital for the country's broader longer-term survival. Even more crucial in Albania than in most other developing societies is the obvious dilemma that the country's major potential tourist destinations are highly sensitive and fragile, both environmentally – mountains, sea coasts, lakes and rivers – and culturally (Hall, 1993a).

Although the level of environmental concern amongst tourism authorities varies considerably within Central and Eastern Europe, Albania's post-Communist decision-makers do appear to be among the more committed in the region to sustainable forms of tourism development (Atkinson and Fisher, 1992; Spaho, 1992, 1993a, 1993b): but then they need to be. The previous prescriptive nature and low level of international and domestic tourism development – numbers of foreign visitors peaking in 1990 at 30,000 (EIU, 1991a, p. 44; Hall, 1991) – was no reliable indicator of the country's potential for mass tourism and its consequences. Albania is very vulnerable to environmentally insensitive and semi-colonial tourism development from multinational groups. An economy of shortage looking for a short-cut route to economic growth can easily underestimate the negative impacts and be over-optimistic in assessing the rewards that such development might bring.

Certainly, the political appeal of hard currency generation and job creation is strong when a country's economic fortunes and

Box 9.1 *Albania: tourism marketing elements*

1. A still enigmatic land at the meeting point of European and Asian cultures.
2. The cradle of an ancient − Illyrian − civilisation, with many surviving elements from classical times.
3. One of the last environments in Europe unspoilt by tourism (and hopefully to remain so), allowing the development, virtually from scratch, of one of Europe's first environmentally sound tourism destinations.
4. A country of great diversity within an area no larger than Wales or Belgium: long stretches of sandy beaches, high, unexplored mountain ranges, large lakes with abundant fish life; wide expanses of forests, abundant and varied wildlife and a variety of climatic regimes from Mediterranean to Alpine, all providing opportunities to develop small-scale niche specialist tourism opportunities for individuals and small groups in the remoter interior of the country to help spread the economic benefits of tourism and extend tourism seasons, such as winter sports in the north-east and indoor leisure centres in the urban centres.
5. Coastal conditions to develop yachting and other nautical tourism activities in order to establish a leading role in the field, and to attract cruise ship stopovers.
6. An accessible location within three hours' flying time of most major European markets.
7. A traditionally friendly and hospitable people.
8. Colourful folklore, customs and crafts with some well preserved and restored archaeological and architectural assemblages providing the potential for an exclusive and high quality range of tourist 'products' and services.
9. Longer-term opportunities to promote business tourism, initially based on existing convention and exhibition facilities in Tirana.
10. In response to these elements, to attract high-spending tourists including those who previously would have taken holidays in Yugoslavia, and to develop special interest tours based on archaeological sites, literature, folklore, railways, bird-watching and wildlife, employing high-quality, small-scale tourism transport with guides, and to generate the appeal of small-scale bed and breakfast and farmhouse accommodation.

Sources: Touche Ross and EuroPrincipals Limited, 1992, pp. 37–9; author's fieldwork, 1974–93.

national morale are low. As a short to medium-term palliative for income generation, international tourism may appear to be far less environmentally harmful than, for example, a metallurgical complex or other misbegotten heavy industrial enterprises.

Tourism brings various negative effects, however. Socio-economic disparities between hosts and tourists, as Germans, Britons, Scandinavians and others penetrate hitherto untouched areas of the country will be made starkly apparent. Widening disparities within the host population itself and the generation of internal and international labour migration will be consequent upon the large-scale pursuit of tourism development. Growing recreational pressures and substantially increased traffic flows, particularly along the relatively unspoilt Ionian coast, will bring inevitable environmental deterioration in their wake. The diminution and/or fabrication of culture in order to meet the perceived requirements of mass tourism will also pose a threat. On the other hand, the growth of private initiative and enterprise, to generate appropriate small-scale artisan crafts reproducing traditional artefacts, could represent a positive contribution to the fund of Albanian material culture and indigenous skills, if adequately regulated.

Living through an economy of shortage for several decades has forced upon the Albanian population an innate sense of innovation and the ingenious use of available materials. But large-scale rural to urban migration and emigration, after decades of enforced rural living for up to two-thirds of the population, and a much wider and greater availability of material goods, will inevitably result in a loss and diminution of traditional rural craft skills. Tourism development needs to avoid imposing on Albania an international set of standards of tourism architecture, furnishing, and service, which, while objectively raising standards of 'comfort' and 'efficiency', would reflect mass production, international anonymity and bland-ness, and reduce the requirement for local craft skills still further. Governmental emphasis on national cultural pride, while not being overtly nationalistic in this region of nationalistic poisons, will need to be maintained and supported by funds for the promotion of national culture in vernacular architecture and building conservation, museums, artisan work-shops and artistic performances. The break-down of law and order in the early 1990s threatened the protection and maintenance of much of the country's material culture: reports of the theft of 13 classical sculptures from Apollonia, likely to have been smuggled across the border into Greece, were only the tip of an unsavoury iceberg.

In short, Albania cannot afford to lose much of its apparent 'character'. But is this not simply an outsider's elitist attitude? The patronising notion that funny little Albania should be kept in aspic as a sort of Stalinist theme park on the Mediterranean pleasure periphery would find little favour within the country, apart from the handful of entrepre-neurs ready to go for any profitable scam. So what of a middle way between mass tourism and animated suspension?

9.3.2 Appropriate tourism?

With no little irony, the previous Stalinist 'prescriptive' forms of tourism development, reasonably sympathetic to the country's small-scale and relatively fragile environments, with suitable adaptations might be seen at first glance as one model for appropriate tourism development in the new Albania. For many Albanians, however, after almost half a century of Stalinist excess, there is an understandable reaction against regulation and prescription and anything that smacks of the Hoxha era. Yet, just as Costa Rica has provided something of a model for 'ecotourism' in the developing tropical and sub-tropical world (Boza and Mendoza, 1981; C. Hall, 1985; Boza, 1988; Mayfield and Gallo, 1988; Sheck, 1990; Pariser, 1992), so Albania has been presented with an ideal opportunity to set itself up as a model for 'appropriate' tourism in low income, fragile Mediterranean environments. How far, with a sustainable development strategy (Redclift, 1987; Brookfield, 1988; Butler, 1990; de Kadt, 1990), tourism itself can be a 'sustainable' activity in terms of its ecological and cultural implications, is a matter of no little debate (Richter, 1987; Wheeller, 1992a, 1992b; Cater and Lowman, 1994; Hall and Kinnaird, 1994).

Sustainable tourism may be defined as developing/managing tourism in such a way as to ensure the compatability of income gener-ation, ecosystem protection/enhancement and support of the indigenous population, its activities and well-being. It is normally seen as possessing a number of positive aspects which may be lacking in other forms of tourism development (Boo, 1990, 1992a, 1992b; Eber, 1992; Cater and Lowman, 1994): (a) helping to stabilise the local population and economy; (b) complementing existing employment structures; (c) providing an alternative/additional source of income, such as in farmhouse tourism or conservation warden activities; (d) helping to reduce pressures for agricultural modernisation methods which might threaten local ecosystems; (e) generating regional income to help finance essential conservation work; (f) pursuing an educational function, for the local population, and indeed for the country as a whole, as well as for visitors.

Conditions likely to affect the development of sustainable tourism for vulnerable Mediterra-nean regions such as Albania differ significantly from those in North West Europe: models derived from the experience of developed northern Europe and North America are unlikely to be appropriate. In particular, in confronting the sustainable development requirements of Europe's southern periphery, the very different contextual characteristics to be recognised and built into any model of development include: (a) a high biological diversity; (b) a rich cultural heritage; (c) less well developed nature protection measures; (d) a lower level of infrastructure; and (e) a greater need for information and training (Simpson, 1992).

To believe that the Stalinist 'prescriptive' Albanian model of tourism development (Hall, 1984b, 1990f, 1991) could survive massive political and economic upheaval and meet the above requirements was perhaps over-extending the bounds of naive faith. The major motivation for the 'prescriptive' approach was, of course, ideological, wishing to minimise the 'contagion' of alien influences while at the same time begrudgingly exploiting Albania's considerable natural potential to generate much needed hard currency and project a positive image of the country for foreign consumption. Thus although the minimising of the wider environmental impacts of tourism was perhaps a by-product of overriding ideological paranoia, none the less it was an important consequence, such that while Albania's wetland and upland ecosystems may have been damaged by agricultural intensification and industrialisation, they remained largely untouched by tourism.

9.3.3 Investing in tourism

In their waning months in the early 1990s, the communists had stumbled into what appeared to be a crash development programme for tourism in a vain effort to save the economy and possibly their own political fortunes. Joint-venture contracts were signed in early 1991 for substantial tourist ventures along the coast and inland, including a marina at Sarandë, five Adriatic tourist villages, and an 18-storey, 260 room Sheraton hotel in Tirana (to be built on a central park), all to be completed by 1995, new hotels in Durrës, Divjakë, Vlorë and Berat and the refurbishment of existing ones in Durrës and Shkodër, to be undertaken by Yugoslav, Italian, French, Swiss and German interests

under contracts worth half-a-billion dollars (EIU, 1991c, p. 44). Some of these plans appeared far from realistic, and several involved Illiria Tourist, an 80:20 per cent joint venture between Illiria Holdings, a largely Kosovo Albanian-run organisation with its headquarters in Switzerland, and Albturist, the state tourism organisation.

In March 1992, however, all agreements with Illiria Holdings were summarily annulled, including the 18-storey hotel and the establishment of a joint Swiss-Albanian bank. Similarly, in September 1992, the country's State Control Commission abrogated the agreements also undertaken by the previous communist government with the French joint venture company Ada, which had established Albania's first post-war airline (one second-hand 18-seat Banderainte) and had pursued other diversions which became subject to criminal proceedings subsequently (*ATA*, 6 September 1992).

A greater emphasis upon foreign tourism is important for the post-communist Albanian government not just in economic terms but as a symbol of Albania joining the European mainstream. The most important long-term consequence of this has been Albania joining the EBRD in 1992 and the much maligned bank's subsequent assistance to formulate guidelines for appropriate tourism development as part of economic restructuring. The bank hired consultants to develop a blueprint for the tourism development potential of the country (Touche Ross and EuroPrincipals Limited, 1992) and to produce a guide for the government and foreign investors (Ministry of Tourism and EBRD, 1993). The study involved an environmental consultant, chosen by the EC and financed by PHARE (Murphy, 1992).

For its part, the new Ministry of Tourism, although headed by a macro-economist at the time of writing, sought to work with environmentalists, acknowledging the potential discordance between Albania's interests and the pressures of international capital (Spaho, 1992, 1993a, 1993b). It sought to develop links between tourism and other areas of the economy — agriculture, handicrafts, culture — within an environmentally sustainable framework, and was anxious to establish a tourism plan and strategy prior to major investment decisions (Atkinson and Fisher, 1992).

By early 1993, a yet to be privatised Albturist had about 25 enterprises scattered around the country. A process of decentralisation had been in progress since 1990, but the hesitant nature of this restructuring was both the cause and effect of: (a) a lack of clarity of responsibilities, both within Albturist and between it and the central ministry; (b) a lack of competition, with no legal control over prices for more autonomous enterprises; (c) a shortage of appropriate experience at the enterprise level; and (d) an apparent reluctance of Albturist's head office to relinquish control over negotiations with foreign companies. These factors were conducive neither to coherent planning nor to establishing the strengthened structures required to meet the challenges of tourism strategies which were about to be unleashed upon the country.

The consultants' report argued that a number of key steps were necessary in order to encourage confidence in the investment prospects of tourism. These included: (a) a reorganisation of the ministry of tourism to develop clear roles and responsibilities; (b) establishment of a single point of contact for potential investors; (c) provision of clear planning and environmental control criteria; (d) development of an appropriate manpower training department for tourism; and (e) identification of international aid opportunities for the industry.

Yet the virtual absence of an adequate legal and fiscal framework for investment and co-operation, including insurance guarantees, would inhibit development in the short term. Land and property rights and ownership would be a problem for some time to come, despite the January 1993 law on priority tourism development zones (RAPA, 1993), which established the framework for the Council of Ministers to allocate, and for a tourism development committee to review the progress of, priority tourism development areas within the country. A number of land purchases had already taken place along the coast, with Dema Construction of Illinois a notable buyer. The country's fledgling Green Party called for a halt to such sales until an adequate planning control system was in place. Priority tourism zones were finally demarcated in June 1993 (Ministry of Tourism and EBRD, 1993) (Figure 9.1).

9.3.4 Planning for tourism

An environmentally enlightened framework within which tourism and other development paths could be placed was now essential. Databases, and the means for developing them, would be urgently required, not least to establish a comprehensive environmental inventory. In response, during 1993 WWF began co-ordinating monitoring groups both in the UK and in Albania, the latter made up of representatives of the PPNEA and the universities, to examine the likely environmental consequences of the consultants' reports and of tourism strategies adopted by the Albanian government, and to advise both the EBRD and Albanian government accordingly.

Tourism plan formulation had actually begun to emerge – albeit tentatively – during 1992, with statements made by both the Minister of Tourism (Table 9.1a) and the Director of Albturist (Table 9.1b), the co-ordination/synchronisation of which was a matter of some speculation.

By mid-1992, the country's minister of tourism was arguing that within three or four years 200,000–250,000 Albanians could be employed in tourism. In November 1992, following several visits, a consultants' final report on tourism development guidelines for the country was presented to the Ministry of Tourism by the EBRD, emphasising the objective of developing a 'sustainable, environmentally sound tourism industry' (Touche Ross and EuroPrincipals Limited, 1992, p. 2). This document was interesting not least for concentrating on international tourism almost to the exclusion of any consideration of domestic recreational needs and their relationship with foreign visitors' requirements. The consultants' suggested phased tourism development timetable and visitor target figures are noted in Tables 9.2 and 9.3.

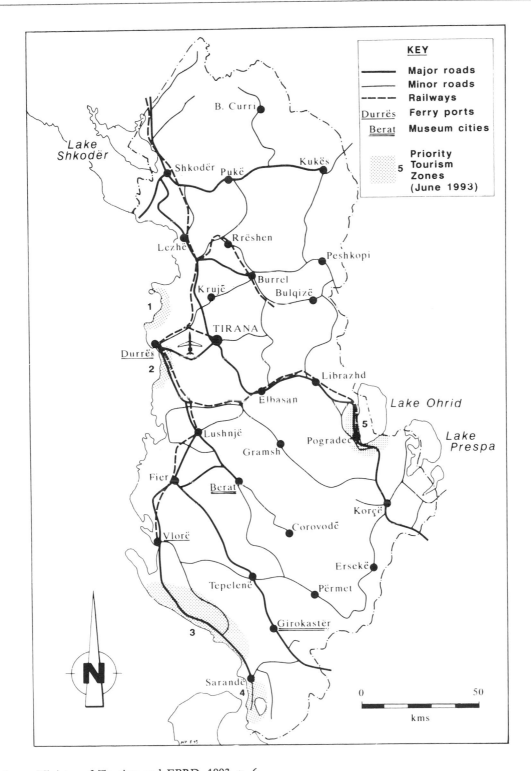

Source: Ministry of Tourism and EBRD, 1993, p. 6.

Figure 9.1 *Albania: priority tourism zones, 1993*

Table 9.1 *Tentative Albanian tourism development plans, 1992*

a. Ministry of Tourism
Phase 1: 1992–96
New bed spaces: Adriatic coast 20,000
                 Ionian coast   15,000
                 Inland resorts   5,000

Total   40,000
Employment in tourism 200,000–250,000

Phase 2: 1996–2000
Increase of total bed spaces to 100,000
Annual total of international tourists: 1,000,000

Employment in tourism 200,000–300,000

b. Albturist
1. 'Medium-level' tourism
To cater for large numbers of tourists, but not spatially concentrated. Accommodation would be in small buildings and villages along the coastline. For example: Vlorë-Fier, Lushnjë-Kavajë, Bay of Shëngjin-northern border.

2. 'High-level' tourism
Limited beach areas surrounded by pine forests; lagoons; intimate surroundings; with an emphasis on a clean environment (implication for 1 above??).

3. 'Elite-level' tourism
This would be pursued in some small rocky bays with deep water and exclusive beaches. Premium tourism tariffs would be sought.

In the mountains there would be winter sports ('white' tourism) and 'green' tourism; both would be based in small-scale accommodation. Sites would be selected for their 'environmental cleanness'.

Sources: (a) Albanian Radio 31 May 1992 and 29 June 1992 (from undated *Rilindja Demokratike* interview with Osman Shehu, then Minister of Tourism); (b) Atkinson and Fisher, 1992.

9.3.5 Tourism development zones

Following very quickly on the heels of the consultants' reports, in June 1993 five priority tourism zones were designated for investment purposes (Ministry of Tourism and EBRD, 1993) (Figure 9.1), within which all economic activities were to be subordinated to tourism. These focused on the Adriatic and Ionian coasts and the lakeside of Lake Ohrid. Overall, five major types of environment were to provide the geographical focus for future tourism development:

9.3.5.1 Adriatic and Ionian coastal resorts and

marinas. Incorporating four of the first five priority tourism zones (Figure 9.1), the Adriatic coast would continue to carry the majority of tourists, while the Ionian coast was likely to be developed for high-quality resorts, all of low-rise buildings, together with boating marinas at Durrës, Vlorë and Shëngjin on the Adriatic, and at Sarandë and Himarë on the Ionian. Protection of adjacent agricultural areas was seen as vital, given the crucial agrarian importance of the country's coastal plain. They would, however, contribute food for tourism consumption. Controlling the spread of tourism development both in the horizontal and vertical dimensions would be a major priority: clusters

Table 9.2 *Albania: suggested phased tourism development*

I Type of development	II Comments
A. Short term: within four years 1. Special interest trips: trekking, archaeology and heritage, railways, nature; chauffered or escorted car and minibus tours.	While all require a relatively modest investment outlay, specific requirements, such as reliable fuel and car spare parts supplies, will require special attention.
2. On-shore excursions for cruise-ship passengers: cruise ships can anchor off Durrës, Vlorë, Sarandë or Shëngjin, and passengers can disembark using smaller boats.	Requires restaurant facilities, opportunities to purchase souvenirs, such as handicrafts, and specific-interest visits. Reliability and synchronisation of organisation is vital. The high level of passenger shipping passing Albania *en route* between Italy and Greece provides substantial opportunities for this form of tourism development.
3. Conventions, exhibitions and meetings arising out of business trips, largely based in Tirana and Durrës.	Requires high-quality urban accommodation. The high-spending and all-year nature of business tourism could present potentially fast returns, given economic stability within the country and political stability within the Balkans.
4. Redevelopment of cultural centres and elaboration of existing events such as the Gjirokastër folklore festival.	Commercial sponsorship may be an inevitably necessary evil.
B. Medium term: four to eight years 1. Development of Adriatic and Ionian coastal resorts, including yachting and other marine activities not requiring marinas.	All require a stable economic and political environment and essential telecommunications and commercial banking systems.
2. Upmarket coach tours.	They emphasise the encouragement of both small-scale, informal, low-spending tourism and upmarket high-spending activities.
3. Small-scale accommodation planned for low impact: camping and caravan sites, bed and breakfast and farm holiday accommodation.	
4. Niche facilities: upland adventure activity sites, indoor facilities, particularly at lake resorts, golf courses.	

Continued

Table 9.2   *Continued*

I Type of development	II Comments
C. Long term: more than eight years. 1. Consolidation and expansion of most of A and B above.	
2. Establishing a major Mediterranean yachting centre.	Given the shortage of boat berths in the Mediterranean region, this could provide lucrative returns for relatively small impacts, although harbour-side serviced village development would be necessary.
3. Promoting the country as an international tax haven to attract such activity.	

Source: Touche Ross and EuroPrincipals Limited, 1992.

Table 9.3   *Albania: projections of numbers of visitors, 1993–2010*

Country of origin	1993	1994	2000	2010
Britain	2,500	3,750	45,000	65,000
Austria	2,000	3,000	38,000	59,500
Germany	1,300	1,950	24,000	66,000
France	1,200	1,800	19,000	18,000
Italy	500	750	14,000	44,500
Switzerland	500	750	9,000	18,000
Others	2,000	3,000	27,000	102,000
Total leisure tourists	10,000	15,000	176,000	373,000
Total business tourists	20,000	30,000	59,000	118,000
Total tourists	**30,000**	**45,000**	**235,000**	**490,000**

Assumptions:

1993: no change in range and quality of tourism services, especially hotel accommodation

1994: beginnings of economic recovery with refurbishment of some ex-Albturist hotels

2000: present ex-Albturist hotels refurbished with additional business hotels in some major centres; three resorts on the Ionian coast of 1,000 beds each, and two resorts on the Adriatic coast of 1,500 beds each. Total beach tourism beds: 6,000. Assume open 26 weeks per year, 70 per cent occupancy, average length of stay 7 days. Business tourism: 500 beds, 65 per cent occupancy, average stay 2 nights.

    Thus: beach tourism   109,000 tourists
          on-shore cruises' excursions   20,000
          business tourism   59,000
          other tourism   47,000
          Total tourists   **235,000**

2010: Five Ionian coast resorts of 1,200 beds and five Adriatic coast resorts of 1,500 beds: 13,500 beds. Assume open 26 weeks per year, 70 per cent occupancy, average length of stay 7 days. Business tourism: 1,000 beds, 65 per cent occupancy, average stay 2 nights.

    Thus: beach tourism   245,000 tourists
          on-shore cruises' excursions   25,000
          business tourism   117,000
          other tourism   103,000
          Total tourists   **490,000**

Source: Touche Ross and EuroPrincipals Limited, 1992, pp. 54–6.

of low-rise developments would be in sympathy with beaches, woods and other local features. Coastal parks would be created with emphasis on the natural environment and sporting activities. Domestic tourism facilities would be provided, with the balance of local and international tourism given careful consideration. All development should employ vernacular building styles and local construction materials wherever possible, and be designed to create minimal impact on the natural environment. Building density of no more than 100 tourist beds per hectare should be observed for tourist village developments.

Preservation of the Ionian coastline as a more exclusive tourist area was likely to be acknowledged with access to some coastal locations restricted to boats rather than through developing motor roads. Avoidance of creeping development up cliff and hill slopes would be a priority. Maximum benefit would be sought by exploiting local views, sunsets and natural topography in building design. Beach environments would require the setting back of development and public access routes. The extent to which existing villages could be both protected and integrated, socially and physically, was a matter of some speculation. Traditional income sources would be preserved as appropriate, although local labour would also be required for tourism activities. Clear potential for conflicting objectives was presented here.

9.3.5.2 Mountain resorts. Providing training skills for the management and maintenance of upland recreational centres, including environmental appreciation and conservation awareness, would be important in counteracting rural depopulation and for inculcating into young people the value of their country's remoter regions and their resources. Well-developed activity holidays such as trekking, mountaineering, rafting and canoeing, could be developed in the more rugged north-eastern and south-eastern uplands of the country, with less arduous rambling and cycling activities, in conjunction with bed and breakfast, farm and camping accommodation. Potential winter sports centres in the north-east and south-east, would require meticulous planning. Emphasis

would be given to compact clusters of vernacular style development, while simple cabins would be appropriate as high mountain refuges for trekkers and climbers. Part-time employment as guides and wardens should be made available to the local population, but not to the extent of completely replacing their agrarian livelihoods. Regional craft industries could be stimulated for marketing throughout the country and overseas if the goods produced were of genuine pedigree and of reasonable quality. Upland tourism construction should not impose on the skyline, but should follow the contours of the landscape, especially above the tree line. Many examples of good practice exist as models, such as the Ben Lawers national nature reserve mountain visitor centre in Scotland (National Trust for Scotland, 1988).

9.3.5.3 Lakeside resorts. Shkodër, Pogradec and Kukës could provide the focus for lakeside activities of both an outdoor and indoor nature, coupled with modest accommodation and appropriate infrastructural improvements and environmental safeguards. Lake Ohrid's lakeside area, centred on Pogradec, has been included as one of the first five priority tourism zones. While Kukës has potential pollution problems from local copper processing, the full potential of both lakes Ohrid and Shkodër requires international agreement (with Macedonia and Montenegro respectively). The less accessible lakes of Prespa in the south-east and of Lurë in the north-east would require strict environmental protection.

9.3.5.4 Museum cities and other heritage centres. Special interest niche holidays focusing on culture, architecture and heritage generally would be based in these centres, although Berat, Fier (for Apollonia) and Gjirokastër possessed the least satisfactory Albturist hotels. Small-scale accommodation could be integrated into the urban fabric, preferably employing existing structures converted to a standard found in, for example, the house employed in Gjirokastër as an ethnographic museum. Existing controls in these heritage centres, despite their communist pedigree, should be reinforced with an aim, for example, to preventing uncontrolled development up the slopes of highly visible mountains and hills (ironically, given that such past development has provided much of the character of these centres).

9.3.5.5 Business centres. The major centres of Tirana, Durrës, Shkodër, Vlorë and Korçë would act as the focus for the development of business tourism as and when the Albanian economy picked up and the country consolidated its political and cultural role within Europe. The potential for its relationship with the Middle East and the world of Islam should not be disregarded in this respect. While not easily accessible from North America, the potential of short incentive holiday breaks for favoured European employees could be significant.

In the subsequent parliamentary process political representatives saw the designation of priority tourism zones as a short-cut to local economic prosperity. As a consequence, many lobbied for their own constituencies to be included in the priority list, The result, as indicated by the Tourism Minister in December 1993 (Spaho, 1993b), was little short of a nonsense. Virtually all potential recreation areas of the country were listed as priority development areas, including those with vulnerable ecosystems such as Karavastë Lagoon and Lake Prespa, which the ministry had previously acknowledged as needing priority protection.

A further cause for concern was the fact that while the 'grave' dug in a central Tirana park for the foundations of the aborted Sheraton hotel was left unoccupied, as a gaping eyesore and testament to the follies of the early 1990s, one of the EBRD's first two credits for tourism development in the country was a $12 million facility to build a hotel and business centre on a different city centre site less than a kilometre away. As a four star hotel with 110 rooms, 25 apartments and 25 offices with satellite telephone facilities this development would be the first of its standard in the country (*BEE*, 6 September 1993, p. 9; EIU, 1993e, p. 46). Situated adjacent to the governmental and university quarters, construction of the complex was begun in September 1993. Under

the auspices of the Austrian Rogner construction company, sub-contracting for all of the necessary building materials and labour went to Slovenian companies such that no immediate employment benefits accrued to the Albanians. A starker example of comprehensive tourism economic leakages in pre-operation phase would be hard to find (*Albanian Economic Tribune*, 1993, 6(18), p. 15).

9.3.6   Infrastructural requirements

Even for a sustainable tourism development strategy, which seeks to maintain an equilibrium with the natural and cultural environment, significant infrastructural development would be necessary, given the very poor state of the country's transport, communications, accommodation and utilities. This would include: (a) expansion and refurbishment of the points of entry – border crossings, Rinas international airport, and the port terminals of Durrës, Vlorë and Sarandë (section 8.3.4 above), to cope with increased capacities, together with expansion and improvement in passenger and luggage handling capabilities and onward land transport provision, with a speeding-up and reduction of bureaucratic procedures; (b) improved quality (rather than quantity) of road access between points of entry and main destinations (section 8.3.6); (c) an increased supply of good quality but appropriate scale accommodation throughout the country; (d) a reliable and efficient telecommunications system to support both tourism businesses and tourists (section 8.3.3); and (e) provision both within the country and outside for ongoing education and training in tourism and conservation management skills (sections 3.3.3, 4.4.3.5, 5.3.1, 5.4.1, 8.2.2 above).

The need for regulation in physical, social and financial planning, licensing and classification was essential, as was the development and publication of a framework of stringent environmental standards for tourism developments and operations by the ministries of planning and tourism, and the development and publication of clear planning guidelines, which should be regularly reviewed and evaluated. Establishment of a licensing and registration system for taxi drivers, tour car drivers, tourist guides and key tourism operators was clearly necessary to establish and maintain high-quality key tourism services and promote tourist confidence. A tourist accommodation classification, registration and standards system would also be required.

9.3.7 Sustainable conclusions?

Tourism should not be permitted to become the country's key economic sector. It is too vulnerable to the movement of international capital, changes in fashion, and natural and cultural environmental degradation. But as a supplemental income, particularly in conjunction with agriculture and rural development, appropriate sustainable forms of tourism can provide a valuable economic, educational and social role within the country's post-communist development processes.

By 1993, domestic, regional and international circumstances were still far from ideal for the relaunch of an Albanian tourism industry. In the first half of the year 17,732 foreigners were accommodated in the country's hotels, of whom only 17.5 per cent stated they were there for a holiday. Of 70 joint ventures set up in the Albanian public sector, only three were in tourism, compared to 19 in industry, mining and energy resources and 15 in agriculture and food (section 9.1.2.3 above). A measured approach to post-transition tourism development is, however, both sensible and realistic.

The highly 'prescriptive' Albanian model of tourism development remained unique in Europe for several decades, reflecting the country's particular if anachronistic circumstances (section 4.4. above). It was able to harness 'heritage' in its aims of emphasising: (a) continuity between the post-war communist leadership and past nationalistic aspirations; (b) the distinctiveness and 'purity' of Albanian culture; (c) the persistence of traditional pursuits, thereby making a virtue of the country's low level of economic development; (d) the state's care and protection of Albanian culture; and (e) the self-perceived superiority of Albania's ideological approach. Until the mid-1980s the country's leadership had concluded that strictly controlled and stringently planned tourism could not only present this positive propaganda face to the outside world but also could positively aid national development by both providing hard currency and gradually stimulating the provision of facilities to the benefit of the host population.

When the country is ready to sustain a renewed international tourism development programme, that sustainability will need to be expressed in terms of balance with both the country's natural environment and its material culture. Disregarding either will leave this intriguing society, and those who visit it, forever impoverished.

10

Albania into the twenty-first century

10.1 Past: change

10.1.1 Trade-offs

Despite almost half-a-century of policies supposedly designed to promote equality of access and opportunity both within and between the countries of Central and Eastern Europe, state socialism largely failed to remove the enormous variations in levels of economic development which resulted from the region's diverse historical evolution. By most criteria, Albania remained at the bottom of the economic ladder. Breaking away from the Soviet bloc in the early 1960s and receiving only outdated Chinese technical aid and assistance subsequently, the country's Stalinist stance and high levels of population growth ensured that even by regional standards Albania would remain impoverished.

For half-a-century, an economy of shortage prevailed, which, while socially and economically degrading, did at least allay environmental degradation through innovation, improvisation, import substitution, recycling and low levels of consumerism and material waste. But having survived the long Stalinist experiment, the country's environment, both natural and cultural, is too fragile to permit the luxury of too many mistakes.

Positive environmental benefits are resulting from the closure of heavily polluting and uneconomic industrial plants developed as a result of dogmatic self-reliance, poor transport and distribution systems and sclerotic political leadership. The considerable short- to medium-term unemployment, social disruption and emigration resulting from such structural rationalisation does, however, confront the country's leaders with a difficult balancing act.

10.1.2 Learning from the past?

Albania's post-communist politics of revenge have not been as severe as many had predicted. Following precedents elsewhere in the region, the new government's May 1992 confiscation of the PLA's hard currency account was viewed as a political necessity. Worth some $1,565,000, it was transferred to the state budget, helping a little to fill a large hole in the national exchequer. The accounts of the former communist-controlled trade unions, women's and youth organisations were frozen, and the SPA's main building in Tirana was expropriated. The Albanian Communist Party, a hardline splinter group from the SPA, was banned after parliament had voted to prohibit the activities of fascist and communist parties. But the country would lose a great deal if it turned its back completely on the communist past: much still needs to be learnt from the mistakes made.

The removal of the remains of Enver Hoxha and 12 other leading communists from Tirana's Martyrs' Cemetery in May 1992 was understandable. Thousands of Albanians and their remains had been removed from history under Hoxha's regime, and in many eyes the disinterring of the former leader and his comrades from the country's most important resting place was appropriate justice. That Hoxha's tomb was later recycled as a war memorial for British servicemen who died on Albanian soil during the Second World War was perhaps less justifiable (*EEN*, 14 April 1993, p. 8).

In 1993, the culture ministry argued that there was no longer a market for the literature published by the communists, and all stocks of the 70-odd volumes of Hoxha and his colleagues were to be pulped to provide for 1,000 tonnes of scarce newsprint. These benighted works were also being recycled by street vendors for wrapping snacks and, as the author found on a visit to the border post at Qafa e Morinë, they were providing the focus of some domestic recreation by being folded into shapes resembling table lamps and used for decoration.

10.2 Present: transition

10.2.1 Economic transition

By mid-1993, it could be claimed of Albania that it was the only country of the region to have met every IMF criterion. Certainly, during the transition period of post-communist restructuring, market-led macro-economic considerations were dominating Albanians' lives. The IMF reform programme introduced in the summer of 1992 together with a one-year stand-by arrangement, did appear to have succeeded in checking the decline of the Albanian economy. Rescheduling and deferring an outstanding debt of over $400 million was the government's main priority: the exchequer was empty, yet the country did not wish to been seen as Europe's beggar nation.

During 1992, Albania had been dependent upon some $730 million-worth of foreign aid, representing more than 50 per cent of the country's foreign earnings. Remittances from Albanian workers abroad provided a further estimated $300–400 million, although attempts to regularise labour migration through quota agreements with the EC came to nothing. Yet it was to the mutual benefit of Albania and Western interests to target individual young people for training rather than sink short-term foreign investment into an uncertain Albanian domestic environment.

The high level of debt was certainly a major factor in deterring much potential foreign investment, particularly in larger-scale enterprises: the basic ingredients of a particularly vicious circle. A tendency towards changing and inconsistent legislation did nothing to reassure intending investors. Not least in this context was the question of land and property restitution: May 1993 legislation overturned previous positions, allowing former owners to claim back their land, even if it had been built over. This was bound to generate further property disputes. Both the civil service and local government were experiencing difficulty in coping with legislative instability (Anon, 1993a).

Registered unemployment had reached 14 per cent by the end of 1992 and was predicted to rise to 20 per cent by the end of 1993. Tax revenues in 1992 accounted for just 16 per cent of GDP. As bankruptcy laws became effective and the government introduced mechanisms to impose some measure of financial discipline at enterprise level, factories would be closing on a permanent basis or be forced to lay off large numbers of staff. Yet an estimated 22,000 shops, bars and restaurants had been sold into the private sector by mid-1993 (Keay, 1993b).

Inflation had peaked at 300 per cent in 1992 and was expected to reach 120 per cent in 1993. Reduced subsidies and wage ceilings were aimed at bringing it down. Within this economic climate, the poor provision of basic services – housing, water, heating – made everyday life for many Albanians close to intolerable.

10.2.2   Pre-conditions for the future

For the 'successful' pursuit of capitalism, a society requires a firm rule of law, a social safety net to protect the weakest in society, and a set of ethical values which underpin the role and status of honest work. While Albania under the Democratic-led government appeared to have largely brought law and order under control, little finance was available for social welfare provision.

This was amply illustrated by the media publicity given to the appalling conditions of the country's orphanages and psychiatric institutions (e.g. Hamilton and Solanki, 1992; Martinson, 1993), and the wide range of foreign charities and other voluntary groups providing assistance for the young, old and institutionalised (e.g. see the newsletters of the *Albanian Society of Britain*, the *Anglo-Albanian Society*, and *Friends of Albania*). For example, following September 1993 BBC television and radio reports by Bill Hamilton (also Bond, 1993) on the unit for mentally handicapped children in Berat, a consortium of charities, co-ordinated by *Feed the Children* helped to rebuild the institution using local labour and materials. As one of the most active British charities working in Albania since its launch in the autumn of 1990, *Feed the Children* had helped over 60 institutions and hospitals for the handicapped or sick children in Albania, Bulgaria and Romania, and had been presented with the Mother Theresa award for humanitarian assistance by President Sali Berisha in July 1992.

One particularly disquieting dimension of social welfare shortcomings was the growth in numbers of begging children, and the substantial potential for exploitation of the most unsavoury kind (Buckingham, 1993).

While any concept of a 'Protestant ethic' is at best an ethnocentric perspective, a recurrent theme of conversation with Albanians is the need to change (other) people's mentality, in order to escape from the dependency syndrome. An irony of Hoxha's Albania was that while in its latter years it claimed self-sufficiency at a national level, at a personal and family level there was a necessary dependence upon the patronage of the Party and state, threat of withdrawal of which was a constant means of maintaining subordination. That religious institutions are now competing with each other and with black market values to win the hearts and minds of the Albanian people is a process of no little importance for the country's path to post-communist identity.

10.2.3   Public opinion?

In the meantime, an opinion poll sponsored by the European Commission and co-ordinated by Gallup UK surveyed 18,500 people in 18 countries of Central and Eastern Europe on the processes of reform and related issues. In Albania the survey was carried out over ten days during November 1992: 1,049 people were interviewed. Crucially, the nature of the sampling techniques and of the sample itself were not disclosed in detail: one must assume that, if only for practical reasons, the Albanian sample held an urban bias in this predominantly rural country.

Given that caveat, the Albanian survey suggested widespread support for reform: 77 per cent of respondents said they believed the country was moving in the right direction, 84 per cent that they valued the new political system, and 72 per cent that they had faith in the free market economy. Intriguingly, 71 per cent of Albanians surveyed expected the economic situation to improve in the following 12 months. This was the highest percentage of respondents answering positively to this question of any country surveyed, and could either reflect optimism or the simple fact that towards the end of 1992 many Albanians must have been assuming that matters could get no worse. Some 84 per cent of respondents said that the present government was better than the previous one, but this again was somewhat ambiguous given that the immediately previous government was a relatively short-lived caretaker regime of technocrats. Overall, 56 per cent of Albanians surveyed indicated that they were in favour of speedier economic reforms and of privatisation.

10.2.4 The wider context

If 1992 was year zero for Albania's climb out of the slough of 'self-reliance', then the July local election results of that year (section 6.1.3 above) soon indicated that the newly democratised electorate was getting impatient with both the lack of improvement in living standards and the political bickerings which eventually led to a major split within the ruling Democratic Party. Indeed, only 44 per cent of the respondents in the EC survey said that they were satisfied with the process of democratisation in Albania. Regarding the media, only 45 per cent of the Albanians polled claimed they trusted Albanian Television, and 55 per cent that they had confidence in Albanian Radio. The survey also showed that 91 per cent of the respondents favoured Albanian membership of the EC, while 67 per cent thought that Albania should become a member within five to ten years (Zanga, 1993e; *Flash – Albania*, March 1993, p. 3).

The possibility of political extremism will rarely be far away until Albania is firmly anchored to 'civil' Europe. The threat of Serbian or Greek aggression remains as a possible pretext upon which authoritarian rule or military dictatorship could emerge. By taking the latter path, however, Albania would lose European support and return to an isolation more dangerous than that of the communist era. In such circumstances, any probable assistance would most likely come from the Muslim world. Given the already volatile religious sub-text of Balkan conflict, these ingredients could result in further unimaginable torment for the region.

10.3 Future: development?

10.3.1 A continuing rural-led programme?

Albania's development path has never been easily predictable. Now the country is struggling through one of the most important turning points in its history. Albania has much social, cultural and environmental wealth to be conserved, preserved or nurtured.

'Modernisation' and 'progress' will not be adopted easily; much will be lost and gained along the way. But if Albania and the Albanians are able to survive both the last half century of deadly dogma and the current tortuous period of transition with some measure of independence, well-being and dignity, then future prospects could be exceedingly good.

With electricity theoretically available in every village since 1970, Albania could possibly stabilise a reduced rural population and, with foreign assistance, undertake a technological and conceptual leapfrog by introducing decentralised information technology-based employment opportunities which could be provided at home with appropriate training programmes, thereby by-passing environmentally deleterious industrialisation processes and minimising the adverse impacts of rural depopulation. Although currently there exists a low level of technological sophistication within the country, following decades of isolation from global technological and educational developments, the population's capacity for adaptation and innovation should not be underestimated. Such capacity could complement the enhancement and commercialisation of organic farming together with the encouragement of farm tourism for the maintenance of 'rural'-led development.

10.3.2 Potential for development

The country's potential is substantial. Firstly, Albania has a small but adaptable population. Within the region there are as many Albanians outside of the country's borders as within them, providing a strong potential for trade and commerce given stable regional conditions and ease of movement. The cost of the country's labour is currently extremely low by international standards, rendering it potentially attractive for foreign investment although also vulnerable to exploitation and to the capricious movement of international capital.

Secondly, the country can gain advantage from its location at a physical crossroads between west and east, north and south, with potentially good access to Western and Eastern

Europe, the Middle East and North Africa. As the country with the lowest level of economic development in Europe, and with a population whose religious affiliations have been historically pragmatic, Albania also stands in an advantageous cultural position to act as a bridgehead between the 'North' and the 'South': between Europe and the developing (particularly Islamic) world. Just like the double-headed eagle of its national flag, Albania needs to face both westwards and eastwards (Prifti, 1972b, p. 39).

Thirdly, the resource potential is high. The country is currently impoverished after half-a-century of communism, but is potentially very rich. Petroleum and gas, chrome, copper, iron and water power resources provide the potential for substantial value-added export-orientation. With one of the most benign climates in Europe, coupled with a very fertile reclaimed coastal plain, the agricultural potential, though in competition with far more sophisticated Mediterranean producers for the European market, is considerable (sections 9.1 and 9.2).

Fourthly, climate, an amenable coast, mountains, wildlife and a distinctive cultural heritage also provide the potential for tourism development, but this needs to be set within a framework of sustainability (section 9.3).

With all these positive factors at its disposal, Albania into the twenty-first century could fill several niche roles for Western markets, such as the provision of specialised agriculture, value-added processing, high intrinsic value consumer goods (developing out of craft traditions), and premium cost tourism. Yet this potential

requires both the economic and wider protective blanket of supranational membership (of such bodies as the EU, NATO and CSCE) and a regional co-operation framework. While Milan Panic's call for a Balkan federation represented the rhetoric of a desperate (ex-)politician, the creation of a Black Sea zone of economic co-operation (BSZEC) (Anon, 1992) could provide at least an interim support mechanism. Within this framework, Albania was one of 15 signatories to the 1992 Bosphorous Statement, which committed its subscribers to the basic principles of dialogue, restoration of peace and legitimacy, and opposition to aggression, violence, terrorism and lawlessness. The momentum behind such a bland expression heralded a potentially useful vehicle with which to further develop ties between Albania and Turkey. As the group includes a wide range of non-Muslim states, Albania's membership could also help to allay fears that the country was veering towards a pro-Muslim bias in its sympathies.

There need not be a 'conflict between preservation and progress' (Glenny, 1990, p. 159) in Albania's development path. Social and economic progress can be compatible with the retention of many of the valuable characteristics of 'Albanian-ness'. This requires a combination of judicious international financial assistance, realistic policies for skill enhancement and sustainable development, strengthened trading links and regional stability.

While the first are certainly not unattainable, the latter remains in the realms of conjecture for the forseeable future.

Appendix I
Alternative place-names

Albanian	Classical	Turkish	Italian	Greek	Serbian	Anglicised
Berat/Berati	Antipatra/ Albanorum oppidum/ Pulcheriopolis					
						Berat
Bitol/Bitoli		Manastir			Bitolj	Monastir
Butrint/Butrinti	Buthrotum		Butrinto			Butrint
Cetinjë/Cetinja					Cetinj	Cetinj
Dibër/Dibra	Uscana	Dibra			Debar	Debar
Durrës/ Durrësi	Dyrrachium/ Epidamnos		Durazzo			Durres
Elbasan/ Elbasani	Scampa/ Albanopolis					Elbasan
Fier/Fieri						Fier
Florinë/Florina		Filorma		Florina		Florina
Gjirokastër/ Gjirokastra				Argyrokastro		Gjirokastra
Himarë/Himara	Oricum			Chimarra		Himara
Janinë/Janina				Ioannina		Yannina
Kastorië/ Kastoria		Kezriye		Kastoria		Kastoria
Korçë/Korça	Pelium	Körice	Corizza	Koritsa		Kortcha
Korfuz/Korfuzi	Corcyra			Kerkira		Corfu
Kosovë/Kosova					Kosovo	Kosovo
Krujë/Kruja			Croia			Kruja
Lezhë/Lezha	Lissus		Alessio			Lesh
Ohër/Ohri	Achris/Lychnis			Okhrida	Ohrid	Ochrid
Pojan/Pojani	Apollonia					Apollonia
Pejë/Peja		Ipek			Peć	Petsh
Pogradec/ Pogradeci						Pogradets
Prishtinë/ Prishtina					Priština	Pristina

Continued

Albanian	Classical	Turkish	Italian	Greek	Serbian	Anglicised
Prizren/						
Prizreni					Prizren	Prizren
Sarandë/			Porto Edda/			
Saranda	Onchesmus		Santi Quaranta			Saranda
Selanik				Thessaloníki		Salonica
Selenicë/						
Selenica			Selenissa			Selenica
Shëngjin/			San Giovanni			
Shëngjini			di Medua			Shengjin
Shkodër/						
Shkodra	Scodra	Shkodra	Scutari		Skadar	Shkodra
Shkup/Shkupi		Üsküb				Skopje
Strugë/Struga	Patoae				Struga	Struga
Tepelenë/						
Tepelena	Anticonia					Tepelena
Tetovë/Tetova		Kalkandelen			Tetovo	Tetovo
Tiranë/Tirana						Tirana
Tivar/Tivari					Bar	Bar
Ulqin/Ulqini			Dulcigno		Ulcinj	Ulcinj
Vlorë/Vlora	Aulon		Valona			Valona

References

Abecor, 1979, *Albania*, Abecor, London.

Abulafia, D., 1976, Reflections on a visit to Albania, *The Cambridge Review*, 26 November: 46–51.

Ackerman, E.A., 1938, Albania – a Balkan Switzerland, *The Journal of Geography*, 37(7): 253–62.

Adami, J., 1983, *Rrugë dhe objekte arkeologjike në Shqipëri*, 8 Nëntori, Tirana.

Adhami, S., 1988, Historical monuments, their restoration and use, in Anon, *Legacy of centuries*, 8 Nëntori, Tirana, 3–5.

Adhami, S., Zheku, K., 1981, *Kruja dhe monumentet e saj*, 8 Nëntori, Tirana.

Afezolli, N., 1993, There is no complete strategy on foreign investments, *Albanian Economic Tribune*, 1(13): 11–12.

Aflalo, F.G., ed., 1901, *Sport in Europe*, Sands and Co., London, E.P. Dutton and Co., New York.

Ahmataj, H., Çeku, K., 1984, *Bimët aromatike*, Botimi Shtëpisë së Propagandës Bujqësore, Tirana.

Albanian Economic Tribune, The, Tirana, monthly.

Albanian Foreign Trade, Tirana, irregular.

Albanian Resistance, The, News Bulletin of the National Democratic Committee for a Free Albania, Paris, irregular.

Albanian tourism: investment opportunities, 1993 *Albanian Economic Tribune*, 5(17): supplement.

Albturist, nd., *The tourist map of Albania*, 8 Nëntori, Tirana.

Albturist, 1969, *Tourist guide book of Albania*, Naim Frashëri, Tirana.

Albturist, 1989, *Hotels and tourist centres in Albania*, 8 Nëntori, Tirana.

Aleksi, A., 1985, Aspekte gjeografiko-ekonomike të zhvillimit të transportit hekurudhor në RPS të Shqipërisë, *Studime Gjeografike*, 1: 227–39.

Aleksi, A., 1987 Ndërtimi socialist i vendit dhe ndryshimet në gjeografinë e transportit automobilistik, *Studime Gjeografike*, 3: 203–13.

Alia, R., 1983, *Politike në sherbim te socializmit, lirise dhe pavaresise se atdeut*, 8 Nëntori, Tirana.

Alia, R., 1986, *Report to the 9th. Congress of the Party of Labour of Albania*, 8 Nëntori, Tirana.

Alia, R., 1988, *Our Enver*, 8 Nëntori, Tirana.

Alia, Z., 1990, *The family and its structure in the PSR of Albania*, 8 Nëntori, Tirana.

Alisov, N.V. *et al.*, 1985, *Economic geography of the socialist countries of Europe*, Progress, Moscow.

Alla, I, Rrakacoll, Z., 1991, Landwirtschaft und Umweltproblematik in Albanien, *Südosteuropa Mitteilungen*, 31(2): 115–21.

Allcock, J.B., 1983, Tourism and social change in Dalmatia, *Journal of Development Studies*, 20(1): 35–55.

Allcock, J.B., 1986, Yugoslavia's tourist trade: pot of gold or pig in a poke?, *Annals of Tourism Research*, 13(4): 565–88.

Allcock, J.B., 1990, Tourism and the private sector in Yugoslavia, in Allcock, J.B., Milivojević, M., eds, *Yugoslavia in transition*, Berg, Oxford.

Almagía, R., 1930, *L'Albania*, Rome.

Almagía, R., 1932, Modern Albania: a review, *Geographical Review*, 22: 464–73.

Almond, M., 1988a, A Balkan journey: part 1, *The Rock Garden*, 20(4): 459–66.

Almond, M., 1988b, A Balkan journey: part 2, *The Rock Garden*, 21(1): 76–81.

Almond, M., 1990, The last stalwarts of Stalinism come in from the cold, *The Sunday Correspondent*, 22 April.

Alternativa, Tirana, twice-weekly.

Altmann, F-L., ed., 1990, *Albanien im Umbruch. Eine Bestandsaufnahme*, R. Oldenbourg, Munich.

Ambler, J., Shaw, D.J.B., Symons, L.J., eds, 1985, *Soviet and East European transport problems*, Croom Helm, Beckenham.

A.M.C., 1991, L'Albania alla vigilia delle elezioni tra tensioni sociali e crisi economica, *Est-Ouest*, **22**(1): 16–21.

Amery, J., 1948a, *Forward march*, Macmillan, London.

Amery, J., 1948b, *Sons of the eagle*, Macmillan, London.

Amery, J., 1973, *Approach March: a venture in autobiography*, Hutchinson, London.

Amnesty International, 1984, *Albania: political imprisonment and the law*, Amnesty International, London.

Amnesty International, 1989, *When the state kills: the death penalty vs human rights*, Amnesty International, London.

Amnesty International, 1992, *Amnesty International Report 1992*, Amnesty International, London.

Anagnosti, V., 1985, *The terraces of Lukova*, 8 Nëntori, Tirana.

Anamali, S., 1969, On the ancient culture of the Albanians, in Anon, *The Illyrians and the genesis of the Albanians*, Mihail Duri, Tirana.

Anamali, S., 1972, From the Illyrians to the Arbers, in Anon., *Convention of Illyrian Studies*, Mihail Duri, Tirana.

Anamali, S., Adhami, S., 1974, *Mosaiques de l'Albanie*, 8 Nëntori, Tirana.

Anamali, S., Spahiu, H., 1988, *Stoli Arbërore*, Akademia e Shkencave e RPS të Shqipërisë, Qendra e Kërkimeve Arkeologjike, Tirana.

Andrejevich, M., 1992, The Sandzak: the next Balkan theater of war? *RFE/RL Report*, **1**(47): 26–34.

Anon., 1971a, *Atlas gjeografik i Shqipërisë*, Hamid Shijaku, Tirana.

Anon., 1971b, In the Chairman's footsteps, *The Economist*, 24 July: 38.

Anon., 1972a, City planning and civic beauty, *New Albania*, **26**(4): 12–13.

Anon., 1972b, Ligji i ri: mbi mbrojtjen e monumenteve kulturale e historike dhe pasurive natyrale të rralla, *Monumentet*, **3**: 223–4.

Anon., 1972c, Rregulle për mbrojtjen e monumenteve kultural dhe historike, *Monumentet*, **3**: 225–8.

Anon., 1972, The Bajram Curri city, *New Albania*, **26**(4): 12–13.

Anon., 1973a, *People's health*, Naim Frashëri, Tirana.

Anon., 1973b, Rregullore 'mbi mbrojtjen, restaurimin dhe administrimin e qytetitmuze të Gjirokastrës', *Monumentet*, **5–6**: 211–17.

Anon., 1973c, Rregullore 'mbi mbrojtjen dhe restaurimin e ansambleve dhe ndërtimeve të tjeva me vlerë historike të qytetit të Korçës', *Monumentet*, **5–6**: 219–22.

Anon., 1974, *Atlas për shkollat fillore*, Hamid Shijaku, Tirana.

Anon., 1977, Rregullore 'mbi mbrojtjen dhe restaurimin e qendrës historike të qytetit Elbasanit', *Monumentet*, **13**: 160–62.

Anon., 1978, *The Albanian woman – a great force of the revolution*, 8 Nëntori, Tirana.

Anon., 1979, *35 years of socialist Albania*, 8 Nëntori, Tirana.

Anon., 1980a, A new railway extending towards the north of Albania, *Albanian Foreign Trade*, **125**: 5.

Anon., 1980b, The extension of the iron lines, *New Albania*, **1**: 26–7.

Anon., 1981a, A new railroad, *Albania Today*, **58**: 42–5.

Anon., 1981b, *Republika Popullore Socialiste e Shqipërisë: harta fiziko politike (1:800,000)*, Hamid Shijaku, Tirana.

Anon., 1982a, *Bujqesia në Republikën Popullore Socialiste të Shqipërisë*, 8 Nëntori, Tirana.

Anon., 1982b, *Portrait of Albania*, 8 Nëntori, Tirana.

Anon., 1982c, Tourist Albania: an interview with the director of the Albturist enterprise, *New Albania*, **3**: 34–5.

Anon., 1983, A new appearance for the ancient city, *New Albania*, **4**: 8–9.

Anon., 1984a, *40 years of socialist Albania*, 8 Nëntori, Tirana.

Anon., 1984b, The newest railway of the country, *New Albania*, **1**: 14–15.

Anon., 1985a, Albania comes in out of scientific cold, *New Scientist*, 30 May: 8.

Anon., 1985b, How much is the rent for an apartment?, *New Albania*, **6**: 22–3.

Anon., 1985c, Shkodra – Hani i Hotit railway inaugurated, *Albanian Foreign Trade*, **1**: 10.

Anon., 1985d, *The Enver Hoxha University of Tirana*, 8 Nëntori, Tirana.

Anon., 1987a, A lot of Balkan questions, *The Economist*, 24 October: 50.

Anon., 1987b, Serb pressure for purge on Albanians to prevent swamping, *Times Higher Education Supplement*, 23 October.

Anon., 1988a, Albania and Greece: a door now ajar, *The Economist*, 23 April: 60.

Anon., 1988b, In the interests of good neighbourliness and cooperation in the Balkans, *New Albania*, **2**: 4.

Anon., 1989a, Environment survey part I, *East European Newsletter*, **3**(23): 6–8.

Anon., 1989b, One of the biggest water-collecting objects in the Balkans, *New Albania*, **6**: 8.

Anon., 1989c, The holiday places, *New Albania*, **4**: 26–7.

Anon., 1989d, The second ferrochrome plant, *New Albania*, **6**: 8.

Anon., 1990, Fruitful collaboration, *New Albania*, **6**: 6–7.

Anon., 1991a, Albania: open for business, *East European Markets*, **11**(16): 14–15.

Anon., 1991b, Albania's push for investment, *East European Markets*, **11**(15): 11–13.

Anon., 1992, To date projects of the World Bank for Albania, *Albanian Economic Tribune*, **7**(11): 13–14.

Anon, 1993a, Oh dear, *The Economist*, 5 June: 44–5.

Anon., 1993b, The hope for Albania's economic salvation, *Albanian Economic Tribune*, **1**(13): 30–31.

Archer, B.H., 1982, The value of multipliers and their policy implications, *Tourism Management*, **3**(4): 236–41.

Armstrong, H.F., 1928, Italy, Jugoslavia and Lilliputia, *Foreign Affairs*, **6**: 191–202.

Artisien, P., 1978, Yugoslavia and Albania in the 1970s, *Co-existence*, **15**(2): 219–27.

Artisien, P., 1978, Albanian nationalism and Yugoslav socialism: the case of Kosovo, *Co-existence*, **16**(2): 173–89.

Artisien, P., 1980, *Friends or foes? – Yugoslav-Albanian relations over the last 40 years*, Postgraduate School of Yugoslav Studies, University of Bradford, Bradford.

Artisien, P., 1984, A note on Kosovo and the future of Yugoslav-Albanian relations: a Balkan perspective, *Soviet Studies*, **36**(2): 267–76.

Artisien, P., 1987, Albania at the crossroads, *Journal of Communist Studies*, **3**(3): 231–49.

Artisien, P., Howells, R.A., 1981, Yugoslavia, Albania and the Kosovo riots, *The World Today*, **37**(11): 419–27.

Ascherson, N., 1985, Legacy of the lost Stalinist, *The Observer*, 14 April.

Ash, W., 1974, *Pickaxe and rifle*, Howard Baker, Wimbledon.

Ashton, C., 1979, Australia's Queen Susan, *The Australian Women's Weekly*, 23 May: 14–15.

Åslund, A., 1991, Conclusion: the socialist Balkan countries will follow East Central Europe, in Sjöberg, Ö. and Wyzan, M.L., eds, *Economic change in the Balkan states*, Pinter, London, pp. 161–6.

Åslund, A., Sjöberg, Ö, 1991, *Privatisation and transition to market economy in Albania*, Stockholm Institute of Soviet and East European Economies, Working Paper 27, Stockholm.

ASPSRA (Academy of Sciences of the People's Socialist Republic of Albania), 1984a, *Problems of the formation of the Albanian people, their language and culture*, 8 Nëntori, Tirana.

ASPSRA (Academy of Sciences of the People's Socialist Republic of Albania), 1984b, *Questions of the Albanian folklore*, 8 Nëntori, Tirana.

ASPSRA (Academy of Sciences of the People's Socialist Republic of Albania), 1985, *The Albanians and their territories*, 8 Nëntori, Tirana.

ATA (Albanian Telegraph Agency), Tirana, regular bulletins.

Atkinson, R., 1992, *Report on a visit to Albania, 28 May–1 June 1992*, Ecological Studies Institute, London.

Atkinson, R.I., Bouvier, M., Hall, D., Prigioni, C., 1991, Albania, in IUCN-EEP, *Environmental status reports: 1990. Volume two: Albania, Bulgaria, Romania, Yugoslavia*, IUCN, Cambridge, pp. 1–38.

Atkinson, R., Fisher, D., 1992, *Tourism investment in Central and Eastern Europe: structure, trends and environmental implications*, East West Environment Ltd, London.

Baçe, A., Condi, D., 1987, *Buthrot*, 8 Nëntori, Tirana.

Baci, F., 1992, A step to be consolidated, *Albanian Economic Tribune*, **8**(12): 27–8.

Baci, I., 1981, *Agriculture in the PSR of Albania*, 8 Nëntori, Tirana.

Backer, B., 1987, Self-reliance under socialism – the case of Albania, *Journal of Peace Research*, **19**(4): 355–67.

Backer, B., 1991, Northern Albania, in Watson, D., ed., *Disappearing World: the series*, Granada TV, Manchester, pp. 14–19.

Baker, M., 1990, Albanians note JV details: but little Western interest, *Business Eastern Europe*, **19**(46): 372.

Baker, M., 1993, Copier giant takes regional approach to training EE employees, *Business Eastern Europe*, **22**(22): 6–7.

Balli i Kombit, Tirana, twice-weekly.

Balyrakis, Y., 1974, My year inside an Albanian prison camp, *The Sunday Times*, 7 July.

Banac, I., 1984, *The national question in Yugoslavia: origins, history, politics*, Cornell University Press, Ithaca and London.

Banja, H., 1968, *Establishment and prospects of development of socialist industry in P.R. Albania*, Naim Frashëri, Tirana.

Banja, H., 1981, The geographical distribution of industry, *New Albania*, **1**: 9.

Banja, H., Toçi, V., 1979, *Socialist Albania on the road to industrialization*, 8 Nëntori, Tirana.

Barber, T., 1993, Invasion of the mushroom bunkers, *The Independent*, 13 July.

Barker, E., 1950, *Macedonia: its place in Balkan power politics*, Royal Institute of International Affairs, London.

Barnes, J.S., 1918, The future of the Albanian state, *Geographical Journal*, **52**: 12–27.

Bartl, P., 1993, Religionsgemeinschaften und Kirchen, in Grothusen, K-D., ed., *Albanien*, Vandenhoeck und Ruprecht, Göttingen, pp. 587–614.

Basha, H., 1986, *Tirana et ses environs*, 8 Nëntori, Tirana.

Bashkimi, Tirana, twice-weekly (formerly daily).

Bashkin, M., 1983, Crisis in Kosovo, *Problems of Communism*, **32**: 61–74.

Baumgartl, B., 1993, West provides no new aid to clean up Eastern Europe, *RFE/RL Research Report*, **2**(29): 41–7.

BBC, *SWB (Summary of World Broadcasts): Central Europe and the Balkans (economic reports)*, BBC, Caversham, weekly.

BBC, *SWB (Summary of World Broadcasts): Eastern Europe (economic reports)*, BBC, Caversham, weekly.

Beaver, S.H., 1941, Railways in the Balkan peninsula, *Geographical Journal*, **97**: 273–94.

Bebler, A., 1993, Yugoslavia's variety of communist federalism and her demise, *Communist and Post-communist Studies*, **26**(1): 72–86.

BEE (*Business Eastern Europe*), Business International, Vienna and London, fortnightly.

Begeja, K., 1967, *Women's rights and her role in the People's Republic of Albania*, Naim Frashëri, Tirana.

Begeja, K., 1984, *The family in the PSR of Albania*, 8 Nëntori, Tirana.

Bell, E.A., 1940, Italians process Albanian heavy oil to aviation gasoline, *Oil Weekly*, **98**: 28–30.

Bellows,, H.E., 1993, The challenge of informationalization in post-communist societies, *Communist and Post-communist Studies*, **26**(2): 144–64.

Berg, M., Litvinoff, M., 1992, *Ancestors: the origins of the people and countries of Europe*, Peter Lowe, London.

Berisha, S., 1992, I guarantee that nobody will lose his invested money in Albania, *Albanian Economic Tribune*, **8**(12): 10.

Bernard, R., 1935, *Essai sur l'histoire de l'Albanie moderne*, F. Loviton, Paris.

Bërxholi, A., 1985a, Mbi disa aspekte të zhvillimit ekonomik dhe të shpërndarjes gjeografike të popullsisë dhe vendbanimeve në territorin e përfshirë nga rrethet Gjirokastër, Përmet, Tepelenë dhe Sarandë, *Studime Gjeografike*, **1**: 207–17.

Bërxholi, A., 1985b, *Vlora and its environs*, 8 Nëntori, Tirana.

Bërxholi, A., 1986, *Durrës and its environs*, 8 Nëntori, Tirana.

Bërxholi, A., 1988, Tipare të zhvillimit demografik të zonës së intensifikuar me përparësi, *Studime Gjeografike*, **3**: 191–202.

Bërxholi, A., ed., 1990a, *Atlas gjeografik i RPS të Shqipërisë*, Shtëpia Botuese e Librit Shkollor, Tirana.

Bërxholi, A., 1990b, On the surface – flowers and leaves, underground – silver and gold, *New Albania*, **5**: 6–7.

Bërxholi, A., 1990c, Riprodhim i popullsisë fshatare në vitet 1971–1987, *Studime Gjeografike*, **4**: 203–16.

Bërxholi, A., Qiriazi, P., 1986, *Albania: a geographic outline*, 8 Nëntori, Tirana.

Bërxholi, A., Qiriazi, P., 1990, *Republika Popullore Socialiste e Shqipërisë: harte fizike*, Shtëpia Botuese e Librit Shkollor, Tirana.

Bërxholi, A. et al., 1988, *Gjeografia e Shqipërisë*, Shtëpia Botuese e Librit Shkollor, Tirana.

Besemeres, J., 1980, *Socialist population politics*, M.E. Sharpe, New York.

Bethel, N., 1984, *The great betrayal: the untold story of Kim Philby's biggest coup*, Hodder and Stoughton, London.

Biber, M., 1980, Albania alone against the world, *National Geographic Magazine*, **158**: 530–57.

Biberaj, E., 1985, Albania after Hoxha: dilemmas of change, *Problems of Communism*, **34**(6): 32–47.

Biberaj, E., 1986, *Albania and China: a study of an unequal alliance*, Westview, Boulder and London.

Biberaj, E., 1990, *Albania: a socialist maverick*, Westview, Boulder and London.

Biberaj, E., 1991, Albania at the crossroads, *Problems of Communism*, **40**(6).

Bićanić, I., 1988, Fractured economy, in Rusinow, D., ed., *Yugoslavia: a fractured federalism*, Wilson Center Press, Washington D.C., pp. 120–41.

Binder, D., 1990, Opposition in Albania urges ties to US, *International Herald Tribune*, 26 December.

Birch, J., 1971, The Albanian political experience, *Government and Opposition*, **6**(3): 361–80. Reprinted in Schapiro, L., ed., 1972, *Political opposition in one-party states*, Macmillan, London, pp. 179–200.

Birch, J., 1977, Albania – the reluctant puppet, *Journal of Social and Political Studies*, 269–96.

Bird, B., 1989, *Langkawi – from Mahsuri to Mahathir: tourism for whom?*, INSAN, Kuala Lumpur.

Bird, C., 1992a, Poor little rich girl . . ., *Business Europa*, **1**(1): 9

Bird, C., 1992b, Roll out the barrel . . ., *Business Europa*, **1**(1): 11

Birge, J.K., 1937, *The Bektashi Order of Dervishes*, Luzac, London.

Bismarck-Osten, M. von., 1992, We help the Albanians help themselves, *Albanian Economic Tribune*, **2**(6): 4–5.

Bitincka, F., 1992, Private and state transport side by side, *Albanian Economic Tribune*, **8**(12): 6.

Blanc, A., 1960, Recherches sur les communautés patriarcales et les structures agraires en Albanie du nord, *Bulletin de l'Association de Géographes Français*, **292/3**: 117–28.

Blanc, A., 1961, Naissance et évolution des paysages agraires en Albanie, *Geografiska Annaler*, **43**(1–2): 8–16.

Blanc, A., 1963, L'évolution contemporaine de la vie pastorale en Albanie méridionale, *Revue de Géographie Alpine*, **51**(3): 429–61.

Blanchard, O., Dornbusch, R., Krugman, P., Layard, R., Summers, L., 1991, *Reform in Eastern Europe*, MIT Press, Cambridge Mass.

Bland, W., nd, *A short guide to Albania*, The Albania Society, Ilford.

Bland, W., 1988, *Albania*, Clio Press, Oxford.

Bland, W., 1992, Albania after the Second World War, in Winnifrith, T., ed., *Perspectives on Albania*, Macmillan, Basingstoke and London, pp. 123–36.

Bland, W., Price, I., 1986, *A tangled web: a history of Anglo-American relations with Albania (1912–1955)*, Albania Society, Ilford.

Boardman, A., Vining, A., 1989, Ownership and performance in competitive environments, *Journal of Law and Economics*, **32**: 1–33.

Bogetić, Z., 1993, The role of employee ownership in privatisation of state enterprises in Eastern and Central Europe, *Europe-Asia Studies*, **45**(3): 463–82.

Bogliani, G., 1987, C'e'del verde in Albania – riscopriamo una nazione che cambia, *Airone*, 74, June.

Bollano, P., 1984, The limitation of wage differentials, *Albanian Life*, **29**: 21.

Bollano, P., 1988, *Popullsia e Shqipërisë*, 8 Nëntori, Tirana.

Bollano, P., 1991, Nëpër vite, gjer tek regjistrimi i fundit i popullsisë, *Rruga e Partisë*, **38**(2): 26–42.

Bollano, P., Dari, F., 1984, The transition to state farming, *Albanian Life*, **28**: 15–17.

Bond, M., 1993, Handicapped by life behind bars, *The European*, 23 September.

Boniface, B.G., Cooper, C.P., 1987, *The geography of travel and tourism*, Heinemann, London.

Boo, E., 1990, *Ecotourism: the potentials and pitfalls*, World Wildlife Fund, Washington DC, 2 vols.

Boo, E., 1992a, *The concept of visitor carrying capacity as it applies to developing countries*, World Wildlife Fund, Washington DC.

Boo, E., 1992b, *The ecotourism boom*, World Wildlife Fund, Washington DC.

Bookman, M.Z., 1990, The economic basis of regional autarchy in Yugoslavia, *Soviet Studies*, **42**(1): 93–109.

Bopp, F., 1854, *Uber das Albanesische in seinen verwandtschaftlichen Beziehungen*.

Boppe, A., 1914, *L'Albanie et Napoleon (1797–1814)*, Paris.

Borba, Belgrade, daily.

Borchert, J.G., 1975, Economic development and population distribution in Albania, *Geoforum*, **6**(3/4): 177–86.

Borgatta, G., 1937, L'economia albanese e la collaborazione dell'Italia, *Nuova Antologia*, **394**: 343–6.

Borisov, V.A., *et al.*, 1985, *Okhranyaemye prirodnye territorii mira*, Agropromizdat, Moscow.

Bourcart, J., 1921, *L'Albanie et les Albanais*, Bossart, Paris.

Bourne, E., 1972, Peking firmly advises Albania to seek aid from Western world, *Christian Science Monitor*, 13 July.

Bouvier, M., Kempf, C., 1987, La nature en Albanie, *Le Courier de la Nature*, **109**: 18–23.

Boza, M.A., 1988, *Costa Rica national parks*, Infaco, Madrid.

Boza, M.A., Mendoza, C., 1981, *The national parks of Costa Rica*, Industrias Graficas Alvi, Madrid.

Bozdo, A., 1989, Perestrojka intensifikon shfrytëzimin e popullit sovjetik, *Probleme Ekonomike*, **36**(4): 103–5.

Brailsford, H.N., 1906, *Macedonia: its races and their future*, Methuen, London.

Bratkowski, A.S., 1993, The shock of transformation or the transformation of the shock?, *Communist Economies and Economic Transformation*, **5**(1): 5–28.

Braun, R-R, 1988, *Albanien*, Manfred Klemann, Rielasingen.

Bren, P., 1992, The status of women in post-1989 Czechoslovakia, *RFE/RL Research Report*, **1**(41): 58–63.

Brogan, P., 1990, *Eastern Europe 1939–1989: the fifty years war*, Bloomsbury, London.

Brookfield, H.C., 1988, Sustainable development and the environment, *Journal of Development Studies*, **25**(1): 126–35.

Brown, J.F., 1962, Albania, mirror of conflict, *Survey*, **40**: 24–41.

Brown, J.F., 1984, The Balkans: Soviet ambitions and opportunities, *The World Today*, **40**(6): 244–53.

Brown, J.F., 1991, *Surge to freedom: the end of communist rule in Eastern Europe*, Duke University Press, Durham.

Buckingham, H., 1993, The vulnerability of Albanian children, *Albanian Life*, 1: 11–13.

Buckley, M., ed., 1992, *Perestroika and Soviet women*, Cambridge University Press, Cambridge.

Buda, A., 1957, Rruga e popullit shqiptar drejt 28 nëndorit 1912, *Rruga e Partisë*, 3: 30–44.

Buda, A., 1961, The noble role of women in history, *New Albania*, 2: 10–11.

Buda, A., 1980, About some questions of the history of the formation of the Albanian people and of their language and culture, *Historical Studies*, 1: 165–80. Reprinted in, ASPSRA, 1985, *The Albanians and their territories*, 8 Nëntori, Tirana, pp. 5–32.

Burks, R.V., 1961, *The dynamics of communism in Eastern Europe*, Princeton University Press, Princeton.

Burley, T.M., 1970, Albania's minerals, *Geographical Magazine*, **62**(11): 849.

Busch-Zantner, R., 1939, *Albanien: neues Land in Imperium*, W. Goldmann, Leipzig.

Business Europa, London, bi-monthly.

Bussmann, T., 1990, Hoxha hoaxers? Buncha jokers, *The Guardian*, 2 June.

Butler, R.W., 1990, Alternative tourism: pious hope or Trojan horse?, *Journal of Travel Research*, **28**(3): 40–45.

Cambau, D., 1976, Travel by Westerners to Eastern Europe, *ITA Bulletin*, **40**: 883–99.

Cameron, J., 1969, *Point of departure*, Panther, London.

Campbell-Ferguson, A., 1993, Agriculture, Albania and ICI, *Albanian Life*, 1: 22.

Capps, E., 1963, *Greece, Albania and Northern Epirus*, Argonaut, Chicago.

Çarçani, A., 1986, *Report on the 8th. Five-Year Plan (1986–1990)*, 8 Nëntori, Tirana.

Carp, E., 1980, *A directory of western paleartic wetlands*, IUCN-UNEP, Cambridge.

Carrier, C., 1991, Pace of Albanian reforms picking up, slowly, *Business Eastern Europe*, **20**(44): 389.

Carrière, P., Sivignon, M., 1982, Les rapports ville-campagne et l'urbanisation de l'espace et de la société en Albanie, *Villes en Parallèle*, 6: 149–65.

Carter, F.W., 1973, Albania: some problems of a developing Balkan state, *Revue Géographique de l'Est*, **13**(4): 453–79.

Carter, F.W., 1977, *An historical geography of the Balkans*, Academic Press, London.

Carter, F.W., 1986, Tirana, *Cities*, 3(4): 270–81.

Castle, T., 1990, East rings the changes for telecoms, *The European*, 27 July.

Cater, E., Lowman, G., 1994, *Ecotourism: the sustainable alternative?*, Belhaven, London.

Çavolli, I., 1987a, Autumn days in villages, *New Albania*, 5: 16–17.

Çavolli, I., 1987b, Berat – a living museum, *New Albania*, 4: 6–9.

Çavolli, I, 1987c, The five-storey town, *New Albania*, 2: 6–9.

Çavolli, I., 1987d, Town in the centre of Albania. . . . *New Albania*, 3: 4–7.

Chamberlain, G., 1985, Hoxha era ends in Albania, *The Guardian*, 12 April.

Chazan, Y., 1992, Minority threatens Macedonia split, *The Guardian*, 17 November.

C.H.G., 1946, Greek claims in southern Albania, *The World Today*, 2: 488–94.

Childs, D., 1988, *The GDR: Moscow's German ally*, Unwin Hyman, London, 2nd edn.

Chirot, D., ed., 1989, *The origins of backwardness in Eastern Europe*, University of California Press, Berkeley.

Christie, E.B., 1926, The new Albanian constitution, *American Political Science Review*, **20**: 120–23.

Chung, I.Y., 1959, *Legal problems involved in the Corfu Channel incident*, E. Droz, Geneva.

Cikuli, Z., 1984, *Health service in the PSR of Albania*, 8 Nëntori, Tirana.

Ciulache, S., Ionac, N., 1993, *Public control on rural environment: a case study*, Paper, 3rd British-Romanian Seminar in Geography, University of Sunderland, Sunderland.

Civici, A., 1993, the agriculture today needs a more serious attention, *Albanian Economic Tribune*, **17**(17): 20–21.

Claude, I.L., 1969, *National minorities*, Greenwood Press, New York.

Clogg, R., ed., 1981, *Balkan society in the age of Greek independence*, Macmillan, London.

Çobani, J., 1988, Problems of state in protection of the atmospheric environment, in *Balkan Scientific Conference, Environmental Protection in the Balkans, Abstracts*, Varna.

Çobani, J., 1989, Conservation of the environment in Albania, *Albania Today*, **109**: 47–9.

Cochrane, N.J., 1992, Prospects for Eastern Europe's private agriculture in the nineties, in Lampe, J., ed., *Private agriculture in Eastern Europe*, Woodrow Wilson International Center for Scholars, East European Studies Program, Washington DC, pp. 81–102.

Çoçoli, F., 1989, There the sun does not set with the evening, *New Albania*, 4: 14–15.

Cohen, L., 1983, *Political cohesion in a fragile mosaic: the Yugoslav experience*, Westview Press, Boulder.

Colitt, L., 1985, Hoxha: an enigmatic leader with strong sense of Albania's past, *The Financial Times*, 12 April.

Collinson, S., 1992, The Albanian exodus, 1990–91 and the Italian response: what lessons for the future?, *Albanian Life*, **2**: 25–8.

Cookridge, E.H., 1968, *The third man*, Barker, London.

Coon, C., 1939, *The races of Europe*, Macmillan, New York.

Coon, C., 1950, *The mountains of giants*, Papers of the Peabody Museum of Archaeology and Ethnology, Harvard University, Harvard.

Copani, A., 1992, The democratic process and Albanian security policy, *NATO Review*, October, reprinted in *Albanian Life*, **1**: 20–21.

Corrin, C., ed., 1992, *Super women and the double burden*, Scarlet Press, London.

Costa, N.J., 1987, Kosovo: a tragedy in the making, *East European Quarterly*, **21**(1): 87–97.

Costa, N.J., 1988, Albania – a nation of contradictions, *East European Quarterly*, **22**(2): 233–7.

Council of Europe, 1991, *Report on the situation in Albania*, Document 6496 Geneva, 13 September.

Craik, J., 1991, *Resorting to tourism*, Allen and Unwin, Sydney.

Crawshaw, S., 1990, Albania unlocks the gates, *The Independent*, 11 May, 19.

Crawshaw, S., 1991, Hoxha victims receive no apology for past, *The Independent*, 15 June.

Cristofoli, A.M., 1990, Albania's foreign trade in the post-Hoxha era: more openings to the outside, in Altmann, F-L., ed., 1990, *Albanien im Umbruch. Eine Bestandsaufnahme*, R. Oldenbourg, Munich, pp. 225–46.

Crosfield, J., and Sons Ltd, 1967, *An economic survey of Albania*, Joseph Crosfield and Sons Ltd, Warrington, 2 vols.

Çuedari, A., 1983, The development of the power industry in the PSR of Albania, *Albania Today*, **68**: 6–10.

Culf, A., 1990, Albanians snatch at freedom, *The Guardian*, 29 May.

Culf, A., 1993, 'Balkan feel' for BBC's revived Albanian service, *The Guardian*, 26 February.

Çullaj, A., 1992, *Environmental situation in Albania*, Organization for the Protection and Preservation of the Natural Environment in Albania (PPNEA), Tirana.

Cusack, D., 1966, *Illyria reborn*, Heinemann, London.

Cviic, C., 1991, *Remaking the Balkans*, Pinter/RIIA, London.

Daci, L., 1989, Thelbi antimarksist i Perestrojkë për problemet e riprodhimit, *Probleme Ekonomike*, **36**(4): 95–8.

Dako, C.A., 1919, *Albania: the master key to the Near East*, E.L. Grimes, Boston.

Danas, Zagreb, weekly.

Danermark, B., 1982, Albanien – Några data om urbanisieringsprocessen, befolkningsutvecklingen, stadsplaneringen och den socio-ekonomiska relationen mellan stad och land, *Bidrag till Öststatsforskningen*, **10**(4): 61–113.

Danermark, B., Soydan, H., Pashko, G., Vejsiu, Y., 1989, Women marriage and family – traditionalism vs modernity in Albania, *International Journal of Sociology of the Family*, **19**: 19–41.

Daniels, A., 1991, *The wilder shores of Marx*, Hutchinson, London.

Davis, H., 1992, Chronology of Albanian historical dates I, *Albanian Life*, **2**: 5–6.

Davis, H., 1993a, Albania's origins, *Albanian Life*, **1**: 24.

Davis, H., 1993b, Chronology of Albanian historical dates II, *Albanian Life*, **1**: 25–6.

Dawson, P., Dawson, A., 1989, *Albania: a guide and illustrated journal*, Bradt, Chalfont St Peter.

Dede, S., ed., 1983, *The earthquake of 15 April 1979 and the elimination of its consequences*, 8 Nëntori, Tirana.

Dede, S., 1986, *Rruga e gjeologjisë Shqiptare*, 8 Nëntori, Tirana.

Dede, S., et al., 1985, *Enver Hoxha 1908–1985*, Institute of Marxist-Leninist Studies at the CC of the PLA, Tirana.

Dedijer, V., 1951, Albania, Soviet pawn, *Foreign Affairs*, **30**: 103–11.

de Kadt, E., 1979, *Tourism – passport to development?*, Oxford University Press, London.

de Kadt, E., 1990, *Making the alternative sustainable – lessons from development for tourism*, Institute for Development Studies, University of Sussex, Brighton.

Demiri, M., 1983, *Flora ekskursioniste e Shqipërisë*, Shtëpia Botuese e Librit Shkollor, Tirana.

DeS (Drejtoria e Statistikës), 1962, *Annuari statistikor i RPSH 1961*, DeS, Tirana.

DeS (Drejtoria e Statistikës), 1968, *Vjetari statistikor i RPSH 1967 dhe 1968*, DeS, Tirana.

DeS (Drejtoria e Statistikës), 1991, *Vjetari statistikor i Shqipërisë*, DeS, Tirana.

Deutsch, K.W., 1953, *Nationalism and social communication*, MIT Press, Cambridge.

Deutsch, K.W., 1969, *Nationalism and its alternatives*, Alfred A. Knopf, New York.

Dewar, M.S., 1990, *Personal communication*.

DEYA (Department of Education and Youth Affairs), 1983, *Albania*, Australian Government Publishing Service, Canberra.

Dhamo, D., 1974, *La peinture murale du moyen age en Albanie*, 8 Nëntori, Tirana.

Dhamo, D., 1989, Mbi ikonën dhe miniaturën e periudhës Bizantine në Shqipëri, *Iliria*, 2: 229–40.

Diack, H., Mackenzie, R.F., 1935, *Road fortune: a cycling journey through Europe*, Macmillan, London.

Dibra, J., Vako, P., 1965, La population de l'Albanie d'après les recensements de 1955 à 1960, *Population*, 20(2): 253–64.

Dinga, L., 1988, The protection and enrichment of the vegetation genetic fund, in *Balkan Scientific Conference, Environmental Protection in the Balkans, abstracts*, Varna.

Dizdari, P., 1992, Pendimi është gjeja më vlerë në botë, *Tribuna Ekonomike Shqiptare*, 1(5): 34.

Dobbs, M., 1977, Albania looks for new friends, *The Sunday Times*, 17 July.

Doder, D., 1992, Albania opens the door, *National Geographic*, 182(1): 66–93.

Dollani, K., 1988, Control of radioactivity, in *Balkan Scientific Conference, Environmental Protection in the Balkans, abstracts*, Varna.

Donovan, P., 1991, A drip-feed for the East, *The Guardian*, 15 April.

DPS (Drejtoria e Përgjitheshme e Statistikës), 1974, *30 vjet Shqipëri Socialiste*, DPS, Tirana.

Dragnich, A., Todorovich, S., 1984, *The saga of Kosovo: focus on Serbian-Albanian relations*, Westview, Boulder.

Drakulić, S., 1990, The women who wait, *New Statesman and Society*, 31 August.

Drakulić, S., 1992, *How we survived communism and even laughed*, Hutchinson, London.

Drizari, N., 1968, *Scanderbeg: his life, correspondence, orations, victories and philosophy*, The National Press, Palo Alto.

Durham, M.E., 1905, *The burden of the Balkans*, Nelson, London.

Durham, M.E., 1909, *High Albania*, Edward Arnold, London. Reprinted by Virago, London, 1985.

Durham, M.E., 1928, *Some tribal origins, laws and customs of the Balkans*, Allen and Unwin, London.

Durham, M.E., 1941, Albania, *Geography*, 26: 18–24.

Dyvik, E., 1991, *Personal communications*, Development Banking: Infrastructure, Energy and Environment Department, European Bank for Reconstruction and Development, London, October–November.

Eber, S., 1992, *Beyond the green horizon: principles for sustainable tourism*, WWF UK, Godalming.

Ebiri, K., 1992, Albania a virgin territory for modern industry, *Albanian Economic Tribune*, 8(12): 18–19.

EBNA (Editorial Board of *New Albania*), 1984, *Albania*, 8 Nëntori, Tirana.

EBRD (European Bank for Reconstruction and Development), 1991, *How to work with the European Bank for Reconstruction and Development*, EBRD, London.

EBRD (European Bank for Reconstruction and Development), 1993, *Annual eonomic review*, EBRD, London.

Economist, The, Economist Publications, London, weekly.

Edmonds, P., 1927, *To the land of the eagle*, Routledge, London.

Edmundson, L., ed., 1992, *Women and society in Russia and the Soviet Union*, Cambridge University Press, Cambridge.

EEM (*East European Markets*), The Financial Times, London, fortnightly.

EEN (Eastern Europe Newsletter), 1990a, Albania: cri de coeur, *East European Newsletter*, 4(8): 4–5.

EEN (Eastern Europe Newsletter), 1990b, Albania: reform?, *East European Newsletter*, 4(10): 1–3.

EEN (Eastern Europe Newsletter), 1990c, Albania: the juggling act, *East European Newsletter*, 4(23): 3–4.

EEN (Eastern Europe Newsletter), 1991a, Albania: companies and carpet-baggers, *East European Newsletter*, 5(8): 4–5.

EEN (Eastern Europe Newsletter), 1991b, Albania: the morning after, *East European Newsletter*, 5(7): 3.

EEN (Eastern Europe Newsletter), 1992a, Albania, *East European Newsletter*, 6(25): 9–10.

EEN (Eastern Europe Newsletter), 1992b, Macedonia: pre-meditated murder?, *East European Newsletter*, 6(19): 4–6.

EEN (Eastern Europe Newsletter), 1992c, Serbia: implosion?, *East European Newsletter*, 6(13): 1–3.

EEN (Eastern Europe Newsletter), 1992d, The Balkans: the winter war, *East European Newsletter*, 6(23): 3–4.

EEN (Eastern Europe Newsletter), 1992e, War preparations, *East European Newsletter*, 6(24): 1–2.

Einhorn, B., 1991, Where have all the women gone?, *Feminist Review*, 39.

Eisenhuth, S., 1977, Susan of Albania, *Australian Women's Weekly*, 11 May, 10–11.

EIU (Economist Intelligence Unit), 1990a, *Bulgaria, Albania: country profile 1990–91*, EIU, London.

EIU (Economist Intelligence Unit), 1990b, *Romania, Bulgaria, Albania: country report No. 1 1990*, EIU, London.

EIU (Economist Intelligence Unit), 1990c, *Romania, Bulgaria, Albania: country report No. 2 1990*, EIU, London.

EIU (Economist Intelligence Unit), 1990d, *Romania, Bulgaria, Albania: country report No. 3 1990*, EIU, London.

EIU (Economist Intelligence Unit), 1990e, *Romania, Bulgaria, Albania: country report No. 4 1990*, EIU, London.

EIU (Economist Intelligence Unit), 1991a, *Bulgaria and Albania: EIU country profile 1991–92*, EIU, London.

EIU (Economist Intelligence Unit), 1991b, *Romania, Bulgaria, Albania: country report No. 1, 1991*, EIU, London.

EIU (Economist Intelligence Unit), 1991c, *Romania, Bulgaria, Albania: country report No. 2, 1991*, EIU, London.

EIU (Economist Intelligence Unit), 1991d, *Romania, Bulgaria, Albania: country report No. 3, 1991*, EIU, London.

EIU (Economist Intelligence Unit), 1991e, *Romania, Bulgaria, Albania: country report No. 4 1991*, EIU, London.

EIU (Economist Intelligence Unit), 1992a, *Bulgaria, Albania: country profile 1992–93*, EIU, London.

EIU (Economist Intelligence Unit), 1992b, *Romania, Bulgaria, Albania: country report No. 1 1992*, EIU, London.

EIU (Economist Intelligence Unit), 1992c, *Romania, Bulgaria, Albania: country report No. 2 1992*, EIU, London.

EIU (Economist Intelligence Unit), 1992d, *Romania, Bulgaria, Albania: country report No. 3 1992*, EIU, London.

EIU (Economist Intelligence Unit), 1992e, *Romania, Bulgaria, Albania: country report No. 4 1992*, EIU, London.

EIU (Economist Intelligence Unit), 1993a, *Bosnia-Hercegovina, Croatia, Macedonia, Serbia-Montenegro, Slovenia: country report No. 2 1993*, EIU, London.

EIU (Economist Intelligence Unit), 1993b, *Bulgaria, Albania: country profile 1993–94*, EIU, London.

EIU (Economist Intelligence Unit), 1993c, *Romania, Bulgaria, Albania: country report No. 1 1993*, EIU, London.

EIU (Economist Intelligence Unit), 1993d, *Romania, Bulgaria, Albania: country report No. 2 1993*, EIU, London.

EIU (Economist Intelligence Unit), 1993e, *Romania, Bulgaria, Albania: country report No. 3 1993*, EIU, London.

Ellenburg, H., Damm, K., 1989, *Albanien 1989*, Institut für Geographie, Technische Universität, Berlin.

Elsie, R., 1993, *Anthology of modern Albanian poetry: an elusive eagle soars*, Forest Books, London.

Emerson, J., 1990, *Albania: the search for the eagle's song*, Brewin Books, Studley, Warks.

Ermenji, A., 1968, *Albania*, National Democratic Committee 'Free Albania', Paris.

Escarpit, R., ed., 1990, *Nagel's Albania*, Nagel, Paris and Geneva.

Etherton, P.T., Allen, A.D., 1928, *Through Europe and the Balkans: the record of a motor tour*, Cassell, London.

Falaschi, R., 1992, Ismail Qemal Bey Vlora and the making of Albania in 1912, in Winnifrith, T., ed., *Perspectives on Albania*, Macmillan, Basingstoke and London, pp. 106–14.

Farrell, B.H., Runyan, D., 1991, Ecology and tourism, *Annals of Tourism Research*, **18**(1): 26–40.

Fincancioglu, N., Dinshaw, K., 1982, Fertility and family planning, *People*, **9**: special supplement.

Fine, J.V.A., 1983, *The Early Medieval Balkans – a critical survey from the sixth to the later twelfth century*, University of Michigan Press, Ann Arbor.

Fischer, B.J., 1984, *King Zog and the struggle for stability in Albania*, Columbia University Press, New York.

Fishta, I., 1992, Foreign capital in Albania: a brief 100-year historical survey, *Albanian Economic Tribune*, **7**(11): 34–5.

Flash – Albania, Tirana, weekly.

Fletorja zyrtare e Republikës së Shqipërisë (Official Journal of the Republic of Albania), Tirana.

Flint, J., 1993, Past imperfect that won't go away, *The Guardian*, 13 February.

F. N-B., 1952, The Albanian mystery: Russia's least known satellite, *The World Today*, **8**: 466–73.

Fong, M.S., Paul, G., 1992, *The changing role of women in employment in Eastern Europe*, International Bank for Reconstruction and Development, Washington D.C.

Fontana, D.G., 1975, Recent Sino-Albanian relations, *Survey*, **21**(4): 121–44.

Forbes, N., Toynbee, A.J., Mitrany, D., Hogarth, D.G., 1915, *The Balkans*, Clarendon Press, Oxford.

Foss, A., 1978, *Epirus*, Faber, London.

Foster-Carter, A., 1986, North Korea, *Far Eastern Economic Review*, 26 June: 36–45.

Fowler, B., 1992, Banished for their fathers' sins, *New York Times Magazine*, 17 May.

Frashëri, M., 1988, Hydric resources in the context of Albania's environmental protection problems, in *Balkan Scientific Conference, Environmental Protection in the Balkans, abstracts*, Varna.

Frashëri, S., 1954, Një letër e Sami Frashëri mbi lidhjen e Prizrenit, *Buletin i Shkencave Shoqërore*, **2**: 114–16.

Freedman, R.O., 1970, *Economic warfare in the communist bloc*, Praeger, New York.

Freeman, E.A., 1877, *The Ottoman power in Europe*, Macmillan, London.

Freris, A.F., 1986, *The Greek economy in the twentieth century*, St. Martin's, New York.

Frey, B. *et al.*, 1990, *Human rights in the People's Socialist Republic of Albania*, Minnesota Lawyers International Human Rights Committee, Minneapolis.

Friendly, A., 1971, Albania softens pro-Mao stance, *New York Times*, 31 January.

Funck, R.H., Kowalski, J.S., 1987, Impact of transportation bottlenecks on production – the Polish case, in Tismer, J.F., Ambler, J., Symons, L., eds, *Transport and economic development – Soviet Union and Eastern Europe*, Duncker and Humblot, Berlin, pp. 292–305.

Funk, N., Mueller, M., eds, 1993, *Gender politics and post-communism*, Routledge, London.

Fusonie, A.E., 1974–75, An experiment in foreign agricultural education in the Balkans, 1920–1939, *East European Quarterly*, 8(4): 479–93.

G-24 Coordination Unit, 1993, *Environmental assistance to Central and Eastern Europe*, Commission of the European Community, Brussels.

Gács, J., Karimov, I.A., Schneider, C.M., 1993, Small-scale privatisation in Eastern Europe and Russia: a historical and comparative perspective, *Communist Economies and Economic Transformation*, 5(1): 61–86.

Gajo, A., 1992, Large-scale privatization: the key to the reform, *Albanian Economic Tribune*, 2(6): 24–5.

Galler, A., 1957, *The red book of the persecuted church*, Gill, Dublin.

Gardin, G., 1988, *Banishing God in Albania*, Ignatius Press, San Francisco.

Gardiner, L., 1966, *The eagle spreads his claws: a history of the Corfu channel dispute and of Albania's relations with the West 1945–1965*, Blackwood, Edinburgh.

Gardiner, L., 1976, *Curtain calls: travels in Albania Romania and Bulgaria*, Duckworth, London.

Gashi, A., ed., 1992, *The denial of human and national rights of Albanians in Kosova*, Illyria, New York.

Gasser, E., 1939, Present position of the dairying industry in different countries: (19) Albania, *International Review of Agriculture*, 30(4): 144T–51T.

Geco, P., 1970, L'accroisement de la population urbaine de la R.P. d'Albanie et sa repartition géographique, *Studia Albanica*, 2: 161–82.

Geco, P., 1973, Rendesia e qyteteve të medha në popullsine qytetare të R.P. Shqipërisë, *Studime Historike*, 1: 53–71.

Gegaj, A., 1937, *L'Albanie et l'invasion turque au XVe siècle*, University of Louvain, Louvain.

Gegaj, A., Rexhep, K., 1964, *Albania*, Assembly of Captive European Nations, New York.

Georgevitch, V., 1913, *Die Albanesen und die Grossmachte*, S. Hirzel, Leipzig.

Gianaris, N.V., 1982, *The economies of the Balkan countries: Albania, Bulgaria, Greece, Romania, Turkey and Yugoslavia*, Praeger, New York.

Gianaris, N.V., 1984, *Greece and Yugoslavia: an economic comparison*, Praeger, New York.

Giannopoulos, G.A., 1984, Land transport in south-eastern Europe: situation and principles for improvement, *Transport Review*, 4(1): 1–26.

Gibson, H., ed., 1946, *The Ciano diaries, 1939–1943*, Doubleday, Garden City New York.

Gilberg, T., 1976, Yugoslavia, Albania and Eastern Europe, in Gati, C., ed., *The international politics of Eastern Europe*, Praeger, New York, pp. 103–27.

Gilbert, F., 1914, *Les pays d'Albanie et leur histoire*, P. Rosier, Paris.

Giles, F.L., 1930, Boundary work in the Balkans, *Geographical Journal*, 75: 300–12.

Gill, A., 1990, *Berlin to Bucharest*, Grafton, London.

Gjergji, A., 1978, Klasifikimi i veshjeve popullore Shqiptare, *Etnografia Shqiptare*, 9: 3–56.

Gjiknuri, L., 1988, Fauna and some protection problems, in *Balkan Scientific Conference, Environmental Protection in the Balkans, abstracts*, Varna.

Gjiknuri, L., Çullaj, A., 1993, *Personal interview*, Head, deputy head, Committee of the PPNEA, Tirana, 25 March.

Gjinari, J., 1969, The dialectical demarcation of the Albanian language, *Albanian Life*, 1: 29–33.

Gjyzari, N., 1989, Ekonomia të drejtohet më mirë me metoda ekonomike dhe jo me masa thjesht administrative, *Probleme Ekonomike*, 36(5): 3–14.

Glasgow, G., 1939, Italy, Albania and the Mediterranean, *The Contemporary Review*, 155: 540–51.

Glenny, M., 1990, *The rebirth of history*, Penguin, London.

Glenny, M., 1992, *The fall of Yugoslavia: the third Balkan war*, Penguin, London.

Godwin, P., 1984, Former fascist set to rule Albania, *The Sunday Times*, 23 September.

Gołembski, G., 1990, Tourism in the economy of shortage, *Annals of Tourism Research*, 17(1): 55–68.

Gonsalves, P.S., 1987, Alternative tourism – the evolution of a concept and establishment of a network, *Tourism Recreation Research*, 12(2): 9–12.

Gooding, K., 1991, Albania seeks help with chrome venture, *Financial Times*, 12 August.

Gordon, J., Gordon, C., 1927, *Two vagabonds in Albania*, Bodley Head, London.

Greenberg, K., 1992, Plum wine and here's to King Zog, *The European*, 25 June.

Greenberg, S., 1991, 'Green' board to oversee East European revival bank, *The Guardian*, 19 January.

Griffin, M., Ward, S., 1989, Albanians and Serbs – the conflict continues, *Geographical Magazine*, **61**(5): 21–4.

Griffith, W.E., 1963, *Albania and the Sino-Soviet rift*, MIT Press, Cambridge Mass.

Grimmett, R.F.A., Jones, T.A., 1989, *Important bird areas in Europe*, International Council for Bird Preservation, Cambridge.

Gross, H., 1933, Wirtschaftstruktur und Wirtschafts-beziehungen Albaniens, *Weltwirtschaftliches Archiv*, **38**: 505–51.

Grothusen, K-D., ed., 1993, *Albanien*, Vandenhoeck und Ruprecht, Göttingen.

Guicciardini, F., 1901a, Impressioni d'Albania I, *Nuova Antologia*, **93**: 577–611.

Guicciardini, F., 1901b, Impressioni d'Albania II, *Nuova Antologia*, **94**: 17–54.

Gunther, J., 1949, *Behind the curtain*, Harper, New York.

Gurashi, A., Ziri, F., 1982, *Albania constructs socialism relying on its own forces*, 8 Nëntori, Tirana.

Gurney, J., 1978, Energy needs in the Balkans: a source of conflict or co-operation? *The World Today*, **34**(2): 44–51.

Haastad, D., 1990, Future that's under their feet, *The Guardian*, 14 December.

Hackett, L.W., 1944, Spleen measurement in malaria, *Journal of the National Malaria Society*, **3**(2): 121–33.

Hadzivukovic, S., 1989, La population de la Yougoslavie: structure, developpement et perspective, *Population*, **44**(6): 1189–212.

Haigh, N. *et al.*, 1992, *The integration of environmental protection requirements into the definition and implementation of other EC policies*, Institute for European Environmental Policy, London.

Haigh, W.E., 1925, *Malaria in Albania*, League of Nations Health Organisation, Geneva.

Hajdini, G., 1993, Investments on reconstruction of Laçi copper plant, *Albanian Economic Tribune*, **5**(17): 28–9.

Hajrizi, I., 1993, Religious zealots fight for lost souls, *The European*, 10 December.

Hall, C., 1985, *Costa Rica: a geographical interpretation in historical perspective*, Westview, Boulder.

Hall, D. and Howlett, A., 1976, Neither east nor west, *Geographical Magazine*, **48**: 194–6.

Hall, D.R., 1975, Some development aspects of Albania's fifth five-year plan 1971–5, *Geography*, **60**(2): 129–32.

Hall, D.R., 1981a, A geographical approach to propaganda, in Burnett, A.D., Taylor, P.J., eds, *Political studies from spatial perspectives*, Wiley, Chichester, pp. 313–30.

Hall, D.R., 1981b, Town and country planning in Cuba, *Town and Country Planning*, **50**(3): 81–3.

Hall, D.R., 1984a, Albania's growing railway network, *Geography*, **69**(4): 263–5.

Hall, D.R., 1984b, Foreign tourism under socialism: the Albanian 'Stalinist' model, *Annals of Tourism Research*, **11**(4): 539–55.

Hall, D.R., 1984c, Tourism and social change: reply to Romsa, *Annals of Tourism Research*, **11**(4): 608–10.

Hall, D.R., 1985, Problems and possibilities of an Albanian-Yugoslav rail link, in Ambler, J., Shaw, D.J.B, Symons, L., eds, *Soviet and East European transport problems*, Croom Helm, London, pp. 206–20.

Hall, D.R., 1986a, New towns in Europe's rural corner, *Town and Country Planning*, **55**(12): 354–6.

Hall, D.R., 1986b, North of the divide, *Geographical Magazine*, **58**: 590–92.

Hall, D.R., 1987a, Albania, in Dawson, A.H., ed., *Planning in Eastern Europe*, Croom Helm, London, pp. 35–65.

Hall, D.R., 1987b, Albania's transport cooperation with her neighbours, in Tismer, J.F., Ambler, J., Symons, L., eds, *Transport and economic development – Soviet Union and Eastern Europe*, Duncker and Humblot, Berlin, pp. 379–99.

Hall, D.R., 1989, Cuba, in Potter, R.B., ed., *Urbanization and development in the Caribbean*, Mansell, London, pp. 77–113.

Hall, D.R., 1990a, Albania, in Sillince, J.A.A., ed., *Housing policies in Eastern Europe and the Soviet Union*, Routledge, London, pp. 359–401.

Hall, D.R., 1990b, Albania: the last bastion?, *Geography*, **75**(3): 268–71.

Hall, D.R., 1990c, Change closes in on Europe's last communist bastion, *Town and Country Planning*, **59**(9): 251–4.

Hall, D.R., 1990d, Eastern Europe opens its doors, *Geographical Magazine*, **62**(4): 10–15.

Hall, D.R., 1990e, Introduction: geographic dimensions of change, *Geography*, **75**(3): 239–44.

Hall, D.R., 1990f, Stalinism and tourism: a comparative study of Albania and North Korea, *Annals of Tourism Research*, **17**(1): 36–54.

Hall, D.R., ed., 1991, *Tourism and economic development in Eastern Europe and the Soviet Union*, Belhaven, London.

Hall, D.R., 1992a, Albania's changing tourism environment, *Journal of Cultural Geography*, **12**(2): 33–41.

Hall, D.R., 1992b, Czech mates no more, *Town and Country Planning*, **61**(9), 250–51.

Hall, D.R., 1992c, East European seaports in a restructured Europe, in Hoyle, B.S., Pinder, D.A., eds, *European port cities in transition*, Belhaven, London, pp. 98–115.

Hall, D.R., 1992d, Skills transfer for appropriate development, *Town and Country Planning*, **61**(3): 87–9.

Hall, D.R., 1992e, The challenge of international tourism in Eastern Europe, *Tourism Management*, **13**(1): 41–4.

Hall, D.R., 1992f, The West's nuclear dumping ground?, *Town and Country Planning*, **61**(1): 28–30.

Hall, D.R., 1992g, The changing face of international tourism development in Central and Eastern Europe, *Progress in Tourism, Recreation and Hospitality Management*, **4**: 252–64.

Hall, D.R., 1992h, Transport's road to restructuring, *Town and Country Planning*, **61**(12): 336–8.

Hall, D.R., 1993a, Albania, in Carter, F.W., Turnock, D., eds, *Environmental problems in Eastern Europe*, Routledge, London, pp. 7–37.

Hall, D.R., 1993b, Eastern Europe, in Pompl, W., Lavery, P., eds, *Tourism in Europe*, CAB International, London.

Hall, D.R., 1993c, Green tourism in Eastern Europe?, *Town and Country Planning*, **62**(6): 156–7.

Hall, D.R., 1993d, Impacts of economic and political transition on the transport geography of Central and Eastern Europe, *Journal of Transport Geography*, **1**(1): 20–35.

Hall, D.R., ed., 1993e, *Transport and economic development in the new Central and Eastern Europe*, Belhaven, London.

Hall, D.R., 1993f, Transport implications of tourism development, in Hall, D.R., ed., *Transport and economic development in the new Central and Eastern Europe*, Belhaven, London, pp. 206–25.

Hall, D.R., Kinnaird, V.H., 1993, Eastern Europe, in Cater, E., Lowman, G., eds, *Ecotourism: the sustainable alternative?*, Belhaven/Royal Geographical Society, London.

Halliday, J., 1985, The bandit who made his revolution stick, *The Guardian*, 12 April.

Halliday, J., ed., 1986, *The artful Albanian; memoirs of Enver Hoxha*, Chatto and Windus, London.

Hamilton, B., Solanki, B., 1992, *Albania – who cares?*, Autumn House, Grantham.

Hamm, H., 1963, *Albania – China's beachhead in Europe*, Weidenfeld and Nicolson, London.

Hammond, N., 1992, The relations of Illyrian Albania with the Greeks and the Romans, in Winnifrith, T., ed., *Perspectives on Albania*, Macmillan, Basingstoke and London, pp. 29–39.

Hammond, N.G.L., 1972, *A history of Macedonia*, Oxford University Press, Oxford.

Hamsher, W.P., 1937, *The Balkans by bicycle*, H.F. and G. Witherby, London.

Hana, L., 1989, Perestrojka dhe melanizmi kapitalist i tregtisë së jashtme, *Probleme Ekonomike*, **36**(4): 99–102.

Harding, A., 1992, The prehistoric background of Illyrian Albania, in Winnifrith, T., ed., *Perspectives on Albania*, Macmillan, Basingstoke and London, pp. 14–28.

Harrington, R., 1967, Albania, Europe's least known country, *Canadian Geographical Journal*, **74**: 132–43.

Hasluck, F.W., 1929, *Christianity and Islam under the sultans*, Clarendon Press, Oxford, 2 vols.

Hasluck, M., 1925, The nonconformist moslems of Albania, *The Contemporary Review*, **127**: 599–606.

Hasluck, M., 1954, *The unwritten law in Albania*, Cambridge University Press, Cambridge.

Haxhiu, P., 1986, Personal property in Albania!, *New Albania*, **4**: 20–21.

Hegedüs, J., Tosics, I., Turner, B., eds, 1992, *Housing reforms in Eastern Europe*, Routledge, London.

Heller, C., 1989, Turmoil in the Balkans, *Geographical Magazine*, **61**(10): 18–21.

Helmreich, E.C., 1938, *The diplomacy of the Balkan Wars 1912–1913*, MIT Press, Cambridge.

Henderson, P., 1990, Scramble for freedom, *Daily Mail*, 6 July.

Heseltine, N., 1938, *Scarred background: a journey through Albania*, Lovat Dickson, London.

Hibbert, R., 1990, *Albania's national liberation struggle*, Pinter, London.

Hibbert, R., 1993, Albania revisited, *Albanian Life*, **1**: 14–15.

Hido, M., 1993, How to re-evaluate our minerals, *Albanian Economic Tribune*, **1**(13): 33–34.

Hill, S., 1992, Byzantium and the emergence of Albania, in Winnifrith, T., ed., *Perspectives on Albania*, Macmillan, Basingstoke and London, pp. 40–57.

Hinton, H.C., 1972, *China's turbulent quest*, Indiana University Press, Bloomington.

Hoda, P., 1991, *Personal interviews*, Lecturer in Botany, Faculty of Natural Science, University of Tirana, April/August.

Hoda, P., 1993a, *Personal interviews*, Lecturer in Botany, Faculty of Natural Science, University of Tirana, March.

Hoda, P., 1993b, Wild flowers in Albania, *Friends of Albania Newsletter*, **4**: 12–15.

Hoffman, G.W., 1963, *The Balkans in transition*, Van Nostrand, Princeton.

Hoffman, G.W., 1972, *Regional development strategy in Southeast Europe: a comparative analysis of Albania, Bulgaria, Greece, Romania, and Yugoslavia*, Praeger, New York.

Hofsten, E., 1975, Demographic transition and economic development in Albania, *European Demographic Information Bulletin*, 6(3): 147–58.

Hondius, F., 1968, *The Yugoslav community of nations*, Mouton, The Hague.

Höpken, W., 1989, Erste Ergebnisse der Bevölkerungszählung in Albanien, *Südosteuropa*, 38(9): 541–8.

Hösch, E., 1972, *The Balkans*, Faber and Faber, London.

Hoxha, A., 1992, What is the future of the foreign investments? *Albanian Economic Tribune*, 7(11): 7.

Hoxha, D., 1988, Assessment and protection of land, in *Balkan Scientific Conference, Environmental Protection in the Balkans, abstracts*, Varna.

Hoxha, E., 1968–85, *Vepra*, Naim Frashëri/8 Nëntori, Tirana, 47 volumes.

Hoxha, E., 1971, *Speeches 1969–1970*, 8 Nëntori, Tirana.

Hoxha, E., 1974, *Speeches 1971–1973*, 8 Nëntori, Tirana.

Hoxha, E., 1977a, *Report submitted to the 7th Congress of the Party of Labour of Albania*, 8 Nëntori, Tirana.

Hoxha, E., 1977b, *Speeches, conversations, articles, 1965–1966*, 8 Nëntori, Tirana.

Hoxha, E., 1978, *Yugoslav 'self-administration' a capitalist theory and practice*, 8 Nëntori, Tirana.

Hoxha, E., 1979a, *Imperialism and the revolution*, 8 Nëntori, Tirana.

Hoxha, E., 1979b, *With Stalin*, 8 Nëntori, Tirana.

Hoxha, E., 1980a, *Eurocommunism is anti-communism*, 8 Nëntori, Tirana.

Hoxha, E., 1980b, *The Khrushchevites*, 8 Nëntori, Tirana.

Hoxha, E., 1981, *Report to the 8th Congress of the PLA*, 8 Nëntori, Tirana.

Hoxha, E., 1982a, *The Anglo-American threat to Albania*, 8 Nëntori, Tirana.

Hoxha, E., 1982b, *The Titoites*, 8 Nëntori, Tirana.

Hoxha, E., 1984a, *Laying the foundations of the new Albania*, 8 Nëntori, Tirana.

Hoxha, E., 1984b, *Reflections on the Middle East*, 8 Nëntori, Tirana.

Hughes, T.S., 1830, *Travels in Greece and Albania*, H. Colburn & R. Bentley, London, 2nd edn.

Hutchings, R., 1984, Albania's population boom, *Soviet Analyst*, 13(13): 2–4.

Hutchings, R., 1989a, Albanian industrialization: widening divergence from Stalinism, in Schönfeld, R., ed., *Industrialisierung und gesellschaftlicher Wandel in Südosteuropa*, Südosteuropa-Gesellschaft, Munich, pp. 109–24.

Hutchings, R., 1989b, Albania, in *Pressures for reform in the East European economies*, vol. 2, US Government Printing Office, Washington DC.

Hutchings, R., 1992, Albania's inter-war history as a forerunner to the communist period, in Winnifrith, T., ed., *Perspectives on Albania*, Macmillan, Basingstoke and London, pp. 115–22.

Hutchings, R., 1993, Internal trade, transportation, supply and communications, in Grothusen, K-D., ed., *Albanien*, Vandenhoeck und Ruprecht, Göttingen, pp. 391–416.

Hutchings, R., 1994, *Historical dictionary of Albania*, Scarecrow Press, London.

Hyman, S., ed., 1988, *Edward Lear in the Levant*, John Murray, London.

Iatrides, J.O., 1968, *Balkan triangle*, Mouton, The Hague.

Ilievski, P. H., 1992, The ancient Macedonian language and the name of contemporary *Makedonski*, *Macedonian Review*, 22: 247–57.

Illyria, Boston, twice-weekly.

IMF (International Monetary Fund), 1992, *Albania: from isolation towards reform*, IMF, New York.

Infobotues, 1993, *Tirana. harta e qytetit*, Infobotues, Tirana.

Ingber, D., 1949, Enver Hoxha: Albanian dictator, *The Contemporary Review*, 176: 86–93.

Institute of Marxist-Leninist Studies at the CC of the PLA, 1986, *Enver Hoxha 1908–1985*, Ndermarrja e Perhapjes se Librit, Tirana.

Irwin, Z.T., 1984, The fate of Islam in the Balkans, in Ramet, P., ed., *Religion and nationalism in Soviet and East European politics*, Duke University Press, Durham.

Italiaander, R., ed., 1970, *Albanien, Vorposten Chinas*, Delp, Munich.

IUCN (World Conservation Union), 1967, *Liste des Nations Unies des parcs nationaux et reserves analogues*, IUCN, Brussels.

IUCN (World Conservation Union), 1990, *United Nations list of national parks and protected areas*, IUCN, Cambridge.

IUCN-EEP (World Conservation Union – East European Programme), 1990, *Protected areas in Eastern and Central Europe and the USSR*, IUCN, Cambridge.

Jackson, M.R., 1987, Economic development in the Balkans since 1945 compared to Southern and East-Central Europe, *Eastern European Politics and Societies*, 1(3): 393–455.

Jackson, M., 1990, The impact of the Gulf crisis on the economies of Eastern Europe, *Report on Eastern Europe*, **1**(35): 40–45.

Jacques, E.E., 1938, Islam in Albania, *Moslem World*, **28**: 313–14.

Jähne, G., 1991, *Agriculture and nutrition in Albania*, Duncker and Humblot, Berlin.

Jelavich, B., 1983a, *History of the Balkans: volume I: eighteenth and nineteenth centuries*, Cambridge University Press, Cambridge.

Jelavich, B., 1983b, *History of the Balkans: volume II: twentieth century*, Cambridge University Press, Cambridge.

Jelavich, C., Jelavich, B., 1965, *The Balkans*, Prentice-Hall, Englewood Cliffs.

Jenkins, L., 1976, Albania – the land of eagles, *Port Talbot Guardian*, 13 April.

Jenkins, T., 1992, *Who pays the piper? The operations of multinational development banks in Central and Eastern Europe*, Friends of the Earth, London.

Johnson, D.G., 1982, Agriculture in the centrally planned economies, *American Journal of Agricultural Economics*, **64**(5): 845–53.

Jones, L., 1993, *Biografi: an Albanian quest*, Andre Deutsch, London.

Jones, M., 1989, Day trip to the land where Stalin's clock stands, still, *The Sunday Times*, 27 August.

Jones, S., 1990, Albanian refugee looks back in anger, *Independent on Sunday*, 15 July.

Kabo, M., 1982, The coastal lowlands, *New Albania*, **6**: 24–5.

Kabo, M., Kristo, V., Qiriazi, P., Krutaj, F., Gruda, G., Meçaj, N., Bërxholi, A., eds, 1985, *Studime gjeografike*, Akademia e Shkencave e RPSSH, Tirana.

Kabo, M., Bërxholi, A., Krutaj, F., Gruda, G., Meçaj, N., Qiriazi, P., Kristo, V., eds, 1987, *Studime gjeografike 2*, Akademia e Shkencave e RPS të Shqipërisë, Tirana.

Kabo, M., Bërxholi, A., Krutaj, F., Gruda, G., Meçaj, N., Qiriazi, P., Kristo, V., eds, 1988, *Studime gjeografike 3*, Akademia e Shkencave e RPS të Shqipërisë, Tirana.

Kabo, M., Bërxholi, A., Krutaj, F., Gruda, G., Meçaj, N., Qiriazi, P., Sala, S., Kristo, V., eds, 1990, *Studime gjeografike 4*, Akademia e Shkencave e Republikës të Shqipërisë, Tirana.

Kadare, I., 1971, *The general of the dead army*, W.H. Allen, London.

Kadare, I., 1987, *Chronicle in stone*, Serpent's Tail, London.

Kadare, I., 1988, *Doruntine*, Saqi, London.

Kadare, I., 1990, *Broken April*, Saqi, London.

Kadare, I., 1993, *The palace of dreams*, Harvill, London.

Kadia, I., 1993, Oil in Albania. Hopes are high . . ., *Albanian Economic Tribune*, **1**(13): 3.

Kallfa, A., 1984, *Arritje dhe probleme të ngushtimit të dallimeve thelbësore ndërmjet qytetit dhe fshatit*, Universiteti i Tiranës, Tirana.

Kalo, Y., 1993, Bunker uprooting 1993, *Albanian Economic Tribune*, **17**(17): 24.

Karadimov, I., 1989, *Balkan mayors on the environment*, Sofia Press, Sofia.

Karaiskaj, G., Baçe, A., 1975, Kalaja e Durrësit dhe sistemi i fortifikimit përreth në kohën e vonë antike, *Monumentet*, **9**: 5–33.

Karaiskaj, G., 1989, Kështjella mesjetare në Shqipërinë jugperëdimore, *Monumentet*, **37**: 49–63.

Kaser, M., 1967, *Comecon: integration problems of the planned economies*, Oxford University Press, London.

Kaser, M., 1975, Albania, in Hohmann, H., Kaser, M., Thalheim, K., eds, *The new economic systems of Eastern Europe*, Hurst, London, pp. 251–73.

Kaser, M., 1977, Trade and aid in the Albanian economy, in Joint Economic Committee, US Congress, *East European economies post-Helsinki*, US Government Printing Office, Washington DC, pp. 1325–40.

Kaser, M., 1979, Albania's self-chosen predicament, *The World Today*, **35**(6): 259–68.

Kaser, M., 1982, A new statistical abstract from Albania, *Soviet Studies*, **34**(1): 123–5.

Kaser, M., 1983, Albania's muscular socialism, *Contemporary Review*, **243**: 89–94.

Kaser, M., 1985, Albanien gegen 'Konservativismus' und 'Liberalismus', *Europäischer Rundschau*, **13**(1): 117–18.

Kaser, M., 1986, Albania under and after Enver Hoxha, in *East European economies: slow growth in the 1980s, Vol. 2: Country studies on Eastern Europe and Yugoslavia*, US Government Printing Office, Washington DC, pp. 1–21.

Kaser, M., 1993, Economic system, in Grothusen, K-D., ed., *Albanien*, Vandenhoeck und Ruprecht, Göttingen, pp. 289–311.

Kaser, M., Schnytzer, A., 1977, *The Albanian economy from 1945 to the 1980 plan*, Paper in East European Economics 52, St. Antony's College Oxford, Oxford.

Kaser, M., Schnytzer, A., 1983, The economic system of Albania in the 1970s: developments and problems, in Nove, A., Hohmann, H-H., Seidenstecher, G., eds, *The East European economies in the 1970s*, Butterworths, Boston, pp. 315–42.

Keay, J., 1992, Waiting for change, *Business Europa*, **1**(1): 6–11.

Keay, J., 1993a, Fast and loose on the roads, *Guardian*, 13 July.

Keay, J., 1993b, Life after Hoxha, *Euro Business*, **1**(3): 42–6.

Kedourie, E., 1960, *Nationalism*, Hutchinson, London.

Keefe, E.K. *et al.*, 1971, *Area handbook for Albania*, US Government Printing Office, Washington DC.

Kemp, O., 1992, Our aim today: prepare the market, *Albanian Economic Tribune*, **7**(11): 18.

Kende, P., Strmiska, Z., 1987, *Equality and inequality in Eastern Europe*, Berg, Leamington Spa.

Kennedy, P.B., 1939, Politics and religion in Albania, *Missionary Review of the World*, **62**: 359–60.

King, R.R., 1973, *Minorities under communism*, Harvard University Press, Cambridge.

Kirk, D., 1981, Albania, in David, H.P., McIntyre, R.J., *Reproductive behavior; Central and Eastern European experience*, Springer, New York, pp. 300–304.

Klosi, M., 1969, *25 years of construction work in socialist Albania*, Naim Frashëri, Tirana.

Knight, E.F., 1880, *Albania: a narrative of recent travel*, London.

Kobylka, J., 1992, DHL brings some help to Albanian mail, *Business Eastern Europe*, **21**(28): 459–69.

Kobylka, J., 1993, The business outlook: Albania, *Business Eastern Europe*, **22**(15): 4.

Koenig, A.M., 1993, *An overview of the educational system of Albania*, Educational Credential Evaluators, Milwaukee.

Koha e Jone, Shkodër, daily.

Kolodko, G.W., 1993, From recesssion to growth in post-communist economies: expectations versus reality, *Communist and Post-communist Studies*, **26**(2): 123–43.

Kolsti, J., 1981, Albanianism: from the humanists to Hoxha, in Klein, G., Reban, M.J., *The politics of ethnicity in Eastern Europe*, Westview, Boulder, pp. 15–48.

Kolsti, J., 1982, Albania: retreat toward survival, *Current History*, November: 376–80, 392.

Kolsti, J., 1985a, Albania's new beginning, *Current History*, November: 361–4, 386.

Kolsti, J., 1985b, From courtyard to cabinet: the political emergence of Albanian women, in Wolchik, S.A., Meyer, A.G., eds, *Women, state, and party in Eastern Europe*, Duke University Press, Durham, pp. 138–51.

Kondis, B., 1979, The Albanian question at the beginning of 1920 and the Greek-Albanian protocol of Kapestitsa (May 28th. 1920), *Balkan Studies*, **20**(2): 393–416.

Konini, S., 1989, Zgjerimi i kompetencave të bazës për planifikim bugjësor nxit indicativën e masave për shfrytëzimin më mirë të rezervave të brendshme dhe shtimin e prodhimit, *Probleme Ekonomike*, **36**(1): 39–44.

Konstantinidis, P.T., 1992, Rush with caution, *The Guardian*, 11 December.

Kontos, J.F., 1981, *Red Cross, black eagle: a biography of Albania's American School*, Columbia University Press, New York.

Korkuti, M., 1971, *Shqiperia Arkeologjike*, Universiteti Shteteror i Tiranës, Instituti i Historise dhe i Gjuhesise Sektori i Arkeologjise, Tirana.

Kornai, J., 1980, *Economics of shortage*, Elsevier, Amsterdam.

Kornai, J., 1982, *Growth, shortage, efficiency*, University of California Press, Berkeley.

Kosinski, L.A., ed., 1977, *Demographic developments in Eastern Europe*, Praeger, New York.

Kosmo, M., 1993, Two-part strategy designed to aid Albania's environmental problems, *(World Bank) Environmental Bulletin*, Spring: 9.

Kostanick, H.L., 1977, Characteristics and trends in Southeastern Europe: Romania, Yugoslavia, Bulgaria, Albania, Greece and Turkey, in Kostanick, H.L., ed., *Population and migration trends in Eastern Europe*, Westview, Boulder, pp. 11–22.

Kowalski, J.S., 1983, On the relevance of the concept of the centrally planned economies, *Jahrbuch für Sozialwissenschaft*, **2**: 255–66.

Kowalski, J.S., 1987, Rational expectations in centrally planned economies, in Pejovich, S., ed., *Socialism: institutional, philosophical and economic issues*, Kluwer, Dordrecht, pp. 175–208.

Kowalski, J.S., 1990, Privatisierungsstrategien in Polen: eine ordnungspolitische Aufgabe, *Zeitschrift für Öffentliche und Gemeinwirtschaftliche Unternehmen*, **13**(3): 337–43.

Kowalski, J.S., 1991, Privatisierung in osteuropäischen Ländern: die Erfahrungen der ersten zwei Jahre, *Zeitschrift für Öffentliche und Gemeinwirtschaftliche Unternehmen*, **14**(3).

Kowalski, J.S., 1992, *Personal communication*, Professor, Department of Comparative Economic Systems, University of Münster, 8 July.

KPS (Komisioni i Planit të Shtetit, Drejtoria e Statistikës), 1988, *Vjetari statistikor i R.P.S. të Shqipërisë*, Komisioni i Planit të Shtetit, Tirana.

KPS (Komisioni i Planit të Shtetit, Drejtoria e Statistikës), 1989, *Vjetari statistikor i R.P.S. të Shqipërisë*, Komisioni i Planit të Shtetit, Tirana.

KPS (Komisioni i Planit të Shtetit, Drejtoria e Statistikës), 1990, *Vjetari statistikor i R.P.S. të Shqipërisë*, Komisioni i Planit të Shtetit, Tirana.

Kraja, E., ed., 1976, *Shkodra Almanak*, 8 Nëntori, Tirana.

Kristo, D., 1991, *Personal exchange*, Senior Lecturer in English, Faculty of History and Philology, University of Tirana, November.

Kromidha, T., 1985, *Transporti i nderlidhja në RPSSH*, 8 Nëntori, Tirana.

Kromidha, T., Konduri, P., 1984, Achievements and development of transport, *Albania Today*, **78**: 33–5.

Kuke, S., 1983, High rates in housing construction, *New Albania*, **2**: 14–15.

Kusse, P.J., Winkels, H.J., 1990, *Remarks on desalination and land reclamation in the coastal area of the People's Socialist Republic of Albania*, Dutch Ministry of Agriculture, Nature Management and Fisheries, The Hague.

Laber, J., 1993, Slouching towards democracy, *The New York Review*, 14 January.

Laçi, S., 1990, Aspekte të zhvillimit dhe të shpërndarjes gjeografike të forcave prodhuese në bujqësinë e vendit tonë në periudhën midis dy luftërave botërore, *Studime Gjeografike*, **4**: 223–36.

Laffan, R.G.D., 1918, *The guardians of the gate*, Clarendon Press, Oxford.

Lamani, D., 1960, Albania w drodze rozwo ju, *Przeglad Geograficny*, **32**(1–2): 125–8.

Lamani, G., 1993, *Personal interviews*, Secretary, University of Tirana Foreign Relations Office, January–February.

Lampe, J.R., Jackson, M.R., 1982, *Balkan economic history, 1550–1950*, Indiana University Press, Bloomington.

Lane, R.W., 1922, *The peaks of Shala*, Chapman and Dodd, London.

Lange, K., 1973, *Grundzüge der Albanischen Politik*, Rudolf Trofenik, Munich.

Lange, P., 1981, *Die Agrarfrage in der Politik der Partei der Arbeit Albaniens*, Rudolf Trofenik, Munich.

Lani, R., 1984, The youth are a great revolutionary progressive force *Albania Today*, **77**: 14–18.

Larrabee, F.S., 1978, Whither Albania? *The World Today*, **34**(2): 61–9.

Lascaris, M., 1932, Greece and Serbia during the war of 1885, *Slavonic review*, **11**: 88–99.

Lea, J., 1988, *Tourism and development in the Third World*, Routledge, London.

League of Nations, 1941, *Epidemiological report of the Health Organization of the League of Nations*, League of Nations, Geneva.

Lear, E., 1851, *Journals of a landscape painter in Greece & Albania*, Hutchinson, London.

Lee, M., 1984, Albania's isolation in post-war politics, *Labour Focus on Eastern Europe*, **7**(1): 34–5.

Leiby, J.D., Marra, M.C., 1993, Albanian agriculture: perspectives on the future, *Albanian Economic Tribune*, **1**(13): 24–5.

Leggett, E., 1976, *The Corfu incident*, New English Library, London.

Lemperg, F., 1935, Northern Albania, *The New Flora and Silva*, **7**: 79–83.

Lendvai, P., 1969, *Eagles in cobwebs: nationalism and communism in the Balkans*, Macdonald, London.

Lhomel, E., 1986, Albanie, *Le Courrier des Pays de l'Est*, Supplément, **309–11**: 5–17.

Lhomel, E., 1987, L'économie albanaise en 1986: 'le recentrage', *Le Courrier des Pays de l'Est*, **320**: 57–64.

Lhomel, E., 1988, Stagnation persistante de l'économie albanaise en 1987, *Le Courrier des Pays de l'Est*, **330**: 67–71.

Lhomel, E., 1989, L'économie albanaise en 1988: priorité à l'agriculture, *Le Courrier des Pays de l'Est*, **340**: 64–70.

Lika, Z., 1964, *Disa cështje mbi përmirësimin e mëtëjshem të planifikimit. . .*, Naim Frashëri, Tirana.

Lindsay, M., 1992, *Developing capital markets in Eastern Europe*, Pinter, London.

Lipton, D., Sachs, J., 1990, Creating a market in Eastern Europe: the case of Poland, *Brookings Papers on Economic Activity*, **1**: 75–147.

Lipton, D., Sachs, J., 1991, Privatisation in Eastern Europe: the case of Poland, *Brookings Papers on Economic Activity*, **1**: 293–341.

Lleshi, Q., 1977, Tirana, *Geografski Horizont*, **23**(3–4): 20–26.

Lloshi, X., 1990, *Academy of Sciences of the PSR of Albania*, Publishing Council of the Academy of Sciences of the PSR of Albania, Tirana.

Llukani, L., 1993, Transport: a potential area for foreign investments, *Albanian Economic Tribune*, **1**(13): 35–6.

Logoreci, A., 1942, Albania, *The Contemporary Review*, **162**: 42–8.

Logoreci, A., 1950, Albania and Yugoslavia, *The Contemporary Review*, **177**: 360–64.

Logoreci, A., 1961, Albania: a Chinese satellite in the making, *The World Today*, **17**(5): 197–205.

Logoreci, A., 1967, Albania: the Anabaptists of European communism, *Problems of Communism*, **16**(3): 22–8.

Logoreci, A., 1977, *The Albanians: Europe's forgotten survivors*, Victor Gollancz, London.

Logoreci, D., 1993, Room with a view, *The Independent*, 9 September.

Lombardo, E., 1985, Nuovi dati sulla demografia albanese, *Genus*, **41**(3): 115–25.

Lopasic, A., 1992, in Winnifrith, T., ed., *Perspectives*

on *Albania*, Macmillan, Basingstoke and London, pp. 89–105.

Lorenzoni, G., 1930, *La questione agraria albanese*, Laterza, Bari, 2nd edn.

Lorenzoni, G., 1940, L'Albania agricola, pastorale, forestale, *Giornale degli Economisti e Annali de Economia*, NS, 2(7–10): 437–97.

Louis, H., 1927, *Albanien: eine Landeskunde vornehmlich auf Grund eigener Reisen*, J. Engelhorn, Stuttgart.

Luckwald, G.E. von, 1942, *Albanien: Land zwischen Gestern und Morgen*, F. Bruckman, Munich.

Luxner, L., 1993a, Albanian oil: promises, but few rewards, *Business Eastern Europe*, 22(21): 1–2.

Luxner, L., 1993b, Bible-bashing in Albania, *The European*, 5 August.

Luxner, L., 1993c, Will the son of Zog ever wear Albania's crown?, *The European*, 29 July.

Lyall, A., 1930, *The Balkan road*, Methuen, London.

Lydall, H., 1989, *Yugoslavia in crisis*, Clarendon Press, Oxford.

MacDonald, E., 1992, Orphans find salvation – at a price, *The European*, 22 October.

Mackenzie, D., 1992, Europe continues 'poison my neighbour' exports . . ., *New Scientist*, 7 November, p. 8.

Madhi, R., 1982, The process of strengthening the socialist psychology of property, *Albania Today*, 63: 25–33.

Magaš, B., 1993, *The destruction of Yugoslavia*, Verso, London and New York.

Magnani, M., 1939, Risorse minerarie dell'Albania, *La Vie d'Italia*, 45: 1450–63.

Magnusson, L., 1990, Albania, in Mathéy, K., ed., *Housing policies in the socialist Third World*, Mansell, London, pp. 315–21.

Malltezi, J., 1993, Hunting problems in Albania, in, *A study visit of Albanian environmentalists to the Netherlands, May 7–17, 1993*, Milieukontakt Oost-Europa, Amsterdam, p. 60.

Mandi, P., 1980, Tourist Albania, *Albanian Foreign Trade*, 123: 6.

Mann, S.E., 1955, *Albanian literature*, Bernard Quaritch, London.

Mara, M., 1988, Problems of the state and protection of the natural environment in the PSR of Albania, in *Balkan Scientific Conference, Environmental Protection in the Balkans, abstracts*, Varna.

Marchini-Camia, A., 1992, How to attract Albania within the Community, *Albanian Economic Tribune*, 3(7): 6–7.

Marmullaku, R., 1975, *Albania and the Albanians*, C. Hurst, London.

Martin, M.E., 1992, Conquest and commerce: Normans and Venetians in Albania, in

Winnifrith, T., ed., *Perspectives on Albania*, Macmillan, Basingstoke and London, pp. 58–73.

Martinson, J., 1993, Charity that waits in hope, *The European*, 23 September.

Mason, K., Myres, J., Winterbotham, H.S.L., Longland, F., Davidson, C.F., Turrill, W.B., White, N., Mann, S.E., 1945, *Albania*, Naval Intelligence Division, London.

Masotti Christofoli, A., 1985, Albania's economy between the blocs, in Schönfeld, R., ed., *Reform und Wandel in Südosteuropa*, R. Oldenbourg, Munich, pp. 285–305.

Mather, I., Doder, D., 1993, Serbs begin cleansing of Kosovo, *The European*, 4 March.

Mathieson, A., Wall, G., 1982, *Tourism: economic, physical and social impacts*, Longman, London.

Matthews, R., 1937, *Sons of the eagle*, Methuen, London.

May, V., 1991, Tourism, environment and development, *Tourism Management*, 12(2): 112–18.

Mayfield, M.W., Gallo, R.E., 1988, *The rivers of Costa Rica: a canoeing, kayaking and rafting guide*, Menasha Ridge Press, Birmingham Alabama.

McCulloch, J.I.B., 1936, *Drums in the Balkan night*, Putnam's, New York.

McDowall, L., 1991a, Albania learns the art of wrecking, *New Statesman and Society*, 13 December: 18–19.

McDowall, L., 1991b, Albania's desperate poor die in the fight for bread, *The Guardian*, 16 December.

McDowall, L., 1991c, Democrats pull out of Albania coalition, *The Guardian*, 5 December.

McDowall, L., 1991d, New prime minister installed as 32 die in Albanian food riot, *The Guardian*, 11 December.

McDowall, L., 1992, Dreams revealed as Albania strips away old restraints, *The Guardian*, 1 February.

McDowall, L., 1993, Confused signals in Kosovo, *New Statesman and Society*, 5 March: 12–13.

McIntyre, R.J., 1975, Pronatalist programmes in Eastern Europe, *Soviet Studies*, 27(3): 366–80.

McKinley, E.B., 1935, *A geography of disease*, The George Washington University Press, Washington DC.

Medical Monitor, 1991, Health crisis in Europe's poorest land, *Medical Monitor*, 22 November. Reprinted in *Albanian Life*, 1992, 1: 5–7.

Medlicott, W.N. *et al.*, eds, 1980, *Documents on British foreign policy 1919–1939. 1st series vol. XXII Central Europe and the Balkans 1921*, HMSO, London.

Meksi, A., 1983, *Arkitektura mesjetare në Shqipëri*, 8 Nëntori, Tirana.

Meksi, A., Thomo, P., 1981, Arkitektura pasbizantine në Shqipëri, *Monumentet*, **22**: 99–114.

Meksi, V., 1987, Ample drinking water for all the villages and inhabited centres, *New Albania*, **5**: 13.

Mercer, D., 1991, *A question of balance*, The Federation Press, Sydney.

Meynell, C., 1984, Albania's tortuous opening up, *The World Today*, **40**(11): 449–52.

Meynell, C., 1985, Inside Albania, *Telegraph Sunday Magazine*, 24 February: 14–19.

Mihali, Q., 1984, The Albanian economy in 1983–84, *Albanian Life*, **29**: 34–7.

Miho, K., 1977, Përmirësimi i mëtejshëm i higjienës dhe i shërbimit shëndetësor në fshat kërkojne një kujdes të përhershëm, *Rruga e Partisë*, **24**(5): 54–64.

Miho, K., 1987, *Trajta të profilit urbanistik të qytetit të Tiranës*, 8 Nëntori, Tirana.

Mijatovich, C., 1915, *Servia of the Servians*, Pitman, London.

Milanovich, B., 1991, Privatisation in postcommunist societies, *Communist Economies and Economic Transformation*, **3**(1): 5–39.

Milivojevic, M., 1992, *Wounded eagle: Albania's fight for survival*, Alliance Publishers/Institute for European Defence and Strategic Studies, London.

Miljovski, J., 1992, Capitalism without capitalists, *East European Reporter*, **5**(5): 51–2.

Milo, K., Leka, L., 1984, The development of rail transport, *Albanian Life*, **28**: 19–20.

Milone, F., 1941, *L'Albania economica*, CEDAM, Padua.

Mining Journal, 1992, Albania, *Mining Journal*, supplement, 8 May.

Ministry of Tourism, Department of Marketing and Promotion, 1993, *Albania: land of sun and hospitality*, Ministry of Tourism, Tirana.

Ministry of Tourism and EBRD (European Bank for Reconstruction and Development), 1993, *Albania: investing in tourism*, Albania Ministry of Tourism and the EBRD, Tirana and London.

Minxhozi, B., 1992, What distinguishes Albania from other eastern countries, *Albanian Economic Tribune*, **6**(9): 13.

Misja, V., Vejsiu, Y., 1982, De l'accroisement demographique en RPS d'Albanie, *Studia Albanica*, **19**(1): 3–30.

Misja, V., Vejsiu, Y., 1985, *Demographic development in the People's Socialist Republic of Albania*, 8 Nëntori, Tirana.

Misja, V., Vejsiu, Y., Bërxholi, A., 1987, *Popullsia e Shqipërisë (studim demografik)*, Universiteti i Tiranës 'Enver Hoxha', Tirana.

Mitrovic, A., ed., 1983, *Istorija Srpskog naroda*, Srpska Knjizevni Zadruga, Belgrade.

Mladenović, M., 1978, The policy and system of stimulating faster development in economically underdeveloped republics and the autonomous province of Kosovo in the period 1976–1980, *Yugoslav Survey*, **19**(1): 55–68.

Mladina, Ljubljana, daily.

Modiano, M., 1984, Work camp sisters who swam away to freedom, *The Sunday Times*, 19 August.

Modiano, M., 1985, The world waits for Albania to come out of its shell, *The Sunday Times*, 14 April.

Montgomery-Massingberd, H., 1990, Kings without Kingdoms, *Daily Telegraph Magazine*, 10 February.

Moore, P., 1992a, Islamic aspects of the Yugoslav crisis, *RFE/RL Research Report*, **1**(28): 37–42.

Moore, P., 1992b, The 'Albanian question' in the former Yugoslavia, *RFE/RL Research Report*, **1**(14): 7–15.

Morgan, W.B., 1992, Economic reform, the free market and agriculture in Poland, *Geographical Journal*, **158**: 145–56.

Moschetti, A., 1930, Le miniere in Albania, *L'Industria Mineraria d'Italia*, **4**: 409–32.

Moscos, C.C., 1965, From monarchy to communism: the social transformation of the Albanian elite, in Barringer, H.R. *et al.*, eds, *Social change in developing areas*, Schenkam, Cambridge Mass., pp. 205–21.

Mosko, S., 1984, Town planning in the service of the people, *Albania Today*, **77**: 24–6.

Muka, A., 1978, Banesa fshatare në malësinë e Tiranës gjatë shek. XIX dhe fillimit të shek. XX, *Etnografia Shqiptare*, **9**: 209–312.

Muka, A., 1985, Karakteri i baneses popullore ne fshatrat e Librazhdit, *Librazhdi Almanak*, **1**: 61–91.

Muller, J., 1844, *Albanien, Rumelien und die Öster-reichische-Montenegrinische Grenze*, J.G. Galveschen, Prague.

Murphy, P., 1985, *Tourism: a community approach*, Methuen, London.

Murphy, T., 1991, *Personal communications*, Senior Environmental Consultant, European Bank for Reconstruction and Development, London, November.

Murphy, T., 1992, *Personal communication*, Senior Environmental Consultant, European Bank for Reconstruction and Development, London, 18 August.

Mury, G., 1970, *Albanie: terre de l'homme nouveau*, François Maspero, Paris.

Mury, G., 1973, *Mensch und Sozialismus in Albanien*, Trikont, Munich.

Myrdal, J., Kessle, G., 1978, *Albania defiant*, Stage 1, London.

N'Diaye, S., Private lines – the future of the air traffic, *Albanian Economic Tribune*, **8**(12): 8.

Nallbani, H., 1989, *The Onufri Museum Berat*, 8 Nëntori, Tirana.

Nano, T., 1987, *Bimet mjaltese*, 8 Nëntori, Tirana.

Narayan, N., 1991, Cramped but free, *The Higher*, 8 November.

National Trust for Scotland, 1988, *Ben Lawers nature trail*, National Trust for Scotland, Edinburgh.

Newby, E., 1985, *On the shores of the Mediterranean*, Picador, London.

Newman, B., 1936, The Law of Lek, *Geographical Magazine*, **8**: 143–56.

Newman, B., 1938, *Albanian journey*, Pitman, London.

Newman, B., 1944, *Balkan background*, Robert Hale, London.

Neza, A., Hanka, M., 1993, *Travellers' guide to Albania*, ACO UK, Princes Risborough.

Nickel, H.M., 1989, Sex-role socialization in relationships as a function of the division of labor: a sociological explanation for the repoduction of gender differences, in Rueschemeyer, M., Lemke, C., eds, *The quality of life in the German Democratic Republic*, M.E. Sharp, Armonk.

Nicol, D.M., 1957, *The despotate of Epirus*, Basil Blackwell, Oxford.

NIN, Belgrade, weekly.

Noakes, V., 1985, *Edward Lear 1812–1888*, Weidenfeld and Nicolson, London.

Noli, F.S., 1947, *George Castrioti Scanderbeg (1405–1468)*, International Universities Press, New York.

Norris, H.T., 1993, *Islam in the Balkans*, C. Hurst, London.

North, C., 1990, Into Albania, *The Rock Garden*, **22**(1): 63–71.

Nova Makedonija, Skopje, daily.

Nowack, E., 1921, A contribution to the geography of Albania, *Geographical Review*, **11**: 503–40.

Nowack, E., 1926, *Beiträge zur Geologie von Albanien*, E. Schweizerbart, Stuttgart.

Nowack, E., 1928, *Die geologische Karte von Albanien*, Militärgeographisches Institut, Vienna.

Nuri, F., 1982, Achievements in land reclamation and irrigation, *Albania Today*, **67**: 24–6.

O'Ballance, E., 1966, *The Greek civil war, 1944–1949*, Faber and Faber, London.

Omari, L., Pollo, S., 1988, *The history of the socialist construction of Albania*, 8 Nëntori, Tirana.

Onuzi, A., 1987, *Poçeria popullore në Shqipëri*, Akademia Shkencave e RPS të Shqipërisë, Instituti i Kulturës Popullore, Tirana.

Oslobođenje, Sarajevo, daily.

Ostreni, A., 1974, *Gjeografia e Shqipërisë*, Shtëpia Botuese e Librit Shkollor, Tirana, 4th edition.

Ostrowski, S., 1984, Tourism in protected areas – the case of Poland, *Tourism Management*, **6**(4): 288–94.

O'Sullivan, J., 1972, *The Egnatian Way*, David and Charles, Newton Abbott.

PADU (Protected Areas Database Unit), 1990, *Information from protected areas database*, World Conservation Monitoring Centre, Cambridge.

Page, B., Leitch, D., Knightley, P., 1968, *Philby – the spy who betrayed a generation*, London.

Pajcini, I., 1983, New addresses in a city, *New Albania*, **6**: 14–15.

Paloka, A., 1981, Development of the power industry in PSR of Albania, *Albania Today*, **56**: 32–6.

Pano, N., 1990, Ecological balance in the Mediterranean Sea, *New Albania*, **5**: 28.

Pano, N. C., 1968, *The People's Republic of Albania*, The Johns Hopkins Press, Baltimore.

Pano, N. C., 1970, Albania in the sixties, in Toma, P.A., ed., *The changing face of communism in Eastern Europe*, University of Arizona Press, Tucson, pp. 244–80.

Pano, N. C., 1974, The Albanian cultural revolution, *Problems of Communism*, **23**(4): 44–57.

Pano, N. C., 1977a, Albania in the era of Kosygin and Brezhnev, in Simmonds, G.W., ed., *Nationalism in the USSR and Eastern Europe*, University of Detroit Press, Detroit, pp. 474–94.

Pano, N. C., 1977b, Albania in the 1970s, *Problems of Communism*, **26**(6): 33–43.

Pano, N.C., 1977c, When friends fall out, *Far Eastern Economic Review*, 26 August: 34, 39.

Pano, N.C., 1982, Albania: the last bastion of Stalinism, in Drachkovitch, M.M., ed., *East Central Europe*, Hoover Institution Press, Stanford, pp. 187–218.

Pano, N. C., 1984, Albania, in Rakowska-Harmstone, T., ed., *Communism in Eastern Europe*, Indiana University Press, Bloomington, pp. 213–37.

Papa, A., 1987, Mbi disa veçori të relievit në trevat fushore, *Studime Gjeografike*, **2**: 165–82.

Papa, M., 1972, Mbrojtja ligjore e pasurive kulturale të vendit tonë, *Monumentet*, **3**: 139–45.

Papajorgji, H., 1982, Peopling the countryside and extending the working class to the whole territory of Albania, *Albania Today*, **63**: 14–19.

Papajorgji, H., 1989, Triumph of the correctness of the Party on the countryside, *Albania Today*, **109**: 42–6.

Pariser, H.S., 1992, *Adventure guide to Costa Rica*, Hunter Publishing, Edison, New Jersey.

Parkin, S., ed., 1991, *Green light on Europe*, Heretic Books, London.

Partos, G., 1992, Behind barbed wire boundaries, *The Guardian*, 4 September.

Partos, G., 1993, *The world that came in from the cold*, Royal Institute of International Affairs, London.

Pashko, G., 1991, The Albanian economy at the beginning of the 1990s, in Sjöberg, Ö., Wyzan, M.L., *Economic change in the Balkan states: Albania, Bulgaria, Romania and Yugoslavia*, Pinter, London, pp. 128–46.

Pashko, G., 1993a, Inflation in Albania, *Communist Economies and Economic Transformation*, **5**(1): 115–26.

Pashko, G., 1993b, Obstacles to economic reform in Albania, *Europe-Asia Studies*, **45**(5): 907–21.

Pastor, X., ed., 1991, *The Mediterranean*, Collins and Brown, London.

Peacock, P., 1993, Roman Catholicism in North Albania, *Albanian Life*, **1**: 31–2.

Peacock, W., 1914, *Albania: the foundling state of Europe*, Chapman and Hall, London.

Pearce, D. G., 1987, *Tourism today: a geographical analysis*, Longman, Harlow.

Pearce, D. G., 1989, *Tourist development*, Longman, Harlow, 2nd edn.

Pellumbi, S., 1988, Restructuring – ideological mechanism to deceive the masses, *Albania Today*, **99**: 48–52.

Pepo, A., 1992, 18 months – Albanian or US time?, *Albanian Economic Tribune*, **6**(9): 11.

Pergent, G., 1992, *Field study in Albania on state of protection of marine and coastal sites of ecological interest and endangered species*, RAC/SPA, Tunis.

Permeti, A., 1991, A market economy without economists?!, *Albanian Economic Tribune*, **4**: 22.

Perrin, B., 1940, Le pétrol de l'Albanie, *Revue des deux Mondes*, **57**: 148–60.

Perry, D.M., 1992, The Republic of Macedonia and the odds for survival, *RFE/RL Research Report*, **1**(46): 12–19.

Perry, D.M., 1993, Politics in the Republic of Macedonia: issues and parties, *RFE/RL Research Report*, **2**(23): 31–7.

Peters, S., 1971, Ingredients of the communist takeover in Albania, *Studies on the Soviet Union*, **11**(4): 244–63.

Petrela, S., 1990, A pearl of nature, *New Albania*, **5**: 32–3.

Petrovic, B., 1985, Albania rejects Soviet sympathy, *The Guardian*, 13 April.

Pettifer, J., 1990, Chink of reformist light enters fortress Albania, *The Independent on Sunday*, 11 March.

Pettifer, J., 1992, Albanian forces mass on Kosovo border, *The Times*, 9 December.

Pettifer, J., 1993, *The Greeks: the land and people since the war*, Viking, London.

Peyfuss, M.D., 1992, Religious confession and nationality in the case of the Albanians, in Kerr, D.A. *et al.*, eds, *Religion, state and ethnic groups*, Dartmouth, Aldershot, pp. 125–38.

PHARE, 1993, *Albania: orientation paper*, EC PHARE Office, Brussels.

Philby, H.A.R., 1968, *My silent war*, MacGibbon and Kee, London.

Pick, H., 1985, Golden road to Tirana, *The Guardian*, 11 June.

Pier, R., 1993, Tourismus, in Grothusen, K-D., ed., *Albanien*, Vandenhoeck und Ruprecht, Göttingen, pp. 417–26.

Pigram, J.J., 1980, Environmental implications of tourism development, *Annals of Tourism Research*, **6**: 245–72.

Pipa, A., 1989, The political situation of the Albanians in Yugoslavia, with particular attention to the Kosovo problem: a critical approach, *East European Quarterly*, **23**(2): 159–81.

Pipa, A., Repishti, S., eds, 1984, *Studies on Kosova*, Westview East European Monographs, Boulder.

Piperi, R., Kajno, K., 1990, *Flora mjekësore e Korçës*, Drejtoria e Arsimit Shëndetësor, Tirana.

Plomer, W., 1970, *The diamond of Janina: Ali Pasha 1741–1822*, Taplinger, New York.

Pobjeda, Podgorica, daily.

Politika, Belgrade, daily.

Politikal Ekspres, Belgrade, daily.

Pollo, S., 1983, *The proclamation of independence of Albania*, 8 Nëntori, Tirana.

Pollo, S., Puto, A., 1981, *The history of Albania*, Routledge and Kegan Paul, London.

Polunin, O., 1980, *Flowers of Greece and the Balkans*, Oxford University Press, Oxford.

Poncet, J., 1976, Le developpement du tourisme en Bulgarie, *Annales de Géographie*, **85**: 155–77.

Popa, T., 1974, *Icônes et miniatures du moyen age en Albanie*, 8 Nëntori, Tirana.

Popović, V., Milić, B., 1981, Montenegro after the catastrophic earthquake, *Yugoslav Survey*, **22**(2): 27–48.

Post, T. *et al.*, 1992, At last, a Balkan plan, *Newsweek*, 30 November: 10–11.

Poulsen, T.M., 1977, Migration on the Adriatic coast: some processes associated with the development of tourism, in Kostanick, H.L., ed., *Population and migration trends in Eastern Europe*, Westview, Boulder, pp. 197–215.

Poulton, H., 1989, *Minorities in the Balkans*, Minority Rights Group, report No. 82, London.

Poulton, H., 1993, The Republic of Macedonia after UN recognition, *RFE/RL Research Report*, **2**(23): 22–30.

Pounds, N.J.G., 1969, *Eastern Europe*, Longman, London.

Poznanski, K., 1993, An interpretation of communist decay: the role of evolutionary mechanisms, *Communist and Post-communist Studies*, 26(1): 3–24.

Prampolini, N., 1941, La bonifiche dell'Albania, *Rivista di Malarialogia*, 20(4): 258–70.

Preza, B., Bekteshi, S., 1978, Disa aspekte të zhvillimit të shëndetësisë sonë socialiste, *Buletin i Universitetit të Tiranës – Serija Shkencat Mjekësore*, 18(4): 3–16.

Price, C.A., 1963, *Southern Europeans in Australia*, Oxford University Press, Melbourne.

Prifti, P.R., 1968, *Albania's cultural revolution*, MIT Press, Cambridge Mass.

Prifti, P.R., 1971, *Albania and Sino-Soviet relations*, MIT Press, Cambridge Mass.

Prifti, P.R., 1972a, Albania, in Bromke, A., Rakowska-Harmstone, T., eds, *The communist states in disarray, 1965-1971*, University of Minnesota Press, Minneapolis, pp. 198–220.

Prifti, P.R., 1972b, Albania's expanding horizons, *Problems of Communism*, 21(1): 30–39.

Prifti, P.R., 1973a, Albania and the Baltic republics: mininations in a modern world, in Ziedonis, A. ed., *Mininations of the world*, California State University Press, San Jose, pp. 49–55.

Prifti, P.R., 1973b, Albania and the Sino-Soviet conflict, *Studies in Comparative Communism*, 6: 241–79.

Prifti, P.R., 1974, Armed forces and society in Albania, in McArdle Kelleher, C., ed., *Political-military systems: comparative perspectives*, Sage, Beverly Hills, pp. 191–7.

Prifti, P.R., 1975a, Albania – towards an atheist society, in Bociurkiw, B.R., Strong, J.W., eds, *Religion and atheism in the USSR and Eastern Europe*, Macmillan, London, pp. 388–404.

Prifti, P.R., 1975b, Minority politics: the Albanians in Yugoslavia, *Balkanistica*, 2: 7–18.

Prifti, P.R., 1975c, The Albanian women's struggle for emancipation, *Southeastern Europe*, 2(2): 109–29.

Prifti, P.R., 1978, *Socialist Albania since 1944*, MIT Press, Cambridge Mass.

Prifti, P.R., 1979, Albania, in Bromke, A., Novak, D., eds, *The communist states in the era of detente 1971-1977*, Mosaic Press, Ontario, pp. 189–210.

Prifti, S., 1988, The museum zone of the Shkodra city, in PSR of Albania, *Legacy of centuries*, 8 Nëntori, Tirana, pp. 27–30.

Prifti, V., 1993, Foreign investors are welcome, *Albanian Economic Tribune*, 1(13): 26–7.

Prybyla, J.S., 1967, Albania's economic vassalage, *East Europe*, 1: 9–14.

PSR of Albania, 1977, *Constitution of the People's Socialist Republic*, 8 Nëntori, Tirana.

PSR of Albania, 1988, *Legacy of centuries*, 8 Nëntori, Tirana.

Pucks, K., 1993, Optimizing the value of existing state companies, *Albanian Economic Tribune*, 5(17): 22–3.

Puka, V., 1988, Physical-chemical qualities of river water, in *Balkan Scientific Conference, Environmental Protection in the Balkans, Abstracts*, Varna.

Pumo, E., 1977, Generalità sui giacimenti minerari dell'Albania, *L'Industria Mineraria*, July–August: 262–71.

Puto, A., 1981, *From the annals of British diplomacy*, 8 Nëntori, Tirana.

Qemo, G., Luci, E., 1983, The improvement of planning for the territorial distribution of productive forces and problems which emerge in this field, in Institute of Marxist-Leninist Studies, *The National Conference: on problems of the development of the economy in the 7th. five-year plan*, 8 Nëntori, Tirana, pp. 233–9.

Qerimi, V., 1981, *Chronicle of another battle won (April October 1979)*, 8 Nëntori, Tirana.

Ramet, P., 1984, *Nationalism and federalism in Yugoslavia, 1963–1983*, Indiana University Press, Bloomington.

RAPA (Republic of Albania People's Assembly), 1993, *Law on priority tourism development zone*, RAPA, Tirana.

Raven, S., 1993, The road to empire, *Geographical Magazine*, 65(6): 21–4.

Read, J., 1993, 'My dream for Albania in Europe', *The European*, 3 December.

Redclift, M., 1987, *Sustainable development: exploring the contradictions*, Methuen, London.

Reed, C., 1990, Albania, the final domino, *The European*, 11 May.

Reiquam, S., 1983, Emigration and demography in Kosovo, *Radio Free Europe Research*, 8: RAD/186.

Remérand, G., 1928, *Ali de Tebelen, Pacha de Janina 1744-1822*, Paul Geuthner, Paris.

Republika, Tirana, twice weekly.

Réti, G., 1983, The foreign policy of Albania after the break with China, in Carlton, D., Schaerf, C., eds, *South-Eastern Europe after Tito*, Macmillan, London, pp. 189–99.

Réti, G., 1991, *Albánia*, Panoráma, Budapest.

Reuter, 1985, Albania to maintain its isolation, *The Guardian*, 16 April.

Reynolds, P., Young, P., 1992, *Eastern promise*, Adam Smith Institute, London.

RFE/RL Daily Report, Radio Free Europe/Radio Liberty, Munich, daily.

Richter, L.K., 1987, The search for appropriate tourism, *Tourism Recreation Research*, 12(2): 5–7.

Rieder, I., 1991, *Feminism and Eastern Europe*, Attic Press, Dublin.

Rilindja, Priština, daily.

Rilindja Demokratike, Tirana, daily (formerly twice weekly).

Rimmell, N., 1992, Walking in Albania, *Albanian Life*, 2: 18–20.

Rimms, J., 1993, Into unknown territory, *In Focus*, 7: 6.

Riza, E., 1971, Banesa e fortifikuar Gjirokastrite, *Monumentet*, 1: 127–48.

Riza, E., 1975, Studim për restaurimin e një banese me cardak në qytetin e Kruja, *Monumentet*, 9: 107–25.

Riza, E., 1978, *Gjirokastra: museum city*, 8 Nëntori, Tirana.

Riza, E., 1981a, Banesa popullore në qytetin-muze të Beratit, *Monumentet*, 21(1): 5–35.

Riza, E., 1981b, L'architecture populaire urbaine en Albanie aux XVIIIe–XIXe siècles, *Culture Populaire Albanaise*, 1: 87–111.

Riza, E., 1983, The Institute for the Restoration of Monuments of Culture, *New Albania*, 1: 24–5.

Roche, J., 1992, Shqipëria është me fat, *Albanian Economic Tribune*, 1(5): 14–19.

Rojec, M., Svetličič, M., 1993, Foreign investment in Slovenia: experience, prospects and policy options, *Communist Economies and Economic Transformation*, 5(1): 103–14.

Romsa, G.H., 1984, Comment on Hall's *Foreign tourism under socialism*, *Annals of Tourism Research*, 11: 607–8.

Ronart, O., 1936, L'évolution économique de l'Albanie, *Revue Economique Internationale*, 28: 581–97.

Rose, R., 1993, Contradictions between micro- and macro-economic goals in post-communist societies, *Europe-Asia Studies*, 45(3): 419–44.

Rosenberg, D.J., 1991, Shock therapy: GDR women in transition from a socialist welfare state to a social market economy, *Signs: Journal of Women in Culture and Society*, 17(1): 129–51.

Royal Institute for International Affairs (RIIA), 1939, *South East Europe: a political and economic survey*, RIIA, London.

Ruka, A. *et al.*, 1992, It was, we are, *East European Reporter*, 5(5): 64–5.

Ruli, G., 1992, A reality with numerous investment and development possibilities, *Albanian Economic Tribune*, 7(11): 3–4.

Russ, W., 1979, *Der Entwicklungsweg Albaniens. Ein Beitrag zum Konzept autozentrierter Entwicklung*, Anton Hain, Köningstin am Tanus.

Sandström, P., Sjöberg, Ö., 1991, Albanian economic performance: stagnation in the 1980s, *Soviet Studies*, 43(5): 931–47.

Sarbutt, G., 1992, Rail crisis in Albania, *Modern Railways*, 48(11): 622–3.

Savvides, N., 1992, Albania banks on Islamic help, *The European*, 1 October.

Schmidt-Neke, M., 1987, *Entstehung und Ausbau der Königsdiktatur in Albanien (1912–1939)*, R. Oldenbourg, Munich.

Schmidt-Neke, M., Sjöberg, Ö., 1993, Bevölkerungsstruktur, in Grothusen, K-D., ed., *Albanien*, Vandenhoeck und Ruprecht, Göttingen, pp. 464–90.

Schnytzer, A., 1981, The impact of the Sino-Soviet split on the Albanian economy, in, *East European economic assessment: part I – country studies, 1980*, US Government Printing House, Washington DC.

Schnytzer, A., 1982, *Stalinist economic strategy in practice: the case of Albania*, Oxford University Press, London.

Schnytzer, A., 1992, Albania: the purge of Stalinist economic ideology, in Jeffries, I., ed., *Industrial reform in socialist countries*, Edward Elgar, Aldershot.

Schnytzer, A., 1993, Industry, in Grothusen, K-D., ed., *Albanien*, Vandenhoeck und Ruprecht, Göttingen, pp. 312–42.

Schönfeld, R., ed., *Reform und Wandel in Südosteuropa*, R. Oldenbourg, Munich.

Schöpflin, G., 1993, *Politics in Eastern Europe*, Blackwell, Oxford.

Schwanke, R., 1960, Die landwirtschaftlichen Productionsgenossenschaften in Albanien, *Österreichische Osthefte*, 2(1): 46–53.

Schwanke, R., 1962a, Das neue Erziehungs – und Bildungsprogramm in Albanien, *Österreichische Osthefte*, 4(1): 47–51.

Schwanke, R., 1962b, Wirtschaftsgeographische rayonierung Albaniens, *Österreichische Osthefte*, 4(4): 302–6.

Schwanke, R., 1964, Demographische Probleme Albaniens, *Österreichische Osthefte*, 6(1): 42–8.

Scriven, G.P., 1919, The awakening of Albania, *Geographical Review*, 8(2): 73–83.

Sejdia, A., 1991, Albania cannot develop without the aid of foreign capital, *Albanian Economic Tribune*, 4: 11–13.

Selala, P., 1982, Well-being and its continuous uplift in the PSRA, *Albania Today*, 63: 20–24.

Selfo, L., 1993, *Personal interview*, Chairman, Committee of Environmental Preservation and Protection, Ministry of Health, Tirana.

Senja, N., Kekezi, H., 1982, *The national exhibition of the material culture of the Albanian people*, 8 Nëntori, Tirana.

Senja, N., Xhafa, B., n.d., *The treasures of folk culture*, 8 Nëntori, Tirana.

Sereni, A.P., 1941, Legal status of Albania, *American Political Science Review*, **35**: 311–17.

Seton-Watson, H., 1956, *The East European revolution*, Methuen, London.

Seton-Watson, H., 1967, *Eastern Europe between the Wars, 1918–1941*, Harper, New York.

Sheck, R.S., 1990, *Costa Rica: a natural destination*, John Muir, Santa Fe.

Shehu, M., 1968, *On the stand of the People's Republic of Albania towards the Warsaw Treaty*, Naim Frashëri, Tirana.

Shchu, M., 1971, *Report on the 5th 5-year Plan (1971–1975)*, Naim Frashëri, Tirana.

Shehu, M., 1976, *Report on the 6th Five-Year Plan (1976–1980)*, 8 Nëntori, Tirana.

Shehu, M., 1979, *Magnificent balance of victories in the course of 35 years of socialist Albania*, 8 Nëntori, Tirana.

Shilegu, H., 1987, *Personal interview*, Head of English Section, Albturist, Tirana, July.

Shilegu, H., 1991, *Personal interview*, Director, Tirana Travel Service, Tirana, April.

Shivji, I.G., ed., 1975, *Tourism and socialist development*, Tanzania Publishing House, Dar Es Salaam.

Shkëmbi, H., 1990, Ndryshimet sasiore në popullsinë e rajonit të veriut dhe ndikimi i tyre në problemet e prodhimit bujqësor, *Studime Gjeografike*, **4**: 217–22.

Shkodra, G., Ganiu, S., 1984, *The well-being of the Albanian people and some factors and ways for its continuous improvement*, 8 Nëntori, Tirana.

Shkurti, S., 1978, Shirja e drithërave, *Ethnografia Shqiptare*, **9**: 57–113.

Shoup, P., 1968, *Communism and the Yugoslav national question*, Columbia University Press, New York.

Shoup, P.S., ed., 1990, *Problems of Balkan security: southeastern Europe in the 1990s*, Wilson Center Press, Washington DC.

Shyti, F., 1989, Ristrukturimi i marrëdhënieve të shpërndarjes në Bashkimin Sovjetik kapitalist, *Probleme Ekonomike*, **36**(4): 91–4.

Sigalos, L., 1963, *The Greek claims on Northern Epirus*, Argonaut, Chicago.

Sillince, J.A.A., ed., 1990, *Housing policies in Eastern Europe and the Soviet Union*, Routledge, London.

Simmons, M., 1991, Four million facing hardship, *The Guardian*, 1 November.

Simmons, M., 1992, Win by right expected in Albanian poll, *The Guardian*, 23 March.

Simpson, J., 1993, To play the dictator, *The Daily Telegraph*, 4 September.

Simpson, R., 1992, *Sustainable tourism for protected areas: progress report*, European Federation of Nature and National Parks, Grafenau.

Singleton, F.B., 1975, Albania and her neighbours: the end of isolation, *The World Today*, **31**(9): 383–90.

Singleton, F.B., ed., 1987, *Environmental problems in the Soviet Union and Eastern Europe*, Lynne Rienner, London.

Sinishta, G., 1976, *The fulfilled promise: a documentary account of religious persecution in Albania*, H and F Composing Service Printing, Santa Clara.

Sivignon, M., 1970, Quelques données demographiques sur la République Populaire d'Albanie, *Revue de Géographie de Lyon*, **45**(1): 61–74.

Sivignon, M., 1975, Tirana et l'urbanisation de l'Albanie, *Revue de Géographie de Lyon*, **50**(4): 333–43.

Sivignon, M., 1983, Évolution de la population de l'Albanie, *Méditerranée*, **50**(4): 37–42.

Sivignon, M., 1987, Les disparités régionales en Albanie, *Bulletin de la Société Languedocienne de Géographie*, **21**(1–2): 97–103.

Sizeland, J., Hall, D., 1992, Preparing Czech youth to do its best, *Town and Country Planning*, **61**(6): 183–4.

Sjöberg, Ö., 1989a, A note on the regional dimension of post-war demographic development in Albania, *Nordic Journal of Soviet and East European Studies*, **6**(1): 91–121.

Sjöberg, Ö., 1989b, *The agrarian sector in Albania during the 1980s: a changing regional focus*, Stockholm School of Economics, Studies in International Economics and Geography, Stockholm.

Sjöberg, Ö., 1990a, Infant mortality in Albania: an interim report, *Südosteuropa*, **39**: 709–18.

Sjöberg, Ö., 1990b, *The Albanian economy in the 1980s: the nature of a low performing system*, Stockholm Institute of Soviet and East European Economics, Working Paper 10, Stockholm.

Sjöberg, Ö., 1990c, Urban Albania: developments 1965–1987, in Altmann, F-L, ed., *Albanien im Umbruch – Eine Bestandsaufnahme*, R. Oldenbourg, Munich, pp. 171–223.

Sjöberg, Ö., 1991a, *Rural change and development in Albania*, Westview, Oxford.

Sjöberg, Ö., 1991b, The Albanian economy in the 1980s: coping with a centralised system, in Sjöberg, Ö., Wyzan, M.L., *Economic change in the Balkan states: Albania, Bulgaria, Romania and Yugoslavia*, Pinter, London, pp. 115–27.

Sjöberg, Ö., 1991c, *Urbanisation under central planning: the case of Albania*, Faculty of Social Sciences, Uppsala University, Uppsala.

Sjöberg, Ö., 1992, Underurbanisation and the zero growth hypothesis: diverted migration in Albania, *Geografiska Annaler*, **74B**(1): 3–19.

Sjöberg, Ö., 1993, Social structure, in Grothusen, K-D., ed., *Albanien*, Vandenhoeck und Ruprecht, Göttingen, pp. 491–504.

Sjöberg, Ö., Sandström, P., 1989, *The Albanian statistical abstract of 1988: heralding a new era?*, Department of Soviet and East European Studies, Uppsala University, Working Papers 2.

Sjöberg, Ö. and Wyzan, M.L., 1991, The Balkan states: struggling along the road to the market from Europe's periphery, in Sjöberg, Ö., Wyzan, M.L., eds, *Economic change in the Balkan states*, Pinter, London, pp. 1–15.

Skarço, K., 1984, *Agriculture in the PSR of Albania*, 8 Nëntori, Tirana.

Skenderi, K., Vejsiu, Y., 1983, The development of demographic processes and the socio-economic problems which emerge, in Institute of Marxist-Leninist Studies, *The National Conference: on problems of the development of the economy in the 7th five-year plan*, 8 Nëntori, Tirana, pp. 155–64.

Skenderi, K., Vejsiu, Y., 1984, The demographic processes are inseparable from the socio-economic development, *Albania Today*, **77**: 3–35.

Skendi, S., 1948, Albania within the Slav orbit: advent to power of the communist party, *Political Science Quarterly*, **63**(2): 257–74.

Skendi, S., 1953a, Beginnings of Albanian nationalist and autonomous trends; the Albanian League, 1878–1881, *The American Slavic and East European Review*, **12**(2): 219–32.

Skendi, S., 1953b, Beginnings of Albanian nationalist trends in culture and education, 1878–1912, *Journal of Central European Affairs*, **12**: 356–67.

Skendi, S., 1954a, Albanian political thought and revolutionary activity, 1881–1912, *Südost Forschungen*, **13**: 159–99.

Skendi, S., 1954b, The Northern Epirus question reconsidered, *Journal of Central European Affairs*, **14**: 143–53.

Skendi, S., 1954c, *The political evolution of Albania 1912–1944*, Mid-European Studies Center, New York.

Skendi, S., 1955, Die Islamisierung beiden Albanern, *Jahrbücher für Geschichte Osteuropas*, **3**: 404–23.

Skendi, S., 1956a, *Albania*, Stevens and Sons, London.

Skendi, S., 1956b, Religion in Albania during the Ottoman rule, *Südost-Forschungen*, **15**: 311–27.

Skendi, S., 1960, The history of the Albanian alphabet: a case of complex cultural and political development, *Südost-Forschungen*, **15**: 311–27.

Skendi, S., 1962, Albania and the Sino-Soviet conflict, *Foreign Affairs*, **40**(3): 471–8.

Skendi, S., 1967, *The Albanian national awakening 1878–1912*, Princeton University Press, Princeton.

Skendi, S., 1968, Skenderbeg and the Albanian national consciousness, *Südost-Forschungen*, **27**: 83–8.

Skendi, S., 1980, The complex environment of Skenderbeg's activity, in Skendi, S., *Balkan cultural studies*, Columbia University Press, New York, pp. 167–86.

Smiley, D., 1984, *Albanian assignment*, Chatto and Windus, London.

Smiley, D., 1985, To war with Hoxha, *The Spectator*, **254**(8180): 16–17.

Smith, A.D., 1979, *Nationalism in the twentieth century*, Martin Robertson, London.

Smith, A.H., 1991, The implications of change in East Central Europe for the Balkan socialist economies, in Sjöberg, Ö. and Wyzan, M.L., eds, *Economic change in the Balkan states*, Pinter, London, pp. 147–60.

Smith, H., 1992, Macedonia's outcasts threaten to turn Balkan 'fruit salad' into a powder keg, *The Guardian*, 31 July.

Smith, H., 1993a, Compassion alive on Greek border, *The Guardian*, 22 July.

Smith, H., 1993b, Ex-minister to attack Athens for 'soft' line on Macedonia, *The Guardian*, 19 February.

Smith, M., 1979, The earthquake in Albania, *Albanian Life*, **15**: 1.

Sobell, V., 1988, The ecological crisis in Eastern Europe, *Radio Free Europe Research*, RAD/5.

Spaho, E., 1992, Tourism: promising contracts, *Albanian Economic Tribune*, **6**(10): 17–19.

Spaho, E., 1993a, *Personal interview*, Deputy Minister of Tourism, Tirana, 26 March.

Spaho, E., 1993b, *Personal interview*, Minister of Tourism, Tirana, 10 December.

Spall, N., 1992, *Tourism development strategy for Bulgaria*, Discussion Paper, Sheppard Robson, London.

Spillett, S., 1992, We are a responsive group!, *Albanian Life*, **2**: 21.

Standish, M.J.A., Yates, A.M., 1992a, Foreign capital – investment or invasion? *Albanian Economic Tribune*, **7**(11): 10–11.

Standish, M.J.A., Yates, A.M., 1992b, Two serious disappointments: the foreign investment and profit taxation laws, *Albanian Economic Tribune*, **8**(12): 8–9.

Stanley, D., 1993, Albania, in Costanzo, A., Coxall, M., Driesum, R. van, Mitra, S., Pike, F., Saad, D.,

Steward, S., Waters, K., Williams, J., Williamson, C., eds, *Mediterranean Europe*, Lonely Planet, Hawthorn, Berkeley and Chiswick, pp. 65–100.

Stanley, E., 1932, Italy's financial stake in Albania, *Foreign Policy Reports*, 8: 79–86.

Start, Zagreb, weekly.

Stavrou, N.A., 1975, The political role of the Albanian military, *Intellect*, July–August: 18–21.

Stefani, A., 1993, Will the unemployed be re-employed? *Albanian Economic Tribune*, 1(13): 14–15.

Stern, G., 1977–78, Chinese-Albanian relations: the end of an affair?, *Millennium*, 6: 270–4.

Steen, E., 1988, Albania decides to come in from the Balkan cold, *The Independent*, 25 February.

Stickney, E.P., 1926, *Southern Albania or Northern Epirus in European international affairs, 1912–23*, Stanford University Press, Stanford.

Stipčević, A., 1977, *The Illyrians: history and culture*, Noyes Press, New Jersey.

Stojanović, M.D., 1939, *The great powers and the Balkans, 1875–1878*, Cambridge University Press, Cambridge.

Strazimiri, B., Nallbani, H., Ceka, N., eds, 1973, *Monumente të Arkitekturës në Shqipëri*, Instituti i Monumenteve të Kulturës, Tirana.

Strazimiri, G., 1987, *Berati: qytet muze*, 8 Nëntori, Tirana.

Stretton, H., 1978, *Urban planning in rich and poor countries*, Oxford University Press, Oxford.

Šufflay, M., 1916, Die Kirchenzustände im vortürkischen Albanien. Die orthodoxe Durchbruchszone im Katholischen damme, in Thallóczy, L., ed., *Illyrischalbanische Forschungen*, 1: 188–282.

Šufflay, M., 1925, *Srbi i Arbanisi*, Belgrade.

Sugar, P.F., 1969, External and domestic roots of eastern European nationalism, in Sugar, P.F., Lederer, I.J., eds, *Nationalism in Eastern Europe*, University of Washington Press, Seattle, pp. 3–54.

Suli, L., 1982, Tipologjia dhe arkitektura e banesës se vjetër të zonas së Konispolit, *Saranda Almanak*, 2: 100–107.

Sulko, T., 1988, Tirana is rejuvenated every year, *New Albania*, 1: 10–11.

Sullivan, P., 1992, A day in the life of Sali Barisha, *Sunday Times Magazine*, 22 November, reprinted in, *Albanian Life*, 1993, 1: 18–19.

Sumner, B.H., 1937, *Russia and the Balkans, 1870–1880*, Clarendon Press, Oxford.

Svet, Belgrade, twice weekly.

Swire, J., 1929, *Albania; the rise of a kingdom*, Williams and Norgate, London.

Swire, J., 1937, *King Zog's Albania*, Robert Hale, London.

Szalai, J., 1991, Some aspects of the changing situation of women in Hungary, *Signs: Journal of Women in Culture and Society*, 17(1): 152–70.

Szulc, T., 1992, Scenes in a Greek tragedy, *The Guardian*, 17 November.

Tachtsis, K., nd, Epirus, in King, F., ed., *Introducing Greece*, Methuen, London, pp. 190–208.

Talbott, S., ed., 1977, *Khrushchev remembers. Volume 2: the last testament*, Penguin, Harmondsworth.

Tang, P.S.H., 1978, Albania's challenge to Peking: contribution to communism?, *Asian Thought and Society*, 3(9): 330–37.

Tang, P.S.H., 1980, The Soviet, Chinese and Albanian constitutions: ideological divergence and institutionalized confrontation? *Studies in Soviet Thought*, 21: 39–58.

Tanjug, Yugoslav News Agency, Belgrade.

Tanner, M., 1992, Serbs fail to halt Albanian breakaway poll in Kosovo, *The Independent*, 25 May.

Tarifa, F., Barjaba, K., 1986, Vështrim sociologjik mbi kohën e lirë të punonjësve, *Studime Politiko-Shoqërore*, 11: 116–33.

Tarifa, F., Barjaba, K., 1990, Leisure in Tirana, *Albanian Life*, 48: 11–15.

Tartari, T., 1988, Principal aspects of the protection of the genetic fund of flora and fauna, in, *Balkan Scientific Conference, Environmental Protection in the Balkans, Abstracts*, Varna.

Temo, S., 1985, *Education in the PSR of Albania*, 8 Nëntori, Tirana.

Thomas, J.E., 1969, *Education for communism: school and state in the People's Republic of Albania*, Hoover Institution Press, Stanford.

Thomo, P., 1988, *Korça: urbanistika dhe arkitektura*, Akademia e Shkencave e RPS të Shqipërisë, Tirana.

Thompson, P., 1991, Balkan democratic forces agree to co-operate, *The Independent*, 17 June.

Thomson, I.M., 1988, Alien in the land of Zog, *The Sunday Times*, 5 June.

Tifft, S., 1985, Master of an isolated realm: Enver Hoxha, 1908–1985, *Time*, 125(16): 18.

Tihon, F., 1992, Albanians of Kosovo waging cultural resistance to Serbs, *The Guardian*, 3 August.

Toçi, V., 1971, Amfiteatri i Dyrrahit, *Monumentet*, 2: 37–42.

Toçka, J., ed., 1980, *Korça Almanak 2*, 8 Nëntori, Tirana.

Toçka, J., ed., 1981a, *Elbasani Almanak 1*, 8 Nëntori, Tirana.

Toçka, J., ed., 1981b, *Fieri Almanak 3*, 8 Nëntori, Tirana.

Toçka, J., ed., 1982, *Saranda Almanak 2*, 8 Nëntori, Tirana.

Toçka, J., ed., 1985, *Librazhdi Almanak 1*, 8 Nëntori, Tirana.

Toepfer, H., 1985, Zur Entwicklung der Landwirtschaft in Albanien, *Zeitschrift für Agrargeographie*, 3(2): 136–57.

Tönnes, B., 1982, Religious persecution in Albania, *Religion in Communist Lands*, 10(3): 242–55.

Topia, G., 1992, Where have the three billion gone?, *Albanian Economic Tribune*, 7(11): 22.

Touche Ross, EuroPrincipals Limited, 1992, *Albania tourism guidelines*, The Ministry of Tourism, Government of Albania and the European Bank for Reconstruction and Development, Tirana and London.

Toynbee, A.J., 1934–54, *A study of history*, Oxford University Press, London.

Travis, A.S., 1982, Managing the environmental and cultural impacts of tourism and leisure development, *Tourism Management*, 3(4): 256–62.

Traynor, I., 1990, Albania heals 30–year rift with Moscow, *The Guardian*, 31 July.

Traynor, I., 1991, A prison called Albania, *The Guardian*, 8 March.

Traynor, I., 1993a, Awakened Albania set to shake off charity status, *The Guardian*, 24 July.

Traynor, I., 1993b, Pouring cold water on Albania's lazy 'little pashas', *The Guardian*, 8 July.

Tretiak, D., 1962, The founding of the Sino-Albanian entente, *The China Quarterly*, 10: 123–43.

Trojani, V., 1991, *Personal interview*, Professor of Geography, Faculty of History and Philology, University of Tirana, April.

Turnock, D., 1977, Romania and the geography of tourism, *Geoforum*, 8: 51–6.

Turnock, D., 1986, *The rural development programme of Romania with special reference to the designation of new towns*, University of Leicester, Department of Geography, Occasional Paper 13, Leicester.

Turnock, D., 1990, Tourism in Romania: rural planning in the Carpathians, *Annals of Tourism Research*, 17: 79–112.

Turnock, D., 1991a, Romanian villages: rural planning under communism, *Rural History*, 2: 77–107.

Turnock, D., 1991b, The planning of rural settlement in Romania, *Geographical Journal*, 157: 251–64.

Turnock, D., 1993a, *Agricultural change in the new Eastern Europe*, Stanley Thornes, Cheltenham.

Turnock, D., 1993b, *Agricultural change in the Romanian Carpathians*, University of Leicester Discussion Papers in Geography G93/2, Leicester.

Turrill, W.B., 1929, *The plant life of the Balkan peninsula*, Clarendon Press, Oxford.

Uçi, A., 1969, Familja, martesa dhe çkunorizimi në Shqipëri, *Rruga e Partisë*, 4: 76–9.

United Nations Relief and Reconstruction Agency (UNRRA), Division of Operational Analysis, 1947, *Economic rehabilitation in Albania*, UNRRA, New York.

United States, Department of Interior, 1944, *The mineral resources of Albania*, Bureau of Mines, Washington DC.

Urban, M., 1938, Die Südalbaniens, *Tübinger Geographische und Geologische Abhandlungen*, 2(4).

Valentini, G., 1941, La migrazione stradiotica albanese, *Rivista d'Albania*, 2: 231–9.

Vani, S., 1987, Alongside antiquity, *New Albania*, 5: 6–7.

Vaso, A., 1993, *Personal interview*, Department of Zoology, University of Tirana, Tirana, 11 December.

Vecernje List, Zagreb, daily.

Vecernje Novosti, Belgrade, daily.

Vejsiu, Y., 1981, *Aspekte të zhvillimit industrial dhe të transformimeve demografike në RPSSH*, Universiteti i Tiranës, Fakulteti i Ekonomisë, Tirana.

Vejsiu, Y., 1982a, The natural movement of the population, *New Albania*, 2: 12–13.

Vejsiu, Y., 1982b, What does the shift in population show?, *New Albania*, 6: 20–21.

Vejsiu, Y., 1987, The policy of the Party in the development of the demographic processes of the country, *Albania Today*, 3: 31–7.

Vejsiu, Y., 1989, What do the figures of the recent census show? *New Albania*, 4: 12.

Vejsiu, Y., 1990, The vitality of a population, *New Albania*, 6: 14–15.

Vejsiu, Y., Bërxholi, A, 1987, Aspekte të strukturës dhe shtrirjes gjeografike të popullsisë në vendin tonë, *Studime Gjeografike*, 2: 63–70.

Vickers, J., Yarrow, G., 1988, *Privatisation – an economic analysis*, MIT Press, Cambridge Mass.

Vickers, J., Yarrow, G., 1991, Economic perspectives on privatisation, *Journal of Economic Perspectives*, 5(2): 111–32.

Vickers, M., 1992a, Clouds over a limpid lake, *The European*, 30 December.

Vickers, M., 1992b, Update, *Albanian Life*, 2: 34–5.

Vickers, M., 1993, All the world's a cafe-bar again in sleepy Tirana, *The European*, 22 July.

Vjesnik, Zagreb, daily.

Volpe, G., 1991, Formazione storica dell'Albania, *Nuova Antologia*, 406: 313–32.

V.R., 1950, Albania: a Balkan bridgehead, *The World Today*, 6(2): 73–83.

Vreme, Belgrade, weekly.

Vucinich, W.S., 1951, Communism gains Albania, *Current History*, **21**: 212–19, 345–52.

Ward, P., 1983, *Albania: a travel guide*, Oleander Press, Cambridge.

Weigand, G., 1926, Das Albanesische in Attika, *Balkan Archiv*, **2**: 167–225.

Weiner, R., 1973, Albanian and Romanian deviance in the United Nations, *East European Quarterly*, **7**(1): 65–90.

Weir, D., 1937, *Balkan saga*, Oliver and Boyd, Edinburgh.

Weyr, T., 1992, Women's economic hardship in Albania, *Albanian Life*, **2**: 24.

Wheeller, B., 1992a, Alternative tourism – a deceptive ploy, *Progress in Tourism, Recreation and Hospitality Management*, **4**: 140–45.

Wheeller, B., 1992b, Is progressive tourism appropriate?, *Tourism Management*, **13**(1): 104–5.

White, S., Batt, J., Lewis, P.G., eds, 1993, *Developments in East European politics*, Macmillan, London.

Wildermuth, A., 1989, *Die Krise der albanischen Landwirtschaft: Lösungsversuche der Partei – und Staatsführung unter Ramiz Alia*, Hieronymus, Neuried.

Wiles, P., 1982, Kosovo: the view from Tirana, *South Slav Journal*, **5**(1).

Wilkinson, H.R., 1951, *Maps and politics: a review of the ethnographic cartograpy of Macedonia*, University of Liverpool, Liverpool.

Williamson, A., 1992, Bringing down the other iron curtain, *The European*, 4 June.

Wingfield, W.F., 1859, *A tour in Dalmatia, Albania, and Montenegro*, R. Bentley, London.

Winiecki, J., 1989a, Eastern Europe: challenge of 1992 dwarfed by pressure of system's decline, *Aussenwirtschaft*, **44**(3/4): 345–65.

Winiecki, J., 1989b, CPEs' structural change and world market performance: a permanently developing country (PDC) status?, *Soviet Studies*, **41**(3): 365–81.

Winnifrith, T., 1987, *The Vlachs*, Macmillan, London.

Winnifrith, T., 1992a, Albania and the Ottoman empire, in Winnifrith, T., ed., *Perspectives on Albania*, Macmillan, Basingstoke and London, pp. 74–88.

Winnifrith, T., ed., 1992b, *Perspectives on Albania*, Macmillan, Basingstoke and London.

Wohl, P., 1972, Coolness parts Albania, China, *Christian Science Monitor*, 5 May.

Wolff, R.L., 1956, *The Balkans in our time*, Harvard University Press, Harvard.

Woods, H.C., 1918, Albania and the Albanians, *Geographical Review*, **5**(4): 257–73.

Woods, L., 1989, East European trade with the industrial West, in *Pressures for reform in the East European economies, Vol. 2*, US Government Printing Office, Washington DC, pp. 388–419.

World Bank, The, 1993, *Albania environmental strategy study*, World Bank Report 11784-ALB, New York.

World Bank, The, European Community, The, 1993, *An agricultural strategy for Albania*, The World Bank, Washington DC.

Wright, Q., 1949, The Corfu Channel case, *American Journal of International Law*, **43**(3): 491–5.

Xhaja, A., 1993, Industry is being caught under the falling roof of heavy debts, *Albanian Economic Tribune*, **1**(13): 16–17.

Xhaja, B., Metohu, D., 1988, Shpërndarja sipas punës nxit shtimin e prodhimit e përmirësimin e cilësisë forcon regjimin e kursimit, *Probleme Ekonomike*, **35**(4): 27–33.

Xherahu, Q., Baruti, V., 1975, *Gjeografia e Shqipërisë*, Shtëpia Botuese e Librit Shkollor, Tirana.

Xholi, Z., 1985, *For a more correct conception of national culture*, 8 Nëntori, Tirana.

Xhuvani, P., 1989, Prona e grupit – tipar dallues kryesor i Perestrojkës, *Probleme Ekonomike*, **36**(4): 88–90.

Xhuveli, L., 1984, Albanian agriculture on the road of its ceaseless development and intensification, *Albania Today*, **77**: 19–23.

Yee, C., 1993, Tax incentives for EE investment, *Business Eastern Europe*, **22**(27): 6–7.

Young, A., Prodani, A., 1993, Agriculture in Albania today, *Albanian Life*, **1**: 33.

Zanga, L., 1985, Tirana returns Kosovar escapees to Yugoslavia, *Radio Free Europe Research*, **10**: RAD/119.

Zanga, L., 1986a, Albania and its chrome, *Radio Free Europe Research*, **11**: RAD/178.

Zanga, L., 1986b, Pristina and Teheran press on Kosovo, *Radio Free Europe Research*, **11**: RAD/61.

Zanga, L., 1987, News media coverage of events in Kosovo, *Radio Free Europe Research*, **12**: RAD/223.

Zanga, L., 1988a, Albania expands international participation and cooperation, *Radio Free Europe Research*, **13**: RAD/106.

Zanga, L., 1988b, Albanian foreign minister sets forth Albania's new-look diplomacy, *Radio Free Europe Research*, **13**: RAD/36.

Zanga, L., 1988c, Albania's contacts with the outside world, *Radio Free Europe Research*, **13**: RAD/87.

Zanga, L., 1989a, A freer and more assertive Albanian youth, *Radio Free Europe Research*, **14**: RAD/177.

Zanga, L., 1989b, Census of Albania and its minority groups, *Radio Free Europe Research*, **14**: RAD/142.

Zanga, L., 1989c, Mother Theresa's visit to Albania, *Radio Free Europe Research*, **14**: RAD/155.

Zanga, L., 1989d, Tirana's views on the 'crisis of socialism', *Radio Free Europe Research*, **14**: RAD/183.

Zanga, L., 1990a, A major revision of cultural history, *Report on Eastern Europe*, **1**(20): 1–4.

Zanga, L., 1990b, Albania: approaching the European mainstream, *Report on Eastern Europe*, **1**(52): 1–3.

Zanga, L., 1990c, Albania makes overtures to superpowers, *Report on Eastern Europe*, **1**(19): 1–3.

Zanga, L., 1990d, Ramiz Alia renews Albania's international contacts, *Report on Eastern Europe*, **1**(43): 1–3.

Zanga, L., 1990e, Changes in the 'last bastion', *Report on Eastern Europe*, **1**(21): 1–3.

Zanga, L., 1990f, The Balkan foreign ministers' conference in Tirana, *Report on Eastern Europe*, **1**(49): 1–4.

Zanga, L., 1990g, The defection of Ismail Kadare, *Report on Eastern Europe*, **1**(47): 1–3.

Zanga, L., 1991a, Albania: the state of the press, *Report on Eastern Europe*, **2**(45): 1–3.

Zanga, L., 1991b, Albania: the woeful state of schools, *Report on Eastern Europe*, **2**(41): 1–3.

Zanga, L., 1992a, Albania and Kosovo, *RFE/RL Research Report*, **1**(39): 26–9.

Zanga, L., 1992b, Albania between democracy and chaos, *RFE/RL Research Report*, **1**(1): 74–7.

Zanga, L., 1992c, Albania's local elections, *RFE/RL Research Report*, **1**(37): 27–30.

Zanga, L., 1992d, Daunting tasks for Albania's new government, *RFE/RL Research Report*, **1**(21): 11–17.

Zanga, L., 1992e, Renewed Italian interest in Albania, *RFE/RL Research Report*, **1**(19): 22–5.

Zanga, L., 1992f, The question of Kosovar sovereignty, *RFE/RL Research Report*, **1**(43): 21–6.

Zanga, L., 1993a, Albania and Turkey forge closer ties, *RFE/RL Research Report*, **2**(11), 28–31.

Zanga, L., 1993b, Albania moves closer to the Islamic world, *RFE/RL Research Report*, **2**(7), 28–31.

Zanga, L., 1993c, Albanian president defends his first year in office, *RFE/RL Research Report*, **2**(29), 23–6.

Zanga, L., 1993d, Cabinet changes in Albania, *RFE/RL Research Report*, **2**(19), 14–16.

Zanga, L., 1993e, One year of democracy in Albania, *RFE/RL Research Report*, **2**(14), 26–7.

Zanga, L., 1993f, The media in Eastern Europe: Albania, *RFE/RL Research Report*, **2**(19), 23–4.

Zanga, L., 1993g, Two new journalistic ventures in Albania, *RFE/RL Research Report*, **2**(24), 41–3.

Zarshati, F., 1982, *Monuments of culture in Albania*, 8 Nëntori, Tirana.

Zavalani, D., 1938, *Die Landwirtschaftlichen Verhältmisse Albaniens*, Paul Parey, Berlin.

Zavalani, T., 1944, Resources of Albania, *Geography*, **29**(3): 80–85.

Zavalani, T., 1961, The importance of being Albania, *Problems of Communism*, **10**(4): 1–8.

Zavalani, T., 1969, Albanian nationalism, in Sugar, P.F., Lederer, I.J., eds, *Nationalism in Eastern Europe*, University of Washington Press, Seattle, pp. 55–83.

Zeljazkova, A.L., 1984, Ottoman-Turkic colonization in Albania and some aspects of the ensuing demographic changes, *Etudes Balkaniques*, **2**: 67–84.

Zëri i Popullit, Tirana, daily.

Zëri i Rinise, Tirana, twice weekly.

Zhang, B., 1993, Institutional aspects of reforms and the democratization of communist regimes, *Communist and Post-communist Studies*, **26**(2): 165–81.

Zurick, D.N., 1992, Adventure travel and sustainable tourism in the peripheral economy of Nepal, *Annals of the Association of American Geographers*, **82**(4): 608–28.

Index

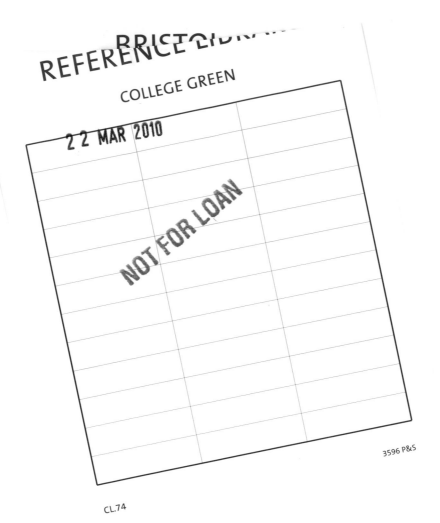